Interviewing principles and practices

Interviewing principles and practices

Third Edition

Charles J. Stewart
Purdue University

William B. Cash, Jr.

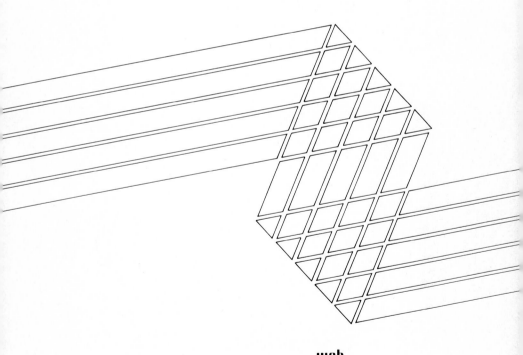

wcb
Wm. C. Brown Company Publishers
Dubuque, Iowa

Book Team

Louise Waller Editor
Laura Beaudoin Production Editor
Mary Heller Visual Research Editor

wcb group

Wm. C. Brown Chairman of the Board
Mark C. Falb Executive Vice President

wcb

Wm. C. Brown Company Publishers, College Division

Lawrence E. Cremer President
Raymond C. Deveaux Vice President, Product Development
David Wm. Smith Vice President, Marketing
David A. Corona Assistant Vice President, Production Development and Design
Janis M. Machala Director of Marketing Research
Marilyn A. Phelps Manager of Design
William A. Moss Production Editorial Manager
Mary M. Heller Visual Research Manager

Photo Credits
Bob Coyle: 59; 185
Robert Gaylord/EKM-Nepenthe: 5; 8; 30; 76; 220; 262
Robert Gaylord: 231; 282
John Maher/EKM-Nepenthe: 80; 141; 274
James L. Shaffer: 35; 120; 168; 244
Courtesy U.S. Catholic Conference: 117; 148

2-04193-03

Contents

Figures

Figures

Preface

We wrote the first edition of *Interviewing: Principles and Practices* to meet a growing interest in perhaps the most common form of planned communication—the interview. Since that time a multitude of new courses and workshops in interviewing have been conducted in high schools, colleges, universities, industries, and professional organizations. For too long the almost daily occurrence of interviewing had led many to believe that what we do often we do well. But that is not the case, and so this third edition of our book reflects the growing sophistication with which the interview is being approached and the effects of equal employment opportunity laws on interviewing practices.

The third edition includes both the general and the specific. The first four chapters treat principles applicable to all interview settings. Chapter 1 defines the interview, compares and contrasts it with other forms of communication, and discusses two approaches to interviewing. Chapter 2 deals with the interview as a process and contains a revised model of that process and an expanded treatment of perceptions, nonverbal communication, and listening. Chapter 3 discusses the structure of the interview and includes new materials on openings and closings. Chapter 4 is an expanded and refined discussion and illustration of the types of questions and ways of using them.

The last six chapters deal with specialized kinds of interviews—survey and journalistic interviews (chapters 5 and 6), employment selection interviews (chapter 7), employment appraisal and discipline interviews (chapter 8), counseling interviews (chapter 9), and persuasive interviews (chapter 10). We have made special efforts to clarify, illustrate, expand, and update concepts and principles and have increased the emphasis on preparing and structuring interviews.

Some discussions of these principles and techniques may seem simple or to dwell on the obvious. In our experience, as both teachers and participants in interviewing, however, we have found that the simple and the obvious are often overlooked and may create major problems in real-life interviews.

The sample interviews at the ends of many of the chapters are provided for analysis and criticism, *not* as perfect examples of interviewing. They illustrate a variety of interviewing types, settings, approaches, techniques, and mistakes.

The role-playing cases at the ends of chapters 5–10 provide students with the opportunity to design and conduct practice interviews and to observe others' efforts to employ the techniques discussed in this book and in the classroom. Suggested readings at the end of each chapter will help those students who are interested in delving more deeply into specific topics, theories, and types of interviews.

This book is designed for courses in such departments as Speech, Communication, Journalism, Business, Industrial Supervision, Education, Political Science, Nursing, and Social Work. It may also be useful in workshops in various fields. We believe this book will be of continuing value to beginning students and seasoned veterans in many fields. We have treated theory and research findings where they are applicable; but our primary concern is with principles and techniques that can be translated into immediate practice in and out of the classroom.

We wish to express our gratitude to the many students at Purdue University and Eastern Illinois University who have provided much of the inspiration and many of the examples contained in this book. Special thanks are extended to Baxter/Travenol Laboratories of Deerfield, Illinois, for permission to include the performance appraisal model in chapter 8; and to Chris Janiak, Sandy Mauck, and Lance Picollo, who helped develop the model and the new material on performance appraisal interviewing. We also wish to thank W. Charles Redding, John Bittner, Gustav Friedrich, Bruce Wheatley, Wayne Shamo, William Brooks, Mary Alice Baker, Lou Duenweg, Robert Minter, Robert Smith, and other past and present colleagues for their suggestions, exercises, theories, criticism, and encouragement.

CJS
WBC

Interviewing principles and practices

To Jane and Jason, Whitney, and Nathan
for Their Continuing Patience and Perseverance

An Introduction to Interviewing 1

A sportscaster, with microphone and television camera crew trailing behind, approached a football coach whose team had just lost a game seven to six and a postseason bowl invitation. "Well," the sportscaster said, "we blew a tough one, didn't we?" The coach replied irritably, "How the hell am I supposed to answer that?" "Oh, I didn't mean to, uh . . ." stammered the sportscaster.

An employer was explaining to a supervisor why salary increases would be "smaller" than expected. "So you see," the employer concluded, "our loss of those two contracts has hurt us badly." The supervisor responded, "I'm obviously not happy with the smaller raise, but I appreciate your explaining the reason. We'll get along, I guess." The boss replied, "Thanks for taking it so well."

A company representative, recruiting on a college campus, asked a graduating senior, "Why do you want to work for Smith Industries?" The student gave a single-word answer, "Money." "Are there any other reasons?" the representative asked.

A member of a public opinion survey team asked a person at the door of his home, "How do you feel about the ERA?" The person responded, "I really don't know." The interviewer then asked, "Do you favor most of its provisions?"

The participants in these situations were taking part in interviews, the most common form of purposeful, planned communication. Because we are involved in interviews so frequently, we take it for granted that the process is simple and requires little, if any, formal training. If you, too, tend to believe that interviewing comes naturally—like swimming to a dog—think of your recent experiences: the inept company recruiter who kept answering her own questions; the car sales representative who was determined to sell you a large sedan when you wanted a small economy car; the counselor who told you all of his problems instead of listening to your problems; the public opinion interviewer who asked biased questions; the encyclopedia sales representative with the canned pitch.

Look again at the situations mentioned earlier. Although each setting is different—with varying purposes, techniques, skills, and degrees of potential success—each involves basic communication principles. There was immediate and direct verbal feedback between the parties and this was undoubtedly accompanied by nonverbal feedback such as frowns, puzzled expressions, raising of eyebrows, and shifting in chairs. Language (our learned symbols that are affected by environmental background, education, experiences, and perceptions of the situation, self, and other party) aided and hindered these interchanges. Each interchange motivated the interviewer and interviewee to respond in a particular manner. How well did interviewers and interviewees listen to one another? Were there times when silence was called for, when neither party would be verbalizing?

The sportscaster, who undoubtedly possessed a good voice and a knowledge of football, was insensitive to the disposition of the coach. The coach's posture and facial expression probably displayed disappointment and reluctance to dwell on the loss. The interviewer's question was not worded to motivate someone in a "normal" state of mind to reply openly and meaningfully, let alone someone who had just suffered a terrible disappointment. The lack of sensitivity would probably preclude communication after a few initial responses. Silence should have replaced the sportscaster's stammering reaction.

The employer has apparently motivated the supervisor to respond agreeably by explaining why raises will be smaller than expected. But how agreeable is the supervisor? Do both parties agree on what "smaller" raises means, or do both *assume* they are using the word in the same way? *Perhaps the greatest single problem of human communication is the assumption of it.* A wise practice is to assume we are going to be misunderstood and to act accordingly. Remember, the meaning of words rests within us; words don't mean, people do.

The applicant for a position with Smith Industries should have been prepared for this question. The answer shows lack of preparation, little interest in Smith Industries or its needs, and no feeling for the way industry is programmed— the way it views the world. The interviewer wisely probes for additional reasons.

The public opinion interviewer assumes the respondent knows what ERA means. The only message the respondent can act upon is the one received. If the respondent does not know what ERA stands for, the response might be a noncommittal "I don't know." The respondent may think ERA stands for Environmental Reclamation Authority instead of Equal Rights Amendment, and answer the interviewer's follow-up question without revealing possible ignorance or misunderstanding.

For years, people were taught to interview by observing "model" interviewers and then practicing what they had learned by observation. This approach passed on the mistakes of the "model" interviewer to the novice and assumed that communication and interviewing could be learned merely from practice. While wines may improve with age and bowlers may get better with practice, this is not necessarily the case with communication, especially interviewing. The old saying "practice makes perfect" should be amended to "practice makes perfect

Perhaps the greatest single problem of human communication is the assumption of it.

if you know what you are practicing." Twenty years of experience may actually be one year of experience repeated twenty times. We must constantly try to improve our communication skills, but copying someone else's style or habits may be a mistake.

We want to show in this and succeeding chapters that there is a vast difference between the effectiveness of skilled and unskilled interviewers. Our purpose is to introduce you to the basic skills applicable to all interviews and to specific skills needed in specialized settings such as survey, journalistic, employment, performance appraisal, counseling, and persuasive interviews. We will begin by examining the nature of interviewing, defining it, comparing it to other communication settings, identifying its approaches and types, and discussing its uses.

Forms and Functions of Interpersonal Communication: The Dyad

Interpersonal communication is direct, unmediated communication between or among individuals in settings such as public speeches, panel discussions, and social conversations. A form of interpersonal communication that involves person-to-person interaction and pervasive feedback between two units or parties in which the roles of speaker and listener alternate, and often merge, is referred to as a *dyad*. The dyad is the foundation of human communication settings and appears in many forms.[1]

Intimate interaction includes dyads that involve husbands and wives, close friends, and family communication—relationships that involve strong emotional attachments. These emotional ties influence the kinds of subject matters discussed, and not discussed, and dictate the setting in which they take place. Intimate interaction situations provide the best opportunities for total communication and the fullest human relationships, but this does not mean that distortion, miscommunication, and other difficulties do not arise. Investment of self with other human beings requires risk-taking behaviors. These risks are filled with positive contributions to both members of the dyad but are fraught with emotionally dangerous consequences.

Social conversation is the most common dyad and perhaps the least understood. Berne, Jourard, and Goffman examined the phenomenon of socialization, or being sociable, and identified a number of games, roles, or postures assumed, depending upon the nature of the conversation.[2] Many social conversations are not dyads. Party conversation, for example, usually involves more than two parties in the exchange of pleasantries. We pass the time of day; we talk about the weather; we comment on food in restaurants; and we often stifle some of our strongest feelings about people and topics because we do not wish to be considered rude, insensitive, or lacking in social graces. Happily or not, social conversation is a must and is often considered an art or artificiality, depending upon the people and the setting.

The *interrogation,* or *examination,* is used to extract information from a source. When police question a suspect, they usually do not take into account what might happen to this human relationship but are bent on solving a crime or extracting valuable information. Whether an attorney is examining a witness on a witness stand or a physician is questioning a dying patient in the emergency room of a hospital, the process is predominantly one way and is highly controlled by the interviewer. The degree of satisfaction may be of no concern to either party. Many psychiatric, medical, and investigatory dyads do involve mutual interest and satisfaction and a sharing of roles.

The *fight* is characterized by a feeling of rightness or of having been wronged in some way by "them."[3] We exclude from fights deeply philosophical or controversial disagreements over such issues as abortion, politics, and religion. The parties in a fight do not communicate about how they are going to communicate or lay down ground rules. A fight's best characterization is an absence of all verbal, and occasionally physical, controls. We would not expect a diplomat at the United Nations to threaten to "kick the hell" out of another representative, but such lack of control or restraint is common in fights. Most fights are serious, and some may be preplanned.

Debates usually have rules by which both sides agree to abide—time limits, switching of sides, no new evidence during rebuttal, and so on. Such rules are common in intercollegiate debating, courts of law, and presidential debates. One professor described debate as "the most civil way to disagree." This formalized and structured system of interaction is designed to balance the interaction and to provide both parties with the same opportunities to present arguments and reasoning. However, the formalized structure of debates prevents a true interchange of behaviors.

This brings us to the *interview*, a special form of dyadic communication that is both similar to (and different from) other types of dyads and may evolve from (or to) another type.

The Interview Defined

We define interviewing as *a process of dyadic communication with a predetermined and serious purpose designed to interchange behavior and involving the asking and answering of questions.*[4] The word *process* denotes a dynamic, everchanging interaction with many variables operating with and acting upon one another, and a degree of structure or system without being fixed. An interview, regardless of its intent, does not occur in isolation. Once a relationship begins, impressions that are inputs into our mental programming are not reversible and may affect our perceptions of the other party, regardless of the length or depth of the relationship. An individual or party who comes into our perceptual field and into a relationship with us cannot ignore or avoid the ongoing dynamic potential of the relationship.

The word *dyad* denotes that the interview is a person-to-person interaction between two parties or units. Thus, more than two people may be involved in an interview (for example, two members of a company interviewing a job applicant, a journalist interviewing three members of a championship team), but never more than two parties—an interviewer party and an interviewee party.

Predetermined and serious purpose means that at least one of the two parties comes to the interview with a purpose or goal in mind—other than mere enjoyment of the interchange—and has planned and organized the interview to focus on some specific subject matter. The predetermined and serious purpose distinguishes the interview from social conversation and from most intimate interactions and fights. This does not mean that polite conversation, chitchat, or reasonable and necessary digressions are not parts of many interviews.

Each participant in the interviewing process has a purpose and some critical content to transact, either consciously thought out in advance or developed within the context of the interview. The degree to which the purpose is achieved is a crude measure of the degree of satisfaction achieved in the interview, which is a way of measuring the success of the interview process. The extent to which we are able to accomplish our objectives, to deal with critical content, and to provide the same opportunity for the other party is a measure of the satisfaction that we can achieve in a fully productive interview.

More than two people may be involved in an interview, but never more than two parties—an interviewer party and an interviewee party.

Interchanging behavior connotes a sharing of relevant programmings and expectations or, if you will, getting it together *together*—a sharing and exchanging of facts, times, names, places, actions, roles, and feelings. The interrogation, debate, and fight, unlike the interview, typically do not involve a mutual sharing of each other, with each other. The interchange of behavior may encourage us to express our total humanness in verbal expressions of joy, fear, loneliness, anxiety, and in nonverbal touches, hugs, punches on the arm, handshakes, winks, and quick looks of concern or knowledge. The free expression of our humanness involves various levels of risk that can be minimized but never eliminated. If one or both parties elect to play it safe, the interchange and the quality of the interview will suffer.

Interchanging behavior also means that each party speaks and listens from time to time. If one party does all of the speaking and the other all of the listening, no interview has taken place. The parties may also exchange roles of interviewer and interviewee. We can see this in the brief interchange between the coach and the sportscaster at the beginning of this chapter.

The asking and answering of questions is crucial to the interviewing process. It is the primary means of interviewer/interviewee interaction and allows both parties to get at crucial subject matter and to achieve their purposes and goals. The mere mouthing of questions and responses, or questions asked solely

An Introduction to Interviewing

for the purpose of politeness or that do not facilitate the progression of the interview toward its goal is a waste of time. Purposeful questions, thought out in advance and used at appropriate times during interviews, are vitally important to the interviewing process.

We will present a model of the interviewing process in chapter 2 and explain in detail each component of the process and how it interacts with other components. Major components include the two parties, the question-anteced-ent-question relationship, pervasive feedback, verbal and nonverbal interactions, and the situation.

Now that we have an understanding of interviewing as a dyad, let's compare it with several common forms of communication.

The Interview and Other Forms of Communication

The dyadic nature of the interviewing process and its frequent reliance upon questions and answers often distinguishes it from other forms of communication. However, there are other distinguishing characteristics that we can understand best by examining a few common settings along a continuum from informal to formal. Informal settings, compared to formal settings, are less structured, participation is more equal, a wider range of subject matter is possible, and the purpose is less predetermined.

At the right end of the continuum in figure 1.1 are the mass media—radio, television, film, newspapers, and magazines. The media are formal, one-way, and allow for little, if any, feedback.

Slightly less formal are public speeches such as the inaugural address of a public official, a graduation address, or an acceptance speech. Applause and "Bronx cheers" may provide the only feedback. Unequal participation, restriction of subject matter (usually one topic per speech), and rigid structure make public speeches very different from interviews. To the left of public speaking on the continuum is the classroom or public lecture. In these settings the interaction is unequal, probably a four to one ratio with the lecturer doing the talking and the audience the listening. A lecture is likely to be less structured than an inaugural address.

Occupying the middle position on the continuum are groups—task groups and group discussions that culminate in accomplishment of a task or plan of action. To be effective, groups must provide an opportunity for equal participation. Forums, symposiums, round tables, and problem-solving or task groups provide an atmosphere in which individuals may hide. We can let someone else talk, volunteer, or respond. The interaction of participants, the subject matter, and interpersonal relationships vary widely according to the type or style of a group. Interaction is shared somewhat, the process is less formal than speeches or lectures, and there is a predetermined purpose.

Intimate Dyads	Conversation	Interviews	Groups	Lectures	Public Speeches	Mass Media
—X—	—X—	—X—	—X—	—X—	—X—	—X—

Informal   Formal

(unstructured, equal participation,   (highly structured, unequal participation,
wide range of subject matter, purpose   purpose known to one or both parties,
may not be determined)   narrow subject range)

Figure 1.1   *The Interview and other Forms of Communication*

The interview is usually located between conversations and groups. It is usually less formal and structured than most groups, lectures, and public speeches, but more formal and structured than conversations and intimate dyads. Participation is more equal in interviews than in communication forms to the right on the continuum, but less equal than in conversations. Many organizations contend that the interviewer who talks more than 40 percent of the time is giving a speech, not interviewing. We believe participation should generally follow a ratio of 70 percent to 30 percent, with the interviewee doing most of the talking, though a few types of interviews—information-giving and sales, for example— may require a reversal of this ratio.

Intimate dyads, at the extreme left end of the continuum, like most conversations, involve a variety of subject matter areas, random interaction patterns, and often no expected outcomes for the participants beyond enjoyment of the interchange. Intimate dyads allow for a wide range of message exchanges and expressions and tend to be highly informal and equal in participation.

There are additional ways in which interviewing differs from other forms of communication.

1. Interviews are more useful in discovering attitudes, feelings, thoughts, beliefs, and what binds them together.

2. Interviewing encourages the use of all kinds and types of questions.

3. Interviewing deals with personal needs or problems, while other communication settings tend to operate in less sensitive areas.

4. Digressions are expected in some communication settings (though often condemned), but they are often necessary and planned in interviews.

5. While all forms of communication require the use of factual data, the interviewer must have documented facts available to support ideas because the interviewee may interrupt and demand evidence at any point during the interview.

6. A speaker, discussant, or lecturer may spend considerable time in formulating language for a presentation, but the nature of interviewing generally does not permit this kind of selectivity except in phrasing questions.

7. In no other communication situation are individuals exposed to the extent they are in an interview; personal risk is often very high.

Kinds and Types of Interviews

Now that we have a basic understanding of the interview and how it compares to other forms of communication, let us examine the various kinds of interviews. There are a wide variety of interviewing dyads, and Redding has developed a "situational schema" or classification into which interviews fit according to the functions they perform. Figure 1.2 is an elaboration of Redding's classification to include virtually all types of interviews.

The first category, *information giving,* includes interviews designed to orient new employees or new members to their organizations or to train, instruct, or coach individuals in particular behaviors. Examples include explaining benefits of an insurance program to an employee, clarifying rules or procedures for meetings, training individuals to fill out application forms, and coaching a door-to-door sales representative on how not to get the door slammed in his or her face. Job-related instructions (orders) also fit under this first category. For example, head nurses in hospitals give reports to shifts of nurses coming on duty. They must give special information or instructions about the conditions, medications, and behaviors of patients. Supervisors in factories often give orders to work crews prior to shift changes.

The second category, *information gathering,* includes interviews designed to gain information from the interviewee and includes surveys, polls, some exit interviews, journalistic interviews, research interviews, and investigation interviews. This category encompasses surveys designed to assess the feelings, attitudes, or trends of belief of a particular audience or market. Exit interviews are often not intended to discover the reasons for an employee leaving but are used as public relations gimmicks to salve the conscience of the employer. An exit interview should ascertain the true reasons why an employee is leaving, with the underlying assumption that no organization can afford to lose a good employee. If the employee's reasons can be discovered and remedied, other employees may not leave for the same reasons. Where it is used to improve the work climate, the exit interview has been a success. The research interview is used primarily to delve deeply into a subject of interest such as product usage, community planning, or recreation facilities. The investigation interview is employed by police, governmental agencies, and other investigatory bodies and is designed to get information from an interviewee about an incident in which the individual was involved or witnessed, or to get information about an event, person, place, or thing. For instance, the investigative interview occurs at the scene of an accident or when a claims investigator seeks information for an insurance company.

The third category, *selection,* includes a broad spectrum of interviews used for screening, hiring, or placement of employees, students, etc. The *initial screening interview* is designed to weed out applicants who do not meet the special qualifications of a particular organization. The screening interview is the most common interview in business, government, and many colleges and universities.

1. Information giving
   a. Orientation
   b. Training, instruction, coaching
   c. Job-related instructions

2. Information gathering
   a. Surveys and polls
   b. Exit interviews
   c. Research interviews
   d. Investigations: insurance, police, etc.
   e. Medical: psychological, psychiatric, caseworker
   f. Journalistic

3. Selection
   a. Screening and hiring
   b. Determination
   c. Placement (internal)

4. Problems of interviewee's behavior
   a. Appraisal, evaluative, review
   b. Separation, firing
   c. Correction, discipline, reprimand
   d. Counseling

5. Problems of interviewer's behavior
   a. Receiving complaints
   b. Grievances
   c. Receiving suggestions or answering specialized questions

6. Problem solving
   a. Objective (mutually shared problems)
   b. Receiving suggestions for solutions
      (especially to problems covering a large group of people)

7. Persuasion
   a. Selling of products
   b. Selling of services
   c. Quasi-commercial selling

Figure 1.2 *Types of Interviews*

The *determination interview,* often referred to as the plant or office interview, usually follows the screening interview. Its basic purpose is decision making; the decision being whether an individual should remain in a formal relationship (hired immediately, tested, given a further interview) with this organization or whether this formal relationship should be terminated. The party with hiring authority may hire a highly qualified individual even though an opening is not available at the moment. Employees are shifted from department to department to provide them with a degree of cross-training. Once a position becomes available within the organization, a third interview, called the *placement or transfer interview,* may take place. This interview is designed to place the most qualified person in the most desirable position for the benefit of the organization. Sometimes corporation employee development departments keep replacement charts (a chart used to plot and plan visually which people might replace others within the organization) and the transfer interview is used as an internal method of selecting the most desirable replacements.

The fourth category, *problems of interviewee behavior,* includes appraisal, evaluation or performance reviews, and counseling interviews dealing with problems related directly to an interviewee's behavior. This type of interview poses difficult and special problems for both interviewer and interviewee and is one of the "big three" interviews in organizations: employment, performance appraisal, and counseling. Besides formally evaluating employees within the framework of appraisal interviews, many organizations conduct disciplinary, corrective, or what are sometimes called reprimand interviews. These interviews are conducted at the insistence of the interviewer and are usually directive in nature. The counseling interview is a common interview, especially in education and business. Counseling interviews are partially nondirective (controlled by the interviewee) because the interviewee often initiates and controls the communication in such situations. An important consideration in counseling interviews is the extent to which the problem is perceived by both interviewer and interviewee. A problem tends to be unimportant until it is *our* problem.

The fifth category, *problems of interviewer's behavior,* deals with perceived problems directly related to the interviewer's behavior or the behavior of the organization the interviewer represents. These interviews involve the receiving of complaints or the accepting or discussing of grievances. These include formal union grievance procedures and other formalized processes in nonunion organizations, and informal grievances such as employee complaints and gripes, customer complaints about faulty merchandise or service, and customers returning unwanted merchandise.

The sixth category, *problem solving,* deals not with problems related to the personal behavior of interviewer or interviewee but with genuinely shared problems of mutual concern. The interview should result in some form of decision making. We are not talking about pseudo problem-solving approaches manifested in the phony, "Now Johnson, what is our problem (meaning your problem) today?" We can best characterize problem-solving interviews as "true" when both parties in the dyad share in the problem and the development of a viable solution.

The seventh category, *persuasion,* is one of the most frequently used and least understood types of interviews. The term persuasion connotes different things to different people. Some time ago, one of the authors was discussing interviewing with a professor of marketing and, when the subject of sales came up, the author said, "Oh, you mean a persuasive interview." The marketing professor shot back indignantly, "I do not deal with that arm-twisting business called persuasion." When we say persuasion we simply mean an effort to bring about a specific change in an interviewee's way of thinking, feeling, or acting without resorting to compulsion or duress. The persuadee maintains the freedom of choice in selecting (perceiving) a message as well as the freedom to act or not to act as a result of the message. The persuader may deal with ideas, events, policy, or with commercial or quasi-commercial matters. Persuasive interviews include sales situations that involve institutional selling or the personalized selling of a product or service.

Two Approaches to Interviewing

Regardless of interview type or setting, the interviewer may select from two basic *interviewing approaches:* directive and nondirective. A *directive interview* is one in which the interviewer establishes the purpose of the interview and, at least at the outset, controls the pacing of the communication situation. An aggressive interviewee may take command of the interview as it progresses, but the intent at the start is for the interviewer to control. Typical directive interviews include information giving, information gathering, employment selection, and persuasive. The names most widely associated with directive interviewing are George Gallup and Louis Harris. The advantages and disadvantages of directive interviewing are as follows.

Advantages

1. It is easy to learn.

2. It takes less time.

3. It provides quantifiable data.

4. It can be used to supplement other methods of data collecting such as questionnaires, interaction analyses, and observations.

5. It can be replicated by controlling variables such as language, voice, sex of interviewer, appearance, etc.

Disadvantages

1. It is inflexible (especially if a standardized list of questions is used and if these standardized questions are scheduled to be asked in a particular order).

2. It is limited in the variety and depth of subject matter.

3. It does not allow the interviewer to use a broad range of techniques.

4. It is often used to replace more effective and efficient means of collecting data.

5. The validity of the information may be questioned because of variables such as voice, facial expressions, appearance, etc.

The following is a directive interview exchange.

Interviewer: Who are you working for at the present time?
Interviewee: The First National Bank.
Interviewer: And how long have you been with the First National Bank?
Interviewee: About two and one-half years.
Interviewer: Apparently you went to work for them as soon as you graduated from college?
Interviewee: Yes, that's correct.
Interviewer: What is your current job title?

A *nondirective interview* is one in which the interviewee, by decision of the interviewer, controls the purpose, subject matter to be discussed, and pacing of the interview. Typical nondirective interviews are counseling, performance appraisal, and problem solving. The father of nondirective therapy and counseling interviews, Carl Rogers, is most widely associated with the concept of nondirective interviewing. The advantages and disadvantages of nondirective interviewing are as follows.

Advantages
1. It provides an opportunity to deal in depth with a wide range of subject matters.
2. It allows the interviewer greater flexibility.
3. It provides the interviewer with an opportunity to establish an ongoing relationship with the interviewee.
4. It allows for the widest possible means of expression on the part of the interviewee.

Disadvantages
1. It is time consuming.
2. It requires acute psychological insight and personal sensitivity.
3. It usually generates nonquantifiable data.
4. It may generate more information than is needed or can be processed.

The following is a nondirective interview exchange.

Interviewer: Tell me about your present position.
Interviewee: I'm in personnel with the First National Bank and have been with the bank since I graduated from college about two and one-half years ago.
Interviewer: Um hum?
Interviewee: I began as a manager trainee and discovered that I really enjoyed working with people, particularly in employee selection and appraisal. When an opening in personnel occurred last October, I applied for the position and got it.
Interviewer: What are your duties and responsibilities in personnel?

Interviewers such as journalists, social service counselors, personnel directors, and sales representatives often find it necessary to use an appropriate *combination* of directive and nondirective approaches. For example, a social service counselor might use a nondirective approach while assessing a family's problems and switch to a directive approach when trying to explain benefits and requirements. A personnel director may use a nondirective approach early in an interview to relax an applicant and establish a feeling of trust and then switch to a more directive approach as the interview progresses. The task of the interviewer is to determine when a particular approach seems most appropriate and when to switch from one approach to the other for maximum effectiveness. Chapter 9 on counseling interviewing contains further discussion of directive and nondirective interviewing approaches.

Uses of Interviewing

Now that we know what interviewing is (and is not), how it compares with other forms of communication, the many types of interviews, and basic approaches to interviewing, let's answer one more question. When should we use an interview instead of a questionnaire, letter, speech, or small group? The answer is many-faceted because it is influenced by type of interview, the interviewing situation, the purpose, the subject matter, and the relationship between interviewer and interviewee.[5] Use an interview—

1. when we need to motivate the interviewee to respond freely, openly, and accurately;
2. when we want to probe into answers;
3. when we want to adapt questions and responses to each interviewee;
4. when we might need to explain questions or to justify them;
5. when we want lengthy answers to questions;
6. when we want to maintain control over questions, responses, interviewees, and the situation;
7. when we want to match interviewees with specific requirements such as age, sex, race, educational level, income range, political beliefs, etc.;
8. when we want to observe the interviewee's nonverbal communication or to evaluate communication skills;
9. when we need to examine in detail emotions, beliefs, feelings, and attitudes that may be undetectable in writing.

Interviews may supplement questionnaires, applications, and other written responses.[6] One technique used to follow up on questionnaire results is the group interview. We can record the interview, cut it up and scramble it, and make a new tape that is an actual voice of the results. More important, the group may provide reasons "why," serve as a validating method, and bind the hard data with verbal expression. Assuming that a group is chosen in a valid manner, it may disprove the questionnaire. This is the risk we take. Videotape may provide a "dramatic" effect without revealing the identity of group participants. This group technique should be used by professionals and with a guarantee of anonymity to participants.

The telephone interview, conference call, and video talk-back meeting are becoming popular ways to use and abuse interviewing. Some telephone soliciting outfits use the cover of conducting a research interview when they are actually selling a product or service. After asking basic questions about the number of persons in your family, the ages of the persons, and the years of education each person has completed, the interviewer begins a pitch for magazines, books, pepper, cosmetics, etc. Many states have outlawed such practices. The use of the video talk-back system and the conference call is increasing among organizations with multiple locations. Its advantages are obvious for a chief executive officer (CEO) or a politician trying to reach campaign workers. The interviewer can talk to many people at one time, answer questions directly, be seen or heard while answering questions, and receive immediate feedback. The time saved, problems solved, and immediacy of communication justify the high cost of the talk-back and conference call.

Interviewing provides us with an opportunity to obtain information about a person, place, thing, event, or idea directly from a particular person. Critics of interviewing ask whether information gained in the face-to-face or person-to-person situation is valid or reliable. Building check questions into the schedule and applying a reliability formula (providing the answers can be quantified) can aid in achieving reliability. Also, we might check the interviewee's responses given in other interviews or questionnaires. Reliability is not an unreachable goal. If the interviewer provides a trusting and supportive atmosphere, respondents will tend to be open and honest. From a theoretical point of view, any response is valid because perceptions of the individual make the expression of personality perfect. An individual's perceptions force responses in a particular manner, and a respondent at that moment and under those conditions is being as honest and trustworthy as one dares.

Interviewing in a face-to-face situation provides us with the opportunity to observe a person's responses to a wide range of behaviors. While one interview should not be the sole criterion by which to judge an individual (and the evaluation should be kept in perspective), it does provide a valuable opportunity to observe an individual firsthand and close up. A student described the interview this way: "It's like being near the wall at the end of a handball court—just as soon as you bounce back an answer, duck, because here comes another question." This atmosphere provides constant input by both parties to fulfill the purpose of the interview. Most successful sales representatives, if given the choice between writing a sales proposal, talking to a person on the telephone, or selling face-to-face, will choose face to face. Why? Because the interview allows them to size up a customer and to adapt to each customer as an individual. Opportunity to clarify material, to interchange behaviors, and to exchange opinions makes the time invested in an interview well spent.

Remember, interviewing is a useful tool on its own and as a supplement; but, like any tool, it is best used by skillfully trained and trustworthy individuals.

Summary

In this chapter, we defined interviewing as a process (dynamic, ongoing, ever-changing, with an interplay of many variables) of dyadic communication (person-to-person interaction and pervasive feedback between two parties) with a pre-determined and serious purpose (a planned, organized effort focused on some specific, serious subject matter) designed to interchange behavior (sharing of programmings, expectations, subject matter, feelings, and roles of speaker and listener) and involving the asking and answering of questions (purposeful, planned questions asked at the appropriate time). This definition encompasses a wide variety of interview settings and two basic approaches—directive and nondirective. Successful interviewing requires training, advance preparation, skill in interpersonal communication, flexibility, and a willingness to expose ourselves to risks involved in an intimate person-to-person situation.

In chapter 2 we will diagram the interviewing process and discuss the many communication variables involved in this process and how they interact.

Student Activities

1. Make a complete list of all of the dyads you are currently a part of. Based upon the characteristics of dyads (especially the interview) presented in chapter 1, discuss the following ideas:

    Sharing: To what degree?

    Caring: How much?

    Risk: What kind and how much?

2. Select two other persons and form a triad. One member of the triad will be person A, another B, and another C. At a given point in time, person A will ask one question of person B. Person B will then ask a question of person C. Person C will ask a question of person A. Questions may cover personal history, interests, likes, and dislikes. Continue the pattern of questioning for ten to fifteen minutes. At the end of this time, discuss the following questions:

    How much do you know about each other?

    What restrictions in this exercise prevented complete communication?

    What problems arose when you asked just one question at a time?

    What were you doing when you were not directly involved in the communication process?

    What did you spend most of your time doing: listening, speaking, preparing answers, preparing questions, observing the other parties?

3. We discussed two basic approaches to interviewing, directive and nondirective. Based on what you know about interviewing, what are their advantages and disadvantages? Which types of interviews tend to require one or the other of these approaches?

4. Interviewing often seems quite similar to conversation. In the next conversation in which you take part, keep track of the number of times the conversation topic changes. Ask yourself these questions:

    Why do people change topics so often in conversations?

    What happens when a particularly sensitive topic is brought up?

    Who initiates changes in topics?

5. By comparing and contrasting interviews with other forms of communication, we identified some distinguishing characteristics of interviewing. What other characteristics make interviewing a unique form of communication?

Notes

1. W. Charles Redding developed this classification of dyads, and he, along with Robert S. Goyer and John T. Rickey, developed the notion of interview "parties."

2. Eric Berne, *Games People Play* (New York: Grove Press, 1964); Sidney M. Jourard, *The Transparent Self* (Princeton, N.J.: Van Nostrand, 1968); and Erving Goffman, *Presentation of Self in Everyday Life* (Garden City, N.Y.: Doubleday Anchor Books, 1959).

3. Anatol Rapoport, *Fights, Games and Delegates* (Ann Arbor, Mich.: University of Michigan Press, 1961).

4. For other definitions of interviewing, see Walter Van Dyke Bingham, Bruce V. Moore, and John W. Gustad, *How to Interview* (New York: Harper & Row, 1959), p. 3; Robert L. Kahn and Charles F. Cannell, *The Dynamics of Interviewing* (New York: John Wiley & Sons, 1964), p. 16; and Robert S. Goyer, W. Charles Redding, and John T. Rickey, *Interviewing Principles and Techniques: A Project Text* (Dubuque, Iowa: Wm. C. Brown Co. Publishers, 1968), p.6

5. See for example, Raymond L. Gorden, *Interviewing: Strategy, Techniques, and Tactics* (Homewood, Ill.: Dorsey Press, 1969), pp. 52–55.

6. Bruce C. Wheatly and William B. Cash, "The Employee Survey: Correcting Its Basic Weaknesses," *Personnel Journal* 52 (June 1973): 456–59.

Suggested Readings

Barker, Larry. *Communication Vibrations*. Englewood Cliffs, N.J.: Prentice-Hall, 1974.

Brooks, William D., and Emmert, Philip. *Interpersonal Communication*. Dubuque, Iowa: Wm. C. Brown Co. Publishers, 1980.

Downs, Cal W.; Smeyak, G. Paul; and Martin, Ernest. *Professional Interviewing*. New York: Harper & Row, 1980.

Huseman, Richard C.; Logue, Cal N.; and Freshley, Dwight, (eds.) *Readings in Interpersonal and Organizational Communication*. Boston: Holbrook Press, 1977.

Johnson, David W. *Reaching Out: Interpersonal Effectiveness and Self-Actualization*. Englewood Cliffs, N.J.: Prentice-Hall, 1972.

Keltner, John. *Elements of Interpersonal Communication*. Belmont, Calif.: Wadsworth, 1973.

Leathers, Dale. *Nonverbal Communication Systems*. Boston: Allyn and Bacon, 1976.

Newman, Mildred; Berkowitz, Bernard; and Owen, Jean. *How to Be Your Own Best Friend*. New York: Random House, 1971.

Pace, R. Wayne, and Boren, Robert R. *The Human Transaction*. Glenview, Ill.: Scott, Foresman, 1973.

Pace, R. Wayne; Boren, Robert R.; and Peterson, Brent D. *Communication Behavior and Experiments: A Scientific Approach*. Belmont, Calif.: Wadsworth, 1975.

Siegman, Aron W., and Pope, Benjamin (eds.) *Studies in Dyadic Communication*. New York: Pergamon Press, 1972.

Tubbs, Stewart L., and Baird, John W. *The Open Person: Self-Disclosure and Personnel Growth*. Columbus, Ohio: Charles E. Merrill, 1976.

The Interviewing Process 2

Smith:	Hey! Glad you could meet with me today. I haven't seen you in weeks!
Jones:	Actually we visited over in the mall about two weeks ago, remember?
Smith:	Oh yes! It seems like months. I guess because I've been so busy.
Jones:	What have you been doing?
Smith:	Actually, I've been worrying a lot.
Jones:	Oh! Cheating on your taxes again?
Smith:	No, not really. We had some problems with my mother, and . . .
Jones:	Gee, I'm sorry to hear that. Anything serious? Can I help somehow?
Smith:	No, not really, but thanks for the offer. She broke her hip, then had the flu, and when you're eighty these things take time I guess. (Pause)
Jones:	Say, did you hear about the Jacksons? Marge just walked out, and Ralph took the boys, sold the business, and moved to Texas . . . Fort Worth . . . Dallas . . . something like that.
Smith:	No. Really? Who would of thought? I never suspected anything.
Jones:	Hey, I was as surprised as anyone. (Pause)
Smith:	Well, the reason I wanted to talk to you concerns the replacement for Elizabeth McMasters. I am really concerned about. . . .

To aid in understanding interview interchanges such as the one between Smith and Jones, we have developed a general summary model of the interviewing process. The Cash-Stewart Model of Interviewing, figure 2.9, contains all of the fundamental elements included in any interview. In this chapter we will explain and illustrate each part of the model and discuss the relationships between the many elements that make the interview a dynamic process.

Two Parties in the Interview

The two parties in the interview—interviewer party and interviewee party—are represented by two overlapping circles (see fig. 2.1). The circles overlap to signify that although each party is unique in many respects, both parties share some experiences, expectations, background, personality traits, beliefs, values, relationships, and so on. For example, both parties in a marriage counseling interview may come from the same city, have experienced similar crises, be

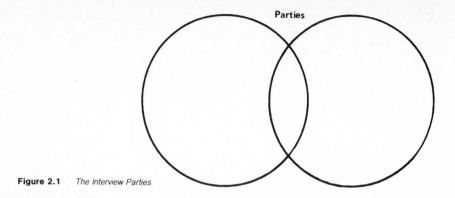

Parties

Figure 2.1   *The Interview Parties*

optimistic, have the same religious beliefs, desire to be treated fairly, want to obtain accurate information, and want the sincere interest and concern of the other party. Interviews are intimate interactions between complex human beings who are both similar and different because of previous programming.

Previous Programming

Previous programming is the sum total of an individual's experiences that causes him or her to behave in a particular manner to a given stimulus. Jess Lair's book, *I Ain't Much, Baby, But I'm All I've Got,* expresses our point that what we are comes with us to the interview.[1] Our attitudes, beliefs, values, ethics, morals, and stereotypes—created from our experiences—are a part of us that we cannot shed for an interview. We may have learned through the socialization process and living in the adult world to cover them up or to hide them in a guise of humor, but they remain an integral part of us.

Our previous programming may be revealed in how we react to language. Why, for example, do some women prefer Ms. to Miss or Mrs.? Why do black men react so strongly to "Boy?" Why do small children use the expression "dumb farmer" or "dumb foreigner?" They have been programmed by their experiences. Take the letters in the word "this" and, using all of them, see how many different words you can make. Do not read any further until you do. If the first word you made was "hits," you are programmed differently from a person who placed the "s" as the first letter.

Notice the client's efforts to avoid the words "died" or "dead" in this interview with a grief counselor.

Counselor:	And what about your father?
Client:	He uh, he left us several years ago.
Counselor:	Your father's alive, then?
Client:	Uh no. He passed away several years ago.
Counselor:	He's dead?
Client:	Yes, he's uh, (in a quiet voice) dead.

Many people have difficulty using and reacting to words such as dead, bankrupt, liar, and fat. Their programming prompts them to make comments such as "he's gone away," "she went out of business," "he exaggerates," and "she's stocky."

Our programming also reveals itself in how we behave toward others. How often have we heard someone profess loudly his or her Christianity and then ridicule a person in church for wearing an old suit or a dingy dress? Then there is the professed liberal who discovers a house he or she likes and can afford, but it is next to a black family. Suddenly the liberal wants to move to the country to find more land. Whether we call them prejudices, preferences, blind spots, or hangups, they are a part of our programmed autopilot and often reveal themselves without our thinking about them.

We are not necessarily talking about nasty, rude, or distasteful actions or with conscious or planned behavior. We are concerned with automatic behaviors. Everyone engages in such behavior, and it may be a barrier to open communication. This automatic behavior may work in positive ways. In the interchange between Smith and Jones, both made instant adaptations to the other's mood. They were sensitive, understood each other, and adapted automatically without much effort. Two principles of behavior are critical in all interviews: (1) we are responsible for what we say; and (2) we are responsible for what we do and how we do it.

Think for a moment. Do we remember which hand we carried our briefcase in this morning? Which shoe we put on first? How do we react to strangers, enemies, friends, interesting people? Take a small sheet of paper. After reading the following instructions, do the exercise before reading further. Place six dashes on the sheet of paper. Then, using the six dashes, write the word *stupid*.

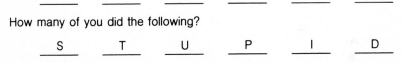

How many of you did the following?

S	T	U	P	I	D

If you did, you are wrong. Remember, we asked you to *write*, not *print*, the word stupid.[2] We might have created less confusion by saying, "Notice we said *write*," but the results would probably have been the same. People are programmed to print when they see dashes and so they ignore the instructions to write. We often engage in habitual behavior without thinking about how others may interpret our actions. Do not become paranoid about unconscious behavior; simply be more aware of the automatic ways we respond to others and how they may feel about the treatment.

How are Smith and Jones programmed? What difference would it make if we could see and hear their interactions? Jones has a sense of humor while Smith seems to be more serious, at least in this situation. Jones seems to enjoy gossip, or was this a means of escaping from an uncomfortable topic? No two people are programmed alike; therefore, no symbol or action can always be interpreted the same way. Smith laughed off Jones' remark about tax cheating, but an Internal Revenue Service agent overhearing this remark might have interpreted it quite differently. People with different backgrounds interpret symbols and interactions differently.

We may extend this concept to selective perceptions. To understand the meaning of selective perception, realize that our senses are constantly bombarded by stimuli.[3] We cannot read all books or magazines, or listen to all records, or talk to everyone, or react to all smells, views, and tactile exposures, or give each and every one our undivided attention. We must select from our exposures those things that are important to us and attempt to deal with them. Our perceptions and selectivity of what we want to perceive are based on complex frames of reference and interlocking value systems.

What we are, our relevant programmings, determines how we respond to the world around us. Some people are at a disadvantage because of poor physical senses or lack of personal sensitivity to people and things around them; others have psychological blind spots and hangups that prevent them from clearly perceiving events, people, or circumstances. Listen carefully the next time you hear two young men talking about a young woman or two young women talking about a young man. One person may refer to one part of the anatomy while the other person may refer to a different part of the anatomy or to a personality or character trait. Different programming influences these perceptions. Suppose two graduates of arch-rival universities focus attention on a player for Southern California; they agree he is quite an athlete. Two plays later he scores on a sixty-five-yard run. All of a sudden he is a devil to the UCLA alumnus while he has become a god to the Southern Cal alumnus.

Observe how the interviewer in the following exchange selects the "possible strike" for emphasis from among several causes of a company's financial problems.

Interviewer: What factors led to your company's current financial difficulties?
Interviewee: Well, I'd say a number of factors: new government regulations; inflated cost of raw materials; a 10 percent pay increase to prevent a strike; high interest rates . . .
Interviewer: (interrupting) I see! Then part of your difficulties were due to labor problems.
Interviewee: Yes, I guess you could say that part of . . .
Interviewer: (interrupting) And how long have you been having labor problems?

This interviewer seems to be "blinded" by selective perception and will come away with the impression, regardless of what the interviewee says, that labor problems caused the company's financial difficulties.

Interchanging Behavior During Interviews

The small circles within each party (see fig. 2.2) contain an R (interviewer) and an E (interviewee) to signify that behavior is constantly interchanged during interviews. Both parties are likely to ask and to answer questions, to speak and

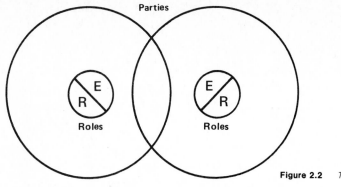

Parties

Roles

Roles

Figure 2.2 *The Switching of Roles*

to listen from time to time, and to take on the roles (including the responsibilities) of interview*er* and interview*ee*. Neither party can sit back and expect the other to make the interview a success single-handedly. For instance, if we feel that a pollster's question is not phrased in a way to obtain our true feelings about a political candidate, we should point this out and explain our answer. During this brief interchange, *we* have taken charge of the interview and have become the interviewer. A short time later the pollster is likely to regain control of the interview and proceed as interviewer. An aggressive interviewee may take command of an interview and become, in reality, the interviewer.

Smith and Jones are the two parties in the opening interchange, and each speaks, listens, and reacts to the other.

Perceptions of the Interviewer and Interviewee

Programming and perceptions affect the way interviewers and interviewees respond to one another and thus the way the interview progresses.[4] We come to each interview with perceptions of the other party (interviewer or interviewee) and of ourselves (interviewer or interviewee) and may modify these perceptions during the interview. These perceptions are symbolized in the model by the double-pointed arrows between the interview parties (see fig. 2.3).

Perceptions of the Other Party   We may be influenced by the other party's reputation—a tough boss, a reporter who asks embarrassing questions, a shady used car dealer, a counselor who cares. Our previous encounters with the person may make us look forward to (or dread) the interview and may pose an advantage (or disadvantage) for the interviewer. One of the authors purchased a large quantity of cookies from a Girl Scout who began her interview, "You may not remember me, but I will never forget your performance at our grade

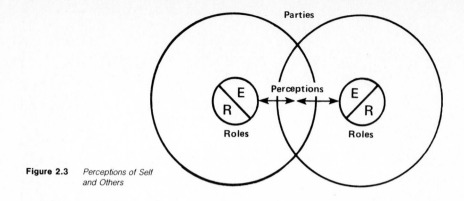

Figure 2.3 *Perceptions of Self and Others*

school Christmas party. You must be the greatest juggler in the world." Such insightful perception could not go unrewarded. Our perceptions may be affected if the other party is endorsed by persons or groups we like or dislike.

Our perceptions of the interviewer or interviewee may be verified or altered during the interview. How does the person answer or react (verbally and non-verbally) to questions and topics? Does the person express himself or herself clearly and effectively? Does the person reason logically and provide evidence for ideas? What about appearance: hair style, manner, appropriateness of clothing, cleanliness?[5] Many government and business groups, for example, react negatively to beards, western-style suits, and dirty fingernails. Some persons believe that sloppy appearance indicates sloppy work habits and lack of pride. A person's age, sex, race, size, or ethnic group and identification with certain groups, people, values, and beliefs may influence our perceptions—positively or negatively. What is our role relationship with the interviewer or interviewee? Are we superior to, equal to, or subordinate to the other party?

Perceptions of Ourselves—Self-Concept   Brooks defines self-concept as "those physical, social, and psychological perceptions of ourselves that we have derived from our experiences and our interactions with others."[6] Our experiences include all of our past behaviors, how *we* have observed and interpreted these behaviors, and how we perceive *others* to have observed and interpreted these behaviors. Our interactions with others include groups we are or have been affiliated with, groups to which we would like to belong, and the roles we have played, or are playing.

Our self-concept may determine whether we are willing to take part in an interview. For instance, we may fear potential failure and refuse to take part in a counseling session. Or we may think we did poorly in a previous counseling session and refuse to take part in another session. We may take part in an

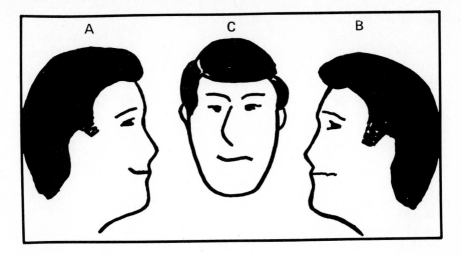

Figure 2.4 *Perceptions of Interviewer and Interviewee*

interview and fail because we were convinced that we would fail. This is a self-fulfilling prophecy: "I told you I couldn't do it"; "I just knew I wouldn't get the job"; "I couldn't help it, that's just the way I am." Our self-concept may influence the kinds of messages we send and receive, how we send and receive messages, the risks we are willing to take, and the degree of self-disclosure we engage in.

In a very real sense, each party creates the other party as the interview process takes place. As John Keltner wrote, in dyadic interchanges, "One and one are not two. Rather it is one and one and two."[7] Figure 2.4 expresses Keltner's idea. Profile A represents the "real" party; profile B represents the unique perceptions of the party by interviewer or interviewee; and profile C represents the "created party," a combination of the real and the perceived. For interviewer or interviewee, however, profile C is the "real" party being dealt with.

In the opening dialogue, Jones apparently perceives Smith to be a person willing to take a joke and interested in gossiping a bit about mutual acquaintances. Smith perceives Jones to be a person who would be sympathetic about his worries, especially about his mother, and one willing to discuss a problem. Both parties seem comfortable with one another. Self-concepts are unclear in these opening exchanges.

Communication Interactions

Communication interactions, symbolized by the series of curved arrows that link each party in figure 2.5, are the most obvious behavioral interchanges during interviews. Each level of interaction differs in the degree of self-disclosure, the amount of personal risk involved, the perceived meaning of the message, and the amount of critical content exchanged.

Level 1 interactions deal with relatively safe, nonthreatening areas of inquiry, and answers tend to be superficial, socially acceptable, comfortable, and replete with ambiguities. These exchanges illustrate level 1 communication interactions.

1. **Interviewer:** How have you been?
   Interviewee: Just fine except for the usual aches and pains.
2. **Interviewer:** How do you feel about your education at Kent State?
   Interviewee: It was okay.
3. **Interviewer:** What do you think about the recent hot spell?
   Interviewee: It was really hot.

Level 2 interactions deal with more intimate and controversial areas of inquiry—our behaviors, thoughts, attitudes, beliefs, feelings—and responses tend to be half-safe, half-revealing. The interviewee strives to satisfy the interviewer while not revealing too much. The following exchanges illustrate level 2 communication interactions.

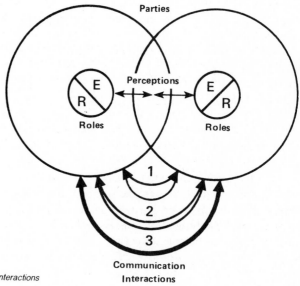

Figure 2.5 *Communication Interactions*

1. **Interviewer:** Tell me frankly, how do you feel about your education at Tulane?

   Interviewee: I think my first two years were a waste of time, but during my last two years, I got a good grounding in accounting and economics. My background in marketing is not strong.

2. **Interviewer:** What are your ideas on attendance?

   Interviewee: We rent a worker's time and, unless it's next to impossible or the worker is sick, we expect perfect attendance.

3. **Interviewer:** What do you think of our new headquarters?

   Interviewee: It's very attractive and seems quite efficient, but it's a long way from the airport and downtown.

Level 3 interactions may deal with highly intimate and controversial areas of inquiry, and answers often reach levels of maximum self-disclosure of feelings, beliefs, attitudes, and perceptions. We are unlikely to achieve level 3 interactions unless and until we have established a high level of trust with the interviewee, a level of trust often unattainable during a first, second, or even third interview with a particular party. The following exchanges illustrate level 3 interactions.

1. **Interviewer:** You seem very hesitant to answer my questions.

   Interviewee: Frankly, I don't trust medical doctors, not since I had a very bad experience with one in Memphis when my father died. I think you're out to make a fortune off people's health problems.

2. **Interviewer:** What did you think of my test?

   Interviewee: Too many of the questions were not worded clearly, and at least a half-dozen went beyond the material we covered. I think you need to prepare your tests more carefully.

3. **Interviewer:** Why has your absenteeism risen in the last quarter of this year?

   Interviewee: Well, my wife and I have been having problems, and we separated a few months ago. I've been having trouble coping with this and have missed work because of appointments with a psychiatrist. You know, I didn't want the guys at work to know that I was seeing a shrink.

The question-response-question sequence (or question-antecedent-question relationship) often makes interaction levels difficult to distinguish in interviews. The interchanges between Smith and Jones reveal three mood changes: joking at the beginning, serious about Smith's mother in the middle, and a bit of gossip near the end. We have all taken part in interviews or conversations that suddenly took a turn for the worse, that deteriorated from level 3 to level 1, from revealing, in-depth responses to guarded, superficial responses. We probably wanted to stop talking before things got worse.

Which levels of interactions occur in an interview depends upon perceptions of self, the situation, and the other party; the level of trust established during the interview; the topics under discussion; defensiveness; the way questions are asked; and level of motivation. Interviews deal with *our* behavior, *our* job performance, *our* reputation, *our* decisions, *our* feelings, *our* loss, *our* money, and *our* future—not some distant or remote person, problem, or decision. Thus, our ego, if not our financial, psychological, or physical survival, tends to be on the line. We tend to do what we want to do or have to do, and we must be aware of what is likely to motivate a particular interviewee or interviewer in a particular situation. Several generalizations may prove useful.

1. People are likely to participate in interviews if they are informed of what is expected and demanded. We should avoid tricks, gimmicks, and lies and be as straightforward and honest as possible. We should introduce ourselves and, if necessary, describe our purpose and interview instrument, and then proceed. If we ask, "May I have five minutes of your time to discuss your mileage report," we should take no more than five minutes. We should be pleasant and polite, regardless of the look or response we get. Remember, the first few minutes of an interview may make the difference between a level 1 and a level 2 or 3 interview.

2. People are likely to take part in interviews and go beyond level 1 interactions if they are interested in the other party or the subject matter of the interview. It may be easier to gather information if the other party knows us or our organization. A self-introduction may create respondent interest. Market survey organizations often pick interviewers who are outgoing, pleasant in appearance, and have an easygoing disposition. Some organizations believe that pleasant and attractive interviewers of the opposite sex may get men or women to talk more openly and freely.

Each person expects our fullest attention and respect.

The Interviewing Process

3. People may be motivated by a tangible or intangible reward. Rewards may include money, a copy of the results, a public or private acknowledgment, a note of sincere appreciation, a feeling of accomplishment, or pride in a contribution to society or a particular organization. We must know the other party in order to determine the appropriate reward that will achieve the kind of cooperation necessary to accomplish a goal.

4. People may be motivated if they are treated as important individuals. They expect our fullest attention and respect. Their views may not be similar to ours and their methods of expression may not be elegant, but they are theirs. Interviewees and interviewers have a right to be treated as persons and to cooperate fully only if we treat them as we would expect to be treated under similar circumstances.

We may encounter individuals who, for whatever reasons, refuse to be motivated or to cooperate even at level 1. This group of individuals is small, but they discourage interviewers. When we have tried our best, terminate the interview and go to another party. Don't be unduly discouraged; it happens to the very best of interviewers.

We might compare communications interaction levels with doors. The door is ajar in level 1 interactions, and some general ideas, feelings, and information may pass through. In level 2, the door is half-open (the optimist's view) or half-closed (the pessimist's view) and more specific and revealing ideas, feelings, and information may pass through. In level 3, the door is wide open and it allows for maximum self-disclosure by one or both parties, and highly specific and revealing ideas, feelings, and information pass through.

Not surprisingly, level 1 communication interactions are most common in interviews, which is the reason for the wide arrow in figure 2.5. This level is particularly common during the early minutes of interviews when parties are "sizing up" one another and the situation. If an interviewer finds it difficult to advance beyond level 1, he or she must try to determine the reason or reasons by observing, listening to, and questioning the interviewee. The reason(s) may be motivational, defensiveness, inability to communicate, situational, or perceptual. Be patient and be perceptive. We should try to ease the other party into level 2 and level 3 interactions. Level 2 interactions are fairly common in many interviews, particularly when the interviewer is acting as an information source or guide and when questions and responses are tactful and nonthreatening. We must avoid evaluative comments such as, "That doesn't make much sense to me." "Now *why* did you do *that?*" or "I resent your insinuation that some lawyers are unethical." Level 3 interactions are the least common in interviews, which is the reason for the thin arrow in figure 2.5. They require high levels of trust, self-concept, and motivation. Level 1 and level 2 interactions do not reveal the intensity of a person's feelings or "hidden" reasons for these feelings as do level 3 interactions.

Interactions or interchanges between interview parties may be verbal or nonverbal and intentional or unintentional. During an interview, it may be impossible to separate the verbal from the nonverbal, but for discussion purposes, we will do so in this chapter.

Verbal Interchanges

Words are merely learned symbols for things, events, ideas, and feelings—they are not the things themselves. Words are vehicles for communication and, since we learn language in a particular environment and under particular circumstances, we come to view the meaning and the word as the same thing and to assume that we share language with any interviewer or interviewee. Remember, the meaning of words rests within us; words don't mean, people do.[8] Both symbol and meaning are learned.

We are reading black type on a white sheet of paper bound in a book, but the word "book" is not this book itself. It simply represents a whole category of things called books in our language. There are fat books, skinny books, interesting books, pretty books, ugly books, short books, long books, well-written books, needless books, and precious books. The word "strike" contains six innocent letters, but the word means different things to different people in different situations. A store manager may hate a strike, while a bowler loves a strike. A baseball pitcher wants to get as many strikes as possible; a batter does not.

How do words get their meanings? One way is by our experiences and programming. "Communism" is simply one *c*, followed by an *o*, plus two *m*'s, a *u*, an *n*, an *i*, an *s*, and another *m*. Call a member of the John Birch Society and a member of the Socialist Labor Party communists and see how they react. The first is likely to react angrily; the second may shrug off the comment or explain the difference between a socialist and a communist. A second way language obtains meaning is through societal usage—dictionary or denotative meanings. A denotative definition of communism, for instance, may be a socio-economic-political theory in which the state is glorified above the individual. A third source of meaning is association with other words. Communism might be preceded with treacherous, dishonest, dirty, barbarous; each gives a particular meaning to the word communism or communist. A fourth way to obtain meaning is by association with nonword symbols. When asked to name a tool that represents communism, we would think of a hammer and sickle. When we see a crossed hammer and sickle, we probably think of the word communism. Geographical region is a fifth influence on language meaning. A recent immigrant from a communist country may react differently to the word communism than a life-long citizen of Chicago, a midwestern farmer, or a retired teacher in Florida.

If words don't mean, people do, what can we do about language in interviews? Here are a few suggestions:

1. Remember that all people do not use the same word(s) in the same way(s).

2. Do not waste time blaming the other party for using the wrong word or for interpreting it differently. Find out how the party is using a word. Mutual understanding is more important than words.

3. Keep up with changes in language, especially slang. For example, bowling alleys are now bowling lanes, gas stations are now service stations, and foreign students are now exchange students. Some groups now refer to traffic lights as vehicular control devices, janitors as maintenance engineers, and cemeteries as memorial gardens. A sports car was "neat" in the 50s, "cool" in the 60s, "tough" in the 70s, and "decent" in the 80s.

4. Expand our vocabulary—the more shades and hues we have at our disposal the more carefully we can paint word pictures. We will address verbal interchanges and problems further when we discuss questions and responses in chapter 4.

Nonverbal Interchanges

When we take part in interviews, we usually observe the other party and listen for verbal and nonverbal clues that reveal how well the interview is proceeding. We may also be keenly aware that the other party is busy detecting everything we *do* and *don't do* and is assigning *meanings* to our simplest behavioral acts: head nods, facial expressions, vocal inflections, speaking rate, pauses, hand and arm movements, leg movements, body movements, posture, touch, yawns, and glances at our watch. The intimate and personal nature of the interview (the parties are often a mere arm's length apart and are directly involved in the topic and outcome of the interview) tends to magnify the importance of nonverbal communication.

Verbal and nonverbal messages are often intertwined. For instance, our nonverbal messages may *complement* our verbal messages. Vocal stress or inflection may call attention to an important word in a sentence: "I am *not* going to give to the United Fund" or "The *net* income last year was $345,000." Vocal inflection to draw out a word may give a specific meaning to the word. Take this example:

Elizabeth: Who do you think we should put in charge of the new account?
William: Delmar Dingfarb.
Elizabeth: Himmm? (in a shocked voice)

Obviously "him" is not a simple, innocent pronoun in this interchange because of the manner in which Elizabeth says it. If we must release an employee, we are likely to complement the verbal message, "I'm sorry Mark, but I'm going to have to let you go," with a serious and sincere tone of voice, deliberate speaking rate, serious facial expression, and direct eye contact. Our nonverbal message accentuates and verifies our verbal message. We often try to combine and to assess the verbal and the nonverbal before interpreting the meaning of messages. For example, if a client remarks, "That's a nice looking outfit; you ought to have it cleaned and burned," we will listen to the client's voice, observe the client's facial expression, and look for a twinkle in the client's eyes in order to determine if the message is a joke or a serious evaluation of our clothing. As we mentioned earlier, language is a collection of imperfect and often imprecise symbols. At times words simply cannot express satisfactorily our inner feelings, the exact meaning we want, or perhaps we don't know or cannot think of a word that expresses an attitude, feeling, or idea in a particular manner. Nonverbal actions may join the verbal in expressing successfully a meaning or subtle feeling.

Some nonverbal messages *repeat* verbal messages. For example, we may nod our head while saying yes or shake our head while saying no. We may emphasize the word stop by extending our arm with the hand and fingers pointing upward. Hello and goodbye are often repeated with waves of the arm and hand. We may point to a chair and say, "Sit here please." "We're number one!" would not be the same without a raised arm and an extended finger. "Give us two beers" is repeated with two raised fingers. "I love you" is repeated and accentuated with a touch, a wink, or a squeeze of the hand. We may claim that the catfish we caught was nearly two feet long and extend our arms and hold our hands approximately two feet apart.

Nonverbal symbols may *substitute* for verbal symbols—the nonverbal being translated instantly into particular words or phrases. All of the actions just discussed as nonverbal repeaters of verbal messages may be used alone. For example, we may point to a chair *without saying,* "Sit here please," and the interviewee will get the message. We may convey "We're number one!" by merely raising and shaking an index finger; say "I don't know" by shrugging our shoulders; or express "I don't care" with a shrug and a sour facial expression. If a person asks, "May I borrow $40 until the first of the week," we may react with a frown and an icy stare; there is no need for a verbal no. We may say "I approve," "please continue," or "I'm interested in what you're saying" by nodding our head during an interview. These nonverbal substitutes—literally a kind of everyday sign language—may be as effective as and less disruptive than verbal messages. A pause or silence may communicate a variety of messages: Go on; I agree (disagree); I do (don't) believe you; I am interested (disinterested); I have confidence (no confidence) in you; You are not finished; or I don't understand. Remember, silence is not a void; communication is taking place. Notice the role of nonverbal substitutes in the following interchange at a football game between a hot dog vendor and a customer seated several people from the aisle.

Vendor:	Hotdogs! (in a loud voice)
Customer:	(raises a hand)
Vendor:	How many?
Customer:	(raises four fingers)
Vendor:	Anything on them? (in a loud voice)
Customer:	(nods head and yells) Mustard!
Vendor:	That'll be $2.70! (in a loud voice)
Customer:	(cups hand behind the ear and looks puzzled)
Vendor:	(holds up two fingers and then flashes ten fingers seven times)
Customer:	(nods head and passes along $3)
Vendor:	(begins to count out change)

The Interviewing Process

Customer: (shakes head, points to the change and then to the vendor, and smiles)

Vendor: (smiles, makes a circle with an index finger and thumb, and shapes lips into "Thanks!")

The majority of this simple transaction takes place through nonverbal symbols that are translated into verbal symbols by the participants. Obviously, nonverbal communication may play a variety of important roles in interviews.

Nonverbal symbols may be *inconsistent* with verbal symbols. For example, if a superior says, "Go ahead and take tomorrow off . . . if you want to," we are likely to listen and to observe the nonverbal messages that accompany the verbal—not merely *what* is said but *how* it is said. We may interpret the "real" message as "I don't approve!" or, "It'll create problems," or, "Do you really care what I say?" We often mean the exact opposite of the verbal symbols we utter. For instance, "Boy, what a choice!" may mean there is no choice; both options are terrible. "That was a tremendous raise" may mean that the raise was ridiculously low. "I can hardly wait" may mean that we dread an outcome and do not want to do something. "That's some car" may mean that we think the car is ready for the scrap heap. "How can I ever repay you?" may mean "How can I get revenge?" A misplaced pause, such as in the following question, may communicate different and perhaps confusing messages: "What's up the road ahead?" or "What's up the road, (pause) ahead?" We must be aware of *how* we are vocalizing language because messages sent and messages received are an inseparable combination of the verbal and the nonverbal. Research suggests that when voice, face, gestures, eye contact, or posture communicate an attitude or feeling that seems inconsistent with the verbal symbols used, the interviewer or interviewee will place the nonverbal over the verbal— the *how* dominates the *what*.[9]

Nonverbal messages may substitute for verbal messages.

Some nonverbal symbols or actions do not complement, substitute, or contradict a particular word, phrase, or sentence but communicate messages of their own. For example, an interviewer may detect a yawn and interpret this as a sign of boredom. Poor posture such as slouching in a chair may communicate sloppy habits, fatigue, laziness, or boredom. Poor eye contact or a limp handshake may "tell" an interviewee or an interviewer that we are untrustworthy, that we have something to hide, that we are timid, or that we are ill. Leaning forward, smiling, head nods, and good eye contact are positive reinforcers—they may communicate empathy, interest, trust, sincerity, and agreement. Our physical appearance and dress may send a variety of messages (ranging from highly positive to highly negative) about intelligence, education, cleanliness, maturity, interest, composure, professionalism, sense of appropriateness, and work habits. A university president once remarked, "One sign of a good administrator is how much time he or she spends on lunch and how he or she eats it. I take each new candidate out for lunch, and the lingerers or sloppy eaters do not get hired."

Our rate of speaking and conducting an interview may communicate urgency (fast speed), the gravity of a situation (slow speed), lack of interest (fast speed), lack of preparation (slow, halting speed), or nervousness (fast speed and breathless voice). Interview participants are likely to notice changes, especially abrupt ones, in vocal tone (from friendly to serious), in speed (from normal to full-throttle), in eye contact (from normal eye contact to a stare or avoidance of eye contact), in posture (from sitting back to sitting on the edge of a chair), in vocal volume (from soft to loud), and in gestures (from none or normal gestures to highly animated movements of hands, arms, legs, or head). And, as interview participants, we are likely to assign meanings and reasons for the nonverbal changes we observe. Eye contact can be a valuable communication asset in the intimate, one-to-one interview, but it can also be a detriment. For instance, unblinking stares or frequent glances at a facial scar, a piece of clothing, or a part of our body is likely to make us feel embarrassed, nervous, or generally uneasy during an interview. We will both wonder and try to guess what the other party is thinking or trying to say nonverbally. Pauses may communicate interest, deep thought, careful consideration of the best way to express an idea, and concern about not rushing the interview or nervousness, inability to express ideas clearly, boredom, and lack of dynamism. As interview participants, we are responsible for and must be aware of our nonverbal messages and the consistency between what we say, how we say it, and what we do.

Remember, any behavioral act—verbal or nonverbal—may be interpreted in a meaingful way by the person receiving it. This message may be intentional or unintentional. The fact that we do not *intend* to communicate boredom by a yawn (we may not know we yawned) is irrelevant if the other party interprets it that way. The boss may approve of our taking tomorrow off, but he or she communicated disagreement. As we noted in chapter 1, perhaps the greatest single problem with human communication is assumption. Faulty assumptions and transmissions are revealed when a person says, "But I didn't mean it *that* way." We may be trying to communicate sincerity, ambition, willingness to learn, and self-confidence, but the interviewer or interviewee may interpret our actions as a show of cockiness or conceit.

To avoid unintentional messages, we should select the most appropriate words and be sure we are sharing language and meanings with the other party. Coordinate the verbal and nonverbal. Don't allow words to communicate one message and face or voice to communicate another. We must be *aware* of what we are doing nonverbally. In other words, we must listen to ourselves.

Feedback

Feedback—represented by the large arrow at the top of the interviewing model (see fig. 2.6)—is the primary means of verifying *what* we communicated to the other party and *how* that party is reacting. Feedback messages are pictured

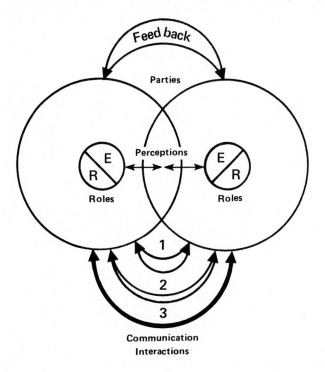

Figure 2.6 *Feedback*

going both ways because feedback between interview parties is continuous. In no other form of communication is feedback so immediate and pervasive as it is in the one-to-one interview situation. A cartoon in a recent issue of the *Wall Street Journal* showed an angry husband whose wife was saying, "If you would only view my comments as feedback rather than nagging, you'd find them easier to take." No interview can progress for any period of time without meaningful feedback.

The interaction process in the interview is diagrammed in figure 2.7. A sends an "original message" to B, and B sends a feedback message to A— B's reaction to the original message. A receives B's feedback message and reacts to it. This message-feedback-reaction process continues until either A or B decides to transmit another original message, then the process begins again.

When Smith and Jones met, Smith said, "Hey! I haven't seen you in weeks." If Jones had responded, "Tire irons and baked beans, thanks!" confusion would have reigned. Fortunately, Jones response signalled to Smith, the initiator of the message, that he had gotten through.

The important question is, What does the sender of an original message do with a feedback message? Feedback is more than a means of checking on word translation. It is a knowledge of results that may be inferred, observed, neither, or both. A response to a question may tell us that the message received was not the message intended or that the message got through. Now, based on previous programming, perceptions, and situational variables, we compare the response to our message with what we had intended; then we decide what to do about a correct or incorrect reception of the intended message.

There are three possible feedback alternatives. We may confirm that we got through, readjust the message, or deny that we got through and try again. To understand the three types of feedback reactions, imagine that an interviewer sends this message: "I want you to work the second shift Saturday." The interviewee sends a feedback message in the form of a frown, an apparent rejection or denial of the original message. The interviewer may reject or deny the feedback message by saying silent or aloud, "I was hoping you would not

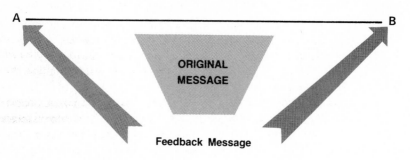

Figure 2.7   *Message-Feedback-Reaction Model*

react that way," or adjust the message to the interviewee's feedback and say, "I know you had plans for Saturday, but this is the first time I have asked you to work late on a Saturday in more than a year." The interviewee may *confirm* the feedback reaction by saying, "Yes, I have had these plans made for more than a month"; or may *deny* the interviewer's feedback, "No, it's really not that big a deal" (essentially denying the frown); or may *adjust* to the feedback by saying, "I'm sorry, you have given me a real break on weekend work; I'll try to change my plans." Caution! The interviewee may only *appear* to agree with the interviewer.

Feedback interchanges are continuous, but whether they are detected and interpreted correctly depends upon the sensitivity, receptivity, and perceptiveness of the participants. For example, an interviewee may avoid intentionally or unintentionally some sensitive area that he or she does not want the interviewer to discover. This person may display uneasiness nonverbally—lowered eyes fidgeting, trembling voice—everytime the interviewer gets close to the sensitive area. A perceptive interviewer will detect this nonverbal signal and adjust the interview to probe into the area or to avoid it.

Here are some guidelines for giving and receiving feedback.[10]

Giving

1. Give feedback in a form that the interviewee/interviewer can handle.
2. Quality feedback is more important than quantity; do not overload the circuit.
3. Give feedback to help the other party, not for self-satisfaction.
4. Pose questions and make statements of substance.

Getting

1. Listen carefully to the feedback message and understand before we defend.
2. Avoiding, suppressing, and denying are methods used to prevent feedback from getting through.
3. Use feedback to discover aspects of communicative behavior and its influences on others.
4. Adjust communicative behavior, this is a small price to pay for better understanding.

Which feedback guidelines can you detect in the following interview exchange? Which guidelines are being ignored? Notice that feedback comes from both parties.

John: Well, what do you think of our new facilities?
Mary: The building or the equipment?
John: Either.
Mary: I think the building is very functional.
John: (serious, somewhat quizzical facial expression) Uh huh?
Mary: By that I mean (quickened pace) it's designed for efficient research and development and ease of communication between departments. It's (slight pause and looking John directly in the eyes) *very functional.*

John: Okay, I *think* I understand what you mean. Any *other* impressions?

Mary: Do you have something *particular* in mind?

John: No (pause) not necessarily, nothing in *particular*. We're proud of our top-of-the-line, state-of-the-art computer facilities.

Mary: Oh yes, of course, (nervous laugh) the computer system is impressive.

Listening

We want to devote special attention to listening because it is vital to effective feedback and communication in interviews. Poor listening habits will guarantee loss of information contained in responses, failure to detect clues in verbal and nonverbal feedback, and failure to motivate an interviewee or interviewer to respond, to listen, and to interact meaningfully. There are three approaches to listening: critical, active, and empathic. Each approach has a particular emphasis that may help us to receive and to process information during interviews.

Critical listening is primarily a "passive" method of receiving content during interviews, in that there is little or no feedback for the other party. Interviewers and interviewees strive to understand content to determine how they may use it or how it might affect them. They focus on what is in it for them and, in this sense, critical listening is selfish listening. The critical listener may conduct a *silent* and *undetectable* debate with an interviewer or interviewee.

Active listening is a method of providing understanding for self-use *and* for instant feedback to the sender of the message. The active listener must be alert to verbal and nonverbal messages because he or she assists the other party in establishing mutual understanding. The concept of active listening comes from the work of Carl Rogers in counseling. There is a close relationship between active listening and secondary questions discussed in chapter 4. Here are six functions of active listening and some possible responses.

Functions	Possible Responses
1. To aid the respondent in opening up.	1. What is bothering you? I understand, go on.
2. To aid the respondent in accurately expressing feelings.	2. This makes you feel. . . . Why do you feel this way? What were your feelings when that happened?
3. To help the respondent to define the situation.	3. Then as you see it. . . . It seems that. . . . From your point of view. . . .
4. To respond to the person's total communication.	4. You appear to be. . . . Then you are saying. . . . You mean. . . .
5. To pinpoint the specific problem or problems.	5. You are having difficulty with. . . . Your problem is. . . . These situations have caused. . . .
6. To summarize the pros and cons or to point to places that need clarification.	6. This job has these advantages. . . . This school can offer. . . . This choice means that. . . .

Active listening during interviews shows interest, understanding, and clear feedback. We do not sit idly by and listen for the things that are important to us. We listen closely and are actively involved in the interviewing process.

Empathic listening is a method of responding to the interviewee in such a manner as to convey understanding that goes beyond the receiving of messages. It lets the interviewee know that we are familiar with and understand the predicament he or she is in. Empathic listening is total response, not a series of principles. It reassures, comforts, and expresses warmth. Empathic listening is closely related to reflective probing questions discussed in chapter 4, and the principles are difficult to learn and to use. Highly personal and emotional problems (terminations, reprimands, demotions, etc.) call for empathic listening. The genuineness of empathic listening is a measure of its success. Empathic listening and responses point the way to actions a person may take. Here are some statements and possible responses.

Statements	Possible Responses
1. *Anger and denial:* I can't be that bad. . . . I know damn well I'm as good as. . . .	1. I can understand your anger; it's often unfair to be compared to others. You do have strengths and have reason to be. . . .
2. *Disappointment:* I really wanted. . . . I just can't believe. . . .	2. We all face disappointments. . . . Yes, it's difficult to believe. . . .
3. *Misunderstanding:* I tried to tell him. He never listens to me.	3. You tried to sit down with Bill and to talk it out? We all feel that way.
4. *Self-Pity:* I never do anything right. I don't know why I try. I never get ahead.	4. Are things really that bad? You do try and that's. . . .
5. *Rejection:* Poor grades No promotion Love rejections	5. I understand how you feel. We all need to look at some ways of getting what we want from time to time.

The expression of understanding is important, but we should not permit the interviewee or interviewer to engage in self-indulgent behaviors. Assist the other party to begin the problem-solving process, to discontinue unproductive behavior. Each sample response is aimed at getting the interviewee or interviewer to examine alternatives, to explore solutions, and to reverse the emotional trends.

Although insightful listening is critical to both parties in interviews, most of us find it difficult to listen, let alone to choose the appropriate listening approach. Listening is an invisible skill (we cannot see, hear, touch, or smell it), and many of us learn to be passive listeners through our roles as children, students, subordinates, and employees. Larry Barker, in his book *Listening Behavior,* lists nine common listening problems.[11]

1. Viewing a topic as uninteresting. Interviewers may make the mistake of thinking that some information or questions may be uninteresting to the interviewee and should not be asked. Nothing is wrong with asking for information that we, the interviewer, deem important, and we can usually explain its importance to the interviewee. The respondent should not look upon routine questions as unimportant; the interviewer may not know where and when we graduated from high school, the courses we took, or our address. The perceptions of both parties determine interest in a topic.

2. Criticizing a speaker's delivery instead of the message. We must not be so concerned about a person's accent, unusual mannerisms, or gestures that we miss the message. Some people's noses wiggle when they talk, but noting this fact is not worth a missed message. Concentrate on the content of the message, not on the means used to deliver the message.

3. Getting overstimulated or emotionally involved. The interviewer may ask a question such as, "How do you feel now that you have finished school?" While answering, the interviewee may express the same reaction the interviewer had when finishing his or her education. The interviewer interjects a lengthy discourse on what it was like when he or she was in school. Valuable time is taken from the respondent. The internal reaction of the interviewer may also damage the interview. For instance, a student interviewing for a job in accounting mentions an affiliation with a student political-action group. The interviewer may become so distracted with feelings about student activism that the information that follows is lost.

4. Listening only for facts. Interviewers may believe in getting the facts, just the facts. They listen for hard-core facts so they may write them down. Facts are important, but often not as important as the reasons behind the facts or the interviewee's feelings about these facts.

5. Preparing to answer questions before fully understanding them. We all love to second-guess a coach on fourth down, the ending of a movie or a book, or the panelist on a quiz show. However, we may find ourselves in an interview saying, "I'll bet she's gonna ask me what courses I liked least because she just asked what courses I liked best in college." While we are engaged in mental speculation, the interviewer may move on to a new area of inquiry, and we may answer the wrong question or have trouble adapting to the new, unexpected one. Wait until the point or question is understood before beginning to answer or to comment.

6. Allowing our attention to be diverted. Interviewing requires the constant attention of both parties, so eliminate as many distractions as possible. Human physiology prevents us from talking much faster than 200 words per minute without loss of listener comprehension, but our thinking processes are at least twice the speaking rate. Thus, if we can think, comprehend, or plan an answer in a fraction of the time it takes to listen, we are certain to occupy our minds in some way, perhaps by daydreaming. Concentrate on what is being said and how it is being said.

7. Listening only to what is easy to understand. It is difficult to become an excellent listener without listening to difficult material. When we are too willing to say, "I don't understand what you mean," we may be admitting that we have made no attempt to understand. When a question or response is not easily understood, ask for clarification; do not admit ignorance or confusion before trying to understand.

8. Allowing emotionally laden words to interfere with listening. Our previous programming creates within us a need to react to the word as if it were the thing. The name of a former boss, lover, partner, hometown, hangout, or labels such as "Pollack," "dago," "spic," "wop," "nigger," or "Jew" may trigger reactions that range from joy to repulsion. Barker suggests, "Identify, prior to listening, those words that affect you emotionally; attempt to analyze why words affect you the way they do; try to reduce their impact upon you by using a defense mechanism."

9. Permitting personal prejudices or deep-seated convictions to impair comprehension. This problem is often identified as closed-mindedness, bigotry, rigidity, or inflexibility. Too often we close our minds as soon as we hear ideas contrary to what we believe. Age, education, or social position may make no difference. We do not wish to believe that a cherished idea could be wrong or out of date, and previous programming may close off options or alternatives. Weigh the potential of the new thought before deciding whether it merits adoption or rejection.

These, then, are some of the problems that hamper listening in interviews.

A simple model of the listening process (see fig. 2.8) may help us to understand the process and to improve our listening skills. The listening process consists of three stages. (1) We detect some *input* or message from the other party. This input is usually a conglomeration of words, sounds, movements, gestures, facial expressions, vocal inflections, and eye contact. (2) We *react* to the input by sorting out and interpreting the variety of verbal and nonverbal

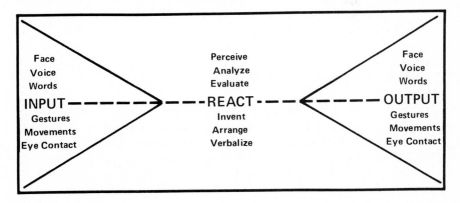

Figure 2.8   *The Listening Process*

signals detected. (3) Our reaction then becomes an *output* that may consist of little more than the poker-faced reaction of the critical listener or as much as the animated, vocal reaction of the empathic listener. A famous football coach used to teach his defensive players to "read" an offensive play (input), to digest the play (react), and to yell "draw," "screen," or "pass" (output). This listening process cannot occur if we are inattentive or preoccupied with matters outside of the interview.

The following checklist of behaviors should help us to listen more effectively as interviewers and interviewees.[12]

1. Listen for the "critical content" and main ideas of interviews.
2. Listen for feelings as well as for "content."
3. Read *all* cues, verbal and nonverbal.
4. Let the other party know that we are listening.
5. Be mentally and physically ready to listen.
6. Be patient.
7. Ask questions for clarification, explanation, and elaboration of content, ideas, and feelings.
8. Be empathic with the other party.
9. Focus attention on the message and the other party, not on the surroundings.
10. Focus attention on this interaction, not on past or future interactions.
11. Do not "replay" poor questions or answers; set them aside and move on.
12. Be wary of evaluative responses during interviews, especially negative evaluations.
13. Be aware of what we are communicating by our actions or lack of actions.
14. Avoid excessive note taking that may cause us to miss important interview content and nonverbal signals.
15. Do not react too quickly (the hair-trigger syndrome) to complete and incomplete comments and questions, especially ones that contain controversial words or ideas.

The Interview Situation

No interview takes place in a vacuum tube in which the parties interchange behaviors oblivious of the world beyond the rarefied atmosphere of the tube. Each interview occurs at a given time and place and is subjected to a variety of situational variables: the type of interview setting, the interviewing approach, the time of day and week, events that precede and follow the interview, location, architecture, temperature, seating arrangement, furniture, distance between interviewer and interviewee, territoriality, noise, interruptions, and privacy.[13] The interview situation is symbolized in the interviewing model (see fig. 2.9) by the

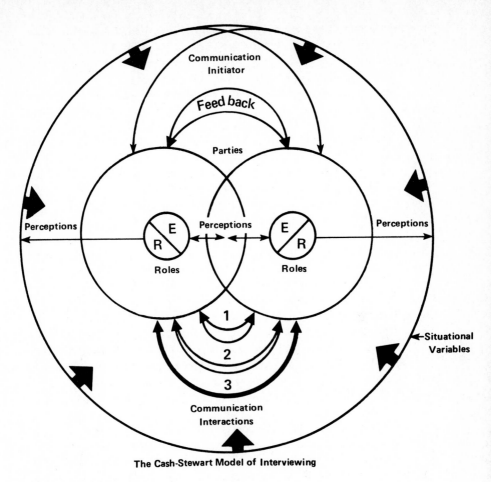

The Cash-Stewart Model of Interviewing

Figure 2.9 *Situational Variables*

circle that encloses the other variables. The arrows pointing inward symbolize the "implosive" effect the many situational variables have on the interviewing process.

Type of Interview Setting   Refer back to figure 1.1, which lists the types and subtypes of interviews. The atmosphere of a screening interview or placement interview is very different from a separation or reprimand interview. A survey or poll creates an atmosphere different from a grievance, sales, or counseling interview. Each type places certain kinds of restraints on the initiation of the process, the parties, and the levels of interchanges. Each type also determines the roles played by interviewer and interviewee and whether these will switch during the interview.

Interviewing Approach   The situation may dictate the basic interviewing approach—directive or nondirective. The type of approach tends to vary with the setting—persuasive interviews tend to be directive; counseling interviews tend to be nondirective; and employment and appraisal interviews may be a little of both. The organization controlling the interview may dictate the approach. For example, survey groups prescribe in detail how each interview is to be conducted. This situational variable will influence other variables during the interview.

Time of Day and Week   People perform and communicate best at different times during the day and week. For example, some people prefer to begin work or to deal with important matters early in the morning, while others prefer late morning, early afternoon, or during the evening. Monday mornings and Friday afternoons are traditional "bad times." Moods tend to be dark and motivation very low at these times. We must know the interviewer or interviewee before we can pick the ideal time for the interview.

Events that Precede or Follow the Interview   Important events that may be related or unrelated to the interview topic may affect the interview. For instance, an accident in the plant, a personal problem, a previous interview, or a national problem may affect the concentration, mood, and ability to communicate of one or both parties in an interview. If the interviewee has a very tough interview that will take place immediately after our interview, he or she may be thinking of the next interview and not really listening to us. Monday afternoons may ordinarily be good times for the interviewee, but not this Monday afternoon. Holidays or seasons such as Christmas, Memorial Day, Thanksgiving, and Yom Kippur may be good times for some people and types of interviews (sales, employment selection, or journalistic) and bad times for other types (dismissals, reprimands, or surveys). Some counselors note marked increases in crisis interviews with lonely people during family-oriented festive seasons such as Christmas and Thanksgiving.

The Location of the Interview   Several location variables may affect an interview: architecture, comfort, noise level, privacy, distance between parties, seating arrangement, and territoriality.[14] Our goal should be to enhance the interviewee's concentration and motivation—to make the other party "feel like" communicating. We are more likely to accomplish these goals in a well-lighted, pleasantly painted, moderate-sized room with a comfortable temperature and proper ventilation than in a dark, drab room the size of a gym or a telephone booth that is too cold or too hot and poorly ventilated. Noise, movements, and interruptions—especially telephone calls—disrupt thought patterns and concentration and may destroy the mood we are trying to create. An interviewee will have difficulty listening and thinking while watching cars on a street outside a window, people moving about in the outer office, or secretaries coming and going from our office. If we do not provide adequate privacy, few interviewees will risk communicating beyond level 1.

Distance between parties is important. Few of us feel comfortable with a person who insists upon communicating nose-to-nose, but we may be equally uncomfortable if the person insists upon sitting across the room or at the far end of a conference table. If a person invades our "territory," we may back up, place furniture between us and the person, or terminate the interview if discomfort

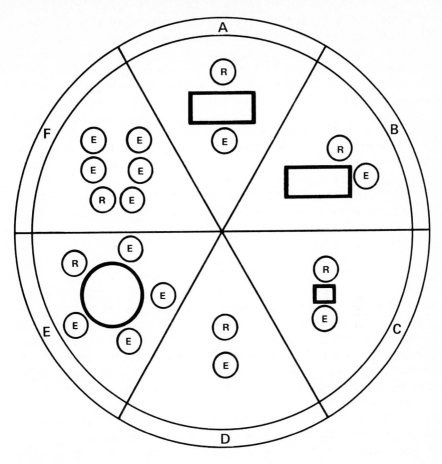

Figure 2.10   *Seating Arrangements*

becomes excessive. Three or four feet—approximately an arm's length—seems to be an optimum distance between interview parties. Remember that seating is highly influenced by status, sex, cultural norms, relationship of the interview parties with one another, furnishings, and personal preferences.

Seating arrangement may help or hinder an interview. For example, a superior and a subordinate may sit across a desk from one another—arrangement A in figure 2.10. This desk arrangement provides an appropriate distance between parties for a formal business setting with a proper place for the subordinate—a chair in front of the desk. Role relationships are quite clear in this setting. Arrangement B, two chairs at right angles near the corner of a desk or table, provides a less formal atmosphere and superior and subordinate tend to be more "equal." Many students have remarked that they prefer this seating arrangement with college professors. Efforts to remove physical obstacles to communication and to reduce the superior-subordinate relationship even further have resulted in seating arrangements such as C—two parties on opposite sides of a small table—and D—two parties seated a few feet apart with no table in between. Seating arrangement E is growing in popularity, especially in counseling interviews, interviews that involve more than two people, and interviews in which there is a need to write, pass around materials, or serve refreshments. The circular arrangement, with or without a table, avoids the head-of-the-table position. The horseshoe arrangement portrayed in F has many of the advantages of the circular arrangement and usually does not involve a table. A potential disadvantage of the horseshoe is that someone must take on the task of assuring that all persons are in direct visual contact with one another.

Perceptions of the Situation

Each person comes to an interview with somewhat unique perceptions of the situation. A boss may view the conference room as a neutral setting while an employee may see it as a threatening, hostile environment. One person may prefer arrangement D with no furniture barriers and another may feel naked in such an arrangement. Eight o'clock in the morning may be a great time for us and a terrible time for an interviewee who is a night person. Some people freeze at 72 degrees and others smother at the same temperature. Perceptions of the situation are symbolized in the interviewing model (see fig. 2.9) by the arrows that run from each party to the situational circle.

There are a number of other personal situational variables. For instance, the interviewer and interviewee may have vested interests in the outcome of the interview: the interviewer wants to sell a set of encyclopedias and the interviewee wants to save money or to spend it on a stereo; the journalist wants a major news story and the campaign worker does not want to jeopardize a relationship with the candidate; the employer wants a hard worker and the applicant wants a good paying job with fringe benefits. Each party comes to the interview in a certain mood: happy, sad, serious, angry, optimistic, pessimistic, depressed, lighthearted. Smith seems to be in a serious mood because of problems with his mother, while Jones appears to be in a lighthearted, joking mood. The apparent clash of these moods could affect the remainder of the interview unless adjustments are made by one or both parties.

The physical and mental health of both parties may influence the interview. It is difficult to concentrate and to communicate when we have a severe headache, a touch of the flu, or are worried about a health problem. Our personal involvements, such as Smith's concern for his mother's health, may help or hinder an interview. A counselor may find it difficult to help others if he or she has major family or personal problems. Recent events or happenings—a tragedy, a victory, a financial loss, record earnings for the last quarter, and so on—may determine the outcome of an interview or whether an interview takes place.

The role or roles being played by each party are important situational variables. We must know what roles are being played and, if possible, how each party is reacting to these roles. Each of us plays many roles during each day of our lives, and social pressure is applied to mold us into "typical" mothers, fathers, husbands, wives, bosses, career persons, citizens, lovers, or friends. We may or may not yield to these pressures, and an increasing number of persons are electing to escape roles by dropping out, filing for divorce, changing careers, or moving to another part of the country. Regardless of the natural urge to escape, we are responsible for what we say and do in interviews. When we take on a role, we take on the responsibility that goes with it.

Remember, each party in an interview is the sum total of all previous programmings, perceptions of self and the other party, and unique situational variables. We cannot remove ourselves from these programmings, perceptions, and situational variables even if we desire to do so, for in a very real sense, they and we are one.

Initiating the Interview

The overlapping arrows that emerge from the top of the situational circle in the interviewing model (see fig. 2.9) and touch each party signify that either party—and in some situations both—may initiate the interview. For example, a counselee may walk into a counselor's office and ask for help, or a counselor may ask the counselee to come in for a talk. A politician may contact a journalist about a change in campaign strategy, or the journalist may contact the politician to verify a rumor about an impending change in strategy. The situation often determines who initiates the interview, and *who initiates* the interview may affect the situation in a variety of ways.

All interviews are initiated for a predetermined and serious purpose. The purpose may be singular: the persuader wants to get a signature on a petition, the pollster wants answers to questions about food prices, the employer wants a higher production rate from a worker. Or, the purpose may be shared: two science teachers discussing the best way to handle the next unit in the eighth grade science class, a counselor and counselee trying to solve a marriage problem, the politician and the journalist wanting a good front-page story on the campaign.

Smith apparently initiated the interview process by arranging for the interview, and he initiates the interaction as the interview begins. Several possible purposes emerge during the early exchanges. Smith and Jones want to recognize one another and to share what has been happening since their last meeting. Smith's safe greeting and Jones's safe response seem designed to make the other person feel good, to be social stroking. However, each party desires to go beyond the recognition stage and to share important subject matter. Smith eventually guides the interchange to the serious purpose he has in mind.

Who initiates the interview may determine when, where, and how the interview takes place and the emotional climate of the interview. For example, a counseling interview may be very different when a professor stops a student after class and says, "See me in my office at 3 o'clock!" than when a student approaches a professor after class and says, "Could I meet with you in the union at 3 o'clock?" One is clearly a highly threatening situation and the other is not. We tend to feel secure at home, in our office, or in familiar surroundings. As interview participants, we should take all situational variables into account when arranging and conducting interviews. When *we* initiate interviews, we should be aware of the potential impact this variable may have on the interviewee and the interview. We will return to this issue in chapter 3 when dealing with the opening phase of interviews.

Encoding and Decoding Messages

We have taken you through the model of interviewing variable by variable. Let's return now to the Smith and Jones interchange to see how the variables operate together in encoding (sending) and decoding (receiving) messages.

The shift in moods of Smith and Jones illustrates how individual programmings and perceptions make identical interpretation (decoding) of the same symbol impossible. Conversely, no individual can transmit (encode) all of a message. Smith began the exchange with a jovial greeting. Jones followed with a more serious and corrective kind of response that guided the interview to a serious level. Smith responded in a subdued tone, but Jones shifted gears to a lighter topic by asking, "What have you been doing?" How could these messages be decoded? The mixed signals give Smith a choice of a serious, disclosing statement or a light, off-the-cuff comment. He chose the serious path. Why? Perhaps if we had seen and heard the exchange we might understand better Smith's choice. Apparently Jones's cues signalled to Smith, "You can level if you want," and he did.

Jones decoded Smith's serious comment in a light fashion, almost as if he were testing the response. Interviewers and interviewees often send up test balloons when they are unsure about how to decode a message. If the balloon is shot down, they back off, just as Jones did. Jones's response, "Oh! Cheating on your taxes again?", was a trial balloon shot down instantly by Smith's, "No, not really, we had some problems with my mother." How might we decode this message and encode a message that lets the other party know we understand and are sensitive to the message? Jones picked up the cue immediately and said, "Gee, I'm sorry to hear that."

Previous interactions, nonverbal communication, and words such as "gee," "worrying," and "problems" were apparently the keys to the encoding and decoding processes in the interchange. These processes are not simple. Just as we cannot perceive all of the stimuli that bombard us, we cannot say everything about anything. The encoding process may require several statements, but the actual event may take place in seconds. Encoding consists of taking perceptual inventory of all the stimuli surrounding an event, person, place, or thing and attempting to put these impressions into message form. We then transmit this message to the interviewer or interviewee. But we can never process all of the information available. Our limitations and our perceptions affect our encoding.

Suppose we are told that we have a growth in our stomach and that it must come out. The doctor suggests that we spend the Christmas holidays with loved ones before entering the hospital. The morning before the operation the surgeon remarks that there is a fifty-fifty possibility of cancer. A few hours later we awake and are told that it was *not* cancer. How can we encode all of the relief, joy, happiness, anxiety, and thrills, let alone specific happenings before and during the operation? We cannot say everything about anything because we cannot know everything about anything.

There are other constraints that prevent us from saying everything about anything; one is language. An old maxim goes, "If you cannot put it into words, you really do not understand the event." Nonsense! There are a great many events in life for which words are inadequate. Suppose we are not grouchy but somewhere between bitchy and grouchy. Are we gritchy? We have no words for many of our in-between moods. Many people cannot perceive and translate their perceptions and feelings into language. Language is a greater problem when an individual is distorting the event or is reluctant to communicate. Interpersonal insensitivity and lack of acute sensory perception may further hinder the encoding process. We may encode the event in such a way that it is not understandable to the other party. Smith and Jones are communicating but on a very general level. Moods and problems are suggested, but they are not identified clearly and concretely. Perhaps they would be so identified as the interview progressed.

The sender and receiver in an interview are in a constant response-feedback-response state. The only message a person can act upon is the one received, and the speed of interview interactions does not permit extensive study of a message to discover all facets of the message or to evaluate carefully all possible responses. Suppose we get up in the morning with a dull headache; our shoelace breaks; we burn our finger on the toaster; we have a flat tire on the way to work; and as we walk into the office, a secretary hands us a telegram informing us that a $100,000 lawsuit has been filed against us. A few minutes later, a new employee barges into our office without knocking and says in a happy voice. "Could I see you about something important?" We retort, "Not now! Don't bother me, and knock the next time!" As the employee beats a hasty retreat from our office, he or she will begin to search for an explanation for our reaction: Did the boss see me goofing off yesterday? Is the boss always like this on Monday? Why me?

Which message do we respond to? What if it is not the message the interviewer intended? The message the employee received may be a result of previous programming (experiences with bosses) a warped way of interpreting the event, the interpersonal relationship with the boss, the setting, the time of day and week, and other possibilities. How then do we as individuals keep from being misunderstood in interviews? Quite often we don't because we are both selective perceivers and selective message reactors.

We may employ several means to determine nuances of messages in the necessary seconds. First, we may prevent misunderstandings by using our frames of reference and past interactions with this person to judge the message. When Jones said, "Oh! Cheating on your taxes again?", a smile, tone of voice, or a previous encounter when Smith and Jones had discussed taxes could serve as a means to decode the message.[15]

Second, consider the intensity or nature of the relationship between the interview parties. Someone may see the gossip in the Smith/Jones exchange as a relief from an embarrassing situation or a little bit of nothing. If a comment seems offensive, try attaching a mental disclaimer to it: "I know she didn't mean it that way." This disclaimer may be accurate or inaccurate. Our interpersonal relationship may guide us in selecting possible responses, but it may cause us to read too much into a message. Overanalysis of a message may be as dangerous as no analysis.

Third, consider the subject matter of the message. Depending upon our frames of reference and the relationship we have with the other party, some topics will be treated seriously, such as the illness of Smith's mother, while others will be treated lightly, such as Jones's comment on taxes. Choice of words and nonverbal cues may tell us how a topic is being treated at a given moment.

Fourth, observe all aspects of the interviewing situation. Suppose Smith and Jones were dressed in old, paint-stained work clothes and were meeting in a fast-food diner? Dress and setting would seem to dictate an informal interview atmosphere. But what if they were meeting in a nice restaurant and both were dressed formally? Dress and place might signal a serious discussion about an important subject.

Summary

Interviewing is a dynamic, complicated process between two complex parties operating with imperfect verbal and nonverbal symbols and often guided or controlled by the situation. In this chapter we presented a model of this process and explained the many variables and how they interact. A thorough understanding of the interviewing process is a prerequisite for successful interviewing.

In chapters 3 and 4 we will show how knowledge of the interviewing process aids the interviewer in structuring the interview and in phrasing and using questions.

An Interview for Review and Analysis

Joe is a production foreman with twenty-five years of experience and a very good record. The boss is considering him for a promotion. Company policy stipulates that a foreman is *not* to be informed when being actively considered for a promotion. Hence, Joe does not know he is promotion material. Furthermore, because of company policy, the boss is compelled to avoid tipping his hand. However, company policy would not forbid mention, in general terms, of overall considerations related to the current work force situation or to established company criteria for promotions. This interview is exploratory rather than a final decision-making interview. About two hours before the interview is to begin, Joe receives a telephone message from the boss's secretary to report to the boss. No reason is given.

As you read this interview, think about answers to questions such as: How did situational variables, including who initiated the interview, affect the interview? What are the perceptions of Joe and the boss, and how do these perceptions affect exchanges? When do the roles of interviewer and interviewee switch between parties? At which communication level are most interchanges? Why are they at this level? What kinds of listening are practiced by the two parties? How important is feedback in this interview? What role does nonverbal communication play in the interview? What suggestions would you give to Joe and the boss to improve their interviewing skills, particularly skills necessary for this type of situation?[16]

1. Boss: Well, Joe, come on in. (smiling) Sit down. It's been quite a while since we've had time for a real *chat.*

2. Joe: (sitting in chair opposite desk, facing the boss) Thank you sir. (low, soft voice)

3. Boss: (very serious facial expression and general tone of voice)
How are things moving along these days, Joe? Everything under control in your section?

4. Joe: Oh, yeah, fine. No complaints. (fast speaking rate)

5. Boss: I'm *glad* to hear that there are no complaints. (pause) You think, then, that you're doing a pretty good job?

6. Joe: As good a job as I know how, sir. (shifts weight in chair)

7. Boss: Good. (pause; looks Joe directly in the eyes) By the way, have you ever thought of . . . uh, doing *something else?*

8. Joe: (pause; speaks slowly) Well . . . uh, yes and no, I guess. However, I do like this job very much. (rapidly) It's a job I really know very thoroughly.

9. Boss: Hmmm, I see. You mean you would not like to change your job, then?

10. Joe: Uh . . . no . . . no . . . I really don't think I would.

11. Boss: (looking closely at Joe; measures his words) I see. Just why do you want to stay on your present job?

12. Joe: Well, I get along fine; I know the work real well, and everybody seems to like me.

13. Boss: *Seems* to like you? (looks Joe directly in the eyes)

14. Joe: Oh . . . now and then there may be one or two fellows who don't like one of my decisions. But we always manage to get along.

15. Boss: Some fellows perhaps don't like you then? (sounds accusative)

16. Joe: Well, I wouldn't exactly say *that*. I've had a couple of guys who may have been sore because I didn't give them some overtime when they *thought* they were entitled to it.

17 Boss: You mean that's the *only* reason some of the men haven't been too fond of you?

18. Joe: Really, sir, that's the only thing of any importance I can think of. And even those two guys are not really hotshots. They're not the kind who deserve overtime. They goof off too much. (firm voice, direct eye contact)

19. Boss: You don't like men who loaf on the job?

20. Joe: No, absolutely not! Everyone should pitch in and do his share.

21. Boss: I assume, of course, that you do yours!

22. Joe: Oh yes indeed!

23. Boss: (after a pause) Uh . . . Joe, answer me this: did you ever think of . . . uh, *bettering* yourself?

24. Joe: Think of bettering myself? Well, yes, lots of times. I guess anyone who has any brains or any ambition wants to try to do better.

25. Boss: Just what do you mean by *that*?

26. Joe: Well, I only mean that anyone—or at least almost anyone—could find ways to improve. (looks down)

27. Boss: You think, then, that there's room for improvement in the way you're handling your job right now?

28. Joe: Oh, I'm sure there's always room for improvement. Did you have anything *special* in mind, sir?

29. Boss: Let me put it this way, Joe: have you ever really thought of bettering yourself on . . . *another job?*

30. Joe: Oh, I really do like my job very much, sir! This is a job I feel I know very well—I feel I'm on top of it, if you know what I mean.

31. Boss: I'm not sure you were listening *carefully* to my question, Joe. Let me ask it again: have you thought of bettering yourself on *another* job?

32. Joe: Well, that's hard to answer, sir, because I'm really enthusiastic about my present job.

33. Boss: You haven't considered the *possibility* of another job?

34. Joe: Well, I suppose there are times when anybody daydreams a little bit about how things would be on another job. But I really haven't given it much serious thought.

35. Boss: I take it, then, that you prefer very definitely to *stay* on your present job; is that right?

36. Joe: Oh, yes—definitely. As I have said, I feel very happy in my job. Did you have anything in mind about me being on another job, sir? (rapid speaking rate)

37. Boss: Oh, don't worry about that, Joe. I see I have another appointment coming up in a couple of minutes. It's been good to have a little chat with you. We'll have to get together again before too long. Lots of luck. See you later. (does not look Joe in the eyes, shakes his hand firmly)

Student Activities

1. How are you programmed? List and be prepared to discuss those inputs that make up your previous experiences. What attitudes, thoughts, feelings, and learnings are a part of your programming? Discuss the conflicts between yourself and other persons you deal with. What variables enter into these conflicts?

2. Nonverbal messages enable us to pick up cues that help us to interpret messages. What are some of the nonverbal cues that enable you to interpret the meaning of messages? How aware are you of these cues? How do you use them?

3. Feedback is a crucial factor in any human communication venture. What rules or guidelines, beyond those discussed in this chapter, would you suggest for getting or giving feedback? Set up a feedback system between yourself and another person or between elements of a group to which you belong. Observe the nature of the feedback and how well your system works.

4. Motivation is difficult to talk about and to instill in others. Select one of the major theories of motivation (Vroom, Herzberg, or Maslow) and discuss its application to interviewing.

5. Examine the Cash-Stewart Model of Interviewing. Based on what you know about the interviewing process and communication theory discuss the strengths and weaknesses of this model. Modify the model or create one of your own.

6. Select a local television or radio talk show and record it. Analyze the interactions by using the principles of listening discussed in this chapter. What kinds of listening are taking place? Were more appropriate means of listening available to the parties? How could the interviewer and interviewee improve their listening behaviors?

Notes

1. Jess Lair, *I Ain't Much, Baby—But I'm All I've Got* (New York: Doubleday, 1969).

2. This exercise was created by Robert L. Minter, Dean, School of Business Administration, Northern Connecticut University.

3. Patricia Niles Middlebrook, *Social Psychology and Modern Life* (New York: Alfred A. Knopf, 1974).

4. Donald E. Broadbent, *Perceptions and Communication* (New York: Pergamon Press, 1958).

5. *Playboy,* November, 1976, p. 55.

6. William D. Brooks, *Speech Communication* (Dubuque, Iowa: Wm. C. Brown Co. Publishers, 1974), p. 40.

7. William D. Brooks and Philip Emmert, *Interpersonal Communication* (Dubuque, Iowa: Wm. C. Brown Co. Publishers, 1976), p. 236.

8. Patricia Pliner, Lester Krames, and Thomas Alloway, *Communication and Affect* (New York: Academic Press, 1973); Wendell Johnson and Dorothy Moeller, *Living with Change* (New York: Harper & Row, 1973); and Elwood Murray, Gerald M. Phillips, and J. David Truby, *Speech: Art and Science* (Indianapolis: Bobbs-Merrill, 1969).

9. For discussions of nonverbal communication, see Mark L. Knapp, *Nonverbal Communication in Human Interaction* (New York: Holt, Rinehart and Winston, 1978); Mark L. Knapp. "The Field of Nonverbal Communication: An Overview," *On Speech Communication*, Charles J. Stewart, ed. (New York: Holt, Rinehart and Winston, 1972); and Judee K. Burgoon and Thomas J. Saine, *The Unspoken Dialogue: An Introduction to Nonverbal Communication* (Boston: Houghton Mifflin, 1978).

10. David W. Johnson, *Reaching Out: Interpersonal Effectiveness and Self-Actualization* (Englewood Cliffs, N.J.: Prentice-Hall, 1972).

11. Larry Barker, *Listening Behavior,* © 1971, pp. 61–65. Reprinted by permission of Prentice-Hall, Englewood Cliffs, New Jersey.

12. See Barker, *Listening Behavior,* pp. 73–74; Ralph G. Nichols, "Do We Know How to Listen? Practical Helps in a Modern Age," *Speech Teacher* 10 (March 1961): 118–24; C. William Colburn and Sanford B. Weinberg, *An Orientation to Listening and Audience Analysis* (Palo Alto, Calif.: Science Research Associates, 1976); and Robert O. Hirsch, *Listening: A Way to Process Information Aurally* (Dubuque, Iowa: Gorsuch Scarisbrick, 1979).

13. Richard F. Haase and Dominic J. DiMattia, "Proximic Behavior: Counselor Administrator, and Client Preference for Seating Arrangement in Dyadic Interaction," *Journal of Counseling Psychology* 17 (1970): 320; Knapp, "The Field of Nonverbal Communication: An Overview," pp. 57–72.

14. James T. Kitchens, Timothy P. Herron, Ralph H. Behnke, and Michael J. Beatty, "Environmental Esthetics and Interpersonal Attraction," *Western Journal of Speech Communication* 41 (Spring 1977): 126–30.

15. C. David Mortensen, "The Interpersonal System" *Communication: The Study of Human Interaction* (New York: McGraw-Hill, 1972).

16. This interview has been revised and adapted by W. Charles Redding from an original appearing in Benjamin Balinsky and Ruth Burger. Adapted from pp. 24–25 in *The Executive Interview* by Benjamin Balinsky and Ruth Burger. Copyright © 1959 by Benjamin Balinsky and Ruth Burger. It is reprinted here by permission of Harper & Row and W. Charles Redding.

Suggested Readings

Barker, Larry L. *Listening Behavior.* Englewood Cliffs, N.J.: Prentice-Hall, 1971.

Barker, Larry L., and Kibler, Robert J. *Speech Communication Behavior: Perspectives and Principles,* Englewood Cliffs, N.J.: Prentice-Hall, 1971.

Brooks, William D., and Emmert, Philip. *Interpersonal Communication.* Dubuque, Iowa: Wm. C. Brown Co. Publishers, 1976.

Johnson, David W. *Reaching Out: Interpersonal Effectiveness and Self-Actualization.* Englewood Cliffs, N.J.: Prentice-Hall, 1972.

Knapp, Mark L. *Nonverbal Communication in Human Interaction.* New York: Holt, Rinehart and Winston, 1978.

Lair, Jess. *Hey, God, What Should I Do Now?* New York: Doubleday, 1978.

Lair, Jess. *I Ain't Much, Baby—But I'm All I've Got.* New York: Doubleday, 1978.

Lair, Jess. *I Ain't Well Yet, But I'm Getting Better.* New York: Doubleday, 1976.

Mortensen, C. David. *Communication: The Study of Human Interaction.* New York: McGraw-Hill, 1972.

Pliner, Patricia; Krames, Lester; and Alloway, Thomas. *Communication and Affect.* New York: Academic Press, 1973.

Samples, Bob, and Wohlford, Bob. *Opening.* Reading, Mass.: Addison-Wesley, 1974.

Structuring the Interview 3

How we structure an interview depends upon the type of interview we are going to conduct. We are unlikely to structure an employment interview the way we would a sales interview, or a survey interview the way we would an appraisal interview, or a journalistic interview the way we would a counseling interview. However, there are principles and techniques applicable to all types of interviews. This chapter focuses on these principles and techniques and divides the interview into three major parts: the opening, the body, and the closing.

The Opening

The few seconds or minutes we spend in an opening may be the most important period of the interview, for the primary function of the opening is to motivate both interview parties to participate freely and to communicate accurately in the interview.[1] A weak opening may lead to a superficial or inaccurate interview or to no interview at all. If dissatisfied with the initial approach, a person may say no, walk away, close the door, or hang up the telephone.

A two-step process of establishing rapport and orienting the other party encourages participation in an interview. The relationship between interviewer and interviewee, interviewer preference, and the situation determine which step comes first. Establishing rapport is a process of creating trust and goodwill between interviewer and interviewee. This process typically begins with a self-introduction ("Good morning, I'm Melissa Johnson.") or a greeting ("Good morning Bob.") accompanied by nonverbal actions such as a firm handshake, eye contact, a smile, head nods, and a pleasant, friendly voice.[2] The rapport stage may proceed to personal inquiries ("What's new?"; "How are things going?"; How have you been?") and on to small talk about the weather, sports, company news, bits of gossip, families, current events, and so on. Both personal inquiry and small talk may be flavored with tasteful humor. Customs of the geographical area and organization, status differences between interviewer and interviewee, formality of the occasion, interview type and setting, and past encounters between interview parties determine the appropriate kind and length of verbal and nonverbal rapport building in an interview. Be careful of overdoing this stage of the opening; we can turn off an interviewee or interviewer with too much sweet talk, especially if we appear to be insincere.

Orientation is the second step in the opening and is usually initiated by verbal means. It may consist of explaining the purpose and nature of the interview, what organization is responsible for the interview, what is expected of interviewee or interviewer, how the information will be used, why and how this party was selected, and perhaps how long the interview will take. Obviously, rapport and orientation are often indistinguishable because they may occur at the same time.

The rapport and orientation steps are illustrated in the following opening from a persuasive interview.

Persuader: Good evening, Mr. Warwich. I'm Jessie Addison from World Auto Insurance. I talked to your wife a few days ago.

Persuadee: Oh yes, she said you were coming over this evening. Come in and sit down.

Persuader: You have a very nice home in a lovely neighborhood. How long have you lived here?

Persuadee: This is our seventh year. We enjoy the home and the area. It's been a great place to live.

Persuader: When I called your wife, she said you have two policies coming due, one on a 1974 VW bug and one on a 1980 Ford wagon.

Persuadee: Yes, that's correct.

Persuader: My primary purpose this evening is to introduce you to the policies, benefits, services, and low prices of World Auto. What do you know about our company?

The following are common ways to begin interviews; some may serve as the entire opening, some may aid the rapport building process, and some may initiate the orientation process.[3]

Summarize the problem   This method is particularly useful when the respondent is unaware of the problem (or is only vaguely aware of it) or when the respondent might not know the details of the problem. For example:

> Since final exams were initiated five years ago, there has been a steady decline in their usage by professors (from 73 percent in 1975 to 47 percent last year) and both the student and faculty senates have discussed the situation. I have agreed to conduct a survey of student attitudes on final exam policies and would like to include your opinions in my survey.

There are occasions when clearly stating the purpose of the interview would make achievement of its purpose impossible. This is particularly true, for example, in research interviews and many types of survey interviews. We may need to withhold our purpose or even to disguise it if we are to get the information needed through unguarded and honest responses from the interviewee. These situations are exceptions, however.

Explain how the problem was discovered   This method explains how we became aware of the problem and, in doing so, usually summarizes the problem. Be honest and specific in revealing the sources of information. For example:

A corner seating arrangement is preferred by many interviewers and interviewees.

Last evening I was reviewing our third-quarter audit and discovered that losses to shoplifting increased nearly 12 percent over the second quarter. I would like to get your reactions to some new security procedures I am developing.

Mention an incentive or reward for taking part in the interview
This can be a valuable method if the incentive is appealing to the respondent. Some interviewers offer small monetary rewards for cooperation. Be careful of this opening because many sales representatives use a gift or other incentive to motivate people to listen to their sales pitches. If we begin an informational interview with this opening, we may never convince the interviewee that we are not a sales representative pretending to be a pollster. The following is an incentive opening.

Good morning. I am conducting a survey of attitudes on current meat prices. My study might result in a stabilizing of meat prices in this area.

Request advice or assistance   This is perhaps the most common of all openings because assistance is usually what an interviewer needs. This request is often the beginning of the orientation process, so be clear, precise, and sincere in requests. The following example reveals this method's close relationship to others just discussed.

> Kathy, I'm preparing a market survey for Model X3, which was released to a number of stores two months ago. Would you be willing to help me by responding to a series of questions I have worked out? Please tell me if any of these questions are unclear.

Refer to the known position of the interviewee   This opening refers to the respondent's position on an issue or problem, and may explain why we have decided to interview him or her. Be cautious in using this opening. A tactless opening reference to a known position may place the respondent on the defensive or antagonize the respondent. Here is an example of a tactful use of this opening.

> I am polling this area for the city council concerning the rezoning petition recently submitted by the Gordon Construction Company. I understand you oppose this petition and are proposing a neighborhood park for the undeveloped property.

Refer to the person who sent us to the interviewee   We must be sure the person did send us and use this method only when we are fairly certain the respondent knows and likes the person we name. It could be embarrassing or disastrous if we discover, after using the name, that the interviewee dislikes the person or denies knowing the person. Here is an example.

> Professor Thompson? Professor Tudor in the History Department said you might be able to give me some information on the archeological diggings at Fort Ouiatenon.

Refer to the organization we represent   This opening is much like the previous one, except that we refer to a group (Gallup, Fuller Brush, Market Research, University of Illinois, the Times) instead of a person. Frequently the mere mention of the group we represent will orient the interviewee or motivate the interviewee to respond. For example:

> Good afternoon. I'm from the Consumer Research Center at Eastern State University. We are conducting a study of automobile purchases during the past six months.

Obviously, the respondent's reaction to our company or organization can be negative as well as positive. For example:

Interviewer: Hello, I'm from International Auto and Life Company and would like to. . . .

Interviewee: (cutting in) Your company refused to pay a damage claim for a friend of mine last year, so I'm not interested.

We can lessen the negative impact of such openings if we prepare for their eventuality and/or if we can discover the attitude of the interviewee towards our organization prior to initiating the interview.

Request a specific amount of time This is perhaps the most overused and misused opening. All of us are guilty of asking, "Got a second?" We cannot explain who we are or what we want in a second. When we use this opening, we should state a realistic and specific period of time. At the end of the time requested, either we should have completed the interview or we should begin to close it. If the interviewee has more time or wants to continue, the interviewee can say so. Here is an example.

John, do you have five minutes to discuss a problem with me?

If we tell a person we need forty-five minutes, the person is likely to say no, but if we do not reveal the time needed, the interviewee might have to end the interview in fifteen minutes because of another appointment. Either way, our purpose is not achieved. Perhaps the best solution to this problem is to make an appointment for any interview that requires more than a few minutes.

These eight opening methods are not the only ones available to the imaginative interviewer; however, we should find them useful (with minor alterations) in a variety of interview situations. Frequently we may combine two or more methods into one opening, as in the following.

Good morning. I'm George Williams from the telephone company and would like to have about five minutes of your time to get your opinions on the new dialing system we installed recently.

Good morning. Your neighbor, Mrs. Kelley, said you might be willing to help me with a survey I'm taking for the telephone company. It will take only five minutes of your time and should lead to better telephone service.

An open-ended question may serve as a transition from the rapport-building and orientation functions of the opening to the informational, counseling, or persuasive functions of the body of the interview. The open-ended question provides an additional warm-up period for the interviewee to learn the role to be played and his or her ability to play it successfully. The question should be easy to answer and clearly relevant to our stated purpose. For instance: Tell me how you became interested in medicine. What are your responsibilities as managing editor? Tell me about your family life as you were growing up. What research projects do you have underway at the moment? The opening question should not deal with an embarrassing area or place stress on the respondent. Remember, the respondent may still be unsure of what is expected and apprehensive about the interview. A difficult or embarrassing question at this stage could ruin the remainder of the interview—if the interview continues at all.

Quiz #1 Interview Openings

How satisfactory are the following openings? Consider the interviewing situations and types, the opening techniques used, and what is and is not included. How might each be improved? Do not *assume* that each is unsatisfactory.

1. This is a counseling interview taking place in a professor's office. The student has not made an appointment.

Professor Taylor, got a second? Are we going to do anything important in class on Friday?

2. This is a survey interview taking place at the door of a home. The parties do not know one another.

Good morning. I would like to ask you some questions concerning your feelings about the recent teacher strike in Swiss County.

3. This is a journalistic interview taking place in the hallway near the Senate chamber between a reporter and a United States Senator. The Senator is heading toward a committee meeting.

Senator Smothers, would you comment on your committee's actions on short-term steps to relieve the energy crisis?

4. This is an informational interview taking place in the office of a production line supervisor.

Hi! I've been sent to see you about a problem in my division; one I can't seem to handle.

5. This is a persuasive interview taking place between two business partners in an office.

I got a call last night, near midnight, from a person I won't name. She said you were thinking of altering your position against unionizing our shop. What's going on?

The Body

An interviewer frequently prepares an "interview guide" to aid in preparing for and conducting the main part, or "body," of the interview. An interview guide is simply an outline or checklist of topics and subtopics to be covered in the interview. It can help the interviewer to remember areas of information, to record answers, to recognize relevant and irrelevent materials in answers, and to determine what probing questions to ask.

Sequences

Since the interview guide is an outline, we would be wise to review and practice the fundamentals of outlining, particularly the sequences of topics and ideas that will impose a clear, systematic structure on our interview.

A *topical sequence* follows natural or familiar divisions of a topic. For example, an interview on road repair might be divided into three parts: budget, major projects, and equipment. An interview on the company budget might discuss research and development, production, and sales. Journalists frequently resort to single-word topical guides: what, when, where, who, how, and why.

A *time sequence* treats topics or parts of an interview in chronological order. For instance, an interview explaining a process might progress from stage 1 to stage 2 to stage 3. An interviewer probing into a person's educational background might proceed from junior high school, to high school, to college or vocational training.

A *space sequence* arranges topics according to "space" divisions: left to right, precinct by precinct, top to bottom, east to west to north to south. For instance, an interviewer explaining the physical arrangement of a firm might begin by discussing the business office, then move to the printing area, and finally to the shipping room. Subtopics might explain the arrangement and functions of each office, area, or room.

The *cause to effect sequence* consists of two divisions: the causes of an event, problem, or result and the effect or effects of these causes. Interviewers often decide to describe a certain effect first and then deal with possible causes. For example, we might discuss high employment figures, rising inflation rates, and low industrial production with an economist and then turn to possible causes for this economic situation.

The *problem-solution sequence* also consists of two divisions: discussion of a problem and consideration of one or more solutions to the problem. For instance, a city engineer and a builder might begin an interview by discussing a zoning problem and then turn to how the zoning problem can be solved. See chapter 9 on persuasive interviewing for further examples of the problem-solution sequence.

Let us assume, for instance, that we have decided to interview an experienced, skilled interviewer to gain information that will aid us in conducting future interviews. We should decide, first, on the broad, major areas of information we want. These might include training, interviewing methods, interviewing experiences, and suggestions for the novice interviewer. Now we should place possible subtopics under each major area, as in the following topical sequence.

    I. Training in interviewing
       A. Courses in interviewing
          1. formal
          2. informal

B. Reading about interviewing
    1. books
    2. pamphlets
    3. trade journals
C. Observing interviews
    1. practice interviews
    2. real interviews
D. On-the-job training

II. Experiences in interviewing
A. Information interviewing
    1. when
    2. where
    3. number
B. Employment interviewing
    1. when
    2. where
    3. number
C. Other types of interviewing
    1. when
    2. where
    3. number

III. Methods used in interviewing
A. Preparation
B. Organization or structure
C. Questions
D. Special techniques

IV. Suggestions for the beginner

Some areas may need no subtopics (such as IV) because we may want to assure free and open responses from the interviewee or because we may discover possible subtopics only as the interview progresses.

Of course we may employ two or more sequences in a single interview. The major divisions may be in a time sequence and subdivisions may be topical or spatial. The problem part of a problem-solution sequence may be developed from cause to effect.

After we complete an interview guide we must decide if additional preinterview structuring is needed. We may stop with the guide or turn all or part of the guide into questions. The outline of areas or questions we take with us to an interview—in our mind, on paper, or both—is called an interview "schedule."

Schedules

The *nonscheduled interview* may consist of a detailed interview guide or merely a list of possible topics and subtopics. The nonscheduled interview is most useful when the information area is extremely broad, when the interviewees and their information levels differ greatly, when the interviewees are reluctant or have fading memories, and when the interviewer must conduct the interview with little prior warning. The major *advantage* of the nonscheduled interview is the unlimited freedom to probe into answers and to adapt to changing situations and respondents. Interviewers at press conferences often use a nonscheduled form of interviewing because they do not know when they will be recognized by the interviewee and because they often ask follow-up questions to questions asked by other interviewers. Also, they may have little control over the interviewing situation. The respondent, the respondent's representative, or a senior journalist may conclude the interview at any moment—sometimes to stop a competing journalist or to avoid discussing a controversial issue. Little structure is possible in such situations. The major *disadvantages* of the nonscheduled interview are that it requires a highly skilled interviewer, it is most difficult to replicate, it provides no easy means of recording answers, and it allows interviewer bias to creep into questions that are not planned ahead of time.

The *moderately scheduled interview* contains our major questions and possible probing questions under each major question—the statements or phrases in the interview guide are converted into questions. Like the nonscheduled interview, it offers a high degree of freedom to probe into answers and to adapt to differing interviewees and situations, broad topics, and reluctant interviewees or ones with faulty memories. However, the moderately scheduled interview does impose a degree of structure on the interview, forces a higher level of preparation, is easier to replicate, aids in recording answers, and is easier for an unskilled interviewer to conduct. In short, this type of interview has most of the advantages of the nonscheduled interview and fewer of the disadvantages. The moderately scheduled interview shows the respondent that we have prepared for the interview and, if the interviewee asks to see the questions we want to ask, we have something to show. In certain situations, respondents are very reluctant to grant interviews with no idea of the kinds of questions they will face. Sometimes the interviewee or a representative may delete some of our questions; the chance of this happening is heightened if the interview will be broadcast to the public. Since interviews tend to wander and become unstructured, the listing of questions in a moderately scheduled interview makes it easier to keep the interview on track or to return to a structure when desired. Journalists nearly always use nonscheduled or moderately scheduled interviews, while pollsters and researchers are unlikely to use either. A moderately scheduled interview would look like the following.

1. What things, or events, or happenings bother you the most these days?
   a. What about natural disasters?
   b. What about crime?
   c. What about the economy?

2. What do you think economic conditions will be like four years from now?
   a. What about the economic conditions in this area?
   b. What about the economic conditions in this state?
   c. What about the economic conditions of the nation?
3. How do you feel about the president's handling of racial integration?
   a. Is he pushing too fast, not fast enough, or about right?
   b. What about school busing as a method of integration?
4. What do you think about federal revenue sharing with the states?
   a. Do you approve or disapprove?
   b. Is the sharing adequate or inadequate?
   c. How should the states use revenue sharing?
   d. What about federal control of the ways states use federal revenue sharing?

A *highly scheduled interview* contains all of the questions to be asked, and they are asked in exactly the same wording and order to each interviewee. There is no probing or deviation from the planned list of questions. The questions may be open-ended or closed but are usually closed. Highly scheduled interviews are easier to replicate, easier for unskilled interviewers to conduct, and take less time than either nonscheduled or moderately scheduled interviews. They have the disadvantages of no unplanned probing into answers and no flexibility in adapting to differing respondents. Questions for a highly scheduled interview might look like the moderately scheduled interview minus the "suggested" probes. Probes, if any, are carefully planned into the schedule. A highly scheduled interview might look like the following.

1. Which issue or problem facing us these days bothers you the most?
   a. Why does this issue or problem bother you the most?
   b. When do you think this problem or issue began to bother you the most?
2. Do you think economic conditions will be better or worse next year?
   (If the answer is better, ask) Why do you think economic conditions will be better next year?
   (If the answer is worse, ask) Why do you think economic conditions will be worse next year?
3. How would you describe the president's economic policies?
4. Which group of taxpayers carries the heaviest burden of taxes?
5. Which group of taxpayers carries the lightest burden of taxes?

Highly scheduled, standardized interviews are the most thoroughly planned and structured. All questions and answer options are included, and these are stated in identical language (without alteration) to each interviewee. The interviewee picks an answer and the interviewer notes the answer chosen. The highly scheduled, standardized interview is the easiest to conduct, to record, to tabulate, and to replicate. The most novice of interviewers can handle such interviews. There are serious disadvantages, however. The breadth of information is highly restricted, and there is no possibility of probing into answers, explaining questions, or adapting to different respondents. Built-in bias may be worse than the accidental bias encountered in nonscheduled and moderately scheduled interviews. The respondent has no chance to explain, to amplify, or to qualify answers. Journalists rarely use highly scheduled, standardized interviews because these have no flexibility. The interviewees must be homogeneous in background, language, and information level or the interviews may be confusing and the results worthless. A highly scheduled, standardized interview might look like the following.

1. Which one of the following issues or problems facing us these days bothers you the most and which one the least?
World peace
Taxation
School busing
Inflation
2. Do you think economic conditions will be better, worse, or about the same four years from now?
3. Do you think the national administration is pushing racial integration too fast, not fast enough, or about right?
4. Which one of these groups, in your estimation, carries the most unfair burden of taxation?
Farmers
The wealthy
Senior citizens
The poor
White collar workers
Factory workers
5. Which one of these groups, in your estimation, carries the smallest burden of taxation?
Farmers
The wealthy
Senior citizens
The poor
White collar workers
Factory workers

Concerning the advantages and disadvantages of schedule types, Gorden warns: "Neither should neatness of the interview schedule, efficiency of coding, or reliability of responses be confused with the more important criterion—validity of the information."[4] Choose the schedule best suited to the interviewer, potential respondents, type of data needed, and type of interview. Do not hesitate to employ different schedules in the same interview: perhaps nonscheduled in the opening and early part of the interview, moderately scheduled for material that

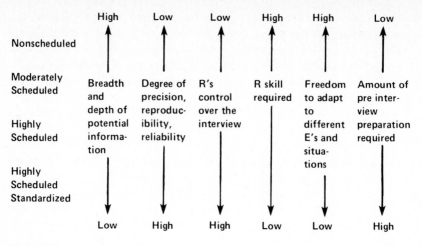

	High	Low	Low	High	High	Low
Nonscheduled	↑	↑	↑	↑	↑	↑
Moderately Scheduled	Breadth and depth of potential information	Degree of precision, reproducibility, reliability	R's control over the interview	R skill required	Freedom to adapt to different E's and situations	Amount of pre interview preparation required
Highly Scheduled						
Highly Scheduled Standardized						
	↓	↓	↓	↓	↓	↓
	Low	High	High	Low	Low	High

Figure 3.1   *Structural Options*

necessitates probing and adaptation to different interviewees, and highly scheduled, standardized for easily quantifiable materials such as demographic data. Although schedules are usually lists of questions, they may range from a topic outline to virtually a "manuscript" for part or all of the interview. We may, for example, write out major arguments for a persuasive interview or instructions to be given in an information-giving interview. Figure 3.1 summarizes major advantages and disadvantages of various types of schedules.[5]

The Closing

Closings, though usually brief, are vitally important parts of interviews. Do not treat them lightly! Once we have asked or answered the last question or made our last point, the temptation is to take a deep sigh of relief that the interview is done and to say goodbye. An abrupt closing, however, may undo the rapport and trust we have worked so hard to establish during the interview. The interviewee may feel like a discarded container—important only as long as the interviewer needs some information. Future interactions between parties may be enhanced by a good closing or irreparably damaged by a poor closing.

There are many common ways to close interviews, both verbal and nonverbal.[6] A number of verbal closings, such as the following, aid in orienting the interviewee or maintaining rapport established throughout an interview.

1. We may signal that an interview is coming to an end by offering to answer questions.

Any questions?

Do you have any questions you would like to ask?

I would be happy to answer any questions you might have.

When we ask for questions, we should be sincere in our desire to answer, and we should give the interviewee adequate time to ask. Do not give a quick answer to one question and then end the interview.

2. Clearinghouse questions allow us to determine if we have covered everything or answered all questions the interviewee might have. They are also a signal that the interview is coming to a close.

I think that takes care of everything I need. Can you think of anything I might have missed?

Anything else?

Is there anything we have not discussed that you would like to bring up at this time?

This closing technique, like the first, can be effective if our request is not perceived as a formality or mere attempt to be sociable but as an effort to ferret out any questions, information, or areas of concern not discussed or discussed completely.

3. We may close an interview by declaring the completion of our purpose or task.

Well, that's all the questions I have.

Okay, that should give me plenty of material for a good report.

With this one last signature, the contract is complete.

The four-letter word "well" probably begins the closings of more interviews than any other word or phrase. When we hear it, we automatically assume the end is near.

4. Personal inquiries having nothing to do with the subject matter of the interview are pleasant ways to close interviews. If we are sincere, inquiries such as the following show a personal interest in the interviewee and allow the interview to end in an informal, relaxed manner.

When are you moving into your new home?

Where are you going on your vacation?

How's your son doing in law school?

Interviewees judge the sincerity of our inquiries by the way we listen and the ways we react verbally and nonverbally.

5. A common closing, particularly in counseling interviews, is the signal that time is up. This closing is most effective when a time limit is announced or agreed upon in the opening or when an appointment is made.

Well, that's all the time we have for today.

Our time's up.

Wow, it's 3:30 already; our time went quickly today.

Be tactful in "calling time," but stick to the time limit imposed on an interview. Try not to give the impression that you are moving interviewees along an interpersonal assembly line.

6. We may close an interview by explaining why we must close at this time.

I have another appointment waiting; perhaps we can. . . .

I'm sorry, but I'm going to have to end our discussion. I have a class in just a few minutes.

I must leave now in order to get to the airport by 5 o'clock.

Be sure our justifications are real. If an interviewee thinks we are making up phony excuses just to end this interaction, future interactions (if they take place) are likely to be strained and with a lower level of trust.

7. Perhaps the most common closing is a note of appreciation or satisfaction, mainly because interviewers usually *want* something: information, help, attitudes, feelings, a sale, a story, and so on.

I've really enjoyed meeting you. Thanks much for your help. That's all the questions I have. Thank you for your time. I think we accomplished a great deal today. I appreciate your willingness to come in early for this meeting.

Be sincere in noting appreciation and satisfaction, and avoid any verbal or nonverbal hint of sarcasm.

8. We often close interviews by expressing concern for the interviewee's health, welfare, future, and so on.

Take care, and I will see you soon.

Be sure to get in touch with me if you run into additional problems.

I hope all goes well for you in this new position as managing editor.

Like the preceding closing, we should be sincere in our concern. "Take care" and other such comments are often little more than verbal habits. Express a concern appropriate for the relationship with the interviewee, for this interview, and for this situation.

9. It is appropriate in many interviews to plan for the next meeting with the interviewee or to reveal what will happen next. Future planning may include date, time, place, topic, content, and purpose.

Let's get together again on the sixteenth at 10:00 A.M. and see how things appear at that time.

Okay, when we meet on the tenth, we should be prepared to review the final draft of the contract.

In about two weeks, we will notify you about the results of this interview and whether we would like you to come to Milwaukee for another interview.

10. A summary is a common form of closing, especially for informational and sales interviews. Summaries frequently include a closing question designed to verify accuracy and agreement.

It's agreed, then, that I will write up a preliminary contract that includes design, labor, and materials cost for phase 1 of the new office complex. You will check our figures with your home office and contact me by Friday if there are any changes. Is this your understanding?

Summaries are valuable means of repeating important bits of information, stages or steps of processes, and agreements and disagreements.

We may signal closings through a variety of *nonverbal actions*—some of which may be unplanned or unintentional. Actions that interview parties often perceive as "leave-taking" signals include straightening up in our seat, leaning forward, standing up, moving our legs from under a desk or away from the other party, uncrossing our legs, placing our hands on our legs as if preparing to rise, breaking eye contact, offering to shake hands, various hand movements, smiling, and looking at a watch or clock. Remember that any behavioral act may be interpreted in a meaningful way by the party observing the act. Unconscious movements such as glancing at a watch may cause an interview party to close an interview prematurely or to feel the pressure of nonverbal "hints" to leave. We must be constantly aware of what our words and actions are saying to the other party.

Interviewers rarely use a single verbal or nonverbal closing technique. They usually combine several techniques into a complete closing, such as the following example.

> Well (glancing at a watch), I see our time is up. (leaning forward and smiling) I think it's been a good session (rising from the chair) and that we are close to agreement on a good course of action. (shaking hands with the interviewee) I appreciate your meeting on such a short notice. Take care of yourself, and I will see you next Monday. (a waving hand motion)

We must decide before or during each interview which combination of closing techniques best suits us, the interviewee, and the situation. Our role in the interview and perhaps our relationship with the interviewee may dictate some techniques and rule out others and determine who will initiate the closing and when.

There are a number of guidelines for closing interviews properly and effectively. Both interviewer and interviewee should be able to tell when the real closing is taking place. Avoid false finishes. When the interview *in fact* or *psychologically* has come to a close, do not try to resurrect it. Do not introduce new topics during the closing. Neither party is ready to devote satisfactory attention to a new topic when the interview appears to be over. Do not expect all interviews to finish like a neatly wrapped package. Be sincere and honest in closings. Make no promises that cannot be kept because of personal limitations, company policies, time limits, and so on. Leave the door open for future contacts. Never rush the closing. If additional contact is required, explain what will happen next, when, where, and why.

Quiz #2 Interview Closings

How satisfactory are the following closings? Consider the interviewing situations and types, the closing techniques used, and what is and is not included. How might each be improved? Do not assume that each is partially or completely unsatisfactory.

1. This is a counseling interview taking place in an academic counseling office.

Interviewer: Well, (straightening up) our time's up. I think we accomplished a great deal today. You're making remarkable headway. (sitting back) What are your reactions to today's session?

Interviewee: I think I'm beginning to. . . .

2. This is an employment interview taking place in a college placement center.

(standing up) I've enjoyed talking with you this morning, Pete. (shakes hands) We'll be getting in touch with you soon. Good luck! (vocal stress)

3. This is a persuasive interview taking place in a used car lot.

Well, Jan and Frank, (smiling) it's been nice meeting you both. (waving) Come back.

4. This is a political survey taking place at the front door of a home.

(looking at the interview form) That's all the questions I have. Really a nice evening, isn't it?

5. This is an appraisal interview taking place in a supervisor's office.

Interviewer: Well, keep up the good work, Ida. (looking at a wall clock) How's your son doing in college?

Interviewee: He's doing just fine. He made the Dean's list last semester and was selected as the outstanding junior in management.

Interviewer: (moving toward the door) See you soon.

Summary

This chapter has divided the interview into three structural parts—the opening, the body, and the closing. All three parts are vital to an interview's success. If during the opening the interviewer does not create the proper atmosphere for free and accurate communication, the best lineup of questions, arguments, or information during the body will fail. If the closing turns off the interviewee, the achievements of the opening and body may be lost. There are many structural principles and techniques available to the interviewer; it is the interviewer's task to select the most appropriate ones for a particular interview situation. The many variables of the interviewing process should serve as selection guides.

Later chapters on survey, journalistic, employment, appraisal, counseling, and persuasive interviews will discuss structural divisions, techniques, and strategies peculiar to each. Chapter 4 will discuss questions and question sequences used in the body of interviews.

Student Activities

1. Take a note pad and, during a twenty-four-hour period, keep a record of how the dyadic interactions you observe (including those on television) or take part in are opened. What openings and combinations of openings are employed? Are most openings combinations of methods? What methods are employed that are not discussed in this chapter? How does the type of dyadic encounter (conversation or interview—survey, journalistic, employment, appraisal, counseling, persuasive, etc.) affect the openings?

2. Select a current topic of local, national, or international interest. First, conduct a ten-minute nonscheduled interview with a fellow student, worker, or neighbor. Make note of the information gained and how the interview progressed. Second, using the same topic, conduct a ten-minute moderately scheduled interview. Once again note the information gained and how the interview progressed. Third, using the same topic, conduct a ten-minute highly scheduled or highly scheduled, standardized interview. Now, compare the results of the three kinds of interviews, problems encountered during the interviews, and advantages and disadvantages of each schedule.

3. Select interviews from various chapters. Try to construct an interview guide for each. What kinds of sequences were employed; how many interviews contained more than one sequence? What difficulties did you encounter in trying to reduce interviews to interview guides and in trying to identify possible organizational sequences? Which schedules were employed? How did interview type and situation seem to affect selection of sequences and schedules?

4. During a week, keep a record of the leave-taking means used to close dyads you observe or take part in. Note the kinds of leave-taking employed. Which are most common? Are certain means of leave-taking characteristic of specific kinds of interviews? How frequently did you encounter false finishes in interviews? What causes them and how can we avoid them?

5. Make an appointment with an experienced interviewer. Discuss the methods used in opening various types of interviews. How does the interviewer determine which methods to employ? Discuss the methods the interviewer uses in the body of interviews—which organizational sequences and which schedules. How often and under which circumstances does the interviewer combine sequences and schedules? How does the interviewer close interviews? How does the interviewer determine which leave-taking methods to employ?

Notes

1. Leonard Zunin and Natalie Zunin. *Contact: The First Four Minutes* (Los Angeles: Nash Publishing, 1972), pp. 8–12.

2. Paul D. Krivonos and Mark L. Knapp, "Initiating Communication: What Do You Say When You Say Hello?" *Central States Speech Journal* 26 (Summer 1975): 115–25.

3. For discussion of these and other opening techniques, see Robert S. Goyer, W. Charles Redding, and John T. Rickey, *Interviewing Principles and Techniques: A Project Text* (Dubuque, Iowa: Wm. C. Brown Co. Publishers, 1968), pp. 10–11.

4. Raymond L. Gorden, *Interviewing: Strategy, Techniques, and Tactics* (Homewood, Ill.: The Dorsey Press, 1975), p. 49.

5. This figure is based on one in Bernard Berelson and Gary Steiner, *Human Behavior: An Inventory of Scientific Findings* (New York: Harcourt Brace Jovanovich, 1964), p. 30.

6. Mark L. Knapp, Roderick P. Hart, Gustav W. Friedrich, and Gary M. Shulman. "The Rhetoric of Goodbye: Verbal and Nonverbal Correlates of Human Leave-Taking," *Speech Monographs* 40 (August 1973): 182–98.

Suggested Readings

Benjamin, Alfred. *The Helping Interview.* Boston: Houghton-Mifflin Co., 1980.

Bingham, Walter Van Dyke; Moore, Bruce Victor; and Gustad, John W. *How to Interview.* New York: Harper & Row, 1959.

Gorden, Raymond L. *Interviewing: Strategy, Techniques, and Tactics.* Homewood, Ill.: The Dorsey Press, 1975.

Goyer, Robert S.; Redding, W. Charles; and Rickey, John T. *Interviewing Principles and Techniques: A Project Text.* Dubuque, Iowa: Wm. C. Brown Co. Publishers, 1968.

Knapp, Mark L.; Hart, Roderick P.; Friedrich, Gustav W.; and Shulman, Gary M. "The Rhetoric of Goodbye: Verbal and Nonverbal Correlates of Human Leave-Taking," *Speech Monographs* 40 (August 1973): 182–98.

Krivonos, Paul D., and Knapp, Mark L. "Initiating Communication: What Do You Say When You Say Hello?" *Central States Speech Journal* 26 (Summer 1975): 115–25.

Richardson, Stephen A.; Dohrenwend, Barbara S.; and Klein, David. *Interviewing: Its Forms and Functions.* New York: Basic Books, 1965.

Zunin, Leonard, and Zunin, Natalie. *Contact: The First Four Minutes.* Los Angeles: Nash Publishing, 1972.

Questions and Their Uses 4

As we stressed in chapter 1, questions play a major role in most interviews; they are the "tools of the trade." Whether we are conducting a poll, hiring an employee, counseling a student, getting task information from a supervisor, or talking with a government official, our knowledge of the types of questions and skill in their use are vital to our success as an interviewer. Even when giving information we are likely to employ questions in clarifying information or in checking to see if we have transmitted the information accurately. The good sales representative relies on skillful questioning to discover a customer's needs and desires and to aid the sales effort. This chapter will introduce the basic types of questions—their uses, advantages, and disadvantages—criteria for phrasing questions, and question sequences.

Types of Questions

Although a listing of types and subtypes of questions can stretch as far as an author's imagination,[1] we may classify questions in three ways: open or closed, primary or secondary, and neutral or leading.

Open Questions

Open questions are broad in nature, often specifying only the topic to be covered. They allow the *respondent* considerable freedom in determining the amount and kind of information to give. Some questions are *highly open-ended* with virtually no restrictions, such as the following:

> Tell me about yourself.
> What do you know about Ford Motor Company?
> What was Disney World like?
> What are your feelings about legalized abortion?
> How do you think this city can be improved?

An open question lets the respondent do the talking and allows the interviewer to listen and observe.

Other open-ended questions are *moderately open* with some restrictions, such as the following:

> Tell me about your hobbies.
> What do you know about the foreign operations of Ford Motor Company?
> Tell me about the campground at Disney World.
> How do you feel about Congressman Smiley's stand on legalized abortion?
> How do you think the parks in this city can be improved?

Market researchers and public opinion surveyors may hand a statement, picture, or product offer to an interviewee and ask, "How would you respond to this statement?" or "What comes to mind when you look at this picture?" or "What are your feelings about this offer?"

Open questions have several *advantages*.

    1. They let the respondent do the talking while the interviewer listens and observes.

    2. They may communicate interest and trust in the respondent and the respondent's answers because they give the respondent considerable freedom to determine the nature and amount of information to be given.

    3. They tend to be easy to answer and pose little threat to the interviewee, the reason why interviewers often begin interviews with open questions.

4. They may reveal what the respondent thinks is important.

5. They allow the respondent to volunteer information the interviewer might not think to ask for.

6. They may reveal a respondent's lack of information or misunderstanding of words or concepts.

7. Answers to open questions may reveal a respondent's uncertainty or intensity of feeling toward an issue or person.

8. Lengthy answers to open questions may bring out the respondent's frames of reference, prejudices, or stereotypes.

Open-ended questions are not without *disadvantages*.

1. Answers to open questions may consume a great amount of time; an interviewer might have time to ask only three or four questions in a ten-minute interview.

2. The respondent may dwell on information the interviewer does not want.

3. The respondent may give a brief answer to a broad question, necessitating several follow-up questions to get the information desired.

4. The respondent may withhold valuable information because it may appear irrelevant or too obvious.

5. The interviewer's verbal and nonverbal behavior (head nodding, looking on the schedule for the next question, glancing at a watch) may affect both quantity and quality of responses.

6. The interviewer must be skilled in controlling open-ended interviews; stopping or redirecting an interviewee in mid-response can have serious repercussions on the interview.

7. Interviewers must be skilled in recording answers, especially if several interviewers are involved.

8. Results from lengthy, rambling answers, usually unorganized and phrased differently by each respondent, may be all but impossible to code and to tabulate.

9. Replication of interviews in a series is difficult because each respondent determines the nature and results of each interview; this problem is magnified when more than one interviewer is involved in a project.

Closed Questions

Closed questions are restrictive in nature. They limit answer options available to the interviewee, often supplying all possible answers in the questions themselves. Some questions are *moderately closed* and ask the respondent to volunteer a specific piece of information, such as the following:

Who is your current Congressional representative?
What was your salary on your last job?
How old are you?
How long has it been since your last physical examination?
What brand name comes to mind when you think of canned fruit?

Other questions are *highly closed* and ask the respondent to select the appropriate answer from among those provided in the question. Multiple-choice questions, such as the following, are common in market and public opinion surveys.

Which of these brands of gasoline did you buy last?

_____ Standard

_____ Arco

_____ Phillips 66

_____ Texaco

_____ Gulf

_____ Sunoco

_____ Citgo

_____ Union 76

_____ other _____

What educational level have you achieved?

_____ some high school

_____ high school graduate

_____ some college

_____ college graduate

_____ some graduate work

_____ a graduate degree

If the election were being held today, who would you vote for?

_____ Brownlow

_____ Grable

_____ undecided

I would like you to rate the following brands of coffee on a scale from one to five. If you strongly like the brand, give it a five. If you like the brand, give it a four. If you neither like nor dislike the brand, give it a three. If you dislike the brand, give it a two. If you strongly dislike the brand, give it a one.

Folgers	1	2	3	4	5
Maxwell House	1	2	3	4	5
Sanka	1	2	3	4	5
Nescafe	1	2	3	4	5
Stewart	1	2	3	4	5

You said you opposed the building of the reservoir in this area. On this card are several reasons frequently cited for opposing the project. How would you rank them in order of importance?

_____ relocation of homeowners

_____ loss of tax base for the area

_____ cost of construction

_____ bad environmental impact

_____ excessive silting

_____ removal of a cemetery

The *bipolar* question is a very common and frequently misused and over-used closed question. It limits the respondent to one of two choices, such as the following:

Do you agree or disagree with the president's veto of the foreign aid bill?
Do you approve or disapprove of the new labor contract?
Are you going to vote in the primary election, or not?
Do you think the cost of living will be higher or lower next year?

The yes/no bipolar question is perhaps the most common two-choice question. The choices may be stated or, as in the following examples, merely implied.

Did you vote in the last presidential election?
Do you smoke?
Are you familiar with the new labor contract?
Are you going to the game tonight?
Do you agree with the Reverend Williams' position on abortion?

Two assumptions undergird bipolar questions: that there are only two possible answers and that the answers are poles apart: like/dislike, hot/cold, approve/disapprove, high/low, rich/poor, yes/no. Such choices do not account for respondents who are undecided, have no opinion, or do not know the answer. Other respondents may feel that inflation will be about the same next year, or may be mildly in favor of or mildly opposed to a president's veto, or may agree with some parts and disagree with other parts of a union contract. The interviewer would be wise to review all bipolar questions for erroneous assumptions. We suspect that most interviewers do not really want yes or no answers to bipolar questions, such as, "Do you think the football team will have a good season?" They phrase questions this way through habit or carelessness.

Closed questions have several *advantages* over open questions.[2]

1. The interviewer can control questions and answers more effectively.

2. The interviewer can ask more questions, in more areas, and in less time.

3. The interviewer can ask for a specific piece of information without waiting for the interviewee to volunteer it.

4. Answers are easier to replicate, code, tabulate, and analyze.

5. Unskilled interviewers can handle closed questions and record answers more reliably.

6. Closed questions require less effort from the respondent.

7. Answers to closed questions do not require explanations or justifi-cations and thus may be less threatening to respondents.

An answer to a closed
question may not reveal why
the respondent feels a
certain way.

Closed questions have several *disadvantages.*

1. A closed question (especially a bipolar one) may obtain too little information, thus requiring several follow-up questions that task the reliability of both interview and interviewer.

2. An answer to a closed question may not reveal why the respondent feels a certain way, the degree to which a respondent may like or dislike, approve or disapprove.

3. A closed question may force the respondent to take a specific position (often a polar one) early in the interview; a forced position that may adversely affect the remainder of the interview.

4. The interviewee has little or no chance to volunteer potentially valuable information.

5. The restrictiveness and rapid-fire manner of closed questions may inhibit communication because the interviewee may feel the interviewer has little interest in him or her or the answers.

6. To use closed questions effectively, the interviewer may need to know the knowledge level, language level, and frames of reference of all potential respondents—an impossibility in many interviewing situations.

7. A respondent can rate, rank, select an answer from a list, or say yes or no without knowing anything about the subject matter, a state of ignorance the interviewer might fail to detect.

Figure 4.1 illustrates the major advantages and disadvantages of open and closed questions.[3] As the interviewer applies more constraint to the question, the amount of data tends to decrease. As the amount of data decreases, the interviewer's control over the interview increases, less interviewer skill and time

Type of Question   Nature of Response

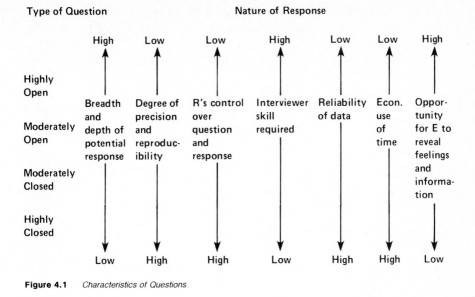

Figure 4.1   *Characteristics of Questions*

are required, and the degree of precision, reliability, and reproducibility increases. On the other hand, as the interviewer lessens constraint on the question, the amount of data tends to increase. As the amount of data increases, the interviewee is likely to reveal knowledge level, understanding of the question, reasons for feeling or acting, hidden motives, and valuable information the interviewer might have overlooked. Obviously, many interviews include a variety of open and closed questions with varying degrees of constraint. The point is, select the most appropriate question for the information desired, the interviewee, and the purpose of the interview.

Primary and Secondary Questions
We may also classify questions as primary and secondary.[4]

Primary questions introduce topics in an interview or new areas within a topic. They can stand alone out of context and still make sense: Where were you when the tornado struck your home? What is your favorite hobby? Tell me about your last accounting position. All examples of open and closed questions in the previous sections of this chapter were primary questions.

Secondary questions attempt to elicit more fully information asked for in a primary question or a previous secondary question and may be either open or closed. They are often referred to as "probing" or "follow-up" questions. Interviewers use secondary questions when answers to primary questions (especially open questions or moderately closed questions) seem incomplete, superficial, vague, suggestive, irrelevant, inaccurate, or when the interviewee gives no response.

If, as interviewer, we feel the respondent has *not completed* an answer or is *hesitant* to go on, we might remain *silent* for a few moments (perhaps using eye contact, facial expressions, or head nodding) and let this pause encourage the respondent to continue. If this fails, we could employ "nudging" probes, such as the following:

I see.
Go on.
And then?
Tell me more.
Please continue.
Yes?
What happened next?
Uh huh?
Hmmm.

If we feel the interviewee has given a *superficial* answer, we might use phrases such as the following to begin our secondary question.

Tell me more about. . . .
What happened after . . . ?
How did you react to . . . ?
Explain further the point that. . . .
What did you do after . . . ?
Why did you . . . ?

If we think the answer is *vague,* perhaps including generalities or specialized terms, we might respond:

I'm not sure I understand your point.
What did you have in mind when you said . . . ?
Please define "middle school" for me.
What do you mean by "a great deal of money?"
Just how large was your school?

If an answer seems to *suggest* a feeling or attitude, we might ask:

Why do you feel that way?
Why do you think that happened?
What do you mean by *seems?*
How do you feel about that?
How did you react?

An answer might be *irrelevant,* such as in the following exchange.

Interviewer: What are your attitudes toward the new work rules?
Interviewee: A lot of people around here don't like them. They say they're dreamed up by somebody who never saw an assembly line, let alone worked on one.
Interviewer: What are *your* attitudes toward the rules?

In this case the interviewer simply restated the question with stress on "your" to get the answer to the original question. The interviewer could have rephrased the question, asked another question, asked a secondary question to probe into the answer to get the relevant information, or remained silent for a few seconds to encourage a more direct answer—a silent probe. No one option is inherently better than another.

An answer might be *inaccurate.* For example, the respondent might give a wrong year, 1975 instead of 1976; or a wrong numerical figure, million instead of billion or two times instead of three times; or an inaccurate quote, leaving out the word probably or maybe or not. The *reflective probing question* is a valuable technique in cases of real or suspected inaccuracy. The reflective probe literally reflects the answer given and may aid in clarifying a vague, unclear answer as well as a possible inaccuracy because the interviewer is in essence double checking an interpretation of the answer. The interviewer, in these cases, might ask:

You mean 1976, don't you?
Was that million or billion?
Didn't you return home three times the first year you were in the army?
He did not qualify his intention?

Interviewers must be cautious when probing into possible inaccurate responses or when using reflective probes. We must communicate to the interviewee that we are interested in a clear and accurate interpretation of the answer and are in no way expressing disbelief or attempting to trick or to trap the interviewee. If the probe appears to question the respondent's integrity, intelligence, or knowledge, the result may be inhibited communication or termination of the interview.

We may be *unsure* of what an interviewee has said or implied in an answer and want to determine the accuracy of our comprehensions, impressions, or assumptions. Reflective probes, such as the following, can help us to resolve uncertainties by clarifying and verifying the messages we receive during interviews.

You think, then, that you can make the new deadline?
Are you saying that a "good raise" is one in excess of 13 percent?
You think you were *tricked* into signing the petition?
Your supervisor *didn't* tell you about the monthly performance reviews?
Am I correct in assuming that you would take the job if it were offered?

The *mirror,* or *summary,* question is closely related to the reflective probing question. The mirror question summarizes a series of answers or interchanges to ensure accurate understanding of what has been stated, implied, or agreed upon. For example, an employee might ask a mirror question to be certain of instructions received from a supervisor: "Okay Bill, let me see if I've got this straight. You want me to put three people on the Smith job, four on the Tompson job, and keep two here to repair some of the equipment?" An employment interviewer, after asking several questions concerning an applicant's educational record, might ask: "It's my understanding, then, that you have a major in public relations and strong minors of eighteen or more semester hours in psychology, marketing, and supervision and that you will take additional courses in graphics and industrial relations before graduation. Correct?" A salesperson might ask a question such as the following after probing into a customer's needs and desires: "You want a used station wagon about two or three years old, preferably middle-sized, and capable of pulling a large boat—right?" Like reflective probes, mirror questions can communicate disbelief, pressure, or entrapment if we do not phrase and ask them carefully. If asked properly, mirror and reflective questions can help us to avoid costly errors caused by *assuming* we understand clearly and accurately what a respondent has stated or implied or what both parties have agreed to.

It is conceivable that the interviewee will *not respond* to a question. If this happens, we might restate the question, rephrase it, or ask *tactfully* why the respondent did not answer. Be careful; do not interpret a pause or hesitation (to gather thoughts to include in the answer) as no response. The unskilled interviewer often jumps in with a rephrased question or a different question if the interviewee hesitates for even a moment. A respondent may state why he or she cannot or will not answer a question. Listen to these reasons carefully before deciding on the next question. Be ready to abandon the area of questioning, to explain why we need the requested information, to explain the potential use of such information, to rephrase the question, or to explain the kind of answer or information we desire.

There are many reasons why an interviewee may give an inadequate response, especially when we consider the complex and intimate nature of the interview. The following reasons are based on ones given by Kahn and Cannell.[5]

1. The respondent may be unsure about how much information or detail we want, especially in a question such as, "Tell me about yourself?"

2. The respondent may be unsure of the kind of answer we want; should the respondent give a yes or no answer to a bipolar question or explain an answer or give a detailed answer?

3. The respondent may not understand the question because of language or phraseology.

4. The respondent may not have the information asked for because of faulty memory or never obtaining it.

5. The respondent may feel the question is irrelevant or none of the interviewer's business.

6. The respondent may be unable to express inner feelings because of emotional trauma, lack of training, language barriers, low intelligence, or societal traditions and practices.

7. The respondent may feel we could not understand an answer: the topic is too technical, too personal, too foreign to us and our frame of reference.

Our initial task is to determine if the answer to a primary question (or even a secondary question) is adequate. If it is not, we must decide what is wrong with it and why the respondent may have answered that way. Then we must decide whether to probe further to get an adequate response or to go on to a new area or another primary question. If the decision is to probe further, we must select the best course of action to pursue in one or more secondary questions. The analysis and decision making must take place in a matter of seconds. A pause of more than two or three seconds may damage the interview by increasing the respondent's anxiety, by seeming to question the respondent's integrity or knowledge, or by making us appear unskilled or unprepared. The answers to the questions in the following quiz are inadequate. Why are they so, and what secondary question should we use to obtain an adequate answer?

Quiz #1—Supply the Secondary Question

1. **Interviewer:** How did you like your last job?
   Interviewee: At first it was quite interesting.
   Interviewer:

2. **Interviewer:** What kind of person was your supervisor?
   Interviewee: So, so.
   Interviewer:

3. **Interviewer:** How do you feel about close detail work?
   Interviewee: That depends.
   Interviewer:

4. **Interviewer:** Define cooperation for me.
   Interviewee: (no response)
   Interviewer:

5. **Interviewer:** What do you envision a sales job would be like?
   Interviewee: I think the product is important. I like to have a product worth being sold and with a good application. I want to sell something with a real and definite purpose.
   Interviewer:

6. **Interviewer:** Which presidential candidate do you plan to vote for?
   Interviewee: Oh, I don't know.
   Interviewer:

7. **Interviewer:** How many cups of coffee do you drink each day?
   Interviewee: Several.
   Interviewer:

8. **Interviewer:** What do you think of my painting?
   Interviewee: It's interesting.
   Interviewer:

9. Interviewer: How do you feel about this work schedule?
   Interviewee: It's . . . not bad.
   Interviewer:
10. Interviewer: How is John doing on the football team?
   Interviewee: He didn't make the starting nine.
   Interviewer:

The use of secondary questions separates skilled from unskilled interviewers. The unskilled interviewer tends to think ahead to the next question on the schedule and is in a hurry to move along through the list of questions. The skilled interviewer listens carefully to responses and selects the best secondary question to assure attainment of clear and complete information asked for in the primary question. Skilled interviewers know that secondary questions make respondents feel the interviewers are listening and interested in them and their answers, thus heightening motivation.

But secondary questions are not foolproof and may cause problems when not phrased carefully. Payne illustrates how the meaning of a simple "why" question can be altered by stressing different words.[6]

Why do you say that?
Why *do* you say that?
Why do *you* say that?
Why do you *say* that?
Why do you say *that?*

"Why" questions can easily communicate disapproval, disbelief, or mistrust. They can put interviewees on the defensive because they appear to *demand* justifications, explanations, and rationales. A secondary question may alter the meaning of the primary question, or it may bias the response. Be careful not to misquote the interviewee or to give the impression of putting words into the respondent's mouth. The respondent may feel we have not listened to the answer. Do not interrupt the respondent in mid-answer or interpret a hesitation as a nonresponse or an incomplete response. Avoid *curious* probing for information we do not need, especially if further probing might embarrass the interviewee.

Neutral and Leading Questions

All questions discussed in previous sections of this chapter are "neutral questions." That is, the respondent could decide upon an answer without direction or pressure from the interviewer. Even in bipolar situations, the interviewee could choose freely and without pressure between two equal choices: yes/no, approve/disapprove, higher/lower.

We now want to discuss questions in which the interviewer suggests implicitly or explicitly, the answer expected or desired. As Kahn and Cannell have stated, the leading question "makes it easier or more tempting for the respondent to give one answer than another."[7] The respondent merely agrees with the direction the interviewer appears to be providing. The direction may be intentional or unintentional, implicit or explicit, verbal or nonverbal. The important point is that the respondent perceives a direction.

The varying degrees of direction and the distinction between neutral and leading questions are illustrated in the following questions.

Leading Questions	Neutral Questions
1. You like close detail work, don't you?	1. Do you like close detail work?
2. You're going with us, aren't you?	2. Are you going with us?
3. Do you oppose the union like most workers I have talked with?	3. What are your attitudes toward the union?
4. Wouldn't you rather have a Buick?	4. How does this Buick compare to other cars in the same price range?
5. How do you feel about these asinine government claims?	5. How do you feel about the government's claims?
6. When was the last time you got drunk?	6. Tell me about your drinking habits.
7. Have you stopped cheating on your exams?	7. Did you cheat on your last exam?
8. Would you classify yourself as a conservative or a radical?	8. Would you classify yourself as a reactionary, conservative, moderate, liberal, radical, or other?
9. Don't you think amnesty is unfair to the loyal Americans who died in the war while draft dodgers were having a great time in Canada?	9. How do you feel about the argument that amnesty would be unfair to the Americans who died in the war?

All nine of the leading questions make it easier, if not necessary, for the interviewee to respond in a particular way; the high potential for interviewer bias is obvious in each question. The setting of the interview (persuasion, reprimand, information getting, counseling, news gathering), the tone of the interview (formal or informal, serious or relaxed), and the manner in which the interviewer asked each question (smiling, frowning, normal voice, gruff voice) would determine the respondent's ability to ignore the direction provided.

The first four questions are mild in direction. Notice that each asks for a yes or no response. This is typical of leading questions, so one way to avoid leading questions is to avoid bipolar questions. Respondents could ignore the direction of question 1 if they did not feel their being hired depended on a yes answer or if they were not in desperate need of a job. Question 3 uses a bandwagon (follow-the-crowd) technique. The respondent's answer would depend upon attitudes toward the union, feelings toward other workers, and past experiences. If the respondent has no strong feelings about the matter, he or she might just go along with the answer we seem to want.

The last five questions provide strong direction, virtual dictation of the appropriate answer, and are usually called *loaded* questions. Questions 5 and 9 illustrate the loading of questions through emotionally charged words and name calling. Questions 6, 7, and 8 provide varying degrees of entrapment. Question

6 assumes the respondent has been drunk at least once. Question 7 charges the respondent with cheating in the past, and either a yes or a no will keep the respondent in hot water. Question 8 polarizes possible choices by eliminating all middle ground such as moderate or liberal. Neither choice may please the respondent, but the respondent is likely to choose conservative over radical. "Are you for us or against us?" is a typical loaded question of the polarized variety.

Since leading questions—whether mild or loaded—have high potential for biased responses, we should avoid them *unless we know what we are doing.* Introductory phrases such as "As you know," "According to the law," "As studies have shown," and "According to John Expert, a leading authority on," may lead the respondent to give what appears to be the most acceptable response rather than reveal true feelings. Remember, we can turn a neutral question into a leading question by the manner in which we ask it. A great many leading questions are unintentional; the interviewer does not realize the question contains an implicit or explicit direction.

Leading questions have some valuable uses. For instance, employment and appraisal interviewers sometimes want to see how the interviewee will respond under stress or to see how much they can get the interviewee to go along with their directions. Persuasive interviewers make frequent use of leading questions, especially when conducting sales efforts: "I'm sure you want a good education for your child?" Reporters ask leading questions to produce unguarded replies or to provoke a reluctant interviewee into responding. Some social workers and attitude pollsters have discovered that questions such as "When was the last time you got drunk?" show the interviewee that the whole range of possible answers are acceptable, that an answer will not shock the interviewer. Respondents might be reluctant to admit, in answering a neutral question on drinking, that they ever got to the point of being drunk.

Do not confuse neutral mirror questions and reflective probes with leading questions. Mirrors and reflectives do appear to direct the respondent toward a particular answer, but their purpose is clarification of a previous answer or series of answers. Often the only way to distinguish these neutral questions from leading questions is by studying the context and manner in which they are asked. If the intent seems to be directed toward a particular answer, the question is leading or loaded. If the intent seems to be clarification or verification, the question is a mirror or reflective probe.

Figure 4.2 compares the general types of questions available to interviewer and interviewee. Identify each question in quiz #2 in three ways: open or closed, primary or secondary, and neutral or leading. Also, note if the question is a "special type": bipolar, mirror, reflective probe, nudging probe, or loaded.

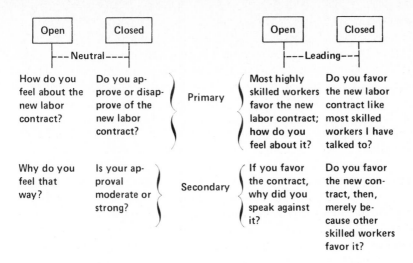

Figure 4.2 *Types of Questions*

Quiz #2—Identification of Questions

1. By middle school, then, you mean grades fifth to eighth?

2. What is your favorite sport?

3. Let me get this straight. We will leave at 7:30 in the morning and will arrive in Chicago at 9:45. The first session will begin at 10:00 and end at 12:00 noon. Is this correct?

4. Do you think we should continue our overly generous support of the United Nations?

5. How can you explain that?

6. Tell me about your previous working experiences.

7. Is your income tax report accurate and honest?

8. Go on.

9. How do you feel about the proposed bypass on US41?

10. Did you vote in the last primary election?

Phrasing Questions

Selecting the appropriate type of question is the first step. Phrasing the question is the second, and perhaps most important, step because careful wording can motivate and enable the respondent to answer freely, accurately, and in the detail desired. Phrasing a question is not a simple and quick task. We should develop each question with at least five factors in mind: (1) language, (2) relevance, (3) information level, (4) complexity, and (5) social and psychological accessibility.

Language

Interviewer and interviewee must share language and meaning if successful communication is to take place. Kahn and Cannell suggest that we use "language that communicates successfully to the least sophisticated respondents involved and at the same time avoids the appearance of oversimplification."[8] They do not mean to mimic respondents by using their jargon or slang, but to use common language—"going to college" instead of "matriculating"; "drunk" instead of "inebriated"; "interviewing" instead of "dyad"; "liar" in place of "prevaricator"; "mercy killing" for "euthanasia."

Be careful! Many common words and names have many meanings. If we are "raising a tent," are we putting it up or taking it down? If we are "moved by a gesture," do we mean physically or emotionally? Are "politicians" all government officials, or currently "elected" officials, or anyone running for office, and what about campaign staffs, office staffs, and party members? Our frames of reference often determine the meanings we apply to words. For example, when we asked twenty students to write down the first thing that came to mind when we said "game," we got the following responses: monopoly, football, basketball, tennis, bridge, baseball, deer, pheasant, sport, fun, cards, wild animal, willing to try something new. What do words such as ball, shipping, engineer, and grass mean to you? To your husband or wife? To your roommate? To a friend in Florida, or Maine, or California?

Be watchful for common words with vague meanings: much, many, most, average, fair, hot, cold, a lot, large, small, excellent, and superior. Does the statement "Most supervisors come up the ladder from assembly line jobs," mean 51 percent, 65 percent, 75 percent, or none of these? A "hot" day for one person may be "just right" for a second and "a bit cool" for a third. To some people "excellent" is always the top rating with "superior" one notch below. Others would reverse this order. Students used the following questions in survey projects.

Do you watch television much?
Do you obey the speed limit most of the time?
Are you familiar with the new contract?
Are you a heavy smoker?

Key words in each of these questions are so vague that unexplained yes or no answers would be meaningless. Respondents would interpret each question from their own unique viewpoints. In the fourth question, is the interviewer asking about smoking habits or the weight of the respondent? Following a classroom interview on "large" versus "small" high schools, the instructor asked the parties to define a large high school. The interviewee said 600 or more students, and the interviewer said 2,000 or more students. The parties had argued from very different frames of reference.

Other common words are used with the assumption that they are synonymous. For instance, could, should, ought and would are often carelessly tossed into questions. Respondents may perceive important differences. How would you respond to each of the following?

1. What rights *could* a woman have in deciding on an abortion?
2. What rights *should* a woman have in deciding on an abortion?
3. What rights *ought* a woman have in deciding on an abortion?
4. What rights *would* a woman have in deciding on an abortion?
5. What rights *does* a woman have in deciding on an abortion?
6. What rights *will* a woman have in deciding on an abortion?

Numbers 1 and 6 may lead to speculative comments on "future" rights. Numbers 2 and 3 may provoke discussion of moral and legal rights a woman has, whether or not they are currently recognized by society. Numbers 4, 5, and 6 may elicit comments on rights a woman has at present, depending upon a particular hospital or geographical area.

Similar sounding words may cause confusion: very and fairly, steal and steel, bull and bowl, cereal and serial, weather and whether. Provide context, transitions, or a preview that will limit or alleviate possible misunderstanding. Listen to answers for hints that the respondent has heard the wrong word.

Be on guard against words and phrasing that may bias responses. In a survey on television programming, an interviewer first asked parents if they "controlled" their children's television viewing. A large majority said no. Later the interviewer asked if they "allowed their children to watch any program they wanted to." A large majority of respondents said no. These contradictory results may have been due to words such as controlled, allowed, and program. In a recent survey, the following questions were asked a few minutes apart.

Is it okay to smoke while praying?
Is it okay to pray while smoking?

An overwhelming number of respondents said no to the first question and yes to the second. The events may be the same, but respondents apparently saw them as very different because of the wording. If we suspect that wording may influence results—a particular arrangement of words, a positive or negative phrasing, or word choice (mercy killing vs. death with dignity)—ask the question differently in several interviews and check results for evidence of bias or loading.

Relevance

Respondents must see the relevance of each question to our stated purpose and their expectations. If not, respondents may become reluctant to communicate freely or to cooperate further. When there is a possibility that a question or series of questions may appear irrelevant to the interviewee, explain the rationale for each and phrase each carefully to avoid obtrusive language.

The placing of questions in an interview is important. For instance, ask for demographic data such as age, salary, political party, and religious preference at the beginning or end of the interview, not scattered throughout. The end of the interview may be best for such data because we will have had the bulk of the interview to establish trust between ourselves and the respondent. Also, if we say we are conducting a political survey, for example, and our first question is "How old are you?" the respondent may feel justified in countering, "What does that have to do with politics?"

Demographic data often appears irrelevant or none of our business. Explain why this information is needed and how we will use it. If we do not need a precise age, salary, or educational level, offer answer categories such as the following:

Stop me when I mention the range that includes your age: 18 to 25, 26 to 35, 36 to 50, 51 to 65, 66 or over.

Was your salary last year under $10,000, $10,000–15,000, $15,000–25,000, over $25,000?

Offer adequate answer categories so the respondent does not feel forced to choose among distasteful alternatives. A person who belongs to no particular religious denomination or to one that does not fit into one of the following may resent our question.

Is your religious affiliation Protestant, Catholic, Jewish, Atheist?

Information Level

Just as the respondent must be able to understand the language of our questions, the respondent must also have a store of knowledge that will allow him or her to respond in what is perceived to be an intelligent manner. Questions above the respondent's knowledge level may cause embarrassment or resentment. Either feeling decreases motivation to communicate freely and accurately. Ask for information in common categories or frames of reference. For instance, ask for pounds of sugar a family uses per month, not how many teaspoonfuls. Ask about electric costs in dollars, not kilowatts. Persons may be able to give us an accurate estimate of how many hours they spend watching television in a typical evening, but not in a given year.

An added danger is that interviewees may fake answers rather than admit they do not have the information. A few years ago a student tested information-level problems by asking several people what they thought of the news report that the Avis Candy Company (both news report and company were fictitious) was a communist front. Some said they doubted its truth; some said they were surprised when they heard the report; and some said they had not heard the report. One person replied, "It's funny you ask that. They contacted me just last week." An interviewer simply cannot assume respondents know what they are talking about.

On the other hand, questions beneath a respondent's level of information may insult the respondent's intelligence. This may occur because of overly simple words, requests for elementary information from an expert, or too much explanation of what is wanted. The interviewer must know if the respondent is a lay person, a novice, or an expert on the subject and if public opinion on a subject or authoritative opinion or knowledge is desired. For instance, the following question would be acceptable in a survey of the general public but not for communication professionals: "What do you think of the FCC's (Federal Communication Commission) ban of X-rated films from television?"

In determining proper information level, be cautious of assumed knowledge. Large numbers of people cannot name their senators, congressional representatives, or governors, do not know the populations of their cities, their annual incomes, or their wedding dates. Current trends, recent world events, new books, unemployment figures, and so on are known by a surprisingly small number of people. Abbreviations or full names can cause problems in questions. A respondent may be familiar with the TVA and CBS but not be aware that they stand for the Tennessee Valley Authority and the Columbia Broadcasting System. A respondent may have a definite opinion on the Equal Rights Amendment but think ERA is a detergent.

Complexity

Questions should contain a simple, clear request for a reasonably delimited amount of information. Avoid complex questions that defy an interviewee to answer them. If we must ask a complicated question, such as the following, consider some sample answers to explain the scale or give the respondent a small card containing the scale and a sample or two.

> Now, I would like your opinion on some leading brands of detergent. I would like you to rate these brands by using the numbers from plus five to minus five. If you like the brand that I mention, give it a number from plus one to plus five. The more you like it, the bigger the plus number you should give it. If you dislike the brand, give it a number from minus one to minus five. The more you dislike it, the bigger the minus number you should give it. If you neither like nor dislike the brand, give it a zero.

Some questions need not be complex; they end up that way because of poor wording, often a sign of inadequate preparation. This question was used in a research project on marriage relationships.

> Pick the most appropriate response. You feel that you understand each other, but you have never told them this.
> 1. You have never felt this way, or you have felt this way and have told them this.
> 2. You occasionally have felt this way, but you have never told them this.
> 3. You frequently have felt this way, but you have never told them this.

The multiple question in which two or more questions are asked at the same time is a common error, especially among novice interviewers. The following example shows how a perfectly good question is turned into a weak multiple question.

Why weren't you happy with the clinical psychology department? It didn't live up to your expectations? It didn't provide the experiences you wanted, or what?

Ask one question at a time. Neither the interviewer nor the respondent is likely to remember a bundle of questions, even if they are simply phrased. The respondent must decide which question to answer and is likely to answer the last one.

The mini-oration under the guise of a question is another frequent problem. This "question" was raised in a question-answer period following a city council meeting.

I wonder if you would explain the council's decision on the contracts for the new auditorium? It seems to me that a delay now would only postpone the inevitable and eventually the taxpayers would have to pay a much higher price for the facility. With building costs jumping 10 to 20 percent a year, we could end up paying several million dollars more for the auditorium. Your decision strikes me as being very short-sighted.

Accessibility

Accessibility refers to the ability of the interviewee to answer questions because of social, psychological, or situational constraints.[9] As we grow up, we learn not to praise ourselves, but to be humble. Even if we believe we are beautiful, intelligent, creative, or generous, we do not say so. We wait for others to say such things about us and then pose an "Aw shucks, it was nothing" attitude.

Some topics (and therefore questions and answers) are or have been off limits in polite society. When an interviewer poses questions in a taboo area— sex, personal income, religious convictions—he or she is probably asking for answers not easily accessible to many respondents. If such topics are to be investigated, the interviewer must pay particular attention to situational variables such as privacy, seating arrangement, location, time of day, and relationship between interviewer and interviewee.

We may be psychologically unable to relate our true feelings toward a supervisor, teacher, friend, parent, or loved one; or to recall details and feelings about an accident, illness, or other traumatic happening. If such questions are necessary, design them to lessen social and psychological constraints and to avoid offending the respondent. Do not ask these questions early in an interview before trust has been established between interviewee and interviewer.

As you will see in chapter 7, some questions are not merely socially or psychologically taboo, they are illegal because of equal employment opportunity legislation, court decisions, and right-to-privacy laws.

Critique the questions in quiz #3, keeping in mind the five factors of question phrasing—language, relevance, information level, complexity, and accessibility. Rewrite each question to make it satisfy these standards.

Quiz #3—What's Wrong with These Questions?

1. (First question in an interview on the Equal Rights Amendment) Are you familiar with the proposals of the ERA?

2. (Asked midway through an interview on lowering the drinking age to eighteen) Are you a registered voter?

3. What effects do you believe euthanasia would have on various age groups and religious groups and what influence do you believe these two groups would have on legalization of euthanasia?

4. What are your reactions to the abortion case now going on in Boston?

5. Would you say that the president is doing a good job or that he could do better?

6. Do you obey the speed limit personally (a) most of the time, (b) when convenient, or (c) seldom?

7. How do you feel physically and mentally after watching a violent television program?

8. (First two questions on mercy killing) (a) Do you agree or disagree with mercy killing? (b) What do you consider mercy killing to be?

9. The energy crisis affected who the most, (a) upper class, (b) middle class, (c) lower class?

10. Please place yourself into one of the following classes: I drink very little, some, quite a lot, a lot.

Question Sequences

A glance at the sample interviews at the ends of chapters reveals that questions are often interconnected, not only primary with secondary questions, but primary with other primary questions. These interconnections may form a sequence for the entire interview or sequences within topics and subtopics. Common types are the funnel sequence, inverted funnel sequence, quintamensional design, and the tunnel sequence.

Funnel Sequence

A funnel sequence begins with a broad, open-ended question and proceeds with ever more restricted questions. The following is a funnel sequence.

1. What are your reactions to the new employee communication program?
2. What kinds of communication media do you use?
3. Which one is most effective?
4. What is the cost per employee?
5. Is the program worth it?

The funnel sequence is appropriate when respondents know the topic well and feel free to talk about it or when the respondents are in an emotionally charged situation and would like to express their feelings. Since open-ended questions are usually easier to answer, pose less threat to respondents, and get respondents talking, the funnel sequence is an advantageous way to start an interview. Also, it avoids possible conditioning or biasing of later responses. For instance, if we begin the interview with a closed question such as "Do you think amnesty should be granted to all strikers?" we might place the respondent in a positive or negative state of mind for the remainder of the interview. The respondent might feel a necessity (perhaps unconsciously) to defend the stance taken. An open question such as "What are your feelings about granting amnesty to all strikers?" on the other hand, may avoid polarization and bias; we can always ask more restricted questions as the interview progresses. And, of course, starting with open-ended questions often eliminates the necessity for many closed or probing questions because the interviewee may volunteer materials needed.

Inverted Funnel Sequence

The inverted funnel sequence begins with closed questions and gradually proceeds toward open-ended questions. An inverted funnel sequence looks like this.

1. Is your employee communication program worth the cost?
2. What is the cost per employee?
3. Which communication medium is the most effective?
4. What kinds of communication media do you use?
5. What are your reactions to the new employee communication program?

The inverted funnel sequence is particularly useful when we need to motivate interviewees to respond freely. Respondents might not want to talk about an unpleasant happening, might feel they do not have the ability to answer or do not have the information we want. Perhaps a respondent's memory needs a bit of assistance. An initial closed question or questions may serve as a necessary warm-up. For example, when an interviewer asked a person to respond to an open-ended question on mudslinging in political communication, the person replied: "I don't know much about politics. You ought to try someone else." The interviewer then resorted to a few closed questions pertaining to mudslinging. Within minutes the reluctant interviewee was giving amazingly sophisticated views on political communication in general and mudslinging in particular. The closed questions had worked when an open-ended question had failed. Also, if we want to obtain a final judgment from the interviewee, the inverted funnel sequence allows us to proceed toward a generalization. A series of closed questions can always work toward a final question such as, "Is there anything else you would like to add?"

Quintamensional Design Sequence

The quintamensional design sequence is used by George Gallup and other attitude and opinion research firms to determine the intensity of the opinion or attitude held by an individual.[10] It is usually a five-step approach, as its name implies, but this is not a requirement and often an interviewee will answer one of our future questions before we get to it. The five steps, with sample questions, are as follows.

1. *Awareness*—"Tell me what you know about the new employee communication program."

2. *Uninfluenced attitudes*—"What, if any, are the contributions of the employee communication program?"

3. *Specific attitude*—"Do you approve or disapprove of the employee communication program?"

4. *Reason why*—"Why do you feel that way?"

5. *Intensity of attitude*—"How strongly do you feel about this—strongly, very strongly, not something you will ever change your mind on?"

Tunnel Sequence

A tunnel, or "string-of-beads," sequence is a series of similar questions—all open or all closed—and usually allows for little probing. The primary concern would be with initial answers to each question. This sequence is common in interviews where the purpose is to get reactions or attitudes toward people, places, or things and the interviewer wants to quantify the data. The tunnel is unlikely to obtain the kind of in-depth attitude information the quintamensional design can obtain. The following is a tunnel sequence.

1. Do you approve or disapprove of the new employee communication program?

2. Do you think it is more or less effective than the previous employee communication programs?

3. Are you personally more or less involved in this program than in previous employee communication programs?

4. Do you prefer a weekly plant newspaper or daily bulletins?

5. Do most employees you work with approve or disapprove of the new employee communication program?

The tunnel sequence is appropriate for many simple informational interviews or parts of interviews, but it may not allow for the kind of in-depth probing or adaptation to differing interviewees possible with the funnel, inverted funnel, or quintamensional sequences.

Quiz #4—Question Sequences

Which question sequence or combination of sequences would you employ in each of the situations described below. Why would you use this sequence or combination?

1. You are conducting a market survey to assess the effect of a recent advertising campaign for a new brand of dishwasher soap.

2. You are a claims adjuster for an insurance company and must interview a family only hours after its home was totally destroyed by fire.

3. You are conducting a preelection attitude and opinion survey for a newspaper chain.

4. You are interviewing a person for the company newsletter who has just been promoted to Director of Research and Development.

5. You are interviewing applicants for positions in sales and supervision.

Summary

The interviewer has a limitless variety of questions to choose from, and each type of question has unique characteristics, capabilities, and pitfalls. In this chapter we have categorized questions into open and closed, primary and secondary, and neutral and leading. Questions must be constructed carefully with several factors always in mind—language, relevance, information level, complexity, and accessibility. The interviewer must select and phrase the kinds of questions and the sequence(s) best suited to the interview's purpose and objectives. Sequences such as funnel, inverted funnel, quintamensional design, and tunnel may be selected for the entire interview or for one or more areas of the interview. Obviously, an interviewer may not employ any type of sequence in an interview.

Later chapters on survey interviewing, journalistic interviewing, employment interviewing, counseling interviewing, and persuasive interviewing will delve further into types and uses of questions and question strategies.

A Sample Interview for Review and Analysis

This is a medical school admissions interview between a medical school faculty member and a prospective medical student. Observe the types of questions used and what they are designed to achieve. How appropriate and effective is each question? What question sequences, if any, are employed?

1. *Interviewer:* Tell me how you became interested in medicine.

   Highly open, neutral, primary question designed to obtain information.

2. *Interviewee:* I guess there were a number of things that gradually turned my attention to medicine. My uncle was a physician and often took me to

his office when I was growing up. He seemed to have a very fulfilling life. My family has been medically oriented with my dad being a pharmacist and my mother being a nurse.

3. *Interviewer:* (silence)

Highly open, neutral, secondary (silent probing question) designed to keep the interviewee talking.

4. *Interviewee:* I've always had an interest in science and would like to get involved eventually in medical research.

5. *Interviewer:* In what ways do you see medicine providing a "fulfilling way of life?"

Moderately open, neutral, secondary question designed to obtain an explanation of a vague response.

6. *Interviewee:* In medicine I would be working with people and helping them both physically and psychologically. I like to work with people.

7. *Interviewer:* If you prefer to work with people, why do you plan to move into medical research?

Moderately open, neutral, secondary question designed to investigate an apparent inconsistency in responses.

8. *Interviewee:* I see research as a very direct way of helping people. I would never want to devote all of my life to research.

9. *Interviewer:* Okay. How happy have you been with your choice of Purdue University for your undergraduate studies?

Moderately open, neutral, primary question designed to assess feelings and attitudes.

10. *Interviewee:* Well, I chose Purdue because I was interested in engineering when I graduated from high school. I have been very satisfied with Purdue.

11. *Interviewer:* Are you saying that you would have selected a school other than Purdue if you had not been interested in engineering?

Highly closed, neutral, secondary (reflective probe) question designed to verify an impression.

12. *Interviewee:* Well, yes and no.

13. *Interviewer:* Yes and no?

Moderately open, neutral, secondary question designed to obtain an explanation of a confusing response.

14. *Interviewee:* I'm not sure at this date what I would have done because engineering dominated my thoughts at the time.

15. *Interviewer:* When and why did you switch from engineering to premed?

Moderately open, neutral, secondary question designed to obtain facts and explanations.

16. *Interviewee:* I made the final decision at the end of my second year. I was not happy working with machines.

17. *Interviewer:* Are you thinking of a specialty in medicine?
18. *Interviewee:* Yes. I think I would like to specialize in pediatrics.
19. *Interviewer:* Uh huh?
20. *Interviewee:* I have always enjoyed working with children in church groups and scouts and think I could work well with children.
21. *Interviewer:* How do you feel about abortion?
22. *Interviewee:* I am opposed to it.
23. *Interviewer:* Are you saying that there are no circumstances that justify an abortion?
24. *Interviewee:* Well . . . (long pause)
25. *Interviewer:* Most physicians I know believe that grave danger to a woman's life justifies an abortion. Wouldn't you agree with them?
26. *Interviewee:* I know many doctors feel that way, but I have read articles by doctors who claim that they have never encountered a situation in which the live fetus was endangering a woman's life.
27. *Interviewer:* Frankly, neither have I. If I were your patient and you discovered that, beyond any doubt, I had terminal cancer, would you tell me I was going to die?
28. *Interviewee:* Yes I would.
29. *Interviewer:* Why?
30. *Interviewee:* I feel strongly that patients have the right to know if they are going to die, to know their chances of survival.
31. *Interviewer:* How would you tell me?
32. *Interviewee:* I'd gather all of the test results and, after getting you comfortably seated, would tell you as simply and as factually as possible.
33. *Interviewer:* Which one of the following ailments do you think is most frightening to patients: cancer, heart attack, leukemia, diabetes, arthritis, or stroke?

Highly closed, neutral, primary (bipolar) question designed to obtain a single fact.

Highly open, neutral, secondary (nudging probe) designed to encourage the interviewee to continue talking.

Moderately open, neutral, primary question designed to assess feelings and attitudes.

Highly closed, neutral, secondary (reflective probe) question designed to see if an interpretation is accurate.

Highly closed, leading, secondary question designed to see if the interviewee will alter a view when under pressure.

Highly closed, neutral, primary (bipolar and hypothetical) question designed to discover an attitude.

Moderately open, neutral, secondary question designed to obtain an explanation.

Moderately open, neutral, secondary question designed to obtain an explanation.

Highly closed, neutral, primary (multiple choice) question designed to assess knowledge and opinion.

34. *Interviewee:* Cancer, by far.

35. *Interviewer:* Why do you think cancer is the most feared?

Moderately open, neutral, secondary question designed to assess knowledge and opinion.

36. *Interviewee:* Most people have family members or friends who have died of cancer and their deaths have often been very painful.

37. *Interviewer:* Don't you think the danger of cancer is greatly exaggerated?

Highly closed, leading, secondary question designed to assess the strength of a belief and to place mild stress on the interviewee.

38. *Interviewee:* No. No, I don't think so.

39. *Interviewer:* Come now. I don't know of a single reputable physician who would agree with you.

Highly closed, leading (loaded), secondary question designed to place heavy stress on the interviewee.

40. *Interviewee:* Well . . . I read a survey published last year by the AMA that stressed the growing danger of cancer to all ages. People have a right to be afraid.

41. *Interviewer:* I get the impression that you are not easily swayed from a position, and I seem to hear you saying that you like and trust people and their judgments. Correct?

Highly closed, neutral, secondary (mirror) question designed to verify a number of impressions.

42. *Interviewee:* Yes, I think so.

Student Activities

1. Select several interviews and note how questions are used by both parties in differing settings. How, for instance, are types and uses of questions different in persuasive, counseling, and market survey interviews? How do the questions satisfy the five factors of question formulation discussed in this chapter?

2. Prepare two sets of questions—one with neutral questions and one with leading questions—on a current national controversy or crisis. Interview ten people using the neutral questions in five interviews and the leading questions in five interviews. Then answer these questions: How did the differing lists affect the interviews as you conducted them? How did answers vary, if at all? Did certain kinds of people (age, sex, education, occupation, etc.) react differently to the leading questions?

3. Tape record an evening news program that includes interviews with government leaders, people in crises, community leaders, and sports figures. What kinds of questions are employed in these interviews? How much does the setting, the event, and the interview affect the types and uses of questions? How much reliance is there upon secondary questions?

4. Select a lengthy interview from the *New York Times, Playboy,* or another current source. See if you can discover a sequence or sequences of questions within the interview. If there are several sequences, try to perceive why the interviewer used the differing sequences. Was the interviewee reluctant? Did various topics demand differing sequences? Did the occasion determine the selection of sequences? Did the length of the interview determine sequences used?

5. Select a current controversial issue and then conduct two five- to ten-minute interviews with fellow students, workers, or neighbors. Use only primary questions in one interview—no probing into answers. In the second interview, rely mainly on secondary (probing) questions into answers from a few basic primary questions. How does information gained from these two procedures differ? How did you prepare for each interview? What kinds of primary questions did you employ when you knew you could not probe into answers?

6. Make up a brief list of words or names—all may be real, all may be fictitious, or the list may be a combination of real and make-believe. Ask fifteen to twenty people to identify the names or to define the terms. Observe carefully both verbal and nonverbal reactions of the interviewees. How did they react when they did not know the names or definitions? How many respondents gave honest "I don't know" responses? What do these brief interviews tell you about phrasing questions for interviews?

Notes

1. See Stanley L. Payne, *The Art of Asking Questions* (Princeton, N.J.: Princeton University Press, 1951), for an excellent discussion of many types and uses of questions and the difficulties in phrasing questions.

2. P. B. Sheatsley, "Closed Questions Are Sometimes More Valid Than Open End," *Public Opinion Quarterly* 12 (1948): 12.

3. This figure is modeled after one in Bernard Berelson and Gary Steiner, *Human Behavior: An Inventory of Scientific Findings* (New York: Harcourt Brace Jovanovich, 1964), p. 30.

4. Robert L. Kahn and Charles F. Cannell, *The Dynamics of Interviewing* (New York: John Wiley & Sons, 1964), p. 205. Reprinted by permission of John Wiley & Sons.

5. Kahn and Cannell, *The Dynamics of Interviewing*, pp. 217–20.

6. Payne, *The Art of Asking Questions*, p. 204.

7. Kahn and Cannell, *The Dynamics of Interviewing*, p. 127.

8. Ibid., p. 112.

9. Ibid.

10. George Gallup, "The Quintamensional Plan of Question Design," *Public Opinion Quarterly* 11 (Fall 1947): 385.

Suggested Readings

Allen, I. L. "Detecting Respondents Who Fake and Confuse Information about Question Areas on Surveys." *Journal of Applied Psychology* 50 (1968): 523–28.

Cantril, Hadley. "Experiments in the Wording of Questions." *Public Opinion Quarterly* 4 (1940): 330.

DeVito, Joseph A. "Relative Ease in Comprehending Yes/No Questions." *Rhetoric and Communication*. Edited by Jane Blankenship and Hermann Stelzner. Urbana, Ill.: University of Illinois Press, 1976.

Dohrenwend, Barbara S. "Some Effects of Open and Closed Questions on Respondent's Answers." *Human Organization* 24 (1965): 175–84.

Dohrenwend, Barbara S., and Richardson, Stephen A. "A Use for Leading Questions in Research Interviewing," *Human Organization* 23 (1964): 76–77.

Gorden, Raymond L. *Interviewing: Strategy, Techniques, and Tactics*. Homewood, Ill.: The Dorsey Press, 1975.

Goyer, Robert S.; Redding, W. Charles; and Rickey, John T. *Interviewing Principles and Techniques: A Project Text*. Dubuque, Iowa: Wm. C. Brown Co. Publishers, 1968.

Kahn, Robert L., and Cannell, Charles F. *The Dynamics of Interviewing*. New York: John Wiley & Sons, 1964.

Lagemann, J. K. "The Delicate Art of Asking Questions," *Reader's Digest* 86 (June 1965): 87–91.

Long, Lynette; Paradise, Louis V.; and Long, Thomas J. *Questioning: Skills for the Helping Process*. Monterey, Calif.: Brooks/Cole, 1981.

Payne, Stanley L. *The Art of Asking Questions*. Princeton, N.J.: Princeton University Press, 1951.

Richardson, Stephen A. "The Use of Leading Questions in Nonscheduled Interviews," *Human Organization* 19 (1960): 86–89.

Richardson, Stephen A.; Dohrenwend, Barbara S.; and Klein, David. *Interviewing: Its Forms and Functions*. New York: Basic Books, 1965.

Stewart, Charles J., ed. *On Speech Communication*. New York: Holt, Rinehart and Winston, 1972.

Informational Interviewing: The Survey Interview 5

Informational interviews come in all shapes and sizes and serve a multitude of purposes. Some are brief and informal, such as asking a professor to explain an assignment or asking an employee how a new production procedure is working out. Others are lengthy and formal, such as market surveys and public opinion polls. News broadcasts and newspapers bring us interviews with national leaders, revolutionaries, sports figures, doctors, and construction workers. We observe television interviews with celebrants of victories, grieving families, survivors of disasters, and the defeated. But regardless of length or formality or setting, the general purpose of informational interviews is the same—to get the needed information as accurately and completely as possible in the shortest amount of time.

Many of our failures to get this information occur because we assume the process is simple and requires little training or preparation. Successful interviews are rarely accidental, however; they are planned carefully and conducted by skilled interviewers. Chapters 5 and 6 focus on how to conduct two common types of informational interviews—the survey interview and the journalistic interview. Let's turn first to the survey interview.

Stages in the Survey Interview

The survey is the most meticulously planned and executed of all informational interviews because its purpose is to establish a solid base of fact from which to draw conclusions, make interpretations, and determine future courses of action. Manufacturers conduct surveys to gauge consumer desires, intents, and trends. Advertisers use surveys to judge the success of advertising campaigns and methods. Politicians rely upon survey interviews to determine voter preference, concerns, and beliefs. Journalists are beginning to employ survey techniques to get solid facts on which to base news reports and interpretations— what is being called "precision journalism."[1] Universities and colleges conduct

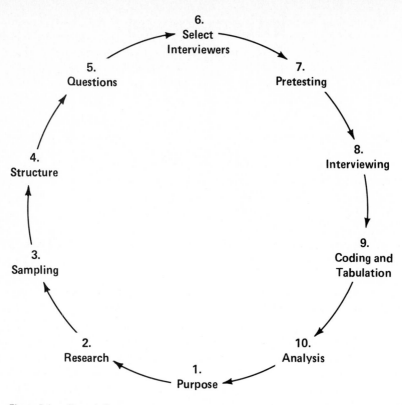

Figure 5.1 *Stages in Surveys*

surveys to determine how students feel about proposed changes in programs of study, housing policies, and school calendars. Students conduct surveys to determine which music groups to invite to campus for convocations or how fellow students feel about proposed changes in student government or the student bill of rights. Uses of surveys seem endless, and most of us are or will be involved in surveys on a regular basis.

Few groups can afford to rely upon sloppy preparation and techniques, so they tend to follow a series of stages, illustrated in figure 5.1, for reasonable assurance of obtaining valid, relevant, and sufficient data.[2] The process begins by determining the purpose of the survey and proceeds stage by stage until that purpose is fulfilled.

Stage 1—Purpose

Stage 1 begins as soon as a topic is selected for the survey: intercollegiate sports, the presidential candidates in the upcoming election, interviewer bias, a recent advertising campaign for Brand Z shampoo, the move to unionize the plant. What do we want to discover about this topic? Our specific purpose might be to discover current attitudes or changes in attitudes of college students toward intercollegiate athletics, or to discover how much voters know about the current presidential candidates, or to measure the effect of blatant interviewer bias on respondent behavior, or to determine how the Brand Z advertising campaign affected consumer buying habits. The purpose of an interview will affect the nature of the survey because each interview demands certain kinds of structure, questions, topic areas, interviewers, and degrees of precision and accuracy.

We should consider several factors when delineating the purpose of a survey.

1. How soon must the survey be completed and the results compiled? A college professor might have years to devote to a project, while a market surveyor may have weeks and a journalist only days.

2. How much time can we devote to each interview? Respondents will not stand on a street corner or in a supermarket for thirty-five to forty minutes to answer questions. But what can we accomplish in five or ten minutes? Besides, long interviews (thirty-five to forty minutes) not only cover more areas but they tend to be more reliable than brief interviews.

3. How will we use the information obtained in our survey: in a class research report, for corporate decision making, in a brief news story, in a lengthy article or series of articles, or to predict the outcome of a sales or political campaign? The specific use of our survey is likely to dictate how accurate and precise the survey must be. For instance, if the outcome of the survey will determine whether or not a multimillion-dollar advertising campaign will commence, our results must be highly accurate. Demands for accuracy and precision affect the nature of our schedule, questions, and both the number and type of people that we survey.

4. What are our short-range and long-range goals? Are we only interested in assessing opinions, attitudes, and feelings at a specific point in time: at the end of a sales campaign, immediately after an event such as a tornado, or after a political convention or debate? If so, then a *cross-sectional* study is sufficient. However, if we want to determine trends or to assess opinions, attitudes, and feelings at various stages during a campaign or at various intervals following an event, then we need to develop a *longitudinal* study. Our short-range goals may preclude our long-range goals if our objectives, procedures, and expectations are too demanding or unrealistic.

5. What are our resources? A grand purpose may be unrealistic if we have limited time, funds, interviewers, and means of analyzing data. Surveys are expensive, and the editor of the *Daily Bugle* may have a mild heart seizure when asked to budget $7,000 or $8,000 for a survey of the gubernatorial election. Is observation of respondent reactions important? If so, less expensive and faster telephone techniques are not feasible.

Stage 2—Research

Once our specific purpose is delineated, we must research the topic. Check every potentially valuable source: newspaper files and archives, letters and in- terviews with experts in the field (perhaps interviewing experts), government documents, newsmagazines, books, and earlier surveys on this topic. Research should reveal what information is available in other sources and, therefore, need not be obtained in this survey. If we become a mini-expert on the topic, we will become familiar with terminology and technical concepts (especially with unique uses of terms and differing versions of concepts) and may detect weaknesses in previous surveys. The search may reveal past attitudes and opinions or spec- ulations about current attitudes and opinions. A thorough knowledge of the topic might enable us to detect intentional or unintentional inaccuracies in answers during our interviews. We may gain insights into the nature and size of the population or group we must sample. Finally, familiarity with the complexities of the issue will allow us to determine areas of information needed and to prepare an interview guide. The following guide was developed for a countywide survey of the needs and interests of persons over age sixty.

1. Demographic data (age, sex, race, educational level, income)
2. Who the person lives with
   a. owner of the property
   b. renter of the property
3. How the respondent gets around the community
4. Family or friends in the area
5. Health and medical care
6. Preparation and kinds of meals
7. Interests and hobbies
8. Skills
   a. how they are being used
   b. willingness to share skills
9. Memberships in senior citizen's groups
10. Financial supports
    a. social security
    b. retirement benefits
    c. earnings
    d. public welfare

Journalists may discover that the traditional journalistic guide will serve the pur- pose: what, when, where, who, how, and why.

With purpose and limitations clearly in mind and research completed, begin the process of selecting respondents.

Stage 3—Sampling

When the respondent population is small—members of a football team, workers in a small factory, the state supreme court, residents in an apartment complex— it's possible to interview *all* potential respondents. However, the majority of surveys are concerned with large "populations" that far exceed time, financial, and personal limitations. (The term population refers to the total of individuals occupying an area, belonging to an organization, sharing a characteristic, or meeting a qualification.) The population may consist of all beer drinkers over eighteen years of age, or all 5,000 full-time employees in Plant 3, or all registered voters in Jefferson County, or all married females of childbearing age in the United States. Obviously an interviewer, or dozens of interviewers, could not interview 100 percent of these populations, so the interviewer resorts to a sample of the identified target population.

Since we cannot interview all married females of childbearing age, for instance, we interview *some* of them and then extend our findings to *all* of them. This can be a tricky business. Sampling automatically solves time, financial, and personnel problems, but poor sampling methods may reduce our data to much statistical garbage.

Systematic sampling techniques are governed by several important principles.

1. We must have a clear definition of the population to be surveyed: all undergraduates at the University of Tennessee, all registered voters in Florida, all hourly employees of Ford Motor Company who have been on the job a minimum of six months.

2. The sample we select to interview must truly "represent" the total population. It must be a miniature version of the whole with all groups and subgroups represented according to their proportion in the total population.

3. Each potential respondent from a defined population must have an equal chance of being selected as a representative of the whole.

4. We must know the probability of each person being selected so we can determine the "margin of error" of our survey. The precision of the survey is the "degree of similarity between sample results and results from a 100 percent count obtained in an identical manner."[3] Most surveys are designed to attain a 95 percent level of confidence. In other words, the mathematical probability is that, 95 times out of 100, interviewees will give results within 5 percentage points either way of the figures obtained if the entire population were interviewed. Our best sampling methods will never be as accurate as interviewing everyone in a population.

5. The size of the sample is usually determined by the size of the total population and the margin of error that is acceptable in a particular survey. There is no magic formula or percentage of a population that we must interview to assure a valid sample. Some researchers use a minimum of 30 respondents from each group in a population. The Gallup organization produces amazingly accurate national surveys from a sample of 1,500. Although some survey takers brag about the large sizes of their samples, the more important question is, How were the respondents selected? Standard formulas reveal that as a population increases in size, the percentage of the population necessary for our sample declines rapidly. In other words, we may have to interview a larger percentage of 5,000 people than 50,000 people to attain equally accurate results. Formulas also reveal that we must increase greatly the size of our sample if we wish to reduce the margin of error from 5 percent to 4 percent or 3 percent. The reduction of error margin may not be worth the added cost of the larger survey. Philip Meyer offers the following table that shows sample sizes of various populations necessary for a 5 percent error margin and a 95 percent level of confidence.[4]

Population Size	Sample Size
Infinity	384
500,000	384
100,000	383
50,000	381
10,000	370
5,000	357
3,000	341
2,000	322
1,000	278

There are a number of sampling techniques we can use once we have defined the population we want to sample. For example, we might place the names of all members of a given population (or numbers assigned to each) *in a hat* and draw out the number needed for the survey. Or we might assign a number to each potential respondent and then create or purchase a *table of random numbers.* With eyes closed, we place a finger on a number and decide whether to read a combination up, down, across to left or right, or diagonally. If the decision is to read the last digit of the numeral touched (46) and the first digit of the numeral to the right (29), we would contact respondent number 62. This process is repeated until the sample is completed. We might employ a *skip interval* or *random digit* approach. For instance, we might choose every tenth number in the telephone book, or every twentieth name on the employee roster, or every other person who walks into a supermarket, or every tenth number in a table of random numbers.

Several factors may affect our sampling methods. For instance, time of day or location of a supermarket may determine the nature of the sample who walks through the door or the type of person who will be at home during afternoon hours. As much as 15 percent of a population may have unlisted telephone numbers and some groups—students, the poor, migrant workers, and persons who have recently moved—may not have telephones or names in the directory. The employee roster might be divided according to areas of the plant, seniority, and job classification, thus producing a nonrepresentative sample. A "simple" random sampling procedure does not provide adequate sampling of subgroups within a population. They may or may not be represented adequately by the names drawn from a hat.

If a population has clearly identifiable groups (males and females; Catholic, Protestant, and Jewish voters; age levels; educational levels; income levels; and so on), we may want a sample from each to determine if attitudes vary across groups. We can employ a *stratified random sample* technique. Our sample might include a minimum number from each group (a quota) or a percentage representing the percentage of the group in the total population. For example, if Catholics make up 26 percent of the voting population of Massachusetts, Catholic respondents would constitute 26 percent of the Massachusetts sample.

In many public opinion polls, the designer gives a *sample point* to an interviewer—perhaps a four square-block area that includes white, blue-collar workers—with instructions to skip the corner house (corner houses tend to be more expensive) and then try every other house on the outside of the four-block area until completing two interviews with males and two with females. This sample point or block sampling technique gives the designer some control over selection of interviewees without resorting to lists of names, random digits, or telephone numbers.

A major reason for systematic sampling is to eliminate or to reduce problems caused by interviewer's prejudices, tastes, and whims. An interviewer might be tempted to avoid all respondents over fifty years of age because they seem grumpy. Certain neighborhoods, supervisors, races, and sexes may be avoided for a variety of personal reasons. The problem is generally solved if the survey designer can supply a list of names, or addresses, or telephone numbers. Even then, however, the interviewer must be persistent in obtaining respondents. If the interviewer reports too frequently that respondents were unavailable or un-cooperative, the carefully designed sample may begin to crumble. The manager of a survey may contact a sample of respondents to see if they were in fact contacted and interviewed.

Stage 4—Structure

The survey is structured so that all respondents go through an "identical" interview—as identical as possible considering human factors. The *opening* is usually written out in full and recited verbatim to each interviewee. The following opening was employed during a political survey.

Hello, my name is _____ , from Opinion Research Associates, a national polling firm. We are conducting a survey of people's opinions toward government and politics. We have been asking questions of some of your neighbors, and I would like to ask you a few questions. (Go to the first question.)

1. Are you registered to vote? (Go to q. 3. If not registered, ask q. 2.)

　　　Yes _____
　　　No _____

2. Do you plan to register to vote (Go to q. 5) within the next month? *Terminate*

　　　Yes _____
　　　No _____

3. Did you vote in the 1978 senatorial election when Willard Smith and Charles Gibson were running?

　　　Yes _____　1-1
　　　No _____　1-2

4. Did you vote in the 1980 presidential election when Ronald Reagan and Jimmy Carter were running?

　　　Yes _____　2-1
　　　No _____　2-2

Terminate if respondent has not voted in at least one of these elections.

Notice the interviewer identifies himself or herself and the survey organization and gives a general purpose. The interviewer does not identify the group that might be paying for the poll—the Democratic Party, the Republican Party, or a special interest group—or the specific purpose—to determine which strategies to employ during the remainder of the campaign or which party or candidate to support. If a newspaper such as the *New York Times* or the *St. Louis Post Dispatch* were conducting the poll, the paper's name would be used to enhance the prestige of the poll and the interviewer, to reduce suspicion that a candidate or party is behind the survey, and to motivate the respondent to cooperate. The respondent is *not asked* to respond; the interviewer moves smoothly from orientation to the first question without giving the respondent an opportunity to refuse. The first four questions, employing a contingency question format, determine the interviewee's qualifications: the person must be registered or plan to be before election day and must have voted in one of the previous two elections. If the person did not vote in either election, chances are he or she will not do so in the next. The survey organization has provided instructions on the schedule for the interviewer to follow, and questions 3 and 4 are precoded for ease of tabulation.

The *body* of the survey is most likely to be highly scheduled, standardized or a combination highly scheduled and highly scheduled, standardized. We must ask questions in the same manner—verbally and nonverbally—and in the same order in each interview. Do not explain content or language of questions, justify questions, rephrase questions, or probe into answers. Survey organizations often instruct interviewers to repeat questions twice, and after the second repetition, to move to the next question without recording an answer. Any change in a question may alter the nature of the interview and affect the results of the survey.

Review question sequences in chapter 4, and select one or more sequences to suit the purpose. The tunnel, or string-of-beads, sequence is common in surveys when no strategic lineup of questions is needed and standardization is desired. Gallup's quintamensional design (described in chapter 4) or a variation of it is appropriate if we desire to explore depth of attitudes or opinions. Be careful of funnel and inverted funnel sequences because they include open-ended questions that are difficult to record and may pose major problems during coding and tabulation.

The *closing* of the survey is usually brief and expresses appreciation. For example:

That's all the questions I have. Thank you very much for your help.

If the survey organization wants a respondent's telephone number to verify that a valid interview took place, the closing might be:

That's all the questions I have. May I have your telephone number so my employer may check to see if this interview was conducted in the prescribed manner? Thank you for your help.

Respondents are often curious about the survey we are conducting and wish to discuss it with us. Do so if time allows, if the respondent will have no opportunity to discuss the survey with future respondents, and if the survey organization has no objections. A friendly closing might motivate the respondent to cooperate in future surveys.

Stage 5—Questions

Phrase questions with great care because we cannot rephrase, explain, or expand them, and *nonplanned* secondary questions are not allowed. A question, once in our schedule, must be worded clearly, must be relevant to the survey, must ask for or contain information at the respondent's level of knowledge, must not be too complex, and must be socially and psychologically accessible. This is not a simple task. Respondents may be of all ages, income levels, educational backgrounds, degrees of intelligence, occupations, of both sexes, and from widely scattered geographical areas.

Questions may satisfy all of these criteria and still produce inaccurate answers. Leading and loaded questions such as "You're going to vote, aren't you?" and "Should we continue our overly generous support of the U.N.?" may reflect or cause *interviewer bias.* Interviewer bias occurs when the respondent gives the answer he or she thinks (rightly or wrongly) the interviewer desires. Answer scales and sequences may bias results in several ways.[5]

1. Respondents tend to pick the middle options in scales, 2 to 4 instead of 1 or 5.

2. Respondents try to pick "normal" answers.

3. Respondents tend to choose the answer option heard last in a list of names, products, or causes.

4. Respondents are hesitant to censure people, organizations, or products and thus may choose positive rather than negative answers.

5. Respondents who do not know the correct answer may pick the option that stands out, the second answer in a list such as 25 percent, 33 percent, 50 percent, 75 percent, 100 percent.

6. Respondents may be swayed by loaded choices, for example, "Do you think the exhibition is an outstanding collection of modern art or mere rubbish?"

7. Clearly stated options such as "undecided" and "don't know" may invite an unusually large percentage of these answers.

8. The last few products, candidates, or organizations in a question such as "Please give me your reaction to the following" may get negative or superficial evaluations because of respondent fatigue.

Let's take a sample question on highway speed limits through a series of developmental stages.

1. How do you feel about the federally imposed 55-mph speed limit?

"Federally imposed" is unnecessary and may bias results. The openness of the question may obtain a range of responses such as: "Angry," "Frustrated," "It's another step toward socialism," "I don't know," "I think it's a (choice four-letter word) dumb law," or a long treatise on the pros and cons of the speed limit. The variety and length of responses will create a recording nightmare and require secondary questions for clarification. Let's close it up.

2. Are you for or against or have no feelings about the 55-mph speed limit?

For	_____	1–1
Against	_____	1–2
No feelings	_____	1–3

This precoded, closed question eliminates the "federal" bias and solves recording problems and potential difficulties in coding answers in stage 9, but it may be too closed. A respondent may not be simply for or against the speed limit and may feel that 55 mph is unacceptable for interstates and trucks and buses but acceptable for cars and state highways. The "no feelings" option may generate a large percentage of nothing answers. Let's try a third version, one employing a Likert scale.

3. Do you strongly agree, agree, disagree, or strongly disagree with this statement: The 55-mph speed limit should be maintained for all vehicles on all highways?

Strongly agree _____ 1-1

Agree _____ 1-2

Disagree _____ 1-3

Strongly disagree _____ 1-4

Undecided or have no feeling _____ 1-5

Why? (Only for respondents choosing strongly agree or strongly disagree)
_____ 1-6

This version assesses degree of feeling and specifies all vehicles and all highways to avoid potential questions from a puzzled respondent. A secondary "Why?" question is provided to discover reasons for strong feelings. The respondent may reveal concern about the application of one rather slow speed limit to all vehicles and highways. All answers have spaces and are precoded to aid in recording, coding, and tabulating results. Work with each question until it satisfies all basic requirements for phrasing questions and until it is designed to obtain the information desired.

The interviewer may employ any of several question strategies (mini-sequences) to determine an interviewee's knowledge level, consistency, or honesty. Payne recommends a *filter approach* to assess knowledge level.[6] For example:

Interviewer: Are you familiar with the Equal Rights Amendment?
Interviewee: Yes, I am.
Interviewer: What is the Equal Rights Amendment?

A *repeat question* strategy consists of asking the same question several minutes apart to see if the response remains the same. A variation of this strategy is to rephrase the question slightly.

1. Are you in favor of the Equal Rights Amendment?
2. Do you think the Equal Rights Amendment should be ratified?

or another example:

1. What is your annual income?
2. I am going to read a series of annual income ranges. Stop me when I read the range that includes your income.

> Under $6,000 _____
> $6,000–11,999 _____
> $12,000–17,999 _____
> $18,000–over _____

A *leaning question* strategy is designed to reduce the number of "undecided" respondents.

1. If the congressional election were being held today, who would you vote for?
> Jablonski _____ 1-1
> Baker _____ 1-2
> Undecided _____ 1-3

2. Well, who do you lean toward at this time, Jablonski or Baker?
> Jablonski _____ 1-4
> Baker _____ 1-5
> Undecided _____ 1-6

A *shuffle* strategy varies the order of questions or answer options within questions from one interview to the next to prevent "order" from influencing the survey results. The shuffle strategy may eliminate order bias but cause confusion if interviewers are not trained or if coding is not designed carefully. A *chain*, or *contingency*, strategy provides for one or more secondary questions if the respondent gives a specific initial answer. The following is a typical chain strategy for a market survey, including built-in instructions for the interviewer and precoding.

1a. During the past three months, have you received any free samples of toothpaste?
> (20)
> Yes . . . . . . 1—Ask q. 1b.
> No . . . . . . 2—Skip to q. 2a
> (21)

1b. What brand or brands of toothpaste did you receive? (Do not read the list.)

```
                    Clear  . . . . . . 1
                    Ipana  . . . . . . 2
              Ever Bright  . . . . . . 4
                  Gleem  . . . . . . 4
                    Crest  . . . . . . 5
        Other _____  . . . . . . 6
                 (specify)
```

1c. Ask only if Ever Bright not mentioned in 1b, otherwise skip to q. 1d.
Did you receive a free sample of Ever Bright toothpaste?

(22)

Yes . . . . . . 1—Ask q. 1d.

No . . . . . . 2—Skip to q. 2a

1d. Did you use the free sample of Ever Bright?

(23)

Yes . . . . . . 1—Skip to q. 2a

No . . . . . . 2—Ask q. 1e.

1e. Why didn't you use the free sample of Ever Bright toothpaste?

_____(24) _____

There are a variety of *scale* strategies designed to avoid bipolar responses, to supply clear choices to interviewees, to delve more deeply into topics and variables, and to reduce recording and tabulation problems. We have already seen samples of *Likert scales* (strongly agree, agree, disagree, strongly disagree, undecided), *nominal scales* that deal with exhaustive and mutually exclusive variables (lists of candidates, sexes, college majors, religious or political affiliations), and *interval scales* that provide distances between measures (highway speeds, temperatures, salary ranges, frequency of drinking beer). *Ordinal scales* rank order more or less of a variable (from low priority to high priority, from most sophisticated to least sophisticated, from low education to high level of education). The *Bogardus Social Distance Scale* has been used to determine how people feel about social relationships and distances. For example, we might use the following scale if we were interested in determining how male coal miners feel about female coal miners.

1. Are you in favor of allowing women to work in American coal mines?
2. Are you in favor of allowing women to work in West Virginia coal mines?
3. Are you in favor of allowing women to work in your coal mine?
4. Would you be willing to work with a woman in your coal mine?
5. Would you be willing to work under a woman boss in your coal mine?

Stage 6—Select Interviewers

We now have the sample determined, the interview structured, and the questions necessary to elicit the information we need. The final step before interviewing begins is to select the interviewers necessary for conducting the survey. Keep three questions in mind when selecting interviewers.

First, how many are needed? If we plan to interview a small number of persons (ten or twenty) and the interviews will be brief (five to ten minutes), one interviewer will be sufficient. However, we will need a number of interviewers if the interviews are long (thirty to forty minutes), the sample is large (fifty or a hundred or thousands), the time allotted for completion of the survey is limited, or respondents are scattered over a wide geographical area.

Second, what special qualifications are required? A highly scheduled or highly scheduled, standardized interview does not require experts on the topic or skill in phrasing questions and probing into answers. It does require a non-threatening person who is a good listener, can follow instructions, is interested in the interview and topic, and can remain neutral no matter how the interviewee responds. College students and middle-aged homemakers tend to be excellent survey interviewers because they have these qualifications and are not as expensive to employ as professional interviewers. Surveys and polls are expensive, and most companies and news organizations cannot afford large sums of money for professional interviewers. Journalists tend to be poor survey interviewers because their training and experiences make them active listeners and adept at probing into answers and challenging interviewees. They do not like to follow a standardized list of questions or to remain neutral.

Third, what personal characteristics are required? These include age, sex, race, ethnic group, manner of dress, attitudes, personality, and organizational memberships. Such characteristics may denote an in-group or out-group relationship between the interviewer and interviewee.[7] When the interviewer belongs to the interviewee's group (black to black, senior citizen to senior citizen, Italian to Italian, or female to female), there may be no etiquette or communication barriers (especially language problems) and trust may be high since the interviewer is perceived as capable of understanding and being sympathetic with the interviewee's situation. When the interviewer is not a member of the interviewee's group (white to black, young citizen to senior citizen, English to Italian, male to female), there may be no ego threat and the communication may be perceived as a new experience or means of recognition. Buttons, dress (uniform or style), language, hairstyle, and so forth may identify the interviewer and the survey or poll with a political party, manufacturer, or ethnic group and bias the results of the interview by encouraging interviewees to respond in a favorable or unfavorable, open or closed, honest or dishonest manner. Some neighborhoods are off limits to female interviewers, young males with long hair, blacks, and other identifiable persons. When interviewing persons in nursing homes, for example, select interviewers with warm personalities and ones willing to sit and chat for a while. Consider whether the potential interviewer can operate under stress and remain objective.

Trust may be high when the survey interviewer is perceived as capable of understanding and being sympathetic with the interviewee's situation.

Stage 7—Pretesting

Always pretest the interview schedule before a survey or poll to locate potential problems. We can prepare only so much on paper, and the best plans may not work. Conduct the pretest with interviewees similar to ones in the sample, but not part of the sample. Conduct complete interviews. Try out the opening; ask all questions, including secondary questions; and close the interviews as planned. Become accustomed to all aspects of the interview, including adapting to physical surroundings, various kinds of respondents, note taking, and tape recording, if applicable. Do not leave anything to chance. For instance, in a political poll conducted by a college class, interviewers discovered that the question "What do you like or dislike about living in Indiana?" took much time and elicited little relevant information. It was deleted. When given a list of candidates and asked "What do you like or dislike about . . . ?" many respondents became embarrassed or gave vague answers because they did not know some of the candidates. This question sequence was replaced with a five-point scale from strongly like to strongly dislike (including a don't know option), and interviewers probed into reasons for liking, or disliking, only for those candidates ranked in the extreme positions on the scale. Interviewers also discovered that scales tended to confuse older respondents, so special instructions were added to clarify the scale. Scales may be placed on file cards or plastic sheets and handed to the respondent. The interviewer asks the respondent to point, circle, or verbally indicate an answer along the scale. This method helps the interviewee to visualize the scale and possible responses. Ask several questions when pretesting is completed, for example:

1. Did interviewees seem to understand what was wanted and why?
2. Were questions clear without further explanation?
3. Did questions elicit the kind and amount of information desired?
4. How much probing was necessary?
5. Did some questions elicit information already obtained in previous answers?
6. Did interviewees react negatively to some questions?
7. Were answer categories adequate?
8. Was interviewer bias apparent in some answers?
9. Can answers be tabulated easily and meaningfully?

Stage 8—Interviewing
Poor execution of interviews can undo the most thorough preparation. The following comments appeared in critiques of student interviewers by respondents (students, parents, farmers, business managers, construction workers, journalists, police, counselors, etc.) in public opinion surveys. Respondents know what they expect of a person who uses them and their time.

Criticisms of Student Interviewers
Preparation
1. Learn more about the topic before interviewing.
2. Practice more before going into the field.
3. Don't leave out interesting points and areas of the topic.
4. Organize questions more carefully before the interview.
5. Know your questions; don't read them to the interviewee.

Communication Skills
1. Relax and smile.
2. Be more aggressive.
3. Increase self-confidence of the interviewer.
4. Improve eye contact, but don't stare.
5. Speak louder.
6. Speak more clearly.
7. Slow the pace of the interview; don't rush through it.
8. Don't overuse gestures, or fidget, or nod the head.
9. Avoid "you know," "like," and other overworked expressions.

Attitude
1. Show interest in the interview; don't appear resigned to having to do it.
2. Take the interview seriously; don't joke about it.
3. Be positive; don't apologize for the interview.
4. Don't be embarrassed.
5. Show sincere interest in the answers.

Informational Interviewing: The Survey Interview

Questioning Skills

1. Avoid biased questions.
2. Know the questions better.
3. Don't suggest answers if the interviewee hesitates; give the interviewee time to think.
4. Don't mention how others answered.
5. Don't assume too much or take too much for granted.
6. Don't cut people off in their answers.
7. Don't take just any answer given.
8. Avoid yes or no questions.

Orienting the Interviewee

1. Introduce yourself.
2. Explain the purpose of the interview.
3. Know who you are representing.
4. Reveal the topic of the interview.
5. Clarify the type of information needed.

Interviewing

1. Don't take too many notes.
2. Dress appropriately.
3. Don't interview too late at night.
4. Don't talk about your personal life.
5. Stick to the topic.
6. Use visual aids (for example, cards for complex questions).
7. Don't rely too heavily on notes and written questions.
8. Be less conscious of time; avoid looking at your watch.
9. Be more businesslike.

Although some interviewees desire one kind of interview and interviewer and some another, the ideal interviewer is (1) thoroughly prepared, (2) skilled in the fundamentals of communication, (3) sincerely interested in the topic and the respondent, (4) skilled in the art of questioning, and (5) considerate of the respondent's beliefs, desires, and feelings.

Several criticisms pertained directly or indirectly to interviewer bias. The interviewee may perceive that we desire a specific answer because of the vocal manner in which we ask a question, expressed or apparent attitudes, facial expressions, reactions to answers (head nods, frowns, verbalisms such as "uh huh," "okay," "good"), style of dress, or who and what we are. Our reactions and manner may be unintentional. However, the way the *interviewee* receives our message, not *our* intent, determines whether a response will be free and accurate.

Interviewing by Telephone   A growing number of interviewers are turning to the telephone for an easier, faster, and less expensive means of conducting surveys and polls, especially if respondents are scattered over a large geographical area. Recent studies comparing telephone and face-to-face interviews have revealed that—[8]

A growing number of interviewers are turning to the telephone for easier and less expensive means of conducting surveys and polls.

1. the quality of data gained on complex attitudinal and knowledge items is the same with both interviewing methods;

2. the quality of data on personal items is about the same, with some respondents preferring the anonymity of the telephone;

3. respondents are somewhat more likely to give socially acceptable answers in face-to-face interviews;

4. the interviewee rate of refusal to take part in or to complete interviews running forty-five minutes or longer is about the same with either method.

5. interviewees in certain neighborhoods prefer telephone interviews because they do not want to open their doors to strangers;

6. potential interviewees without telephones can be interviewed face to face without distorting data because of mixture of methods;

7. telephone interviews remove dress, appearance, and nonverbal communications as potential biasing factors;

8. interviewer preference for telephone and face-to-face interviews is nearly the same.

These results from recent studies suggest that face-to-face and telephone surveys produce similar results and that advantages and disadvantages of each method tend to be minimal. However, some organizations such as Gallup and Harris prefer face-to-face interviews because of the interviewees they might miss (the poor, the transient, the young, people with unlisted telephone numbers).

Surveys vs. Questionnaires Face-to-face and telephone surveys have a number of advantages over mailed or handed-out questionnaires. For instance, we have no control over *who* in a family or organization might fill out a questionnaire. Thus, a fifty-year-old female instead of the twenty-five-year-old male we need for our sample may answer the questions. Questionnaire respondents are highly unlikely to respond to open questions that require lengthy written answers. (A 30–40 percent rate of return is considered good for questionnaires, even when short responses are sought.) We cannot observe or listen to answers in questionnaires, so we lose the valuable nonverbal clues that survey respondents provide. Respondents to questionnaires cannot ask us to explain questions or answers or methods of recording answers. We cannot "hide" parts of contingency questions or answer options to see, first of all, what respondents will say or recall without our hints or lists. Questionnaire respondents may not read our instructions or follow the guidelines we provide. As interviewers we can explain the rationale for our study and respond to concerns and objections that might lead questionnaire recipients to discard questionnaires. And it is easier to throw away a questionnaire than to say no to a live human being.

Training Interviewers A training session and special written instructions for interviewers will prevent many problems during surveys. Discuss common interviewee criticisms such as those listed earlier in this chapter. Stress the importance of following the question schedule exactly as it is printed. Explain complex questions and recording methods. Be sure each interviewer understands the sampling technique employed. The following is a typical list of instructions provided for interviewers.

1. Study the question schedule and become as familiar as possible with it so you will not have to "read" questions and so you can record answers quickly and accurately.

2. If you make appointments with respondents, be on time—neither too early nor late.

3. Be sure your introduction gives the respondent your name, who you are working for, the subject of the interview, and an assurance that answers will be kept in strict confidence. The sample below is the type of opening we prefer.

Good afternoon. I'm Robert Wiggens, and I'm working with the Wisconsin Dairy Association. We are conducting a statewide survey of dairy farms. If you have a few minutes, I would like to ask you some questions about your dairy operation. Any information you give me will be held in strict confidence and results of the survey will not identify you in any way.

4. Be friendly, sincere, and businesslike.

5. If a person says he or she does not have time for the interview, use statements such as, "This will only take a few minutes" or "I can ask you questions while you're working." If time is too limited, make a definite appointment for later. Do not try to pressure the respondent into taking part in the survey.

6. If a respondent does not answer your question directly or misses the point, repeat the question to make sure that the respondent heard it. Do not rephrase the question because any rephrasing may alter the results obtained.

7. Record answers as prescribed in the survey schedule. Be sure to write or print answers to open-ended questions very carefully and clearly. Do not write anything you don't want the respondent to see.

8. Be sure to ask questions in a firm, clear, neutral voice. Do not bias responses by emphasizing specific words or phrases in questions and answer options.

9. Do not interrupt respondents. Give respondents adequate time to think and to respond.

10. Do not prolong the interview or end it too abruptly. When you have obtained the answer to the last question, express your appreciation for the respondent's cooperation and excuse yourself.

Telephone interviewers may receive special instructions, such as the following.

1. Talk directly into the mouthpiece of the phone, being neither too loud nor too soft.

2. Speak clearly, distinctly, and slowly. The respondent cannot see you, your nonverbal signals, or the materials you are carrying but must rely solely upon your voice.

3. Do not smoke, chew gum, or eat candy while talking on the phone.

4. Do not say anything you do not want the respondent to hear. The respondent may hear your comments even if you have the mouthpiece covered.

5. If you are calling long distance and you get a wrong number, get the name of the city, the wrong number if possible, dial the operator and tell her what happened so you won't be billed.

6. When recording answers, explain pauses by saying, "Just a moment while I write down your answer."

7. Ask your first question as soon as possible to get the respondent involved. Long openings often receive "hangups" in telephone surveys.

Stage 9—Coding and Tabulation

The first step is to code all answers that were not precoded. In most surveys this means answers to open-ended questions. For instance, if question 10b is "Why did you not vote in the last mayoral election?" a variety of answers are possible. Let's say 10b is coded #20; each answer would be coded 20 plus 1, 2, 3, etc.

20-1 I didn't know enough about either candidate.

20-2 Both were crooks.

20-3 My independent candidate was not allowed on the ballot.

All "I didn't know enough about" answers would be coded 20-1.

Informational Interviewing: The Survey Interview

Answers to some open questions may require study before we can develop a coding system. For example, in a study of voter perception of mudslinging in political communication, the interviewer asked, "What three or four words would you use to describe a politician who uses mudslinging as a tactic?" Answers included more than a hundred different words.[9] Careful study revealed that these words tended to fit into five descriptive characteristics: untrustworthy, incompetent, unlikeable, insecure, and immature. A sixth category, "other," was added to account for words that did not fit into the major categories. All words were placed into one of these six categories and coded from one to six.

Interviewers may create chaos by recording answers in a confusing manner. A question in a recent political survey was, "Who is Matthew Welsh?" Interviewers recorded answers such as "Democrat," "governor," and "political candidate." Since Welsh was the Democratic candidate for governor and a former governor, how should the answers be coded? Did "governor" mean present governor, past governor, or candidate for governor? Did "political candidate" mean for governor, senator, representative? Did "Democrat" mean Democratic candidate for governor, Democratic candidate, or just a Democrat? Data from this question defied coding attempts and was discarded.

Once answers are coded, it is a simple process of figuring totals and percentages on a calculator or feeding the data into a computer. Totals and percentages are tabulated in seconds.

Stage 10—Analysis

Once coding and tabulation of results are concluded, the analysis of results may begin. What conclusions can be drawn and with what certainty? To how much of a population can we generalize from the data? What are the constraints imposed by the sample interviewed? By the nature of the interviewing instrument? By the interviewer(s)? Can it be determined why people responded in certain ways to certain questions? Are mountains being built out of molehills or insignificant data? Have unexpected events or changes occurred since our survey was completed? What about undecided and nonresponses to a question such as:

Who do you plan to vote for in November: McWilliams or Adamson?

McWilliams	37 percent	Sample = 1000
Adamson	36 percent	
Undecided	15 percent	
Nonresponse	12 percent	

If we eliminate nonresponses (maybe interviewers failed to record some answers or maybe some people refused to answer the question), the sample equals 880 and the new percentages are:

McWilliams 42 percent
Adamson 41 percent
Undecided 17 percent

What if we discard the undecided? McWilliams and Adamson look better, but the large undecided figure may be the most important finding of the survey. Can we say with confidence that McWilliams is ahead, even if we ignore the undecideds? Probably not. What is the margin of error in our survey? The most sophisticated surveys rarely have a margin of error below 3 percent, so Adamson could be ahead by 2–3 percent or McWilliams could be ahead by 4–5 percent. Journalists must be cautious in headlines, stories, and predictions based on surveys. Organizations must be cautious in basing policy decisions and changes on surveys. As part of our analysis we might want to subject our data to a statistical analysis designed to test significance of results or reliability.

Ultimately we must ask if our purpose and objectives have been achieved.

The Respondent in Survey Interviews

The proliferation of surveys in our society assures that we are likely to take part in surveys (whether written or oral) several times a year. We have the right and power to walk away from an interviewer, hang up the telephone, or discard the questionnaire. If we do so, however, we may be forfeiting the opportunity to play a role in improving commercials, selecting political candidates, influencing legislation, or improving our working, living, or learning environments.

When asked to be a respondent, listen to the interviewer's explanation of the survey. We should learn who the interviewer is, who the interviewer represents, why the survey is being conducted, how our answers will be used, and how we were chosen. After getting the information we need, then decide whether to take part. Don't say no before the interviewer can explain the survey. On the other hand, don't agree to take part and then sabotage the interview by intentionally giving wrong answers.

When taking part in survey interviews, we must listen carefully to *each* question. Avoid replaying earlier answers or questions, especially if we think we "goofed" an answer. Don't try to guess what a question is going to be by the first few words an interviewer utters. We might guess wrong, appear stupid, and force the interviewer to restate the question. If a question or a series of answer options is unclear, ask the interviewer for clarification. Listen to a question; think through the answer; and then give the answer clearly and precisely. We should give the answer we feel best represents our views, not the one we think the interviewer would like to hear. Remember also that we cannot listen carefully and answer effectively while trying to guess which political party is sponsoring the survey, which product is being market tested, or which commercial other respondents prefer.

As respondents we have a number of rights. For example, we may refuse to answer a poorly constructed or leading question. We may refuse to give data that we believe to be irrelevant or an invasion of our privacy. We should expect and demand tactful, sensitive, and polite treatment during each interview. We should insist on adequate time to answer all questions and not to be rushed or pressured in any way. Remember, we can end the interview by walking away or hanging up the phone.

Survey interviews can be fun, interesting, and informative if both parties treat one another fairly and trust one another. Surveys are valuable means of gathering information and assessing feelings and attitudes and are likely to become more common as their sophistication increases.

Summary

The survey interview is meticulously planned and tends to be a circular process. We begin with delimiting a purpose and proceed step by step until we have come full circle back to our purpose that should now be fulfilled. The purpose is to establish a solid base of fact from which to draw conclusions, make interpretations, and determine future courses of action. The survey creator and conductor must make careful choices among sampling techniques, schedules, questions, interviewers, interviewees, and coding and recording methods. Each choice has advantages and disadvantages. There is no single correct way to handle all survey situations.

Survey Interview Schedules for Review and Analysis

As you read through the market and political survey schedules, notice the built-in probing questions, instructions for interviewers, precoding of answers, and inclusion of open questions. What question strategies are used? What question sequences (if any) are used? How are the schedules similar and different? Why?

A Market Survey

This is a typical market survey interview instrument. Its purpose is to measure the results of a major advertising effort conducted for a particular brand of coffee. Every seventy-fifth name in the telephone directories of several cities is contacted by telephone. Notice the built-in instructions for interviewers and the precoded questions.

Speak to any person eighteen years old or older who lives in the household.
Hello, I'm _____ of Market Information, Inc., a leading national product research firm. We are doing a nationwide survey on coffees.

   1a. Do you drink coffee at home?
      Yes 1
      No   2 *(Terminate)*
   1b. How many cups of coffee do you drink at home each day?
      More than two a day   1
      Two a day   2
      One a day   3
      Less than one a day   4 *(Terminate)*

   2. What is the first brand you think of when I say coffee? *(Do not read the list. Circle the number for the brand named.)*

Folgers	1	Hills Bros.	5
Maxwell House	2	Taster's Choice	6
Nescafe	3	Fresh Brewed	7
Sanka	4	Other	8 _____ *(Write in)*

   3. What brand or brands of coffee are you and your family using at present? *(Do not read the list. Circle the numbers of the brands named.)*

Folgers	1	Taster's Choice	6
Maxwell House	2	Fresh Brewed	7
Nescafe	3	Other	8 _____ *(Write in)*
Sanka	4		9 _____ *(Write in)*
Hills Bros.	5		10 _____ *(Write in)*

   4. What *other* brand or brands of coffee have you and your family used in the last six months? *(Do not read the list. Circle the numbers of the brands named.)*

Folgers	1	Taster's Choice	6
Maxwell House	2	Fresh Brewed	7
Nescafe	3	Other	8 _____ *(Write in)*
Sanka	4		9 _____ *(Write in)*
Hills Bros.	5		10 _____ *(Write in)*

   5. If you were buying coffee today, what brand or brands would you buy? *(Do not read the list. Circle the numbers of the brands named.)*

Folgers	1	Taster's Choice	6
Maxwell House	2	Fresh Brewed	7
Nescafe	3	Other	8 _____ *(Write in)*
Sanka	4		9 _____ *(Write in)*
Hills Bros.	5		10 _____ *(Write in)*

   6. What brands of coffee have you recently seen or heard advertised? *(Do not read the list. Circle the numbers of the brands named.)*

Folgers	1	Taster's Choice	6	
Maxwell House	2	Fresh Brewed	7	
Nescafe	3	Other	8	_____ (Write in)
Sanka	4		9	_____ (Write in)
Hills Bros.	5		10	_____ (Write in)

7a. During the past six months, have you received any free samples of coffee?

Yes 1 *(Ask q. 7b)*

No 2 *(Skip to q. 8a)*

7b. What brand or brands of coffee did you receive? *(Do not read the list. Circle the numbers of the brands named.)*

Folgers	1	Taster's Choice	6	
Maxwell House	2	Fresh Brewed	7	
Nescafe	3	Other	8	_____ (Write in)
Sanka	4		9	_____ (Write in)
Hills Bros.	5			

7c. Did you receive a free sample of Fresh Brewed coffee? (Ask *only* if *Fresh Brewed* is not mentioned in answer to 7b.)

Yes 1

No 2

8a. Have you ever bought Fresh Brewed coffee in a store?

Yes 1 *(Ask q. 8b)*

No 2 *(Skip to q. 9a)*

8b. Which Fresh Brewed coffee did you buy, regular or instant?

Regular	1
Instant	2
Both	3

8c. About how many times have you bought Fresh Brewed coffee in the past six months?

_____ *(Write in number of times)*

9a. Which of these phrases best describes how you would feel about buying Fresh Brewed coffee in the future?

Definitely would buy it	1
Probably would buy it	2
Might or might not buy it	3
Probably would not buy it	4
Definitely would not buy it	5

9b. What is the main reason why you would not buy Fresh Brewed coffee? *(Ask only if answer is 3, 4, or 5 in q. 9a)*

_____ 1

Anything else?

_____ 2

10a. Have you recently heard or seen any advertisements for Fresh Brewed coffee?

Yes 1 *(Ask q. 10b)*
No   2 *(Skip to q. 11)*

10b. Please tell me everything you saw or heard in the advertising for Fresh Brewed coffee.

_____ 1

Anything else?

_____ 2

Now I need to ask for some personal information so we can compare how different types of people feel about coffee.

11. I am going to read several age ranges. Please stop me when I read the one that includes your age.

18–24	1
25–34	2
35–49	3
50–64	4
65 and over	5

12. Now I am going to read several income ranges. Please stop me when I read the range that includes your total family income last year before taxes. *(Read list)*

Under $7,500	1
$7,500 to $12,500	2
$12,500 to $17,500	3
$17,500 to $25,000	4
$25,000 and over	5
Refused	6

13. Are you: *(Read list)*

Married	1
Single	2
Divorced	3
Widowed	4

14. Finally, what was the last grade of formal schooling you completed? *(Read list)*

Eighth grade or less	1
Some high school	2
High school graduate	3
Some college	4
College graduate or higher	5

A Political Survey

This is a typical political survey instrument. Its purpose is to determine voter attitudes toward opposing candidates and parties and on a variety of issues and possible solutions. Interviewers will talk with a carefully selected stratified sample of people from specific voter precincts throughout the country. Notice the built-in instructions for interviewers and precoded questions and answers.

Hello, my name is _____ , from National Opinion Research, a nationwide polling firm. We're conducting a poll of people's opinions about the presidential candidates and current issues. We've been interviewing people in your neighborhood and would like to ask you a few questions.

1a. Are you a registered voter? *(Circle answers)*
   Yes 1 *(Go to q. 2a)*
   No 2 *(Go to q. 1b)*
1b. Do you plan to register to vote within the next two months?
   Yes 1 *(Go to q. 2a)*
   No 2 *(Terminate the interview)*
2a. Did you get a chance to vote in the 1980 elections?
   Yes 1 *(Go to q. 3)*
   No 2 *(Go to q. 2b)*
2b. Did you vote in the 1976 election when Jimmy Carter and Gerald Ford were running?
   Yes 1 *(Go to q. 3)*
   No 2 *(Terminate if the interviewee did not vote in either of the past two elections.)*
3a. Do you generally consider yourself a Democrat or Republican? *(If independent ask q. 3b)*

Democrat	1
Republican	2
Don't Know	3
Refuse	4

3b. Well, do you generally vote for Republican or Democratic candidates for public office?

Independent/Republican	1
Independent/Democrat	2
Independent	3

4. How would you rate the job Ronald Reagan is doing as president: excellent, good, average, not so good, or poor? *(Circle answers in the scales provided at the end of q. 6)*

5. How would you rate the job Congress is doing: excellent, good, average, not so good, or poor? *(Circle answers in the scales provided at the end of q. 6)*

6. How would you rate the job the Supreme Court is doing: excellent, good, average, not so good, or poor? *(Circle answers in the scales provided below)*

	Reagan	Congress	Supreme Court
Excellent	1	1	1
Good	2	2	2
Average	3	3	3
Not so good	4	4	4
Poor	5	5	5

7. What national problems should the federal government (president, Congress, and the Supreme Court) be trying to solve right now?

_____ 1
_____ 2
_____ 3
Any others? _____ 4
_____ 5

8. What should the federal government do about each of these problems? *(Name each problem mentioned in q. 7 and record the recommended solutions)*

_____ 1
_____ 2
_____ 3
_____ 4
_____ 5

9. Here is a card *(hand the interviewee a card)* that lists some of the problems people say the federal government ought to take care of. As I read each one, please tell me which political party is most likely to solve the problem. The first problem is _____ .

(Rotate the order from one interview to the next) Do you think the Democratic or the Republican Party is most likely to solve this problem?

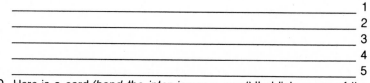

	Dem.	Rep.	Either	Neither	Don't Know
Inflation	1	2	3	4	5
Energy	1	2	3	4	5
Unemployment	1	2	3	4	5
Taxes	1	2	3	4	5
Honesty in government	1	2	3	4	5
Farm prices	1	2	3	4	5
The poor	1	2	3	4	5
Imports	1	2	3	4	5
Abortion	1	2	3	4	5
Arms race	1	2	3	4	5

10. Now please look back over this list and tell me which one of these problems you feel is most in need of solving.

_____ (Write in the problem mentioned)

11. Which is the next most important problem?

_____ (Write in the problem mentioned)

12a. Now I would like to ask you about your impressions of Ronald Reagan.

First, what are some of the things you *like* about Ronald Reagan?

_____ 1

Anything else?_____ 2

12b. Second, what are some of the things you *dislike* about Ronald Reagan?

_____ 1

Anything else?_____ 2

13. Many people tell us that they are very interested in the abortion issue. This card *(hand the interviewee a card)* lists several positions on abortion. Please tell me which one is closest to your feelings about abortion.

There should be a constitutional amendment making abortions illegal 1

Abortions should be legal only when the life of the mother is endangered 2

Abortions should be legal only when the mental or physical health of the mother is endangered, when the child will be deformed, or in cases of rape 3

There should be no restrictions on abortions since it is a matter of free choice 4

Don't know 5

14. Many people feel that inflation is the most serious problem facing America today. This card *(hand card to interviewee)* gives some of the reasons people feel that we have an inflation problem. Which one of these reasons do you feel is the greatest cause of inflation? *(Record answer)* Which is the next most important cause? *(Record answer)* And which would be next? *(Record answer)*

	First	Second	Third
Taxes	1	1	1
Government spending	2	2	2
Farm prices	3	3	3
Foreign oil imports	4	4	4
Union demands	5	5	5
Profits of big corporations	6	6	6
Military spending	7	7	7
Interest rates	8	8	8
Government printing of money	9	9	9
Don't know	10	10	10

15. I'm going to read several statements, and I would like you to tell me whether you strongly agree, agree, don't know, disagree, or strongly disagree with each. *(Record all answers on the scale below)*

    a. We should have a national health insurance plan that would guarantee basic medical care for all individuals and that would be paid for by the national government.

    b. We should place limitations on the number of cars imported into the United States.

    c. Busing is the only way to insure an equal education to all American children.

    d. A compulsory draft should be instituted to replace the volunteer army.

    e. Standards of the Clean Air Act should be reduced to allow the burning of high sulfur coal that could reduce reliance upon foreign oil.

	a	b	c	d	e
Strongly agree	1	1	1	1	1
Agree	2	2	2	2	2
Don't know/undecided	3	3	3	3	3
Disagree	4	4	4	4	4
Strongly disagree	5	5	5	5	5

16. Do you consider yourself to be a liberal, moderate, or conservative?

Liberal	1
Moderate	2
Conservative	3
Don't know	4

17a. Are you currently employed?

Yes 1 *(Ask q. 17c)*

No 2 *(Ask q. 18b)*

17b. Are you unemployed, retired, a student, or a homemaker?

Unemployed	1
Retired	2
Student	3
Homemaker	4

17c. What is your occupation? _____

18. I'm going to read you several age ranges. Stop me when I read the one that includes your age.

18–24	1
25–34	2
35–49	3
50–64	4
65 and over	5

19. What was the last grade level of your formal education?

0 to 8 years	1
9 to 11 years	2
12 years	3
13 to 15 years	4
College graduate	5
Postgraduate	6

20. Is your religious affiliation Catholic, Protestant, Jewish, other, or none?

Catholic	1	
Protestant	2	
Jewish	3	
Other	4	_____ *(Write in)*
None	5	

21. Is your family income level?

Under $6,000	1
$6,000 to $11,999	2
$12,000 to $17,999	3
$18,000 or over	4

22. Which of these statements best describes your affiliation with unions?

Union member	1
Union household	2
Nonunion	3

Survey Role-playing Cases

Desire for a Local Weekly Newspaper

The interviewer is working for a local printing firm that is seriously considering starting a free weekly newspaper. The newspaper would dwell on local news and events and would carry inexpensive ads for baby-sitters, garage sales, local businesses, etc. The firm has assigned the interviewer the task of creating and conducting a survey of community attitudes toward and interest in a free weekly to be called the *Good News Courier.* The interviewer has completed a draft of the public opinion interview to be used in the survey and has made an appointment to pretest the interview on a neighbor.

A New School Calendar

The interviewer is a student at a large state university and has been asked by the student government to create and to conduct a survey of student attitudes toward the current school calendar and a number of proposals for revising the calendar. The student must create a question schedule and determine both the size and the nature of the survey sample. The university has graduate and undergraduate programs in several different schools and a large continuing education program.

A Market Survey

The interviewer works for Market Studies, Inc., and must design a telephone survey instrument that will assess the effectiveness of a recent advertising campaign that promoted an improved version of a long-established brand of toothpaste. The advertising campaign consisted of three phases: full-page ads in major newspapers, thirty-second spots on the three major television networks, and free samples mailed to 200,000 randomly selected homes. The interviewer must create a set of instructions that others will use to train the dozens of interviewers necessary for conducting this survey.

A Political Preference Survey

The interviewer is on the staff of a state senator who is running for a United States congressional seat. The interviewer's task is to design a political preference survey that will determine how people in the congressional district feel about the senator and a number of local, state, national, and international issues. The survey must be done quickly and inexpensively. Thus, the time for each interview cannot exceed fifteen minutes. Major decisions involve which issues to cover; the proportion of each interview to be devoted to local, state, national, and international issues; how to assess the image of the senator; and what demographic data to obtain.

Student Activities

1. Select a current local, national, or international issue and research it. Prepare a twenty-minute highly scheduled, and highly scheduled, standardized interview. Include an opening, all questions, appropriate answer spaces or options, and a closing. Use a variety of questions and interview a variety of interviewees: different ages, sexes, races, educational levels, etc. Write an analysis of your interview experiences, the strengths and weaknesses of your interviewing instrument, and the data obtained.

2. Try a simple interviewer bias experiment. For example, conduct ten brief public opinion interviews on a current issue, political campaign, religious or political group. All questions are to be identical. In five of the interviews wear a conspicuous button or badge that identifies a position—a Republican elephant, a religious symbol, a slogan. In the other five interviews, do not wear the button or badge. Compare results to see if your apparent bias seemed to affect answers received to identical questions.

3. Compare and contrast the market survey and the political survey. How are openings similar and different? What types of schedules are employed? What apparent question sequences are employed? How are questions similar and different? What interviewer skills are required for each interview? How is the information obtained similar and different? How can you account for the differences in these two interviews?

4. Interview a person experienced in survey and poll taking. How does this person or organization prepare for surveys and polls? What kinds of schedules and questions are employed? What sampling techniques are used? How does the person select interviewers? How does interviewing purpose or situation— market survey, research survey, public opinion poll—affect the stages in the interviewing process?

5. Serve as an interviewer for a survey being conducted by a company, political party, or governmental organization. What instructions did you receive? If you were given one or more sample points, how was this decided? What problems did you have with the interviewing instrument? What problems did you have in locating suitable and cooperative interviewees? What problems did you encounter during interviews? What was the most important thing you learned from this experience?

Notes

1. Philip Meyer, *Precision Journalism* (Bloomington, Ind.: Indiana University Press, 1979).

2. Figure 5.1 is based on one in Robert L. Kahn and Charles F. Cannell, *The Dynamics of Interviewing* (New York: John Wiley & Sons, 1964), p. 103. Reprinted by permission of John Wiley & Sons.

3. Morris James Slonim, *Sampling in a Nutshell* (New York: Simon and Schuster, 1960), p. 23.

4. Meyer, *Precision Journalism*, p. 123. For discussions of formulas and tables to determine error margin and sample size, see also Slonim, *Sampling in a Nutshell*, pp. 60–99; and Frederick F. Stephan and Philip J. McCarthy, *Sampling Opinions: An Analysis of Survey Procedure* (New York: John Wiley and Sons, 1958), pp. 31–33.

5. Stanley L. Payne, *The Art of Asking Questions* (Princeton, N.J.: Princeton University Press, 1951), pp. 23, 63, 80, 124; Daniel L. Katz, "Do Interviewers Bias Poll Results?" *Public Opinion Quarterly* 6 (Summer 1942): 248–68; Gardner Lindzey, "A Note On Interviewer Bias," *Journal of Applied Psychology* 35 (June 1951): 182–84; D. F. Wyatt and D. T. Campbell, "A Study of Interviewer Bias as Related to Interviewer's Expectations and Own Opinions," *International Journal of Opinion and Attitude Research* 4 (1950): 77–83.

6. Payne, *The Art of Asking Questions*, p. 21.

7. Raymond L. Gorden, *Interviewing: Strategy, Techniques, and Tactics* (Homewood, Ill.: The Dorsey Press, 1969), pp. 141–43.

8. Theresa F. Rogers, "Interviews by Telephone and in Person: Quality of Responses and Field Performance," *Public Opinion Quarterly* 39 (Spring 1976): 51–65; John Colombotos, "Personal versus Telephone Interviews: Effect on Responses," *Public Health Reports* 84 (September 1969): 773–82; S. Stephen Kegeles, Clifton F. Fink, and John P. Kirscht, "Interviewing a National Sample by Long-Distance Telephone," *Public Opinion Quarterly* 33 (1969–1970): 412–19.

9. Charles J. Stewart, "Voter Perception of Mudslinging in Political Communication," *Central States Speech Journal* 26 (Winter 1975): 279–86.

Suggested Readings

Adams, J. S. *Interviewing Procedures: A Manual for Survey Interviews.* Chapel Hill, N.C.: University of North Carolina Press, 1958.

Alwin, Duane F. *Survey Design and Analysis: Current Issues.* Beverly Hills, Calif.: Sage Publications, 1978.

Atkinson, Jean. *A Handbook for Interviewers.* London: Her Majesty's Stationery Office, 1971.

Babbie, Earl R. *The Practice of Social Research.* Belmont, Calif.: Wadsworth, 1975.

Groves, Robert M., and Kahn, Robert L. *Surveys by Telephone: A National Comparison with Personal Interviews.* New York: Academic Press, 1979.

Hyman, Herbert H. *Survey Design and Analysis.* Glencoe, Ill.: Free Press, 1955.

Meyer, Philip. *Precision Journalism.* Bloomington, Ind.: Indiana University Press, 1979.

Oppenheim, A. N. *Questionnaire Design and Attitude Measurement.* New York: Basic Books, 1966.

Rivers, William L. *Finding Facts.* Englewood Cliffs, N.J.: Prentice-Hall, 1975.

Slonim, Morris J. *Sampling in a Nutshell.* New York: Simon and Schuster, 1960.

Stephen, Frederick F., and McCarthy, Philip J. *Sampling Opinions: An Analysis of Survey Procedure.* New York: John Wiley & Sons, 1958.

Informational Interviewing: The Journalistic Interview 6

If "precision" describes the survey interview, "adaptability" describes the journalistic interview. The journalist is interested more in individuals than a sample of a "population" and usually operates from an interview guide or a moderately scheduled interview that permits maximum probing and adaptation. Obtaining "new" information and gaining unique insights into motives, intents, attitudes, and feelings are the goals of journalists, not replicability, reproducibility, and generalizability. The "journalistic" interviewing guidelines we will discuss in this chapter are applicable to many information-gathering interviews in business, industry, education, medicine, government, and law. Physicians, for example, must often determine both the physical and psychological problems of patients. Their methods are similar to those employed by good journalists: careful questioning, listening, probing into answers, and observation.

Stages in Journalistic Interviews

The journalistic interview, like the survey interview, may follow a series of stages, illustrated in figure 6.1, as means of obtaining the information desired.[1]

Stage 1—Situation and Purpose
In stage 1, the interviewer determines the specific purpose of the interview, considers how the information obtained will be used, and assesses the nature of the interviewing situation. Any one of these goals may control the others. For instance, if the end product is to be a *news feature story* on a specific topic or person, the length and number of interviews, the interviewees, the specific purpose (to elucidate, observe, discover, examine, expose), and the situation may be predetermined by the *use* of the information. If we are going to attend a *news conference* featuring a senator, sports figure, physician, or company president, the *situation* will determine the type and number of questions we can ask and how we will use the information obtained through our questions and

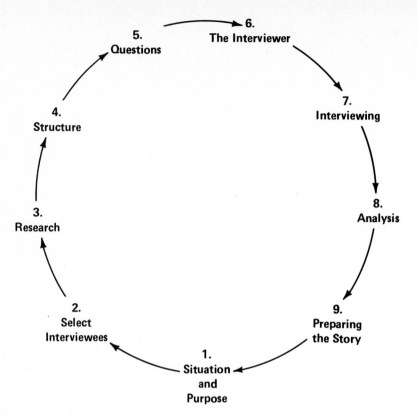

Figure 6.1 *Stages in Journalistic Interviews*

the questions of other journalists present at the news conference. If we want to see how the *person-on-the-street* feels about inflation, the situation, location, and use are determined by our *purpose.* If our intent is to do a *news report* on an accident, natural disaster, football game, or expansion plans of a local factory, *situational factors* such as broadcast or press deadlines, dangers of the situation, psychological state of "victims" and witnesses, and physical setting may determine who we interview, how we interview them, and both the nature and amount of information we obtain. In the case of an interview situation that allows little or no time for preparation, we will go after basic facts and may rely upon the "traditional" journalistic interview guide: *what* happened, *when* it happened, *where* it happened, *how* it happened, *why* it happened, and *who* was involved. The end product is likely to be a *spot news* or *breaking news story* that is both brief and factual.

A variety of situational variables may limit the way we obtain and use information. For instance, a dark and noisy location may prevent us from audio- or videotaping an interview for later broadcast over radio or television. If we can conduct an interview only by telephone, we are denied the opportunity to observe the interviewee and to take pictures. Hostile or reluctant interviewees may not allow us to record interviews, to take notes, to identify them in any way, or to use direct quotations. A verbatim interview report will be impossible if we cannot take extensive notes or use a tape recorder.

Stage 2—Select Interviewees

With situation and purpose clearly in mind, select the interviewee(s) necessary for the report. The situation may determine this selection. For example, when the president calls a news conference, he is the interviewee. If an editor assigns us to interview the high school football coach or Senator Windy or the sole survivor of a plane crash, we can move to stage 3. In many situations, however, we will have to select one or more interviewees from several survivors, witnesses, experts, or persons with differing points of view. Four criteria should guide our selection:

First, does the interviewee have the information we desire? Was the interviewee in a position to observe the event? Was the person involved in determining a policy or course of action? Do we want information from an expert or do we want to determine the expertise of a respondent? Remember, respondents may answer questions whether or not they have accurate data. Raymond Gorden speaks of "key informants"—persons who can supply information on the local situation, assist in selecting and contacting knowledgeable interviewees, and aid in obtaining cooperation.[2]

Second, is the interviewee available? An interviewee might be too far from our home base (don't forget the telephone!), or be available only for a few minutes (when we need an in-depth interview), or may not be available until after our deadline. Many famous or high status persons—the company president, a sports or television star, a senator—may appear to be inaccessible. Do not assume the interviewee is unavailable; at least try to make an appointment. Do we have an acquaintance who might act as a go-between (Gorden's key informant)? Should we go through the public relations department, an aide, or follow a chain of command in reaching the interviewee? Sometimes we will have to be explicit about who we are, with whom we are affiliated, what we want to talk about, how long the interview will take, where it will be held, the areas of information we want to cover, and perhaps provide sample questions or all of our questions.[3] Be careful of excessive interviewee demands.

Third, is the interviewee willing to give us the information? Journalists tend to have few problems in obtaining respondents because people like to get their names, faces, voices, and views in the media. In fact, the journalist must be wary of people who are too anxious to be interviewed. However, a respondent may be reluctant for several reasons: mistrust of us or our organization or the "media," fear of revealing information potentially harmful to self or others, belief that the information is none of our business, or lack of motivation. We might have to convince the interviewee that we can be trusted to maintain confidences and to report information accurately. Usually a person will respond if he or she has an interest in us, the subject matter, or can see some reward to be derived from cooperation. Thus, we might persuade the respondent to provide the information we need by pointing out why his or her interest would be better served if *his or her* views were known. "Your opponent has already agreed to an interview," or "Your opponent has already given his side of the story," or "If you do not give me the information I need, I will have to interpret your position from secondhand information," or "A no comment will look bad in the press." Caution! Heavy handedness may ruin an interview and future contacts with an interviewee.

Some persons are interviewed daily (police chiefs, political leaders, television personalities, political candidates) and are skilled at evading questions or giving vague answers. Many corporate executives attend special courses in which they learn to "confront" reporters. At a press conference where we are only one of many journalists trying to ask questions, the interviewee might refuse to recognize us if we have asked tough questions at other press conferences or earlier in this conference, if we seem hostile, or if we represent an organization the interviewee dislikes or distrusts. The interviewee might respond with a vague or superficial answer and then recognize another journalist in hopes of evading follow-up questions that might force a specific answer. If the interviewee tries to give equal time to all journalists present, we might be recognized only once or not at all if time runs out.

Fourth, is the interviewee able to transmit the information freely and accurately? Any of several problems may make a person unacceptable as a news source: faulty memory, inability to express oneself or to communicate ideas, proneness to exaggeration or to oversimplification, unconscious repression or distortion of information, deliberate lying, and a state of shock. The interviewing situation itself may contribute to interviewee transmission problems at the scene of a murder, tornado, fire, auto accident, or scandal. A father or mother grieving over the death of a small child (and confronted by microphones, lights, and television cameras) cannot be treated like a person commenting on the Christmas decorations in a shopping mall.

Stage 3—Research

We can prepare for many problems if we get to know the interviewee and situation ahead of time. If time allows, the journalist should conduct research into the interviewee as a person, the interviewee's work and accomplishments, and the topic of the interview. Learn the interviewee's biases, values, idiosyncrasies, vested interests, hobbies, reputation, and interviewing traits from articles, other interviewers, the interviewee's books, articles, speeches, and answers during previous interviews. This information may reveal how the interviewee will act and react during our interview. Webb and Salancik write that the interviewer "in time, should know his source well enough to be able to know when a distortion is occurring from a facial expression that doesn't correspond to a certain reply."[4]

Be fully briefed on the interviewee and interview topics.

Be fully briefed on the interview topic so we can go beyond basic, obvious questions and avoid a show of ignorance that may anger the interviewee or embarrass both of us. Few things are more pathetic, for example, than an interviewer trying to discuss a book with the author when he or she has failed to read beyond the title page. Search through news organizations' archives and clipping files, the local library, government publications, corporate reports and publications, periodicals, and various who's who.

As we research the interviewee and the topic, jot down areas and subareas that will develop into an interview guide. If questions come to mind, jot them down for future reference. Our research may reveal other persons to interview or key informants to contact.

Stage 4—Structure

The *opening* of the journalistic interview is the first important step toward establishing an atmosphere of mutual trust and respect that will lead to the accurate, complete information desired. *Usually* this includes identifying ourselves, our organization, and the interview topic and explaining how long the interview will take and how the interview data will be used. Trust is built on truth.

Several common openings are useful to the journalist (see chapter 3). For instance, we might summarize the problem or issue, or explain how we or our organization discovered the problem. A tactful reference to the interviewee's position on the issue could get the interview underway. For example, "I understand you disagree with the new railroad relocation proposal. Would you discuss your reasons for opposing this plan?"

The journalist may engage in a bit of light conversation before asking serious questions. A casual compliment or friendly remark about a topic or person of mutual interest might relax the interviewee. Be careful. The advisability of a rapport-building phase depends upon the interviewee, situation, topic, location, and role relationship between interviewer and interviewee. A busy, important interviewee may be antagonized by time-consuming "small talk." Notice the brevity of the following opening in an interview between a reporter and a United States senator in the hallway near the Senate chamber in the Capitol. The situation is common, the two parties are acquainted, and there is neither time nor need for a lengthy opening complete with rapport building.

Senator Arden, would you comment on your committee's actions on immediate steps to relieve the energy crisis?

The *body* of the journalistic interview (except for a spot news situation) should be moderately scheduled—a listing of all basic questions and some possible secondary questions. The moderate schedule permits the journalist to—

1. digress from the planned structure when deemed necessary;
2. adapt to the interviewee;
3. probe into answers;
4. delete questions that appear unimportant or irrelevant as the interview progresses;
5. bypass questions answered during answers to earlier questions;
6. return to a structure when necessary;
7. concentrate on answers instead of being concerned about phrasing the next question;
8. show preparation for, and a sincere interest in, the interview;
9. conduct a thorough interview without fear of running out of questions.

An interview of one hundred or more questions may employ several sequences or simply be a long list of questions following a topical outline (see chapter 4). The opening question, regardless of sequence, should permit an open expression of views in a favorable manner. This tactic may relax the interviewee and aid in establishing a feeling of trust.

The following are typical opening questions.

1. Tell me what you saw when you arrived upon the scene.
2. What happened, John?
3. What topics did your group discuss today?
4. How do you feel about today's election results?
5. Tell me about your home life when you were growing up.
6. Describe the incident for me.
7. How has the team been doing?

The interview ends when the interviewer has the information needed or time runs out. The interviewer may signal the closing phase with a question such as, "And one final question, when do you think the bill will come to the floor for a vote?" The closing is usually brief with an expression of appreciation, notation when and where results will appear, and congratulations for a good interview. Remember, the interview interaction continues until both parties are beyond sight and sound of one another. The interviewee may relax when the questioning stops and reveal important information about himself or herself or the topic during "unguarded" moments. Listen and observe as long as possible.

Stage 5—Questions

We are now ready to phrase our basic questions. Keep several rules in mind during both preparation and interviewing phases of the journalistic process.

    1. Don't ask bipolar questions.

    2. Use clear, precise language, avoiding qualifiers, abstract words, and words with several meanings.

    3. Don't make statements; ask questions.

    4. Ask relevant questions, determined by topic and purpose.

    5. Avoid loaded questions.

    6. Provide clear, fair options for multiple-choice questions.

    7. Avoid lengthy, complex, or multiple questions.

    8. Ask questions that are specific and to the point.

    9. Ask searching, challenging questions.

    10. Avoid nonverbal cues that signal how we feel about an answer.

    11. Don't allow the interviewee to wander too far off target.

The press conference poses special problems for the journalist. Individually we do not control the interview in any way. The interviewee or a staff may announce when and where the conference will take place and may impose ground rules such as length of the conference, topics open for discussion, what information may or may not be recorded or reported, and which journalists may attend. Protocol may allow the interviewee, a member of his or her staff, or a senior journalist to end the press conference without warning—sometimes to avoid or to escape from a difficult interview exchange. We may or may not get to ask the few questions we prepared before the conference and we may not be able to probe into answers. Listen carefully to answers given to other journalists. These answers might provide valuable news material or suggest questions to ask. Remember that any question we ask may be used by other journalists in their news reports. Therefore, we may want to save a particularly insightful question in hopes of meeting the interviewee on a one-to-one basis.

When asking a primary or secondary question, pay close attention to what is being said and how. Don't cut in on an interviewee's answer unless the interviewee is obviously off target or may continue forever. Be tactful! Ask a question even if both parties know it will not be answered; the way the question is evaded may be revealing. Some interviews and interviewees may require strong, almost abrasive secondary questions: "But a few minutes ago you said. . . ."; " Isn't this a very weak proposal . . . ?"; "You did not hesitate to use pressure during the black civil rights debate, why do you hesitate to do so during the female civil rights debate?"

Three special types of secondary questions are effective in journalistic interviews: the clearinghouse probe, the reflective probe, and the mirror question. The clearinghouse probe may appear at the end of a topic or the interview. For example, "Is there anything we have not covered?" or "Are there any other comments you would like to make?" The intent is to be sure that we have not missed something important. The reflective probe and mirror questions check accuracy of note taking, interpretation of ground rules for the interview, and understanding of language and data in answers. For example, "I take it then that you are saying . . ."; "You feel, then, that the new law is . . ."; "You intend to . . ."; "Do I have this correct . . . ?" Our news story may affect people's lives and actions, our organization's reputation, and our job. Prepare questions carefully and be certain that we understand answers and can reproduce them accurately.

Stage 6—The Interviewer

Sherwood writes that the ideal interviewer is a person "who can ask 160 or 170 questions over a space of a few hours, then write a coherent, organized, interesting report on what he has learned."[5] The ideal interviewer, we would add, is also an excellent observer and listener, skilled at asking secondary questions, and has the ability to record and to interpret answers correctly. However, the interviewing situation (including location) or the interviewee may require an ideal interviewer to be of a specific age, sex, race, or ethnic group or with a certain personality type or style of dress. For example, a known conservative reporter or columnist may be the worst person to interview a liberal political candidate. Thus, we may create the interview but not be able to conduct it if accurate, unbiased data is desired.

Some interviewees will not grant interviews to what they consider to be low-status organizations and people; say, The Sandcut Gazette's cub reporter. As a result, some groups give important sounding titles to all of their representatives: traveling sales representatives become vice-presidents, reporters become editors, assistants become associates, pollsters become research directors.

Which status relationship between interviewer and interviewee is most advantageous; the interviewer is superior to the interviewee, the interviewer is equal to the interviewee, or the interviewer is subordinate to the interviewee? Each relationship tends to offer unique advantages for the interviewer.[6] (Remember R represents the interviewer and E represents the interviewee.)

R Superior to E	R Equal to E	R Subordinate to E
1. R can easily control the interview.	1. Rapport is easily established.	1. E will not feel threatened.
2. E may feel motivated to please the R.	2. Fewer communication barriers.	2. E may feel freer to speak.
3. R can observe E under pressure.	3. Fewer social pressures.	3. R does not have to be an expert on the subject.
4. R can arrange the interview easily.	4. High degree of empathy possible.	4. E might feel sorry for the R and want to help.
5. E might feel honored.	5. R and E at ease.	
6. R can reward E.		

We must know ourselves and the limitations of an interviewing situation before launching an interviewing project.

In each of the following situations, what would be the ideal status relationship between interviewer and interviewee: the interviewer as superior to the interviewee, equal to the interviewee, or subordinate to the interviewee?

1. A student in mechanical engineering wants to talk to someone about the types of positions available for engineers in general and mechanical engineers in particular.

2. The owner of a small (thirty-employee) trucking firm wants information on group health insurance plans.

3. A newspaper wants to interview the president of General Electric about frequent rumors that General Electric may merge with a French corporation.

4. A cancer research specialist at one university wants information about research developments at another university.

5. An employer wants to know how supervisors feel about the new grievance procedures.

Stage 7—Interviewing

An atmosphere of mutual trust and respect is essential to successful journalistic interviews and *how* we conduct the interview determines this atmosphere. Ault and Emery comment, "Treat the average person with respect, and he will do the same to you."[7] Sherwood warns that "no techniques, no tricks, no ploys will substitute for the impression you make as a person . . . they will ultimately respond to you not as a journalist but as another human being."[8]

The following do's and don'ts, if followed, will help to establish an atmosphere of trust and respect *and* to achieve our purpose and goals.

Do's

1. Be courteous.

2. Listen carefully to all answers.

3. Keep the interviewee on track (tactfully) and maintain control of the interview.

4. Probe to draw out understandable, newsworthy answers.

5. Observe personal mannerisms, characteristics, appearance, nonverbal communication.

6. Be cautious of overeager interviewees.
7. Be patient.
8. Try to put the interviewee at ease.
9. Maintain self-control under the most trying circumstances.
10. Prepare the interviewee if recorders, cameras, and lights will be used.
11. Strive for accuracy in every aspect of the interview.
12. Consider changing interviewing style as the interview changes: critical to friendly, approving to disapproving, cool to warm.
13. *Be prepared!*

Don'ts

1. Prolong an interview needlessly.
2. Assume the answer is completed or is going nowhere.
3. Provide verbal and nonverbal cues that reveal pleasure or displeasure.
4. Use jargon or $5 words.
5. Allow personal biases to intrude into questions and manner.
6. Badger the interviewee without justification.
7. Talk instead of listen.
8. Strive to be a "media personality," a "prima donna of the free press."
9. Make assumptions about the topic, the interviewee, the situation, our questions, the answers.
10. Be argumentative, an interrogator instead of a journalist.

Whether we should take notes during an interview, use a tape recorder, or avoid both depends upon the journalist we talk to. Some say we should never take notes; others warn against too few or selective notes; others say the tape recorder is the only way to record data; still others say they never use the contraptions. Select the means of recording data best suited to the objectives, the interview, and the interview schedule. Extensive note taking or tape recording may be necessary during lengthy nonscheduled or moderately scheduled interviews. Memories are often grossly inadequate to recall exact figures and statements, even immediately after an interview, and *how* an answer was given may be impossible to recall. Brief notes or no notes may be satisfactory during short interviews or highly scheduled interviews.

Note Taking   If we take notes, we do not have to worry about a machine breaking down or running out of tape. We can be selective in what we write down and later can choose data more quickly from notes. Listening to entire interviews on tape to pick out important bits of information is time-consuming, and transcriptions of tape recordings are costly in time and money. However, we can rarely take notes fast enough to record everything that is said, especially if a respondent speaks rapidly, and it may be difficult to concentrate on the question-answer process of the interview while trying to take lengthy notes.

Note taking may hamper the flow of communication. In a recent in-depth interview with a newspaper publisher, a student discovered that whenever she began to write, the interviewee would stop answering until she stopped writing— seemingly to let her catch up. Before long he was trying to arrange his seating so he could see what she was writing. Failing to accomplish this, he would occasionally ask her to read what she had written and noted what she could and could not cite in her report as direct quotations. Halfway through the interview he became concerned about her dull pencil and interrupted to sharpen it and to provide additional pencils.

The following guidelines can reduce problems in taking notes and may make note taking more effective.

1. To avoid interfering with the communication climate of the interview, maintain eye contact while taking notes, be as inconspicuous as possible, use abbreviations or shorthand to speed note taking and to avoid gaps in the interview while writing, or learn to remember materials so all information will not have to be written down.

2. To avoid communicating to the respondent what we think is important, do not begin to take notes frantically during or immediately after an answer, take notes throughout the interview (even if we must pretend to do so at times), or delay note taking on an answer until the respondent is answering another question.

3. To avoid excessive respondent curiosity or concern about what we are writing, ask permission before taking notes, explain why note taking is necessary, show notes occasionally, or ask the interviewee to check our notes for accuracy.

4. To avoid respondent concern about how we will use the information, agree to follow ground rules for the interview, explain how and when we will use the material, or agree to let the respondent see the results of the study, report, or article before it is made public.

5. To assure accurate reporting from notes, review notes as soon after the interview as possible.

Tape Recording   When using a tape recorder, we can relax and concentrate on questions and answers. Following the interview we can rehear everything that was said and how it was said; a taped record can protect the interviewer from charges of misquoting. A tape recorder may record unwanted discussions in a noisy crowd, but it also can pick up answers that might be inaudible to the interviewer at the time. Unfortunately, tape recorders may not work. A student, during a lengthy interview for a class project, used a tape recorder and took no notes. When he returned to his room to transcribe the interview, he discovered the tape had not recorded a single word. He was left with only his memory. Some people view a tape recorder as an intruder in the intimate dyadic situation and fear it because it may reveal faulty grammar and poor voice quality and provides a permanent, undeniable record of answers.

The following guidelines can reduce the problems of tape recording interviews.

1. To avoid mechanical problems with the tape recorder, get to know it thoroughly *before* the interview, take more tapes to the interview than are needed, and test the recorder before and during the interview.

A taped record can protect the interviewer from charges of misquoting.

2. To reduce fear of tape recorders and to enhance the communication climate, ask permission to use the recorder, let the interviewee hear himself or herself on tape, place the recorder in an inconspicuous place (out of sight if possible), and use a good, small microphone that need not be stuck in the respondent's face or jabbed from our face to the respondent's and back for each question and answer.

3. To avoid problems with a respondent who is afraid of being quoted too accurately, state that we will be happy to turn off the machine whenever desired, reveal how the recording will be used (possible audio/video broadcast of all or portions of the interview, a verbatim report of the interview, for reference only), volunteer to let the respondent check and edit statements (within reason) before using them, and agree to reasonable ground rules.

4. To avoid problems with telephone interviews, be sure the interviewee knows we are recording the interview and explain how we will use the recording.

Remember that interviews should be pleasant, conversational experiences. Everything we do, from verbal inflections to recording answers, should aid in creating this atmosphere.

Handling Difficult Situations   Free-wheeling informational interviews of the journalistic variety in which interviewers probe into feelings, attitudes, and reasons for actions often hit "raw nerves" and may evoke reactions ranging from tears to hostility. The settings for such interviews—disasters, crimes, scandals, victories, defeats, ceremonies—are often tense, emotional, and embarrassing. Therefore, we must be prepared to cope with a variety of difficult interviewing situations. Many counseling principles discussed in chapter 9 may prove useful to the informational interviewer. Let's look at six common situations and how interviewers might handle each.

1. *Emotional respondents.* It is not unusual for respondents to burst into tears during journalistic interviews. The problem is not helped by family or friends who exclaim, "Oh, God!" or "Now, stop that Mom!", by interviewers who burst out, "Want a kleenex?", or by photographers who crowd in for a "good shot." Interviewer reactions such as the following may help if they are used *tactfully.*

Don't be embarrassed; it's perfectly okay to cry.

Take your time; we're in no hurry.

Would you like me to come back later?

If we have a close relationship with the interviewee, we might hold the person's hand, touch the person's arm, or put our arms around the person's shoulders. Remember the value of silence. Give people opportunities to feel, to think, and to gather thoughts and composure without interruption. They will be ready in a few minutes to continue the interview.

2. *Hostile respondents.* When we detect hostility in an interviewee, we should try to determine the cause of the hostility. For example, a person may feel angry, depressed, helpless, or frightened because of a tragic accident, and we become a convenient target when these feelings are released. The interviewee may have negative feelings toward us, our organization, our profession, or the way information is likely to be used. Bad experiences with other interviewers may lead an interviewee to expect "the worst" from us. An interviewee may become hostile because of a particular question, the timing of a question, the way we ask a question nonverbally, or if our questions are pushing too far. Avoid pressure tactics; the journalistic interview should not resemble a police interrogation. Let an interviewee "blow off steam" and then try to reduce hostility through careful orientation, by avoidance of any actions that might exacerbate the hostility, and by remaining nondefensive and friendly. Never reply in kind. We may have to *prove* that we are not "one of those."

3. *Reticent respondents.* If a person seems unwilling or unable to talk, try to discover why. Perhaps the person is inhibited by us, the situation, the surroundings, other people, or microphones and cameras. Reticence may be a family or personal characteristic that we cannot resolve during one brief interview. If we are using open-ended questions, we might switch to closed questions until the interviewee is "warmed up" and ready to give lengthy answers. A careful self-introduction and orientation about the nature, purpose, and use of the interview might open up a reticent interviewee. Use silence to encourage people to talk, nudging probes to keep people talking, and good listening techniques so people will feel like talking. Discuss easy, nonthreatening topics during the early minutes of interviews that respondents can address easily and openly. Don't walk up to a mother who has just seen her child struck by a car and say, "How did you feel when you saw the car hit your little girl?" and expect her to talk in a calm, detached manner. Unfortunately, radio and television news reports are replete with such insensitive questions by reporters.

4. *Evasive respondents.* Interviewees often try to evade questions that might force them to reveal inner feelings or prejudices, to take specific stands on issues, to make decisions, to reveal decisions that we have already made, to give specific information, or to incriminate themselves. Common evasive strategies include humor, "put on" hostility, counter questions, efforts to answer a different question, requests for rephrasing questions or explaining the nature and rationale for questions, and long, impressive answers that say little and avoid direct answers. The following exchange took place between an interviewer for *Phi Delta Kappan* and then Vice-President Richard Nixon during the 1960 presidential campaign.[9]

Kappan: Mr. Vice-President, do you favor an expansion of federal aid to education?

Nixon: In my opinion, as far as education is concerned in this country, there are three needs. There is a need for buildings. There is a need for better compensation and recognition as well of teachers. And there is also a need for better quality standards. The greatest and most important of these, of course, is standards. Directly related to that, and more important than buildings, is of course, raising the salaries of teachers. This is a vital need, and certainly all over the country at all levels of education it is one that our local communities, our state legislatures, our school boards must face up to and do far more effectively than we have.

Our primary strategy in handling evasive respondents is use of very carefully worded and tactful questions. On occasion we may have to provoke responses through carefully selected leading or loaded questions.

5. *Embarrassing respondents:* Respondents may intentionally or unintentionally embarrass themselves, interviewers, or both. "Blupers" are difficult enough to handle in a tactful manner when we are alone with a respondent, but they are much more difficult to handle if others are present or are witnessing the interview by radio or television. Art Linkletter was the host of the CBS program "House Party" for a number of years. A feature of the show was brief interactions with young children, and these interchanges often produced embarrassing situations such as the following.[10]

Linkletter: What animal would you like to be and why?

Youngster: I'd like to be an octopus, so I could grab all the bad boys and bad girls in my room and spank them with my testicles.

Linkletter: (interrupting hastily) An octopus has eight *tentacles,* Johnny, and he . . .

Youngster: (breaking in and clutching Linkletter's arm impatiently) Mr. Linkletter, you've got that all wrong. Not *tentacles, testicles.*

The best approach to many embarrassing situations is to drop the subject before it gets worse. If necessary, come back to the topic later.

6. *Confused respondents:* Closely related to embarrassing situations are those in which respondents are confused by the topic or the phrasing of questions. We must be prepared to handle confused respondents without making

them feel embarrassed or hostile and in a manner that enables us to get the information we need. The following interactions occurred during a study of doctor-patient interviews.[11]

Doctor: Have you ever had a history of cardiac arrest in your family?
Patient: We never had no trouble with the police.
Doctor: How about vericose veins?
Patient: Well, I have veins, but I don't know if they're close or not.
Doctor: Multiple births?
Patient: (long pause) I had a retarded child once.

A repeat question strategy (see chapter 5), in which we rephrase a question and ask it later in the interview, is perhaps the best way to handle confused respondents. We must not embarrass them by our verbal and nonverbal reactions.

Stage 8—Analysis
We are now ready to review the data and observations obtained during the interview—jog the memory, read through notes, or listen to the tape recording. Sift through hundreds or thousands of words, statements, facts, opinions, and impressions to locate the "newsworthy" items. Check answers with other sources, especially if we suspect the interviewee lied or merely "exaggerated."

If we are preparing a verbatim account for publication, should we include grammatical errors, mispronounced words, "expletives," and vocalized pauses such as "uh," "and uh," "um"? Readers or listeners might enjoy the account, but the interviewee may suffer and we may never get another interview with this person or organization.

When quoting from notes or memory, strive for accuracy. Do not put words into the interviewee's mouth. Be sure proper qualifiers are included. Do not understate or overstate an interviewee's opinions, attitudes, or intentions. Be honest and fair.

Stage 9—Preparing the Story
The technical steps of story preparation are beyond the scope of this book (see the suggested readings at the end of this chapter), but we want to close with a few final cautions. Remember the ground rules agreed to and which materials were "off the record." Violations of agreements will harm us and future journalists. Sherwood reminds us that the journalist asserts that a statement was made, not that it is true.[12] Be patient. Be careful of assumptions, especially when language is involved. Not long after the Chinese leader Mao Tse-tung died, a television network interrupted its programming to announce that Mao's wife and other radicals were dead. An overzealous journalist had assumed that a report of "liquidation from the party" meant death. It did not, much to the network's embarrassment. Strive for accuracy in every fact and interpretation.

This nine-step process should result in a good story or report that is of interest and value to the reader, viewer, or listener and is a credit to us and our organization.

The Respondent in Journalistic Interviews

One of the major problems we encounter in journalistic types of informational interviews is our role relationship with the interviewer. Television, radio, and newspaper interviewers, for example, have become celebrities during the last few decades, and we may be overawed by their presence: "She wants *my* opinion;" "There's Dan Rather!" We are likely to feel subordinate and obligated to answer whatever questions they ask. The presence of cameras and microphones turn some people into "silly putty." We may react the same way when called in to speak to the CEO (chief executive officer) of our organization or the president of our college or university.

We must try to maintain our equilibrium and to determine whether we should speak to a particular person at a particular time and place. There may be no choice if the interviewer is our boss or if as a public relations officer, our job is to meet the press and to explain company plans, policies, and problems. If possible, we should defer interactions until we are informed and mentally ready to cope with tough questions. Each evening we can observe persons making statements at the scenes of accidents, crimes, or controversies that we know they will regret the next day. In some instances they will be fired for their verbal "indiscretions." When we decline interviews, journalists may state ominously into their microphones: "John Prosky was unavailable for comment" or "Officials of Bluebird Corporation refused to grant us an interview." Such statements infer a degree of "guilt," but they may be preferable to foolish comments that become headlines. We have the rights of privacy and silence and should feel free to invoke them at times even when interviewers might make our decisions sound sinister.

We may want to establish some ground rules for an interview. For instance, we may specify which topics are off-limits or off-the-record, whether the interview or parts of it can be tape recorded, who the interviewer(s) will be, and when or where the interview will take place. Occasionally, we may require that questions be submitted in advance. The situation, of course, will often determine how much control we have or want to impose on the interview. If it is to our advantage to have an interview, we may impose no controls and take steps to make the interview as effective as possible for the interviewer.

When we decide to grant an interview, we should listen carefully to each question. Is the question blatantly leading ("Wouldn't you say that your administration has failed miserably in its efforts to show a profit?") or more subtle ("How can you explain this action by members of your administration?")? Many interviewers try to bait interviewees with tricky questions or provoke defensive or hostile reactions. "Keep your cool" is the best advice we can give. A simple, calm "Yes" or "No," or perhaps a "No comment," may take care of a leading question and send the interviewer into a frantic search for a probing question. We may ask the interviewer to rephrase a question or to repeat a long, complex question. The rephrasing or repetition may result in a clearer, less threatening question. At the very least, it will give us an extra few seconds to create an appropriate answer.

Insist that interviewers allow adequate time to think through answers and to present adequate answers. If an interviewer cuts us off in mid-answer or apparently does not want explanations, go along only as long as it suits *our* purpose. If such actions are likely to compromise us or our organization, simply refuse to continue with the interview until given adequate time to think and to respond. If the interviewer refuses or tries to "plow" ahead, terminate the interview.

Do not try to second-guess an interviewer by phrasing an answer while the question is still being asked. Listen to the entire question and pay close attention both to what it says and to what it implies. When asked bipolar questions, be sure that the two choices are fair choices and that a simple yes or no, agree or disagree, is sufficient. If not, insist on giving an explanation or qualifying the answer. Be sure the two choices represent the only options available. Take a look at this question: "Do you think coal or synthetic fuels is the best answer to our future energy needs?" Solar energy, for example, is not included as an option. If solar energy is the answer, give it even though it is not included or qualify the answer such as, "Of the two choices you have given, I think synthetic fuels is the best; however, I think solar energy is the best solution for our future energy needs." Another tactic is to rephrase the question into our own words and then answer the new question: "If you're asking, 'If there were *only* two means available to meet our future energy needs, coal and synthetic fuels, which would I choose?' I would say synthetic fuels."

The point we are making is that we need not be passive participants in journalistic interviews. We should *share* control of the interview with the "journalist" and not submit meekly to whatever is asked or demanded. The result will be a better interview for both parties.

Summary

The journalistic interview, like the survey interview, tends to be a circular process. We begin with a purpose and proceed step-by-step until we have come full circle back to our purpose, which should now be fulfilled. The purpose may be to elucidate, observe, discover, examine, or expose. The end product (feature story, spot news item, report, verbatim account of the interview) and the medium (radio, television, newsmagazine, newspaper) affect the purpose and nature of the journalistic interview. Adaptability is the most important requirement for the journalistic interviewer and interview.

A Journalistic Interview for Review and Analysis

This interview took place between *Maclean's* (Canada's newsmagazine) Foreign Editor David North and General Binyamin Peled, former commander of the Israeli Air Force and one of the masterminds behind the famous Entebbe raid that rescued the hostages from a hijacked airliner who were being held prisoner at Entebbe, Uganda. This was the first interview General Peled granted after the raid.[13]

Notice the use of probing questions and an occasional loaded question to spark a reaction from the interviewee. Many of the interviewer's questions are bipolar. Why does this practice not harm the interview on this occasion? Which questions would you phrase differently? Which question sequence or sequences is the interviewer using? Who controls this interview? What is the status relationship between interviewer and interviewee? How does this relationship help or hinder the interview?

1. *Maclean's:* What is it like sitting in an airplane, knowing that the raid you planned is going on down below and maybe something you did wrong is going to cost the lives of hundreds of people?

2. Peled: You must remember that it's not a new experience for me. Not long before that operation, we had a full-scale war on, where much more was at stake. There were moments of tension, of course, and of anxiety and excitement. But you learn to control those and try and take what comes and make a decision.

3. *Maclean's:* How carefully did you calculate the risks?

4. Peled: When one says "calculated risks," he means that he took into account while he was thinking about it all the possible parameters of failure and success that he could possibly put down. And maybe he will forget or neglect, but if he feels that he took all the parameters into account and the final count says it's feasible, he's willing to take the risk. . . .

5. *Maclean's:* And you wouldn't lie awake at night wondering if you had forgotten anything?

6. Peled: I would, I would think, like any other rational man, that nothing is perfect in this world and there are some things that you cannot control. And maybe the harshest thing is that you know before hand that success will have many fathers, and failure will be an orphan. But you live with it. I was not too emotional about the operation itself, because I felt that even if it failed it would have been the right thing to do instead of dealing. So it had to be done in any case, under any circumstances; so anything that might go wrong was in the context of the necessity to do it. There was no question of not doing it.

7. *Maclean's:* Was the whole operation in fact all your idea?

8. Peled: No, no, I can't say that. My part in it was to propose the feasibility of reaching out there and landing and controlling a certain area for any length of time necessary to perform any type of ground operation that would probably be carried out by the ground forces. These proposals were called for; I put them down and they met with some skepticism at the military level, but it didn't take me too long to convince them that it was feasible and we were quite capable of doing that.

9. Maclean's: Did it all go exactly as you thought it was going to go?

10. Peled: No. There were little things that didn't go according to plan. One little thing: we were supposed to get some late information about some of the landing conditions and it arrived quite late. Actually it arrived while the aircraft were taking off. And the messenger who had that information, in the form of photographs, didn't find his way to the right place on the airfield. Everyone was bustling, and he didn't know who was where and so this very important piece of information got to the tail aircraft and it was not distributed because the people who got it thought it was for them. They didn't think the others should get it.

11. Maclean's: But there always comes a point where having made your plan you are at the mercy of events.

12. Peled: That is true. I find myself surprised every time when I speak to normal, rational people and they speak of our military operation and they look for perfection that they don't usually practice in their own lives. Life is not perfect, even in the military. And I would say even more so because the military works under conditions where there is much less control than in business, insurance, or holiday-making or film-making.

13. Maclean's: Is it more important to be right or is it more important sometimes to make a decision?

14. Peled: Well, I'd say, there was a certain trade-off. If you have time, if you have enough resources, if you have enough patience, I would say you should gather all possible information. But you should also realize that if you work for 100 years preparing the plan, you will never get all the information you need. So, at a certain point in your planning, you must start trading-off . . . if you wait any longer the chance of doing anything would be gone. Some people do this. I call these people activists in retroactive actions. They always know what they should have done after they didn't do it.

15. Maclean's: Do you rather like it when something crops up and you have to extemporize? Is this how you get your kicks?

16. Peled: This is one of the ingredients of wanting to be a leader. If everything is cut out for you, you don't need a leader.

17. Maclean's: What were you before you joined the air force?

18. Peled: I was a high school student . . . then I did one year of national service (1946) in the Jewish Settlement Police Force. We were expected to volunteer for one year's service after finishing high school and I did. But I wanted to be an aeronautical engineer. I had all my admittance papers written out to the Massachusetts Institute of Technology because we didn't have an aeronautical faculty in Haifa at that time. But as things were brewing up in Palestine I didn't think it was right to drift off to the United States. So, I enlisted in the Technion and I only had one semester until the eve of '47 when everything blew up. After serving for about three months on an infantry battalion of Technion students who took part in some operations, I heard that an air force was being set up. I really wanted to be a pilot. I went into some office of the Tel Aviv air club which was then the headquarters of the air-force-to-be. I presented myself and said I wanted to be a pilot. And they said, ''Well you're a nice guy, but we only take people who have had private flying lessons. We can't afford to start from scratch. Why don't you join our mechanics school?''

19. *Maclean's:* Was the war going on at this time?

20. Peled: Skirmishes, shootings, incidents, it was not full-scale war. Full-scale war happened on May 15.

21. *Maclean's:* And by that time you had had your three months training?

22. Peled: Yes, in March I was posted as a flight mechanic. And on May 14 I was suddenly called up and told: ''You pack up your things and go home, pick up some money and clothing''—we didn't have anything and the army was not in being at the time—''and if you can borrow a pistol from your father or someone do it. We're going to send you down to an abandoned British airfield because we're setting up a base there.'' That was on the fourteenth. The next morning the war was on. I'm proud to say that I was the first Israeli mechanic to paint the first Israeli emblem on the first fighting aircraft.

23. *Maclean's:* By the time the 1967 war started, what position did you hold?

24. Peled: I was a wing commander, a fighter wing commander, not in headquarters, the way many people have it now.

25. *Maclean's:* And you were involved in an incredible lightning operation which must be one of the most successful, preemptive strikes by any air force?

26. Peled: Well, the outcome was very successful. And I don't know why people insist on calling it a preemptive strike. It was more of a no-choice decision. I think it is well to remember that on May 15, 1976, we were openly threatened and former Egyptian President Gamal Abdel Nasser made it public that this time he was going to wipe us out, and we believed it. The question arose, could we defend ourselves on the present borders? It was very hard for the chief of staff to give an answer but he did. He said, ''I can't.'' And from then on it was obvious that we were to start and we might have a chance of surviving. If we stayed put we would have a chance of sinking. To call it a preemptive strike sounds scheming. Sure, we had contingency plans for that. But I think it was a decision of no choice. If you remember the obituaries that were running in the world press about Israel at the time, you get the feeling that the right decision was made. It then became a problem with the ground forces and they said, "Yes, we can proceed, but we have a few conditions: First, we have to have complete air superiority." That was turned back to the air force and the air force had to say how, when, and where it could guarantee these conditions. So, we always had pre-conditions. It was a big gamble.

27. Maclean's: It was another of those occasions when you make a plan and then await events. Did you find it exhilarating?

28. Peled: No, I felt this is it. If we don't succeed on the first strike we're going to have to pay.

29. Maclean's: So, it was really quite cold-blooded?

30. Peled: Yes, at any cost because there was no other way. And the cost was quite high. I don't think people like to examine the losses when the war is very successful. That gets pushed aside. But if you look at the losses in the raids, we did pay. We lost about 46 of the 245 pilots we had in absolute numbers.

31. Maclean's: Were there people whom you knew well among those pilots?

32. Peled: Well, about twelve of them I knew well.

33. Maclean's: Do you ever get tired of sending people who are your friends into battle and having them not come home?

34. Peled: Tired? No. I become sad. But you must remember that serving in an air force, you get used to losing your friends along the way. I guess you will find the same feelings in circus performers, tunnel diggers, miners, high-wire artists, builders. They lose people from time to time. It's got to be part of your life. You develop a numbness, you know, this is your way of life. The hardest part was visiting the families right after the war.

35. Maclean's: You were saying earlier that success has many fathers. I would like to turn that around and ask if the German commando raid at Mogadishu was a child of Entebbe?

36. Peled: No, if you look right down into it, Mogadishu was a repetition of an operation we carried out against a Sabena aircraft that was held hostage in Lod—the break-in into an aircraft in a friendly airport.

37. Maclean's: Alright, but what was your reaction when you heard about Mogadishu?

38. Peled: I was very glad, because I couldn't understand the ease with which in previous instances—they gave 5 million dollars to a group of terrorists who took an aircraft and flew to Yemen—the great German people parted with their sovereignty.

39. Maclean's: But, of course, it isn't just up to the country that is most involved as to whether it mounts an operation of this kind. You chose to act at Entebbe for very particular reasons. It was, if I may say so, a characteristic Israeli response. But if you are going to have regard for legalities. . . .

40. Peled: If you have to violate another man's property in order to do those things, is that what you mean?

41. *Maclean's:*	Yes.
42. **Peled:**	Well, do you remember what the Americans did to North Africa when they had the piracy problem there? About 150 years ago? And, if you study a little bit of what happened in the Caribbean when piracy on the high seas was the norm, what the other countries did? If you are driving me to answer a question: if it's morally or internationally legal to violate another country's borders in order to carry out such an operation, it really depends. If the country that hosts those terrorists is in cahoots with them, I wouldn't have any moral restraint. If a country is helpless, I may offer my help. But under no circumstances should one deal.
43. *Maclean's:*	But in a sense Mogadishu was a "first," was it not—the first instance where a country voluntarily allowed a foreign anti-terrorist squad to operate on its soil?
44. **Peled:**	I'm on the verge of trying to be little cynical, if you don't mind. I'm not sure that if Mogadishu had not been able to secure a promise by Western Germany for massive help in its fight with Ethiopia this permission would have been granted. It's a harsh world.
45. *Maclean's*	Do you think that it is desirable that this precedent should be followed?
46. **Peled:**	Yes, but the difference between desirable and possible depends on human nature and expediency. If people recognize that it's a common interest not to let this terrorist game be profitable to anybody, I'd be very glad.
47. *Maclean's:*	But you don't think it's going to happen?
48. **Peled:**	I think we're in for factors, some possible future places, where this will not be possible out of expediency. So, I'm not trying to delude myself that everything is going to be smooth sailing from now on.
49. *Maclean's:*	It's sometimes said that these people do this sort of thing because they are psychologically deprived and want to attract attention. Do you subscribe to this theory?
50. **Peled:**	Yes. I think they want to get public attention. I think they want to become a problem. They have things that they want to get. This is the basis for my assumption that these people are not insane. They are not suicide prone. That is why a no-deal policy will work.
51. *Maclean's:*	Do you think, then, that they can be deterred?
52. **Peled:**	Yes.
53. *Maclean's:*	What do you think will deter them?
54. **Peled:**	That when they calculate the risks of operating this way that they will come up with a certain answer every time—that they will get nothing from it.
55. *Maclean's:*	So, if what they want is publicity, in part, what do you say about the attention the world media give them?
56. **Peled:**	That publicity will be positive for them only if they succeed. But if they fail every time . . . the world doesn't like failures.

Informational Interviewing: The Journalistic Interview

57. Maclean's: No. So you're not for putting a security blanket on news coverage?

58. Peled: No, I think it should be let known that if anybody tries he is going to be trapped; he is not going to succeed even if he gets caught alive.

59. Maclean's: What about the problem, though, that you catch terrorists, that you jail them and then some other terrorists hijack somebody else and demand they should be set free?

60. Peled: No deal.

61. Maclean's: But do you think public opinion will take the fact that 50 or 60 hostages may die?

62. Peled: I don't think the hostages will die. I think these people are not insane. If they know it's not real, why should they kill. . . .

63. Maclean's: So, in fact, what you're saying is that the threat is unreal.

64. Peled: The best way to save the hostages is *"no deal!"*

65. Maclean's: Is it the adventurous spirit, the spirit of Entebbe that wins the hearts of many people who think of Israel? There are also occasions that disappoint and one of them was the air force strike in Lebanon. A lot of people got killed. How do you feel about this? It's your air force.

66. Peled: I know. Listen. Did you notice that you just pointed out the events that make us likeable or adorable? All those are events of war. How come? Do you think we are a warlike people?

67. Maclean's: I am afraid that you may have become one.

68. Peled: We're not. We're being praised for all of the wrong reasons. Look, did you ever sit down and think what is the basic policy of Israel? I must bring this out because I am glad that, as a military man, I am extolled for being an adventurous knight-errant, successful. But this is not what we should be praised for. . . . At the inception of the Zionist movement immediately after Herzl said that the solution to the Jewish problem is becoming sovereign again there was a big question of "How do we go about it?" If you look back into the recent history at the turn of the century there was a big division of opinion among the people who finally made up the Zionist movement about how to go about it. Some people like Zapotinski said that we should not be bashful, we should take it. It's ours and we'll take it—by force if necessary. The other part, which was the majority, led by Weizmann said, "No. We are a moral people. We have a tradition to uphold. We invented Zion, we invented Jesus. We cannot come out against that tradition. We shall do it in another way. We should set up funds to buy the land from the Arabs who want to sell. We shall work hard to get the benediction and blessing of the enlightened world. We will go to the United Nations, we'll speak our minds, we'll try to influence people of our rights, we shall never put up arms in order to gain our political ends." That's been the basic premise of Israel as a sovereign nation, never to take up arms to achieve its political ends.

69. *Maclean's:*	Nevertheless . . .
70. **Peled:**	Nevertheless, the things we're being praised for is the war we make.
71. *Maclean's:*	Yes, and I don't think that that's an accident.
72. **Peled:**	Alright, now I come back to the question: from time to time we do something that seems gory. It's not up to the standard, the high moral level of Entebbe. Why do you want to spoil it by killing 100 civilians? And it's my air force, you say. Let me ask you a question. Which act would you prefer? Try to hurt a place where we have prior intelligence that the group that just fired the rockets is hiding—in a camp or in a house, or in an orchard. Or would you rather that we mobilize two or three divisions, took over southern Lebanon, and started filtering the bad guys from the good guys—and we'll have to stay there for about three months to do it?
73. *Maclean's:*	Yes, obviously you can justify it on those grounds.
74. **Peled:**	I'm not justifying it. Personally, I am against using the air force on technical military errands. I call it misuse of air power. During the period between 1967 and 1973 we did a lot of it, and my biggest argument with the deputy chief of staff, who is now the defense minister, was that I said that this is a misuse of air power. I, as an airman, do not advise it.
75. *Maclean's:*	So you feel that the Israelis are miscast by world opinion as a warring people?
76. **Peled:**	Nobody extols the fact that we've made the country into a garden, that we are the best in the world in agriculture; that we have become a center of science; that we have become a melting pot, a social experiment of the highest order in amalgamating people from the differences in culture of 2,000 years and making them back into one nation. Nobody mentioned that. Everybody mentions Entebbe, the Six-day War, the fact that we are professional amateur soldiers.

Journalistic Role-playing Cases

A Case of Cheating?

A student named Pat Fullmer has been accused of cheating by two instructors at Florida Central College. The instructors questioned a couple of students about the incident and then took the matter to the student court. The student court has reviewed the evidence and heard testimony by several people. As yet it has not reached a final decision on this case. The interviewer is a reporter for the *Student Daily* at Florida Central and wants to write one or more articles on the case that has captured the attention of students, faculty, and administration. He has made an appointment with Mr. Roy Brown, twenty-seven years old, one of the instructors in the English Department who accused Pat Fullmer of cheating. Pat Fullmer is a junior in history and a C+ student.

A Police Brutality Case?

A few months ago John T. Sawyer, fifty-six years old, was stopped and arrested in a Chicago park. There seems to have been much confusion at the time and charges were never filed against Sawyer. Not long after the incident, Sawyer brought charges against the arresting officers. After an initial hearing, the police department took minor disciplinary actions against the officers, but this did not satisfy Sawyer. He is continuing to press charges. The National Association of Law Enforcement Officers has sent an interviewer to Chicago to get material for a report on this case. He has made an appointment with Lou Harris, a local attorney who has questioned all persons involved in the case and attended the police department hearing on the charges.

A Hero Citation?

Several years ago a natural disaster struck a Scout camp near Queens, Kentucky. A local resident has written the national office of Bravery Beyond the Call of Duty, an organization that makes awards to people of all ages who show heroism in coming to the aid of their fellowman without an obligation to do so. The resident, Sam Browning, is forty-nine years old and a lifelong resident of Queens. He is urging that Max Whitmore be awarded Bravery Beyond the Call of Duty's silver medal for actions during the natural disaster. The Bravery Beyond group has sent an interviewer to Queens to interview Sam Browning, who has gathered facts and community feelings about Max, his actions, and whether the silver medal should be awarded to him.

A Case of Murder or Self-defense?

A few years ago Matt Dye was shot and killed near his home in Cottonville, Mississippi. The interviewer is twenty-six years old and a graduate student in criminology at the University of Mississippi. He would like to write a special projects paper on Matt Dye, the case, and the trial. He has located a former resident of Cottonville, Marian Murphy, living near campus. Marian attended the trial, talked to those involved, and listened a great deal. The interviewee will answer all questions asked, but she will not volunteer information on her own.

Student Activities

1. Compare and contrast the sample market survey and the journalistic interview. How are openings similar and different? What types of schedules are employed? What apparent question sequences? How are questions similar and different? What interviewer skills are required for each interview?

2. Interview a newspaper journalist and a broadcast journalist about their interviewing experiences and techniques. How does the nature of the medium affect the interviewer and the interview? How does the medium affect the interviewee? How does the end product differ and what constraints does this place on each interviewer?

3. Conduct two twenty-minute interviews. Take detailed notes in the first and no notes in the second. After each interview, reconstruct the information gained during the interview, and note interviewee actions, reactions, and attitudes. Which interview worked out best? How did note taking or lack of note taking affect the interviews? How much information did you get from each interview? What recall problems did you encounter after the interviews ended? Try this same experiment with tape recording instead of note taking.

4. Attend a press conference where one person (government official, business representative, political candidate) is answering questions from several journalists. How is this interviewing situation similar to and different from a one-on-one journalistic interview? What skills are required of interviewer and interviewee? Which situation, press conference or one-on-one interview, tends to obtain the most quotable material? How can you account for this?

5. Interview a journalist about the skills and techniques required in conducting a variety of journalistic interviews: press conference, sophisticated survey or poll, a person-on-the-street informal poll, an in-depth interview with one person, interviews at the scene of a tragedy. How does the person's journalistic organization select interviewers for various types of interviews? How does the interviewer select interviewees? What are the major problems encountered in each type of interview?

Notes

1. Figure 6.1 is based on one in Robert L. Kahn and Charles F. Cannell, *The Dynamics of Interviewing* (New York: John Wiley & Sons, 1964), p. 103. Reprinted by permission of John Wiley & Sons.

2. Raymond L. Gorden, *Interviewing: Strategy, Techniques, and Tactics* (Homewood, Ill.: The Dorsey Press, 1975), p. 106.

3. Hugh C. Sherwood, *The Journalistic Interview* (New York: Harper & Row, 1972), pp. 22–38 contain excellent suggestions on how to get an interview.

4. Eugene J. Webb and Jerry R. Salancik, "The Interview or the Only Wheel in Town," *Journalism Monographs* 2 (November 1966): 18.

5. Sherwood, *The Journalistic Interview*, p. 3.

6. Raymond L. Gorden, *Interviewing: Strategy, Techniques, and Tactics*, pp. 137–53; Robert K. Bain, "The Researcher's Role: A Case Study," *Human Organization*, Spring 1950, pp. 23–28; Lewis Dexter, "Role Relationships and Conception of Neutrality in Interviewing," *American Journal of Sociology* 62 (September 1956): 153–57.

7. Phillip H. Ault and Edwin Emery, *Reporting the News* (New York: Dodd, Mead and Co., 1959), p. 125; see also George M. Killenberg and Rob Anderson, "Sources Are Persons: Teaching Interviewing as Dialogue," *Journalism Educator* 31 (July 1976): 16–20.

8. Sherwood, *The Journalistic Interview*, p. 5.

9. *Phi Delta Kappan*, May 1960, p. 349.

10. Art Linkletter, *Kids Say the Darndest Things!* (Englewood Cliffs, N.J.: Prentice-Hall, 1957), p. 25.

11. Roger W. Shuy, "The Medical Interview: Problems in Communication," *Primary Care* 3 (September 1976): 376–77.

12. Sherwood, *The Journalistic Interview*, p. 18.

13. © 1977 by *Maclean's Magazine*. Reprinted by permission.

Suggested Readings

Anderson, David, and Benjaminson, Peter. *Investigative Reporting.* Bloomington, Ind.: Indiana University Press, 1976.
Ault, Philip H., and Emery, Edwin. *Reporting the News.* New York: Dodd, Mead and Co. 1959.
Bittner, John R., and Bittner, Denise A. *Radio Journalism.* Englewood Cliffs, N.J.: Prentice-Hall, 1977.
Charnley, Mitchell V. *Reporting.* New York: Holt, Rinehart and Winston, 1966.
Hohenberg, John. *The Professional Journalist.* New York: Holt, Rinehart and Winston, 1973.
McCombs, Maxwell; Shaw, Donald L.; and Grey, David. *Handbook of Reporting Methods.* Boston: Houghton-Mifflin, 1976.
Metzler, Ken. *Creative Interviewing: The Writer's Guide to Gathering Information by Asking Questions.* Englewood Cliffs, N.J.: Prentice-Hall, 1977.
Meyer, Philip. *Precision Journalism.* Bloomington, Ind.: Indiana University Press, 1979.
Sherwood, Hugh C. *The Journalistic Interview.* New York: Harper & Row, 1972.
Tyrrell, Robert. *The Work of the Television Journalist.* New York: Hastings House, 1972.

Employment Interviewing: The Selection Interview 7

The process of hiring, promoting, compensating, and discharging employees has changed dramatically during the last twenty years. Congress has enacted a number of laws designed to eliminate discrimination in the selection of employees and created a variety of agencies to enforce compliance with these laws. If we are involved in any way with the hiring process, then a "passing acquaintance" with equal employment opportunity laws is inadequate. As an *employer*, knowledge of these laws is necessary to assure compliance with them and to avoid lawsuits. Employers can no longer ignore discrimination legislation, especially if (1) they deal with the federal government, (2) they have more than fifteen employees, (3) they have more than $50,000 in government contracts, and (4) they engage in interstate commerce. As an *applicant*, knowledge of discrimination laws is necessary to determine what information we may reveal and what information we need not give to prospective employers.

The Laws and the Agencies

The Civil Rights Act of 1866 was designed to prevent discrimination based on race or national origin. Enforcement was left primarily to the federal court system, however, so it had little influence on hiring or employment. Almost 100 years later, the 1963 Equal Pay Act came into being.[1] Four criteria were used to determine if a person holding a job was receiving equal pay for work similar to another employee: skill, effort, responsibility, and working conditions. The 1963 Equal Pay Act essentially provided equal pay for men and women doing similar work.

The Civil Rights Act of 1964, especially Title VII, spelled out for the first time what employers were prohibited from doing in the entire employment process, including recruiting and hiring.[2] Selection of employees, whether intentional or not, could not be based on race, color, sex, religion, or national origin. Title VII made it obligatory for all employers to discover discriminatory practices and to eliminate them. Congress created the Equal Employment Opportunity Commission to insure that employers complied with the spirit and the letter of the law. The government was concerned with the *results*, not *intents*, of hiring practices.

With regard to *religion*, the 1964 act required organizations to provide to each employee "reasonable accommodation" to religious practices without creating "undue hardship" to the organization. With regard to *sex*, the act prohibited employers from refusing to hire because of (1) the assumption that men could handle certain jobs better than women, (2) personal preference for a man, (3) the assumption that coworkers, clients, or customers would prefer a male, (4) common stereotypes of the sexes or, (5) state laws designed for the "protection of women." With regard to *national origin*, the act prohibited (1) tests in English where English language skill is not a job requirement, (2) height and weight requirements that are not necessary for job performance, or (3) denial of work to persons married to or associated with persons of a specific national origin, to persons who belong to lawful organizations that promote the interests of national groups, to persons who attend schools or churches commonly utilized by persons of a given national origin, or to those whose names reflect a certain national origin.

Executive Order 11246, issued in 1965 and amended in 1967, not only prohibited discrimination but required government contractors to take affirmative action to ensure that applicants were treated equally during the employment process, including hiring, selections for training compliance, recruitment, and recruitment advertising.[3] The Age Discrimination in Employment Act of 1967 was passed to protect older employees. It had become nearly impossible to find a job after age forty.[4] The 1967 act prohibited employers of twenty-five or more persons from discriminating against persons of ages forty to seventy in any area of employment because of their age. Exceptions could be made where *bona fide occupational qualifications* (BFOQ) were involved or there was a bona fide seniority system. Employers were told to avoid generalizations, to evaluate applicants on their individual merits, and to document employee performance.[5] The Rehabilitation Act of 1973 ordered federal contractors to hire handicapped persons. Among the handicaps defined by the law were alcoholism, asthma, rheumatoid arthritis, and epilepsy. The Vietnam Era Veterans Readjustment Act of 1974 encouraged employers to hire qualified, disabled, and Vietnam veterans.

One of the most serious problems that has *surfaced* recently is sexual harassment. Many individuals engage in subtle forms of sexual discrimination because they mistakenly believe that EEO laws do not apply to them, that any woman (employee or applicant) is fair game, or that all "liberated" women want to be treated "that way." The following guideline issued in June of 1980 by the EEO makes it clear that treating someone as a sexual object will not be tolerated.[6]

Unwelcome sexual advancements, requests for sexual favors, and other verbal or physical conduct of a sexual nature constitute sexual harassment when (1) submission to such conduct is made either explicitly or implicitly a term or condition of an individual's employment, (2) submission to or rejection of such conduct by an individual is used as the basis for employment decisions affecting such individual or (3) such conduct has the purpose or effect of substantially interfering with an individual's work performance or creating an intimidating, hostile, or offensive working environment.

Interviewers should refrain from making comments about an applicant's physical attributes, which might be construed as asking for something other than a business or professional relationship, and any physical contact beyond traditional handshaking. Court cases have clearly established that organizations are responsible for preventing and correcting any sexual harassment directed toward applicants and employees.

Now that we have reviewed a number of laws that pertain to discrimination in hiring practices, let's test our knowledge about what we can and cannot ask during selection interviews. Rate each question in the EEO quiz below as either *lawful* (can be asked during an employment interview) or *unlawful* (cannot be asked during an employment interview).

EEO Quiz

1. Would you mind if I called you by your first name?
2. Could I have a picture of you attached to the application blank?
3 Are you a citizen of the United States?
4. Your chances for this job might be better if you went out with me for dinner and drinks so we could get to know each other much better . . . how about it honey?
5. What foreign languages can you speak or write?
6. What is your reaction to occasionally having to entertain customers in the evenings?
7. Who will be baby-sitting with your children while you work?
8. Where did you graduate from college?
9. Will you expect to have your religious holidays off?
10. What kinds of drugs did you try while in the service?
11. What kind of discharge did you receive from the service?
12. Describe for me your greatest strengths as an employee.
13. Are you married or do you live with someone?
14. Would you mind traveling at least 30 percent of the time on this job?
15. Why would you, a blind person, apply for this job?
16. Where did your parents come from?
17. Were you ever arrested for a crime?
18. Which courses did you like most in school?

19. What fraternity (or sorority) did you belong to when you were in college?

20. What professional societies do you belong to?

21. Would you mind pronouncing your name for me?

22. How have you kept such a great body if you graduated from high school in 1959?

23. Will your wife be home to answer the phone when customers try to call?

24. What kinds of people do you enjoy working with the most?

Remember that many applicants today are familiar with antidiscrimination laws and that ignorance of the law is no excuse. Obviously any question can be open to interpretation, but from the most recent information, here are the answers to the EEO quiz.

1. Lawful. To avoid the cumbersome and formal Ms., Miss, Mrs., Mr., Dr., and so on, it is often a good idea to use the applicant's first name.

2. Unlawful. A picture can lead to discrimination based on sex, age, race, or national origin.

3. Lawful. We cannot ask, however, how citizenship was obtained unless it involves national security. If the answer is no, we may ask, "Do you intend to become a citizen" or "Do you have legal sanction to remain in the United States?"

4. Unlawful. This approach is tactless and a basis for sex discrimination or harassment charges. Social contact is not a BFOQ.

5. Lawful. The skills of being able to speak or write a foreign language may be a BFOQ. Notice that no attempt is made to discover how the person learned the language or where.

6. Lawful. Entertaining customers, clients, or executives may be a BFOQ.

7. Unlawful. How a person takes care of his or her family is not a criterion for a job.

8. Lawful.

9. Lawful, if the applicant has stated religious preferences that would require special time arrangements beyond the employer's capability.

10. Unlawful. This question assumes guilt and should not be asked. A person's life-style or what a person has done in the past is none of the employer's business and is not a BFOQ.

11. Unlawful. This question is suspect because many minorities, drug users, and homosexuals were given dishonorable discharges. Type of discharge is not a BFOQ.

12. Lawful.

13. Unlawful. Marital status is not a BFOQ.

14. Lawful. Travel may be a BFOQ, and the reaction of the applicant may reveal the person's desire for the position.

15. Unlawful. Organizations are required to make reasonable accommodations and adaptations for handicapped applicants. The phrasing of this question is in very poor taste.

16. Unlawful. This is not a BFOQ and may reveal national origin.

17. Unlawful. If the position requires a person to be bonded, then we can ask, "Have you ever been convicted of a felony?"

18. Lawful.

19. Unlawful. The "old boys" or "old girls" network is unlawful. Membership in a sorority or fraternity is not a BFOQ.

20. Lawful.

21. Lawful.

22. Unlawful. Not a BFOQ and may be used as the basis for a sex discrimination charge.

23. Unlawful. Being able to reach an applicant may be a BFOQ, but having the wife available to receive calls is not. This question also probes into marital status.

24. Lawful, if the employer and applicant avoid characteristics such as age, sex, race, etc.

How many did you get correct? Unfortunately, even experienced personnel professionals miss some of these questions. While only attorneys can keep up with every subtle change in the laws and their application, we *must* keep constantly abreast of such laws. Too many managers and executives believe that the EEO laws apply only to personnel folks or to very large companies. We cannot afford to be the reason for lawsuits against our organizations.

The Employer and the Selection Interview

We and the organizations for which we work should make interviewing a structured and systematic part of the selection and hiring procedures. Interviewing can be a useful tool in the selection process if the interviewer is well trained, knows the kinds of behaviors to look for, and can use appropriate tests. Keep records on employees who do and do not succeed on the job so we can refine the employee selection process.

Preparation is crucial to the employment interviewing process. Experienced interviewers often believe that they can "wing it" and conduct a good interview. When we ad-lib an employment interview, the chances are good that we will miss critical content and violate EEO guidelines. We can improve employee selection and adherence to EEO laws by following a series of steps or stages such as the following: (1) review laws that pertain to hiring practices, (2) determine the nature of the position to be filled, (3) advertise the position, (4) prepare materials to be used in the selection process, (5) review information on each applicant, (6) conduct the interview, and (7) evaluate the applicant and the interview.

Step 1—Review Laws that Pertain to Hiring Practices

Review the laws discussed earlier in this chapter and keep up to date on the latest decisions and interpretations. Federal laws supercede state laws *unless* the state laws are more restrictive. Remember that the EEOC is not concerned about *intent* but *effect*.

Our organizations are open for potential lawsuits if the information used is unlawful even if we did not solicit the information but happened upon it by accident. What if an applicant volunteers the information? Once the unlawful information is out (and let's assume we did not ask questions to obtain the information), we are subject to complaints. Cut the applicant off immediately and explain that we are *not* interested in such information. Do not panic or be rude; simply explain that the information is not needed and that our organization does not use such information for hiring purposes. Explain that we are following EEOC guidelines and our organization does not wish to discriminate. Some applicants know the law better than interviewers and may tell interviewers that they are asking unlawful questions or that certain information need not be provided. Many applicants do not know guidelines or laws, but they may be able to see that we are making every effort to comply with the law.

Do not write or make notes on the application blank.

Do not write or make notes on the application blank. If you notice that specific information is missing, such as a home phone number, ask the applicant to fill in the missing information. If the applicant refuses, ask if he or she would be willing to initial and date the information if we fill it in. If the applicant says no, forget it. In the past, some organizations used notes or codes to indicate race, religion, ethnic group, or general appearance. Some filed applications by color: red for Indians, brown for blacks, white for whites, and yellow for oriental applicants. These practices are unlawful. Doodling on an application blank may appear to be a code. One employment director we know was severely reprimanded for coloring in the round letters on the printing of the application blank. If too much information is missing, ask the applicant to fill out another application blank and give him or her the old one.

Step 2—Determine the Nature of the Position to be Filled

Determine in writing the bona fide occupational qualifications for each position. These include *specific* levels of education or training, experience, and skills. If we decide, for example, to require a high school diploma or college degree, we must be prepared to prove that the requirement is both job related and an accurate predictor of job success. If we wish to require specific standards of moral or social behavior (ranging from criminal convictions to divorce), we must be able to show that they are job related and apply *equally* to *all* applicants. There should be no "surprises" when an applicant applies or interviews for a position. Remember, we may need to go to court with a particular job description in hand.

Step 3—Advertise the Position

Advertise each position where *all qualified* applicants have a *reasonable opportunity* to learn about the opening. Typical outlets for job advertisements include newspapers, school placement centers, union offices, company bulletin boards, company publications, and professional journals and publications. The advertisements should reveal the nature of the position and major qualifications.

Step 4—Prepare Materials to be Used in the Selection Process

A first principle to remember is that we, the interviewers, *are* the company to the applicant. A bad impression of us means a bad impression of the company. If we are doing campus recruiting, we should provide the college with up-to-date materials on ourselves and the company. A tremendous number of pamphlets are sent to college placement services and are never read because they are not written for the potential applicant. Many job candidates hesitate to read company literature because it is often too complicated or unrelated to their needs. A short history of the company and a listing of its products and services is interesting, but keep such material simple and to the point. Get to know what interests young people entering the labor market. Common questions of concern to applicants are—

How much influence will my ideas have in the company?
Do they welcome suggestions in the system?
Will they keep me advised of my progress?
Will they encourage me to do charity work?
What are their feelings about political activities?
Can I get financial help and encouragement to further my education?

A great many applicants are not as concerned about money as with opportunities to make an individual contribution to the company or to people. They tend to rate the professions, especially teaching and government services, higher than business careers in personal fulfillment. See if specific questions, such as those preceding, are answered in the company's recruiting literature. Encourage interested applicants to correspond with us personally or with the company. Be sure correspondence is answered promptly and, preferably, not with a form letter.

The *application forms* we employ must be appropriate for the particular position we are trying to fill. A form that is appropriate for an office manager opening may be inappropriate for sales representatives, engineers, secretaries, or maintenance people. Eliminate "traditional" categories such as marital status, physical characteristics (height, weight, color of eyes, complexion), age, arrest records, credit references, and type of military discharge. Do *not* ask for a picture. Do provide adequate space for applicants to answer all questions thoroughly.

The selection interview is designed to make one decision: whether or not the interviewee will continue in a formal relationship with our organization after the interview. This decision should not be taken lightly. The interview should be structured—at least moderately scheduled—and interviewers should be trained to ensure that each interviewer is obtaining the same information and that each applicant is being measured by the same yardstick. Undoubtedly most of us would prefer the "give-and-take" of the unstructured interview. However, research reveals the many hazards of *unstructured* employment interviews.[7]

1. Interviewers tend to talk more than applicants. The reverse should be the case.

2. Interviewers tend to make their decisions early. Decisions should not be made until all possible information is obtained.

3. Only factual, biographical information (that is, easily obtainable through written application forms) is covered consistently.

4. General suitability ratings of applicants have extremely low inter-rater reliability.

5. Ratings of applicants tend to differ among an organization's interviewers concerning particular applicants for the same position.

6. If behaviors essential to job success can be specified, then we can structure the interview to search for examples of these behaviors in an applicant's record. Intelligence or mental ability are the only traits judged consistently in "typical" interviews.

Step 5—Review Information on Each Applicant

Read and prepare for each candidate. Scan the completed application form and résumé for completeness. Are all necessary blanks filled in? Is there a phone number where the applicant can be reached? Has the applicant included a list of previous employers? Look for significant time gaps that may give some hints about the person's work history. Be careful of probing too deeply into time gaps because the gap may have nothing to do with the requirements for the position we have open. Has the applicant included references? There are some pluses and minuses in checking references. Former employers, because of various privacy laws, may only verify employment dates or salary paid.

Remember, if we solicit, retain, or use unlawful information to make a hiring decision, we may be subject to a lawsuit. Check the résumé for unlawful information such as a picture, age, marital status, physical characteristics, religion, and national origin. Delete these materials before other members of our organization might see them. We cannot be accused of using what we do not have.

What about reference letters? They are usually not worth the paper on which they are written. Applicants pick out references who will support them, and few people will put damaging information in a letter. Letters may tell us that an individual knows the applicant and that an applicant can get letters of recommendation. Ninety percent of all reference letters are pleasant and do not address a person's past or future performance.

The best predictor of future performance is past performance. The chances that a person's performance will change drastically for the better is not good. Even if an applicant has had no full-time work history, performance on part-time jobs can give us an idea of previous work performance. Past jobs or assignments can give us an idea of the person's view of his or her performances and preferences for types of work and work settings. If the applicant has been in sales, we might develop questions about commissions made, awards won, highest dollars ever sold, or the most difficult sale.

Check out the applicant's educational record, including places, diplomas, degrees, and type of training. In general we should try to detect if this individual has been exposed to appropriate knowledge and training.

Step 6—Conduct the Interview

Do not attempt to accomplish more in an interview than the schedule and allotted time allow. Guard against stereotyping applicants or making a decision until the interview is over. We have control of the interview, at least at the outset, and the tone we set for the interview will often determine success or failure. We should try to avoid interviewing applicants if we feel it is an imposition upon our time or ability. If we have an "I don't give a damn" attitude, how can we expect the interviewee to care?

Beginning the Interview   When ready to begin the interview, greet the applicant warmly and by name to make a good first impression. We should introduce ourselves so that the interviewee will be able to use our names. A handshake is welcomed by most interviewees. If we are going to take notes, inform the interviewee as to what we are doing and why. We should stop taking notes if this action seems to make the interviewee nervous or appears to hamper the smooth flow of questions and answers. Some companies use audio and videotape recordings to assure accurate recording of all information. If we are going to tape an interview, explain why. Some companies are submitting such tapes to personality specialists for analysis. Whether we can reveal this intention to the applicant is probably a matter of company policy, but we should inform the applicant that we are going to tape the interview.

There are two views on how to begin interviews. The traditional view is that the interviewer must spend some time establishing rapport with the interviewee by chatting about the weather, sports, or some local well-known event. It is assumed that this rapport building relaxes the interviewee and creates goodwill. The result may be just the opposite. Idle chatting may heighten tension by creating anxiety and suspense: "When will the *real* questions begin!" The interviewee knows why he or she is there and probably would prefer to get down to the business at hand rather than postpone it while pleasantries are swapped.

So-called ice-breaker questions can backfire and freeze-up the interviewee. Take for example the interviewer who, after introducing himself or herself, says, "Gee, it's really a beautiful day out. Boy it's the kinda day that makes you want to go out and play golf or tennis. Say, what kind of sports do you like to play?" The applicant's response might well be, "None—why?" The applicant is unlikely to believe the interviewer's question was just idle chatter; there must have been a reason for asking that question. The rapport establishing technique also wastes valuable time. Sincere interest in the interviewee and desire to obtain material about him or her will establish rapport. If we really want to relax the interviewee, put the interviewee to work. This does not mean rapid-fire questioning designed to snow applicants. Get people talking and they are likely to forget their nervousness. If a particular applicant is too nervous to respond adequately to our opening questions, we may have to alter our tactics, even change the location of the interview. We may work on rapport enroute to the new location.

An interviewer we know had a person apply for a job as assistant personnel director. The person was obviously uptight. The interviewer suggested they go for coffee because he had not had breakfast. On the way back to the office, the applicant remarked, "I feel so much better; I think I can go ahead with the interview now." The applicant was unaware that much of the interview had already taken place. Some interviewers employ throwaway questions that are

Employment Interviewing: The Selection Interview

not used to gain decision-making information. They might open by asking, "Tell me about yourself." They are more interested in relaxing interviewees and making them communicative than in the information obtained. This technique can backfire because some interviewees are afraid of open-ended questions. We feel that a friendly, warm greeting followed by the first of our questions, ones that are easy to answer, is the best means of starting most employment interviews.

The Questioning   As we move into questioning the applicant, here are some basic guidelines for clear and effective questioning.

1. Make all questions audible; do not mumble.

2. Avoid memorizing the schedule of questions; memorization makes questions sound mechanical.

3. Do not waste time questioning about information we already have or do not need.

4. Avoid asking questions already answered on the résumé or application form.

5. Be aware of what we are communicating nonverbally in questions by tone of voice, eye movement, or shifting in our seat.

6. Avoid evaluative responses to answers.

7. Do not employ a machine gun approach to questioning; give the applicant time to answer each question even if a few seconds pause seems like hours.

8. Use loaded or leading questions *only* for definite and predetermined purposes.

9. Use trick questions only when absolutely necessary; the interview is not a contest between interviewer and interviewee.

10. Use speculative questions with the understanding that we will get speculative answers. For example, "Where do you hope to be professionally in ten years?"

11. Avoid questions that can be answered yes or no.

12. Avoid questions that might violate equal employment opportunity guidelines and legislation.

13. Ask questions that delve into bona fide occupational qualifications.

14. Give the applicant an adequate opportunity to ask questions.

Quiz on Employment Questions   Use the preceding guidelines for employer questions and determine what is wrong with each of the following questions. Rephrase each question to make it good. The position is for a sales representative, and the interviewer has a résumé and a completed application form.

1. Do you like to travel?

2. Where did you go to college?

3. *Why* (vocal stress) do you say that?

4. I assume you would prefer a minimum of supervision?

5. What are your marriage plans?

6. What social group do you belong to?
7. Have you thought about your future in this field?
8. You like to work with people, don't you?
9. Well, we were looking for someone with a little more experience; (brief pause) tell me about your internship with Ford.
10. What jobs have you had during college?

A major problem facing all employment interviewers is how to handle sensitive information. Determine how important this information is to our decision. If it is unimportant, drop the subject. If it is important, we have three alternatives: (1) pursue the line of questioning and attempt to get a clear answer; (2) put off probing questions until later in the interview so the applicant will not be affected during the majority of the interview; (3) drop the subject and hope to get further information on it from another source such as a reference.

The following are typical employment questions that meet our criteria and are lawful under current EEO guidelines. Interest in our organization:

1. Why would you like to work for us?
2. Where or how did you hear about this opening?
3. What made you apply for this position?
4. What material have you read about our company?
5. What do you know about our products and services?
6. What do you know about our organization, including its history?

Work related:

1. Tell me briefly about your work history.
2. What previous work experiences do you think prepare you for this position?
3. Which position has given you the most satisfaction?
4. Which position was the most frustrating for you?
5. Describe for me one or two of the most important accomplishments in your career to date.
6. What kinds of supervision have you experienced in your previous jobs?
7. Describe for me your favorite supervisor.
8. What kind of supervisory style would you use with your subordinates?
9. What might your subordinates say are your strengths and weaknesses?
10. What would you say are your work strengths? Weaknesses?
11. What has been your biggest career disappointment?
12. Why did you choose this career?
13. Why are you leaving your current position?
14. What would make you leave us?
15. What kind of coworkers do you like best?
16. What kind of organization would you like to work for?
17. How does the position we have open fit into your career plan?
18. What new knowledge or experience did you gain from your last job?
19. Why should we hire you?
20. What did you do that was innovative or new on your last job?

Education and training:

1. What kind of formal training have you had?
2. What special certificates have you received?
3. What special skills do you have?
4. What aspects of your education or training have prepared you for this position?
5. Which courses did you like most in college?
6. Which courses did you like least in college?
7. Describe for me the most enjoyable experience you had in college.
8. If you could do it all over again, which courses would you take?
9. How did teachers and professors influence you to pursue this profession?
10. How has your education or training helped you to perform jobs better?
11. Why did you choose _____ as your major?
12. Why did you choose _____ as your minor?

Career plans and goals:

1. Why did you select this area of work?
2. Who influenced you most in your career choice? How? Why?
3. Where would you like to be in my organization in five years?
4. What are your long range career goals?
5. What are you doing to prepare yourself for advancement?
6. What factors do you believe are most influential in determining a person's chance for advancement?
7. Describe for me your ideal boss?

Job performance:

1. Describe the performance appraisal system used by your last company.
2. Tell me how you were evaluated during your last two evaluations.
3. What areas of improvement were pointed out to you during your last performance appraisal?
4. What do you believe are the most important performance criteria in your area of expertise?
5. All of us have pluses and minuses in our performance; what are some of yours?
6. When your performance has slipped, what have you done to put it back on track?
7. What is the longest period of time you have ever been absent from any job? Why?
8. As a supervisor/manager, how would you handle an employee who is chronically late or absent?
9. What do you think is a good attendance record?

Salary and benefits:

1. What kind of salary would you need to join us?
2. What would you consider to be a good annual salary increase?

3. Which fringe benefits are most important to you?

4. If you had to do without a fringe benefit, what would it be?

5. How does our salary range compare to your last job?

Career field:

1. What do you know about the history of your field?

2. What do you think is the greatest challenge facing _____ today?

3. What do you think will be the next major breakthrough in _____ ?

4. How do you feel about government controls in your field?

5. Describe for me a typical work day for a _____ .

6. What do you think is the greatest single problem facing your field today?

7. What do you see as the major trends in your field today?

8. Which area of your field do you think will expand the most?

9. (for a person interviewing for a position in transportation) What effect do you think deregulation of the railroads will have on the transportation industry?

As we listen carefully to an answer, we should be determining whether the answer is adequate. If it is not, we should design probing questions that will get specifics, explore "suggestions," clarify meanings, and force the applicant to reveal inner feelings, preferences, and level of knowledge. Remember that there are always two applicants present in each interview, the *real* and the *make-believe*. The employer's task is to determine which is which. We have a better chance of doing this if we let the *applicant* do the talking.

Closing As the interview draws to a close, have a standard explanation of the follow-up procedure, that is, of what happens next. If we have the authority to hire on the spot (rarely in a campus interview but perhaps always for hourly workers being interviewed in a personnel office), offer the position or terminate further consideration. If we do not have hiring authority, explain specifically what the interviewee can expect after the completion of the interview. For example: "Well, Elizabeth, as you know we interview a number of people for these positions and then select several applicants to go through an additional interview at our home office. You will be notified by mail from my office within the next week to ten days whether or not you will be asked to come for an additional interview. Do you have any final questions?"

Close the interview in neutral. Too often a company makes an enemy by saying, "Gee, Elizabeth, you're the kind of person we have been looking for and I know the job is yours; it's just a matter of formalities." A few weeks later Elizabeth gets a letter (often a mimeographed form with her name scrawled in ballpoint pen next to the "Dear") that says, "At the present time we do not anticipate hiring anyone in your specialization. However, if we see a need in the future, be assured that you will receive every consideration."

The opposite can also happen. The interviewer tells the interviewee at the end of the interview, "Well, I've really enjoyed talking with you but, frankly, I don't see where a person with a major like yours fits in with our needs." A few weeks later the candidate, who has written our firm off his or her list (perhaps angrily), gets an offer from our firm. Simply tell interviewees what happens next, thank them for their time and information, give them our address and telephone number (perhaps a business card), and encourage them to write or call us personally if they have any questions. Do not encourage or discourage candidates. While we might not be able to use a particular candidate for the current position we have available, he or she is still a potential candidate for some other job in our organization and is a potential customer.

Be sure that our offices follow up on all prospects. Do not send out dittoed form letters signed with a rubber stamp. If possible, have all letters typed and signed by the interviewer. This personal touch will go a long way in maintaining a feeling of goodwill among current and future applicants.

Step 6—Evaluate the Applicant and the Interview

The Applicant   As soon as possible after the interview is completed, we should record our impressions of the applicant. Many organizations provide interviewers with "standardized" evaluation forms. If the interview was a *screening* interview, we must decide whether to maintain an interest in the applicant and, perhaps, when to invite the applicant to take a "plant trip." If the interview was a *determinate* interview conducted during a plant trip, we must decide whether to offer the position to the applicant or to write a rejection notice—often referred to as a "ding letter."

A postinterview evaluation may consist of two parts: a set of standardized questions and a set of open-ended questions. The evaluation form, regardless of its construction, should focus on job-related topics and be thorough enough so we can make a decision that is best for the applicant and our organization. The standardized portion of the evaluation may look like the following.

	Poor	Fair	Good	Very Good	Excellent
Interest in the job	_____	_____	_____	_____	_____
Attitude	_____	_____	_____	_____	_____
Maturity	_____	_____	_____	_____	_____
Motivation	_____	_____	_____	_____	_____
Self-confidence	_____	_____	_____	_____	_____
Ability to get along with others	_____	_____	_____	_____	_____
Ability to communicate	_____	_____	_____	_____	_____
Appearance suitable for this job	_____	_____	_____	_____	_____
Knowledge of the company	_____	_____	_____	_____	_____
Knowledge of the field	_____	_____	_____	_____	_____
Training for this job	_____	_____	_____	_____	_____
Experiences for this job	_____	_____	_____	_____	_____

The standardized part of the postinterview evaluation process is often followed by a series of open-ended questions that allows interviewers to make appropriate comments. The following are typical open-ended questions.

1. What are the applicant's strengths?
2. What are the applicant's weaknesses?
3. How does the applicant compare with other applicants for this position?
4. How well would this applicant fit into our organization?
5. How well do the applicant's abilities, strengths, interests, and future goals fit into the company's present and future needs?
6. What is the applicant's capacity for growth and development?
7. For which type of work is this applicant best qualified?
8. How mature and realistic is the applicant's self-concept?
9. How accurate and realistic is the applicant's conception of what is entailed in this position?
10. Should we hire this person? If not, why not?

The Interview   We should do frequent evaluations of our own interviewing skills and performances. It is easy to develop bad habits and to become complacent, if not bored, with the whole process. Questions such as the following can serve as guides for our self-evaluations.

1. How thoroughly did I review the applicant's credentials prior to the interview?
2. How did I try to create an informal, relaxed atmosphere for the interview? How successful were these efforts?
3. How did I try to encourage the applicant to speak freely and openly?
4. How well did I explore and observe the applicant's ability to communicate, physical bearing, personality and human relations skills, maturity, motivation, emotional stability, experiences, knowledge, integrity, and preparation?
5. Did I provide information that the applicant needed and did not know prior to the interview?
6. Did I provide adequate time for the applicant to ask questions?
7. Did I follow all EEO guidelines to the letter?
8. How effectively did I close the interview?
9. Did I reserve judgment until the interview was completed, or did I allow first impressions to control my decision?
10. Did I follow up on all promises I made the applicant?

As we become more experienced as interviewers, we may want to add questions and subquestions to this list. The organizations we work for and the positions we want to fill may dictate the nature of our self-evaluations. The important point, however, is that we must continue to learn and to grow as interviewers.

The Applicant and the Selection Interview

The applicant, like the employer, must prepare thoroughly for each selection interview. If *experienced* interviewers cannot "wing it" during interviews, *inexperienced* interviewees are likely to have many disappointments if they try to ad-lib. We can improve our chances of obtaining good positions and helping employers adhere to EEO guidelines if we follow a series of steps in our job searches: (1) conduct a self-analysis, (2) prepare our credentials, (3) do extensive background study, (4) conduct a job search, (5) take part in the interview, and (6) evaluate each interview.

Step 1—Conducting a Self-Analysis

The first step in seeking a job is to conduct a thorough and insightful inventory of ourselves, including needs, desires, weaknesses, dislikes, and experiences. Self-analysis is often painful, partly because most of us have never done so and partly because we prefer to analyze others. It seems safer for our self-concepts to let well enough alone. However, we cannot prepare adequately for selection interviews and future careers if we do not perform this crucial first step. As John Crystal and Richard Bolles have written, "You have got to know what it is you want, or someone else is going to sell you a bill of goods somewhere along the line that can do irreparable damage to your self-esteem, your sense of worth, and your stewardship of the talents that God gave you."[8] The following questions can serve as guides for our personal inventories. Remember to be thorough and honest; no one will be listening but ourselves.[9]

1. What are my personality strengths and weaknesses?
2. What are my intellectual strengths and weaknesses?
3. What are my communicative strengths and weaknesses?
4. What have been my accomplishments and failures?
5. What things and activities give me the greatest satisfaction?
6. What do I need to be a satisfied human being?
7. What are my special skills and abilities?
8. What are my professional strengths and weaknesses?
9. What are my professional interests and disinterests?
10. Why did I attend _____ and how happy am I with the training I have received there?
11. Why did I study _____ and how happy am I with this choice of major or specialty?
12. What are my on-the-job strengths and weaknesses?
13. What do I want in a position at this time?
14. What do I want in a position in the future?

Companies expect us to have given some thought to our futures and perhaps to have developed some pretty definite ideas about our personal and professional lives. We should think about current events, politics, religion, ethics, and morality. We need not have a ready-made answer for every question, but thinking about these areas before the interview will provide us with some starting points. Give serious consideration to the world around us and how we, our family, and our new employer would fit into the scheme of things.

By now we should have a list of short-term objectives, a self-inventory, and perhaps a series of life goals or mission statements. A goal is a destination or place where we want to be within a time frame. Begin now to plan a strategy to reach a short-term goal, a stopover on the way to a long-term goal. Do not think that because we desire a particular job we will be successful at it, satisfied with it, or able to obtain it. But if we know what we want, where we are going, and how to get there, the chances are greater that we will achieve our goals. Do not set an objective on a particular title or job description. There will be job possibilities that have not yet been created. Focus on the kinds of things that give satisfaction.

Step 2—Prepare Our Credentials

Once we have analyzed ourselves thoroughly, we should prepare the necessary job credentials: résumés, cover or application letters, references or letters of recommendation, and application forms. The question What do we want to communicate? should be ever present in our minds. Employers usually see our credentials before they see us, so our credentials often determine *if* an interview will take place and, if it does, whether we enter the interview with a favorable or an unfavorable *image*. We simply cannot afford to take shortcuts when preparing our credentials.

The Résumé   The résumé is our silent sales representative, so it must be professional in the best sense of the word. There are many varieties of résumés. The choice of paper, typeface, and format are up to us and the type of position we are seeking. Some people prefer the "book" format using the four sides of two pieces of 8½ x 11 paper; others prefer a letter format that can be folded and addressed on the back; but most applicants and employers prefer a single sheet of 8½ x 11 paper that is typed on one side. Avoid odd sizes of paper (11 x 14 or 6 x 9) that are difficult to mail, to file, and to handle.

The basic "data sheet" or "paragraph" (or "story résumé") is preferred by most employers.[10] Keep BFOQ and EEO guidelines in mind when designing a résumé. The résumé *must* include the following information:

1. Who we are
2. Where we can be reached
3. Our current employment
4. Our past employment history
5. Our education and/or training
6. Our business and professional accomplishments, awards, and other forms of recognition

The résumé *may* include the following information:

1. Our activities and interests, especially ones that reveal leadership, skills, and important personality characteristics
2. Our career objectives

```
                         Roberta D. Anderson
                           1721 N. Meridan
                        Fort Worth, Texas 75218
                        Home Phone: (214)763-4118
                          Office: (214)765-2403


   Career Objective: National or Regional Marketing Manager for
                     a large consumer goods organization. My
                     general interest is market research and
                     analysis along with market strategy and
                     media planning.

   Work History: 1980-present--Employed as the senior market
                 analyst for Radio Shack. My duties and
                 responsibilities include market surveys,
                 analysis, and preparation of marketing
                 plans for all small unit sales.

                 1976-1979--Market Survey Coordinator, Chow
                 Division, Ralston Purina, Checker-board
                 Square, St. Louis, Missouri. My responsi-
                 bilities included the development, staffing,
                 and tracing of Agriculture Survey teams.
                 These teams surveyed feed stores, mills, and
                 farmers for various types of product infor-
                 mation.

                 1974-1976--Job Placement Specialists for A & G
                 Employment Services, Clayton, Missouri. I
                 started as an interviewer hiring summer and
                 seasonal employees. After finishing school, I
                 worked full-time in recruiting from January
                 1975, until I left for the position with
                 Ralston.

                 Other work experience--Like others, I have worked
                 in a ladies' wear shop, as a waitress in a Pizza
                 Hut, and did baby-sitting while in junior high
                 school.

   Education:    1970-1974--Graduated from Fairview Heights High
                 School, Fairview Heights, Missouri in 1974.

                 1974-1977--Graduated from Washington University
                 with a B.S. in Business. Major: Marketing/Ad-
                 vertising, Minor: Statistics

   References:   Furnished upon request
```

Figure 7.1 *Data Sheet Résumé*

3. A list of references

4. Our publications, memberships, and engagements that are professional or business related

The résumé *should not* include the following information:

1. A picture

2. Physical data such as age, sex, race, height, weight

3. Personal data such as marital status and memberships in religious, political, or social organizations

The "data sheet" résumé (see fig. 7.1) should provide an employer with a basic knowledge of what we have done or achieved, where we have done it, and what we are looking for now. The résumé provides an objective and factual description of us. When using this style of résumé, be sure to include only BFOQ data. Data about ourselves should come first, then education and training, and finally skills and work experiences. The approach is straightforward and gives the employer information about us. We save the selling for the cover letter that usually accompanies the data sheet.

The "story" or "paragraph" résumé (see fig. 7.2) is a new method, and there are two general reactions: "it's too much like a sales pitch" or "it's super." The story résumé *is* a sales approach that presents the facts in a more interesting fashion. Once we have read a story résumé, we should want to meet the individual. There are three patterns: (1) we can use the journalistic pattern: who, what, when, where, how, and why; (2) we can use the pattern of the data sheet résumé and simply put it into paragraph form; or (3) we can use the first paragraph to give the basic data and the remaining paragraphs to present recent events and then move backward in time.

The Cover Letter   Produce an "original" cover letter or letter of application for each position and, if possible, address the letter to a specific person in the organization. Be sure to use proper business form, good grammar, and no abbreviations, especially for courses and areas of study. For example, does Eng. stand for English or engineering? What is CS 200 or AUS 450? Each letter we write communicates a great deal about us, so it should be neat, on good quality bond paper, and typed with a new ribbon and clean typewriter keys.

Harold Janes conducted a survey among the Fortune 500 companies and discovered the following preferences about letters of application.[11]

1. The letter should be short, usually no more than one page.

2. The letter should reveal particular reasons why the applicant is interested in the position and the organization.

3. The letter should indicate when a person will be available for an interview.

4. The letter should reveal specific areas of interest.

5. The letter should omit the "soft soap."

6. The letter should reveal how the applicant learned about the job opening and/or the company.

```
            Jason G. Janiak
            1408 E. Eastman
    Arlington Heights, Illinois 60015
      Home Phone: (312) 495-3011
         Office: (312) 307-3465
```

Jason is currently employed as the Manager of
Training and Development for Abbott Laboratories
and has been in this position for more than a
quarter of a decade. His responsibilities include
needs analyst and development and staffing of
all supervisory and management courses. In addition,
he supervises a staff of eight professionals
(three with Ph.D.s, two with M.A.s and three with
B.A.s) and three clericals who also conduct
opinion surveys, O.D. intervention, and other
services upon request.

Before Jason joined Abbott Laboratories, he
was the senior consultant in Management Development for Consumer Light and Power in Chicago.
While with Consumer, Jason taught the Basic
Supervision Course, the Management Action Program,
and the Leadership Development Workshop. Not
only did he supervise two professionals and one
clerical, but he also had responsibility for
working with client departments dealing with
various human management problems.

Before joining Consumer, Jason was a consultant with ABC Training Group in Gary, Indiana.
His job was to work with medium to small industries
in developing specialized and custom training
programs and in some cases actually conducting
the training. He was with them for about three
years while finishing his M.B.A. at Northwestern
University and also managed to publish several
articles in the ASTD Journal, Personnel, Management
Review, and a chapter in Motivating the Sales
Force by Alex Duckworth.

His outside interests include writing, tennis,
golf, and dancing.

Figure 7.2   *Story Résumé*

7. The letter should amplify and not merely repeat the résumé.

8. The letter should be original and "somewhat creative"; it should not be a "canned" or a "form" letter.

9. The letter should be an introduction and need not tell the comprehensive, "life" story.

References and Letters of Recommendation Many employers realize that letters of recommendation are of little value in hiring employees, but they still request them as part of the data gathering process. We should select persons who know us well and who can make insightful comments about (1) our training and work experiences, (2) our abilities to perform the tasks required in the position for which we are applying, and (3) our abilities to work with others. If possible, we should select persons whose judgments the employer is likely to respect. Always ask a person's permission to use his or her name as a reference.

Application Forms Fill out application forms neatly, completely, and honestly. Be precise in answers and avoid abbreviations if possible. Always come to interviews with pen and pencil and note paper. Forms are a part of all job searches, and the way we complete them adds to or detracts from our images.

Step 3—Do Extensive Background Study

Once we have prepared our credentials, we should do intensive background study. For instance, we should learn everything we can about our *field*. Areas of study should include our field's history, developments, trends, areas of specialization, leaders, and current and future problems. We should develop a mature perception of what people in our field do during a typical workday.

We should learn everything we can about each *organization* to which we apply for a position. Areas of study should include the organization's products and services (old, new, and future), locations (of plants, divisions, offices), expansion plans, potential mergers, reputation in the field and with the public, history, major competitors, financial status, and nature of ownership.

Companies are like people; each has a personality all its own. Select the companies to interview by their potential for us. We should not waste our time and the company's time shopping around. If we know, for instance, that a company requires conservative dress and behavior, and we deem this to be crass organizationalism, do not interview with that company. If we dislike the commission-only sales system, do not interview with a company utilizing this system.

As Janes discovered in his study, companies expect us to have some knowledge about them and the services or products they sell. While it is the company's primary responsibility to make themselves known to us, take the initiative and seek out the information needed. There are several sources in addition to company annual reports and recruiting materials: *Dun & Bradstreet Reference Book, Moody's Manuals, Standard's and Poor's Corporation Records.*

Select the companies you want to interview by their potential for you.

We can always write to a company and it will be happy to send the necessary materials. A pamphlet may not answer some of our questions, but we can jot these down and ask them during the interview.

Also learn about the *type of position* and the *specific* position for which we are applying. Try to discover the responsibilities and duties, required experiences, type of supervision, advancement potential, location, starting date, job security, fringe benefits, training programs, salary and commissions, relocation possibilities and policies, and rate of turnover.

We should be up to date on *current events*. Employers expect applicants to be aware of what is going on in the world and to have developed mature views of current events. We should read a good daily newspaper and periodicals such as *Newsweek, Business Week,* and *Fortune.*

We should learn everything we can about what happens during interviews. What do employers look for in applicants? What turns employers off? What kinds of questions do employers ask and what are they looking for in these questions? What kinds of interviewers will we face: the skilled professional, the inexperienced nonprofessional, the "recruiter," the "interrogator?" We will see this whole range of interviewers from the highly skilled to the "deadwood" employee sent out to interview because the company has nothing else for him or her to do.

Step 4—Conduct a Job Search

With our credentials prepared and intensive background study completed, we are ready to begin the job search in earnest. Where do we start looking? Figure 7.3 gives a wide range of places to begin the search and a rough estimate of the likely percentage of success through each place or strategy.

Approach getting a job in a serious manner. We should be selective in the jobs for which we apply, but choose a range of jobs we think we would be happy with. For example, instead of being set on a job as a cost accountant, try to get a job with a good firm with the hope of moving into cost accounting.

When looking for a job, begin with the most readily available sources: friends, relatives, former employers. When asking about job opportunities, get names of people to contact. Do not write an open-ended letter to the personnel director or employment manager. Nothing sounds as impersonal as a "Dear Sir" letter.

A second source of employment contacts is placement agencies. Almost every college and university has a free placement agency that will provide contacts and interviews with prospective employers. Other agencies are connected with professional organizations for teachers, management majors, music majors, speech communication majors, and others. There are many "percentage" agencies that will place us for a fee. The fee is usually a percentage of our first month's or yearly salary. Most of the "for-hire" agencies have what is known as "fee-paid" jobs. This means that a company has either retained them on a fee basis or if we are what they want, the company will pay the fee. If we use a percentage agency, remember the following:

1. Many agencies charge a registration fee that ranges from $10 to $50 to discourage "shoppers" and to pay for the preparation of materials and records.

2. Before signing a contract, have an attorney, from within the state where the agency is located, read the contract for hidden charges (for example, so much per interview) or trick clauses.

3. Do not allow the agency to send us out to interview for jobs in which we are not interested or for which we are not qualified.

1%	1.	Professional Placement Organizations
2%	2.	State Placement Offices
10%	3.	University or Alumni Placement Offices
40%	4.	Professional Associations Placement Offices (AMA, SCA, ASTD, etc.)
25%	5.	Relatives
75%	6.	Professional Associates, Former Colleagues, Friends
30%	7.	Former Teachers
25%	8.	Newspaper and Magazine Ads
5%	9.	Mass Mailing to Job Lists
10%	10.	Mass Mailing to the *Fortune 500* List
50%	11.	People Holding a Similar Job
?	12.	Personnel Directors
5%	13.	Leads from Former Employers
10%	14.	Social Acquaintances (clubs, PTA, Scouts, etc.)
60% long-term 15% short-term	15.	Workshops or Seminars
50% long-term 1% short-term	16.	Take Your Classes on Field Trips
1%	17.	Create Your Own
5%	18.	Write Corporate Officers
60%	19.	Fellow Students, Fraternity Brothers, or Sorority Sisters, etc.
15%	20.	Voluntary Organizations (United Fund, Community Center, etc.)
5%	21.	Gimmicks (mail a folder showing your face in the Chairman's or President's Picture)
15%	22.	Work with the Local Chamber of Commerce
10%	23.	Start Your Own Business
2%	24.	Advertise Your Qualifications in Particular Journals, Magazines, and Other Publications

Figure 7.3   *Strategies for Getting a Job*

A third source of employment potential is newspaper ads. While perhaps not the most elegant way to get a job, it is better than being unemployed. Check through the ads and select the jobs we are qualified for. Write to the advertisers; be sure to include a résumé and a request for an interview. Few people are hired on the basis of the application blank alone. If we can obtain interviews, we stand a chance of selling the interviewers on us and our qualifications.

The percentage of success of strategies 1 to 4 depends upon our professions and the particular employment services. Strategies 5 to 7 may be good beginning points and sources of advice. Eight to 11 may prove useful if our searches are not very successful or if other strategies are not applicable for specific jobs or professions. We have placed a question mark by 12 because many personnel directors do not do the hiring and may not know that a very specialized or exciting job will soon be available. Thirteen and 14 are weak possibilities. Fifteen and 16 are sources for teachers who are interested in making contacts outside of teaching. Seventeen takes nerve but it may work. In 18 we might obtain a copy of the organizational chart, draw in a box with our name on it, and send the chart with a cover letter and résumé to a corporate officer. Nineteen has the greatest potential for a young applicant. Strategies 20 to 24 provide possible but limited chances for success.

Which of these strategies should we use? *All of them.* There is no way we can predict which strategies will land the jobs we want. Play the numbers game. Send out twenty-five résumés per week until we get some bites. We should do everything we can to get interviews. When we get interviews, we have opportunities to sell ourselves to organizations.

Step 5—Take Part in the Interview

Now that we have contacted the company and know something about it, we are ready for the interview. Realize from the start that our attitudes can make interviews enjoyable and profitable or miserable for both parties. It is like taking a required course or doing something we feel obligated to do. If we go into the situation with the attitude, "Well, I'm gonna do it, but I know I won't like it," we probably will not. If we enter the interview with the attitude, "All I want is a job, any old job," that is what we will get.

Too many students, even after completing four years of college, are unaware of basic social niceties in the interview situation. Be on time for the interview. Punctuality indicates interest and good manners. If for some urgent reason you cannot keep an appointment, inform the interviewer by phone immediately. Get the interviewer's name before or during the interview and use it. Be neat. Albert Einstein and Thomas Edison might have entered an interview looking disheveled, but few of us are Einsteins or Edisons. Philosophically it might be wrong to judge a person by how he or she dresses, but we in fact do just that.

Take our high school and college experiences, for example. When we entered a classroom and the teacher looked like an unmade bed, we probably thought, "Boy, what a mess! I can imagine what this class is going to be like." Frequently we were wrong, but it took time for that bad first impression to wear off. Interviewers react the same way and we do not have a semester to change our images, only a few minutes. A clean shirt, nicely pressed dress or suit, polished shoes, and combed hair do not require a big financial outlay. Most business firms are not interested in hiring clowns, so avoid outlandish makeup and apparel. A neat, appropriate appearance can add greatly to the images we establish at the start of the interviews. Research results stress how critical the first few minutes are to the interviewee.

1. Interviewers establish their biases early in interviews, and these biases determine the nature of their decision.

2. Interviewers are influenced more by unfavorable than favorable information, and the earlier in the interview the unfavorable information comes, the greater the negative effect.

3. Most interviewers make their decisions in the first four minutes, and the decisions are usually based on the absence of negative information and the interviewer's preferences.

Interviewer complaints occur when the applicant—[12]

1. is caught lying;
2. shows lack of interest in the interiew, merely shopping around;
3. has a belligerent attitude, is rude or impolite;
4. lacks sincerity;
5. is evasive concerning information about himself or herself;
6. is concerned only with salary;
7. is unable to concentrate;
8. displays a lack of initiative;
9. is indecisive;
10. has an arrogant attitude;
11. has a persecuted attitude;
12. tries to use pull to get a job;
13. has dirty hands or face;
14. is cynical;
15. is intolerant and has strong prejudices;
16. is late for the interview;
17. has a limp-fish handshake;
18. is unable to express himself or herself clearly;
19. shows lack of planning for career;
20. has not done research into history and products of the company;
21. wants to start in an executive position;
22. lacks maturity;
23. has low moral standards;
24. presents extreme appearance;
25. oversells case.

The interviewer's job is to get pertinent information about us to make intelligent employment decisions. He or she cannot do the job unless we are willing to cooperate fully. We should enter each interview ready to give freely of ourselves and our knowledge. The result will be a profitable interview for us and the employer. Research reveals that our backgrounds and financial status may affect the way we respond to questions. For instance, as our education increases, so does our willingness to respond to questions concerning personal history, interests, and values. Applicants with low levels of education think questions concerning finances are more acceptable than do applicants with high levels of education. Applicants from urban backgrounds think that inquiry into family background is more an invasion of privacy than do applicants with rural backgrounds. Urban applicants think that questions concerning interests, values, and finances are less an invasion of privacy than do rural applicants. The higher our level of income, the more favorable we look toward items concerning personal history and social adjustments. However, the opposite is true when questions concern personal finances.

Nervousness is natural. If we concentrate on giving the interviewer the information asked for, we will soon find our nervousness disappearing. There seems to be an inherent characteristic in questions that put us on guard. Perhaps our exposure to tests, questions in classes, the television image of the cross examining attorney, and the potential threat of revealing our inner selves condition us to react negatively to questions. Remember that almost no transfer of knowledge takes place without questions. The interviewer is not interested in getting information for a scandal sheet but is trying to get answers that will provide the necessary information to make a selection. The interviewer would not conduct the interview if he or she could get this information through other means. We have the right to refuse to answer questions we think are too personal, but these questions are rare. When we are asked to elaborate on information already in the interviewer's possession, we should not be afraid to discuss these achievements. This is not an open invitation to brag, but if we are good at something, we should tell the interviewer. Answer questions thoroughly but to the point. If the interviewer wants more detail, he or she will ask for it.

Answer every question honestly. Even the slightest diplomatic lie may trip us up later in our relationship with the firm. Start with a clean slate and no hidden information. If we are asked why we got a bad grade in history and if the reason is that we did not like the teacher, say so. If we quit a job because the work was too difficult, say so. Do not be evasive or vague, and above all do not blame others for our inabilities.

We may be asked questions that we do not understand. Try paraphrasing these questions in our own words or simply ask for clarifications. Interviewers assume that we understand questions unless we state otherwise. Suppose the interviewer asks, "What values would you place at the zenith of your hierarchy of values?" Now admittedly this is vague, but the interviewer probably has a clear picture of what it means. Do we? This question could have several meanings. Ask the interviewer, "Do you mean moral values, ethical values, or general American values?" Asking for clarification is far better than answering a question when we do not know where we are going. Never answer a question just to be answering a question.

Occasionally an interviewer will delight in asking questions that may startle or even embarrass us. Do not panic. Take a few seconds to think about the question. Suppose the interviewer asks, "If you could give one executive order as president of the United States, what would it be?" Do not blurt out an answer or say, "Golly, that's a tough one," or "Who knows?" If we cannot answer, admit it. An elementary school supervisor/interviewer for a midwestern university town used to delight in asking newly wedded wives of graduate students, "And what kind of birth control are you practicing?" Losing our composure in answering tough questions may cost us a job. Relax, think, and then answer.

Try not to overrate or underrate abilities. We should have a realistic estimation of where our abilities fit into the company. If we are not scientifically oriented or trained, do not apply for a sales job with a chemical company. Interviewers do not like braggarts or expressions of false modesty. If we are fairly good at math, accounting, and computer science, say so. We should try to be objective about ourselves and know our strengths and weaknesses.

Usually the interviewer will give us an opportunity to ask questions. If not, take the initiative and say, "Pardon me, but there are a few questions I would like to ask about the company and position." Some interviewees feel obligated to ask superficial questions if they have no important questions in mind. If we get this urge, suppress it. Our questions can reveal a great deal about our values, interests, and intelligence, so ask them carefully and thoughtfully. Get enough information from interviewers to make intelligent decisions about continuing our relationships with their organizations. Our questions should satisfy the question guidelines suggested earlier for employer questions. Questions should be open-ended, neutral, tactful, and job related. We should avoid a series of "me, me, me" questions aimed at what organizations can give us but not what we will give in return.

The following are typical interviewee questions:

1. What kind of support would I have for going back to school?
2. What kind of training program would I go through?
3. What methods do you use to evaluate your employees?
4. What is the normal salary range for someone with my background?
5. How much choice would I have in selecting geographical location?
6. How does the cost of living here compare with the midwest, say Minneapolis?
7. How much choice would I have in being transferred to another plant?
8. What are my chances for advancement with your company?
9. Do you pay moving expenses if I am forced to move to another plant?
10. What major fringe benefits does your company provide?
11. What is the average length of time between promotions?
12. Why should I go to work for you?
13. How old would my supervisors be and what chance do they have of being promoted?
14. How much supervision would I get as a new employee?
15. Do relocations usually mean a promotion?
16. Other than money, what kinds of rewards can I expect from your company?
17. Describe your ideal employee for me.
18. What weaknesses do you see in my background? In my training?
19. How creative can I be on the job?
20. Who is your biggest competitor?

Provided no decision is made at the end of the interview, follow up the interview with a note thanking the interviewer for his or her time and repeating that we would like to hear from him or her as soon as possible. If we have submitted no résumé, attach one to the letter. This thank-you note provides us with an excuse to contact the interviewer and to provide additional information that might help the company to decide in our favor. End the letter by offering to send any additional information he or she might like to have.

Here are a few additional observations about and guidelines for taking part in selection interviews.

1. Be interested in the interview, the position, and the organization.

2. Listen carefully to each question, and do not interrupt or try to second-guess the employer.

3. Do nothing merely for the sake of making a good impression; experienced interviewers can detect a phony applicant.

4. Do not prepare canned answers to common questions; the employer can destroy a canned answer with a single, well-placed probing question.

5. Do not try to become a stereotyped applicant. Research shows that each interviewer tends to develop his or her own stereotype of a good applicant and that these stereotypes differ considerably within the same organization.

6. Interviewers place greater emphasis on achievement, motivation, and being informed about the organization and the position than on academic performance.

7. Applicants who disagree with the interviewer may get the position, but they will receive a lower starting salary.

8. Applicants' decisions tend to be based on their perceptions of the interviewer's personality, manner of delivery, and adequacy of job information.

9. Although being interviewed by several interviewers from an organization may be more stressful than a single interview and interviewer, the first situation produces the most reliable results.

10. The face-to-face interview may have more impact on the hiring decision than grades, job performance, campus activities, and references.

11. Characteristics of a previous applicant may be as influential on an interviewer's decision as our own traits; in other words, we may be in trouble if the previous applicant was brilliant.

Step 6—Evaluate Each Interview

We should do a thorough review of each interview with the goal of repeating our strengths and eliminating our weaknesses. We must be careful, however, not to overreact to our impressions and the interviewer's feedback. Our perceptions of what happened during the interview, how the interviewer reacted, or what specific nonverbal actions meant may be exaggerated or wrong.

Here are some questions we might ask during our postinterview evaluations.

1. How adequate was my preparation: background study, credentials, questions?
2. How effective was my role during the opening?
3. How comfortable was I during the interview?
4. How appropriate was my dress?
5. Which questions did I handle well?
6. Which questions did I handle poorly?
7. Did I pass up opportunities to sell myself?
8. How thorough were my answers?
9. How well did I adapt my questions to this employer, organization, and position?
10. Did my questions and answers reveal my true interest in the organization and the position?
11. Did I ask questions that were job related?
12. Did I provide adequate information that was job related and consistent with EEO guidelines?
13. Did I obtain enough information on the position and the organization to determine if I want to remain interested?

Suggestions for Changing Jobs or Careers

Many people get trapped into a job by marriage, parents, or the diploma race—they needed courses to fill a major or to get a certificate and this led to a particular job. Too many employees are bored, restless and spend the greatest part of their waking hours doing something they hate. They kid themselves into believing their work is not boring or that all work is boring and turn to outside activities or the television set.

We do not believe a job has to be living hell. But let's splash reality onto the situation. Every job has routine or donkey work attached to it. Bosses are seldom perfect, but neither are employees. Every organization and job has advantages and disadvantages. If we want fulfilling careers, we can have them. However, it takes work, patience, and persistence.

A Career Plan
No organization can compete in a free market economy unless it inventories its assets and plans a marketing strategy. We must do the same, and here is a place to begin. Our purpose is to provide some general guidelines and suggestions; we might want to expand our planning through one of the excellent manuals or courses on career planning. Two books will help us if we have been fired, demoted, or are in the process of wanting to change careers: Richard N. Bolles, *What Color Is Your Parachute?* (revised edition) and John C. Crystal and Richard N. Bolles, *Where Do I Go From Here With My Life?*

Strategic Planning for the Beginner

Our first jobs are important to launching our careers; it is not fatal if we pick the wrong one. Select the first job as a stepping-stone either for preparation in that field of jobs or as a means for exploring a kind of industry or organization. Ask these questions about the first job.

1. Does it satisfy the *must* objectives?
2. How many of the *want* objectives does it satisfy?
3. What are the new skills, techniques, or experiences I can learn on this job?
4. Is it a stepping-stone in my career plan?

We may have invested twelve to eighteen years in education, so be selective. No organization ever has enough good people. Select the job that appears to have the most potential. Do not be stampeded by a fast-talking recruiter, and do not be arrogant about objectives.

During the first year we are with organizations, we should observe, learn, and make initial evaluations. At the end of the first year, we should examine our skills inventory and add new items to the list based on our experiences. Remember that in most entry-level jobs we will cost the organization money the first six months. If we wait one full year, we will be a productive employee and in a better position to make a judgment.

Do not panic if we find ourselves in a terrible setting. The worst thing we can do is to quit without having another place to go. Set a target date for leaving the unhappy situation and then begin to look at other job opportunities in a systematic fashion.

If we have developed mission statements or series of life goals, we are ready for the first important step in the evaluation process. (See fig. 7.4.) Assume that we begin our careers in our early twenties. Figure 7.4 will help us to visualize our career progress. The steps do not indicate the number or kinds of jobs but the levels of development within our career paths. Our steps may be more or fewer because of changes in careers, promotions, demotions, or other career problems and opportunities.

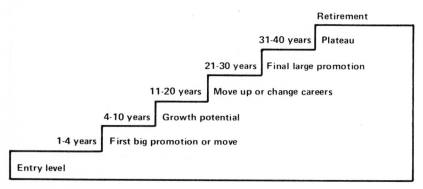

Figure 7.4   *Career Stages*

The evaluative step at the entry level is important. Now that we have had some experience in sales, teaching, broadcasting, or nursing, What are our feelings about our professions? Do we need more experience? What have we learned? Will this profession provide us with the satisfaction we need or want? While we may seek advice, the decision is ours. If we keep a goal in view, chart our progress, and take corrective action when necessary, chances are good that we will reach our career goals.

There are two ways of "getting ahead": the traditional "moving-up" approach and the newer "up-or-out" approach. These two approaches are diagrammed in figure 7.5. Both approaches have benefits and risks.

The traditional approach is to find an organization we wish to stay with and then get promoted. This upward movement is fine if it happens. Unfortunately, there may be someone, such as our boss, blocking our promotion path. The opportunity to move to another line or staff position may be unavailable. The traditional method assumes that each organization has as much interest and need to advance us as we do. It was thought in the past to be somewhat disloyal to leave one organization for an advanced position with another organization. The truth is that many organizations do not return such loyalty to their employees.

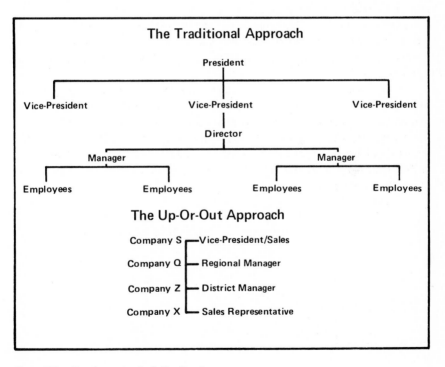

Figure 7.5 *Two Approaches to Getting Ahead*

Career planning, pathing, or development is usually left up to the individual; that is particularly true in education and government. So, we must take charge of our careers.

The up-or-out approach requires a willingness to move when we see a career path block. This approach gives us a chance to experience other organizations and to learn new methods. The major risk is making a wrong choice in a new organization. We may lose months or years in our career advancement and development. The learning experience, however, may be worth the risk. We work not only for a new organization, but for a new boss and with new colleagues and employees. These experiences often make us even more valuable for other organizations and positions.

The up-or-out approach takes nerve because it means risks of failure and several job changes throughout a career. Suppose we graduated from college at age twenty-three and set our career target to be a vice-president of sales by age forty-five. Our first job is a field sales trainee, and at the end of two years, we become a full-fledged sales representative. During the next four years, we continue to grow and to learn. We receive at least one top sales award in our district and we become one of the top twenty sales representatives in the corporation. At age twenty-nine or thirty, a district manager's job becomes available, but we are not selected. Everyone tells us how talented we are and to "hang in there" and our turn will come. Now it is either up-or-out. We put out the word to friends and other companies, look in the trade publications, and contact search firms. Within six months we have found a new job that meets our criteria: more money, more responsibility, a chance to learn and grow, and a whole new product line. Setting the up-or-out criteria is important. When we reach a level where we are making the stay-or-go decision, we should ask ourselves:

1. What are my chances if I stay?
2. What do I need to make me leave this position?
3. What kind of organization do I want to be part of?
4. If I make a wrong decision, can I recover?

Remember that it is our life and career. We each have 168 hours in a week, and roughly 25 to 30 percent of that time is spent in earning the money that allows us to live and to enjoy the other 75 percent. Manage a career somewhat selfishly. Look with some justified skepticism at the old organization myths that persistence can overcome all opposition, that the longer we are around the greater the chance for advancement, that hard work alone will get us ahead. View careers as journies that we can and should control.

Summary

The employment interview can be a productive two-way communication setting. Whether it reaches its goal depends upon the participants. Each must be familiar with recent equal employment opportunity legislation and recent research into the selection process. Both employer and applicant must be prepared and approach the process in a systematic manner. As an applicant, we must know our capabilities (education, knowledge, experiences, and skills) and our career goals before beginning the job search. We should employ a variety of strategies and sources and carefully prepare cover letters and a résumé, and strive to make each interview a sharing of information and insights that will allow employer and applicant to make the best decisions.

An Employment Selection Interview for Review and Analysis

This simulated employment selection interview is between two management majors at Purdue University. The applicant, Steven C. Mitchener, is applying for a position as a consumer lending officer with the National Department of Mellon Bank, one of the nation's largest wholesale banking operations. The interviewer, Mary Ann Ellabarger, is acting as personnel director and college recruiter for Mellon Bank.[13]

How satisfactory are the opening and closing of this interview? How well do employer and applicant questions meet EEOC guidelines and guidelines suggested for questions? What image does the applicant create during this interview? How well does the employer cover relevant areas of information? Does the employer probe sufficiently into answers? How adequate are the applicant's answers? How well does this interview meet the guidelines for structuring employment interviews? Does the employer control the interview too much, too little, or about right?

1. Employer: Good morning; Steve Mitchener?

2. Applicant: Yes.

3. Employer: I'm Mary Ellabarger, Personnel Director of Mellon Bank of Pittsburgh. Won't you have a seat? And how are you today?

4. Applicant: Just fine, thanks. I had a good trip out.

5. Employer: What I would like to do today is, first of all, to ask you some questions concerning yourself and your interests, then I would like to tell you a bit about what Mellon Bank has to offer you, and finally I will be more than happy to answer any questions that you have for me.

6. Applicant: Fine. I have been looking forward to the interview.

7. Employer: First of all, what made you decide to come to Purdue?

8. Applicant: Well, I'll go back to my senior year in high school. I took a computer science course in high school, and I really enjoyed it. I thought I would enjoy programming and data processing. In my decision to attend Purdue University, I sought out some colleges that I thought had good computer science programs. Purdue has an excellent program. It offers bachelor's, master's, and doctoral degrees in computer science, so I thought I would try it out. I planned to minor in business. Once I got here, I realized that computer science was not what I wanted to do. I would be cooped up in a corner, and I would not be working with people, which is what I enjoy doing more than anything else. So I switched my minor to my major and shifted to an accounting and finance major. So that is how I ended up at Purdue with the major that I have.

9. Employer: You say that you like to work with people. Why do you like to work with people?

10. Applicant: Well, it seems like my whole life has been centered around people. Through the activities and the things that I have done, I see that I am a very people-oriented person. That's something I enjoy; I can't explain why. I just enjoy working with people.

11. Employer: What kind of qualities do you think you possess that would enable you to work well with people on a job and in different situations?

12. Applicant: I think that in several activities that I've been involved with at school, I have learned to understand different types of people. You come to college and you get away from a very condensed version of people in high school. When you come to college, it's diversified. Suddenly you meet people from all different cultures and from different locations across the nation and across the world. This is something that I've learned to deal with, to work with many different types of people.

13. Employer: Um hmmm. Are you speaking of your activities? I noticed when reviewing your application that you've been very active in the Purdue Glee Club and Purdue Service. What is Purdue Service?

14. Applicant: The Purdue Service is the Glee Club Honorary. Within the Glee Club there are twelve servers, and each one heads up a committee within the Glee Club. We have public relations and campus relations, just to name a few. We are elected by our peers to head up particular committees.

15. Employer: And I see that you're the manager of the Glee Club.

16. Applicant: Right.

17. Employer: And what does this position as manager entail? In other words, what are your duties, responsibilities, problems?

18. Applicant: Basically, I act as a liaison between the director and the guys in the Glee Club. I'm responsible for lining the guys up, making sure they know where they're supposed to be, what they're supposed to wear at what particular time. If there are any problems that arise within the Glee Club, I take it upon myself, as my responsibility, to take care of these problems, to put the guys at ease, or to communicate these problems to the director. If the director has something that needs to be said to the Glee Club, he works through me, and I talk to the guys in the Glee Club and, if there's a problem, try to straighten it out or get the information that's needed to them.

19. Employer: You have been manager now for a year?

20. Applicant: Right.

21. Employer: What has been the most difficult situation that you have had to deal with?

22. Applicant: Well, like I was saying earlier, I think each guy in the Glee Club is a different person; no two guys in the Glee Club are alike. And you are going to confront different types of personalities and no one is going to agree on everything. So you have to learn to deal with different types of personalities. Someone is going to like something and another person is not going to like it, and you have to work with each one of these differences and you have to compromise and work with the guys in each case.

23. Employer: If I were to walk into a Glee Club practice session and choose maybe ten members at random and ask them to tell me a little bit about you, what would they tell me about Steve Mitchener?

24. Applicant: This is a kind of conceited question, I realize . . .

25. Employer: I know; that's why I would like for you to tell me.

26. Applicant: I'm sure they would say that I am a very caring individual, that I'm open, willing to listen to problems that they might have, that I do care about each individual in the Glee Club, that I don't show partiality to guys in the club, and if there's a problem, they feel that I'm open and that they can come to me with the problem.

27. Employer: How do you feel that these qualities or characteristics that you possess, that you can work well with people, will help you in a job with Mellon Bank as a consumer lending officer, which is the position you are applying for?

28. Applicant: I feel that not only the experience that I have had within the Glee Club but the people I have met when we do our shows has helped me to get a better understanding of individuals, the way they function and the way they think. And I feel that this equips me to work in many jobs. Specifically relating to Mellon Bank, I feel that it is going to help me in working with people, and helping me with the job so that when I come across problems, we will be able to talk about them openly and to get the solutions that are needed.

29. Employer: Very good. Why are you interested in a position with Mellon Bank?

30. Applicant: My major is accounting and finance, and I realize that banking is included in finance. I'm definitely interested in the banking field, and I feel that my accounting can give me a good background for a job with Mellon Bank working as a lending officer. And again, with my interest in people, I feel that I will be able to go out and work with people and apply my finance and accounting training to the job and to the people that I will be working with at Mellon.

31. Employer: Okay. Please tell me what you think a position as a consumer lending officer would entail?

32. Applicant: The way I look at it, it would be a job where I would be responsible for going out to different companies within the Pittsburgh area and getting them to take out loans from Mellon Bank. For each loan that I would get, I would get credit and I would be paid on a commission basis. I would enjoy a position where I would go out to get people to take loans.

33. Employer: So why should we choose you over other applicants for this position?

34. Applicant: That's a pretty tough question. I feel that the work experience that I have had, that I mentioned on the application, as a student service captain in one of the residence halls has helped me on a work basis, as opposed to being manager with the Glee Club, and has helped me to cope with problems in the actual work process. I've learned to deal with people and their problems and to come up with solutions. This experience, as well as being manager of the Glee Club, and a finance major with an accounting background make me a very strong candidate for the job as a lending officer.

35. Employer: You mentioned something about being a student service captain. Was this during college?

36. Applicant: Yes. This was during the last two years.

37. Employer: What were some of your specific duties and responsibilities in this position?

38. Applicant: I was responsible for about thirty-five waiters, I use the term waiters but they're not really that because it's a cafeteria, where I'm responsible for making sure that the meal is run smoothly, that the waiters know what they're supposed to do and where they're supposed to be, and making myself available for any problems that might arise. I make sure there is enough food on the lines and make sure that each captain is familiar with his or her job. I must be available for whatever comes up.

39. Employer: Going back to your education at Purdue, you mentioned on your application that you chose your major because you had a strong interest in accounting and finance. You've already said that once you got to Purdue University you changed over into this major. Would you please elaborate a little bit more on why the interest in accounting and finance?

40. Applicant: After I got here I realized that being in computer science was not what I really wanted to do. I'm people oriented, I talked to quite a few people who were in computer science and they felt that it was leading up to a programming job where I would be pretty much in a secluded area and I would not have much access to or spend any time with people. Well, after talking to these individuals, I was convinced that that was not what I wanted to do. So I shifted my minor to my major. I chose the accounting and finance major in the School of Management where I knew I would definitely be working with people and where I could apply my strong interests in finance and accounting.

41. Employer: How do you feel about the education that you have received from Purdue?

42. Applicant: Purdue definitely has an excellent management school. I have been very pleased with what I have learned at Purdue. I feel that my grades definitely show how much I have learned. But aside from the academic part, I have learned a lot about myself in terms of the way I think, the way I can function with people, and the way I can solve problems. I have learned to understand other people so much better and to accept their points of view because I have become so much more open-minded from my schooling and the people I've been confronted with.

43. Employer: And that's very important in the type of position that you are applying for. Out of those things you just mentioned, which is the most important thing that you have gotten out of your career as a student at Purdue University?

44. Applicant: I think I'll go back to what I just said. The one thing that really stands out I think, aside from the academic, is that I have become a much more open person. I feel that I can handle any situation, any problem that comes up, because I have become so much more open-minded. I'm open to different points of view and what different people have to say. I'm open to constructive criticism whenever I've done something wrong. I feel that I can accept criticism. If it's something that will improve my well-being, then I'm ready for it. So I would have to say that "open-mindedness" has been the most important thing for me.

45. Employer: Let me tell you a little bit about Mellon Bank and what we have to offer you in the position of consumer lending officer. You would be working in the National Department of Mellon Bank, which is one of the largest wholesale banking operations in the country. Our lending officers are responsible for all aspects of our corporate banking relationships. The scope of this Department's operations is nationwide. We do business with more than 90 of the 100 largest United States corporations and almost three-fifths of the Fortune 500. The department is organized geographically, which provides a broad exposure for you to the United States corporate market as well as financial intermediaries. Lending officers interface with top level officers and specialists in multinational and domestic corporations as well as medium sized and smaller regional companies. The training program that we have available for you when you first start out with Mellon Bank is a short orientation program lasting three to four weeks, depending upon how well you adjust and perform. You'd begin your development in the National Department as a credit analyst, and this initial assignment will provide you with a working knowledge of the basic methods and tools to use in evaluating corporate credit situations. You would be working closely with our experienced corporate lending officers who have been with the company for a while. They would help you to apply your skills and financial analysis early in your work with Mellon Bank. After you have completed this three- to four-week training program and gone into the credit analyst assignment, you would move into our National Department in one of the geographical lending divisions. You would be responsible for commercial loan and business division activities not only for existing customers but also for prospective customers, and you would then move according to your performance and your experience. Since all of our lending and operating activities do require extensive nationwide marketing, the position as a consumer lending officer entails traveling nearly one-third of the time. Do you have any questions for me?

46. Applicant: I have several questions that I'd like to relate specifically to Mellon Bank as a whole. You know as well as I do that over the last year the prime rate has fluctuated tremendously, and more last year than in the previous thirty years. Now, how is this going to affect Mellon Bank in the long run?

47. Employer: Well, of course, any change in the prime rate is going to affect any company. As far as Mellon Bank goes, we will not be affected as heavily as many companies because we are in the lending business and companies, as our customers, are going to have to borrow if they need money to meet deadlines. They are going to have to borrow no matter what the prime rate is. So in the long run it will have no effect on Mellon Bank's lending position or Mellon Bank as a whole.

48. Applicant: So you're saying that the prime rate is not really going to affect Mellon Bank?

49. Employer: Not in the long run.

50. Applicant: I know many states across the nation are now allowing banks to expand into surrounding counties, and banks do not have to limit business just to a particular county. Now, I know that in Pennsylvania banks can expand into counties surrounding their main area, the branches can expand, but they cannot go into the rest of the state. Should Pennsylvania pass laws that would allow banks to expand into other counties within the state, how would this affect Mellon Bank? What are your plans?

51. Employer: This would be very good for Mellon Bank at this time. We have made provisions to expand into other counties. Right now, as you said, we are waiting for the laws to pass. We have already planned out where to place new plants of Mellon Bank and, as soon as the law is passed, which is looking good for within the next six months, we will be expanding into surrounding counties in Pennsylvania.

52. Applicant: How is this going to affect your employment?

53. Employer: This will be excellent. We are recruiting heavily right now because, within the next four to five years, we are going to be moving people around within Mellon Bank nationwide. We do need young people to get in there right now, to start at the bottom level as you would as a consumer lending officer and to begin working. We will be opening new accounts; therefore, we will be requiring new employees because we don't have enough employees right now to expand efficiently and effectively. So we'll be employing many new people, especially in the area you're interested in.

54. Applicant: I would like to turn now to your training program. You mentioned that it is a three- to four-week training program. Is this a program that is designed primarily to train individuals or one in which you try to weed out the zeros?

Employment Interviewing: The Selection Interview

55. Employer: Well, neither. It's basically an orientation program. You'll be meeting people, getting familiar with Mellon Bank's policies and benefits, working with different individuals within different departments, and you will get familiar with the surroundings. So you're not just thrown out as a consumer lending officer and told to go to it. This program will give you some background. We do have a seminar to orient new employees. You will be trained at approximately the same time as other new employees. So you will be meeting the new people that you will be working with; you will all be in the same boat; and you will be getting familiar with some of the people you will be working with and under.

56. Applicant: So what's the basis for the performance appraisal in this training program?

57. Employer: Anyone that we decide to hire as an employee of Mellon Bank, as you asked in the first question, if they are a zero, they wouldn't be hired in the first place. I think that would be quite evident while just talking to them. As far as performance appraisal, when you are hired for the position you are applying for as a consumer lending officer, we already know in which department you will be placed. There is no performance appraisal in the orientation program. Like I said, it is designed to get you familiar with Mellon Bank as a corporation. You're coming into this completely cold. You know a little bit about the company on the whole but not much about the different divisions that you will be working in or the different departments. So that's all it is. It's just basically getting you familiar with us. You are not judged on your performance in the orientation program. We'll be showing you around the plant and around the grounds and explaining a bit more about our policies.

58. Applicant: So, as long as I were to contribute to the betterment of Mellon Bank, I would be assured of being placed in a management position as a lending officer?

59. Employer: Oh yes, because we're looking right now for people that are interested in this job, and that's what you would be hired as. But there's a process that you go through to get there. The credit analyst position is basically an extension of the orientation program, familiarizing you with our processes, how we go about working with our customers, and how you would contact potential customers. So, like you said, all it is to get you familiar with the company. You would definitely be placed in a management position in, say, the next year or two.

60. Applicant: That's all the questions I have. I would like to add that I'm very interested in a position with Mellon Bank.

61. Employer: I'm glad to hear that. If you don't have any further questions, I would like to tell you that I've enjoyed talking with you. It's been quite interesting. I feel that your qualifications fit quite nicely with what we are looking for as consumer lending officers. You seem to enjoy working with people, and this job requires a lot of contacts with people. I should be getting in touch with you by mail no later than the fifteenth of this month. I'm going to take your application back and review how your interests fit with what we have to offer. I would be able to tell you more then where you might be located. I notice that you have no specific geographic location on your application.

62. Applicant: That's correct. I will be looking forward to hearing from you.
63. Employer: You should be hearing from me within a couple of weeks.
64. Applicant: Thanks a lot.
65. Employer: Do have a good day.

Employment Role-playing Cases

An Accountant for a Metal Company

The applicant, John Roberts, is an accountant in his forties who has spent twelve years working for Hardshelled Metalworking Associates. Twice during the past five years a departmental headship has been vacant and both times an outsider was brought in to fill the position. The same thing happened a third time and John went to his boss to protest what seemed to be an injustice. A bitter argument followed, and John was fired. He is now about to talk to Howard Jones, personnel manager for the All-Metal Stamping Company, about a position similar to the job he held so long. He has a degree in accounting from Ohio State, a record of successful work in two positions prior to going with Hardshelled, and several of his suggestions for improved accounting procedures reduced office costs at Hardshelled. He is not quite sure what to say if Jones asks why he left his last job. He wants the job at All-Metal because the pay is slightly better than at Hardshelled, he has a family to support, and payments are due on a house and car.

The employer, Howard Jones, has a vacancy to fill in the accounting department. The job requires a full knowledge of accounting procedures, initiative, and loyalty to the company. There is not much immediate opportunity for promotion from the position, and whoever is hired will be in a dead-end spot for some years at least. The accounting department has good morale, and the workers get along well together and with the department chief. Howard knows little about John except that he is slightly over forty years old, has a family, and in general has a good reputation in the field of accounting. He would probably make a good man for the job, except that at his age he might be eager for a promotion. Why he left his former employer is uncertain, but he is certainly looking for another position or he would not have called in response to a classified ad. It would be a relief to fill the vacancy with a steady, capable, loyal man.

A Real Estate Salesperson

The applicant, Louise Wood, is in her late twenties. She worked for four years as a salesperson of women's clothing in a department store in Chicago. She was dissatisfied with the low salary, and six months ago decided to take a training course in real estate. She took the state test recently and passed with a very high grade. Now she is going to talk to Mrs. Wanda Connor, owner of Connor and Associates, a well-known realty company in Chicago. When Louise worked as a salesperson at the department store, she had a very good record, and many of her customers requested her to help with purchases. The store did not want Louise to leave but understood her position since it could not offer her an opportunity for advancement. She has a good personality and can talk easily with people. However, she stutters sometimes when she gets nervous. When she speaks with Mrs. Connor, should she tell her about this difficulty? Louise does not want to ruin her chances for the job, since she has a family to support.

The employer, Mrs. Wanda Connor, has an opening for a real estate salesperson. The job requires a person with experience in selling and someone who can talk easily and persuasively with people. Connor and Associates is run on a commission basis, and it offers opportunity for advancement. Mrs. Connor knows little about Louise except that she is in her late twenties and has a family. She knows nothing about her past work experience. Louise evidently wants the job since she called promptly as soon as the job was advertised.

A Car Salesperson

The applicant, James Miller, is a car salesperson in his middle thirties who has spent five years working for Earl Johnson Chevrolet. He was fired from the company because he lied to customers and contributed to the bad reputation Johnson's achieved. He is going to speak with Carl Williams, personnel manager of Manning-Macomb Chevrolet, about an opening he has for a car salesperson. While working at Johnson's, he had helped with the accounting as well as being a salesperson. He seemed able to help out in almost every position in the company. What will he say if Williams asks why he left his last job? He needs the job because he has a family to support and payments to make on a tract of land he purchased recently.

The employer, Carl Williams, is the personnel manager for Manning-Macomb Chevrolet and has an opening for a car salesperson. The job requires a person with experience in selling cars and someone who can be trusted. Manning-Macomb is a well-known company, and the people working there are paid well on a commission basis. Carl Williams knows very little about James Miller except that he has had experience as a car salesperson. He does not know why Miller left his former employer, but Miller seems quite interested in a position with Manning-Macomb.

An Assistant Sales Manager

The employer, Alex Jackson, is the plant manager of a large wax and floor covering company. His sales manager will reach automatic retirement age next year, and Alex will be promoting an aging person to the sales manager position. He is looking for an assistant sales manager with no less than twelve years of experience. Although age is not the most important factor, he does not want to hire a person who will be retiring in ten years. The job pays between $18,000 and $20,000 per year and has excellent fringe benefits. This job requires a keen competitive sense because of very close competition in this field. It also requires a person who can supervise approximately sixty sales representatives. The person hired for this job will have to move to Moine, Utah, the home office. Jackson is about to interview a Roberta Watkins who recently left a competitor.

The applicant, Roberta Watkins, was for eighteen years one of the top four salespersons for a sealer and wax firm. About three years ago she and another salesperson recommended that their company add a new product line consisting mainly of highway and building sealers. The company consented and gave Roberta and her friend two years to bring the new line into the profit margin. They failed and were fired about a year ago. At forty-eight, Roberta has been looking for a position, but almost every job offered has been below her ability and several thousand dollars below her salary level. She wants a good salary and a six-year contract. She also wants a responsible position and adequate compensation if she has to move. She does not want to admit that she was fired from her previous position.

A Branch Bank Manager

The applicant, Marilyn Haney, is a twenty-nine-year-old college graduate with a B.S. and a M.A. in business accounting and economics. She has held three good jobs with banks but has been asked to leave because of various involvements with married male employees. Her marriage is nothing more than a neutral pact between herself and her husband. Because of her family problems she is not always the easiest person to work with and she knows it. She has been out of work for about a month and needs a job badly. Should she tell the interviewer about her difficulties or let him find out on his own?

The employer, Arnold Jacoby, is in charge of a large bank in a large California community. His bank is branching out into the corporate loan area and he needs a young, aggressive person to head this area. He wants someone with experience and some education above the bachelor's degree. The person must have the ability to understand corporate finance and be able to deal with a number of corporate executives. He or she can select a staff, and salary is practically unlimited. Being the old conservative banking establishment in the community, its leaders do not wish to hire anyone who might damage in any way its image that has been maintained for over seventy-five years.

Employment Interviewing: The Selection Interview

Student Activities

1. Select twenty individuals at random. Ask them how they got their jobs. Compare their statements with the twenty-four strategies for getting jobs suggested in this chapter. Which way(s) seems best for which kinds of jobs? Do respondents suggest additional ways of getting jobs?

2. Contact your state employment office and get a copy of your state's fair employment practices legislation. What cannot be asked in employment interviews in your state? How do your state laws compare to federal laws? Which laws are particularly important for you?

3. Make a collection of application forms from various companies or organizations. What information is requested on all of them? What information is requested by only a few of them? What information is missing from these forms? How would these forms affect a fifteen- to twenty-minute interview you might conduct?

4. Select a person in your profession (a personnel manager, a school principal, a supervisor) who conducts employment interviews. Interview this person, asking what he or she looks for in applicants—what interviewing techniques are used. Compare what you find out with the materials contained in this chapter and materials other members of the class obtain. How can you account for the similarities and differences in the materials?

5. Pair up with another person and discuss your "mission statements." Develop a set of objectives for your next job. How do they compare with the job you have now or would like to have?

Notes

1. Ruth G. Shaeffer, *Nondiscrimination in Employment, 1973–1975: A Broadening and Deepening National Effort* (New York: The Conference Board, 1975).

2. *The Equal Employment Opportunity Act— 1972* (Washington, D.C.: U.S. Government Printing Office, 1972).

3. Michaele Snyder Battles et al., *The Manager's Guide to Equal Employment Opportunity* (New York: Executive Enterprises Publications, 1977).

4. *Analysis of Uniform Guidelines on Employment Selection Procedures,* New York: Organization Resources Counselors, September 1978.

5. Jerome Siegel, *Personnel Testing Under EEO* (New York: AMACOM, 1980).

6. Sandra Sawyer and Arthur A. Whately, *Sexual Harassment: A Form of Sex Discrimination* (New York: The Personnel Administrator, January 1980).

7. The research findings reported in this chapter are taken from the following: Roger N. Blakeney and John F. MacNaughton, "Effects of Temporal Placement of Unfavorable Information on Decision Making During the Selection Interview," *Journal of Applied Psychology* 55 (1971): 138–42; Robert E. Carlson et al., "Improvements in the Selection Interview," *Personnel Journal,* 1971, pp. 268–75; Robert E. Carlson, "Selection Interview Decisions: The Effect of Interviewer Experience, Relative Quota Situation, and Applicant Sample on Interviewer Decisions," *Personnel Psychology* 20 (1967): 259–80; Robert Hopper, "Language Attitudes in the Employment Interview," *Communication Monographs* 44 (1977): 346–51; A. Keenan, "Interviewer's Evaluation of Applicant Characteristics: Differences between Personnel and Non-personnel Managers," *Journal of Occupational Psychology* 49 (1976): 223–30; Manuel London and Milton D. Hakel, "Effects of Applicant Stereotypes, Order, and Information on Interview Impressions," *Journal of Applied Psychology* 59 (1974): 157–62; E. C. Mayfield, "The Selection Interview: A Reevaluation of Published Research," *Personnel Psychology* 17 (1964): 239–60; Marvin M. Okanes and Harvey Tschirgi, "Impact of the Face-to-Face Interview on Prior Judgments of a Candidate," *Perceptual and Motor Skills* 46 (1978): 322; Donald P. Schwab, "Why Interview? A Critique," *Personnel Journal* 48 (1969): 126–29; Donald P. Schwab and H. G. Hensman III, "The Relationship between Interview Structure and Inter-Interviewer Reliability in an Employment Situation," *Journal of Applied Psychology* 53 (1969): 214–17; John A. Sterrett, "The Job Interview: Body Language and Perceptions of Potential Effectiveness," *Journal of Applied Psychology* 63 (1978): 388–90; David A. Tucker and Patricia M. Rowe, "Consulting the Application Form Prior to the Interview: An Essential Step in the Selection Process," *Journal of Applied Psychology* 62 (1977): 283–87; Ulrich and D. Trumbo, "The Selection Interview Since 1949," *Psychological Bulletin* 63 (1965): 100–116; Enzo Vlaenzi and I. R. Andrews, "Individual Differences in the Decision Process of Employment Interviewers," *Journal of Applied Psychology* 58 (1973): 49–53; R. Wagner, "The

Employment Interview: A Critical Summary," *Personnel Psychology* 2 (1949): 17–46; P. V. Washburn and M. D. Hakel, "Visual Cues and Verbal Content as Influences on Impressions Formed after Simulated Employment Interviews," *Journal of Applied Psychology* 58 (1973): 137–41; K. H. Wexley et al., "Training Interviewers to Eliminate Contrast Effects in Employment Interviews," *Journal of Applied Psychology* 58 (1973): 228–32; Orman R. Wright, Jr., "Summary of Research on the Selection Interview Since 1964," *Personnel Psychology* 22 (1969): 391–413.

8. John C. Crystal and Richard N. Bolles, *Where Do I Go From Here With My Life?* (New York: Seabury Press, 1974).

9. See the following for self-inventory guidelines: Lois Einhorn, *Interviewing . . . A Job in Itself* (Bloomington, Ind.: The Career Center, 1977), pp. 3–5; Marilyn A. Hutchinson and Sue E. Spooner, *Job Search Barometer* (Bethlehem, Pa.: The College Placement Council, 1975); *Merchandising Your Job Talents* (Washington, D.C.: U.S. Department of Labor, 1975), pp. 3–5; Melvin W. Donaho and John L. Meyer, *How to Get the Job You Want* (Englewood Cliffs, N.J.: Prentice-Hall, 1976), pp. 111–13.

10. For discussions of credentials see Lois J. Einhorn, Patricia Hayes Bradley, and John E. Baird, Jr., *Effective Employment Interviewing: Unlocking Human Potential* (Glenview, Ill.: Scott, Foresman, 1981); and Donaho and Meyer, *How to Get the Job You Want.*

11. Harold D. Janes, "The Cover Letter and Resume," *Personnel Journal* 48 (September 1969): 732–33.

12. See for example Charles S. Goetzinger, Jr., "An Analysis of Irritating Factors in Initial Employment Interviews of Male College Graduates," unpublished doctoral dissertation, Purdue University, 1954.

13. This interview is printed with the permission of Mary Ann Ellabarger and Steven C. Mitchener.

Suggested Readings

Bassett, Glenn A. *Practical Interviewing: A Handbook for Managers.* New York: American Management Association, 1965.

Bermask, Loretta, and Mordan, Mary I. *Interviewing in Nursing.* New York: Macmillan Company, 1964.

Black, James J. *How To Get Results From Interviewing.* New York: McGraw-Hill, 1970.

Bolles, Richard N. *What Color Is Your Parachute?* Berkeley, Calif.: Ten Speed Press, 1972.

Crystal, John C., and Bolles, Richard N. *Where Do I Go From Here With My Life?* New York: Seabury Press, 1974.

Donaho, Melvin W., and Meyer, John L. *How to Get the Job You Want.* Englewood Cliffs, N.J.: Prentice-Hall, 1976.

Einhorn, Lois J.; Bradley, Patricia Hayes; and Baird, John E., Jr. *Effective Employment Interviewing: Unlocking Human Potential.* Glenview, Ill.: Scott, Foresman, 1981.

Hutchinson, Marilyn A., and Spooner, Sue E. *Job Search Preparedness Barometer.* Bethlehem, Pa.: College Placement Council, 1975.

Jackson, Matthew. *Recruiting, Interviewing, and Selecting: A Manual for Line Managers.* London: McGraw-Hill, 1972.

Making the Most of Your Job Interview. New York Life Insurance Company, n.d.

Rogers, Jean L., and Fortson, Walter L. *Fair Employment Interviewing.* Reading, Mass.: Addison-Wesley, 1976.

Shaeffer, Ruth G. *Nondiscrimination in Employment: 1973–1975.* New York:The Conference Board, 1975.

Performance
Appraisal
and
Discipline 8
Interviewing

The changes that have affected the hiring process over the last fifteen to twenty years have had an even greater impact on evaluating and disciplining human performance in organizations. Unfortunately, many organizations still do not understand how laws govern the appraisal and disciplinary processes. Ever greater numbers of employees are filing lawsuits against employers for equal pay, unfair discharge, and disparate treatment in performance appraisal.

After a recent argument with a manager who was being sued for disparate treatment, one of the authors sat down and reviewed the "why" of performance appraisals. Why is performance appraisal, discipline, and discharge covered by the law? Here is a quiz based on this review of research. Remember, if you miss *one* question in the future, you and/or your organization could be in for a lawsuit. Answer each question *true* or *false*.

Performance Appraisal Quiz

1. Performance appraisals are covered under Title VII of the 1964 Civil Rights Act (as amended) and the EEOC and OFCCP interpretations.

2. Only such traits as leadership, attitude, and loyalty can be measured on a performance appraisal form.

3. In order to implement a performance appraisal process, an organization must prove that it is a business necessity.

4. Discipline or discharge is not covered by any current civil rights legislation.

5. For an organization to use a performance appraisal system, it must be able to prove that such a process is essential to the safe and efficient conduct of business.

6. Performance appraisal, while not required by law, must be standardized by form and administration.

7. Compensation must be based on a performance appraisal process.

8. All performance appraisal processes must meet the general test of job relatedness.

9. While it may appear to be more difficult to discharge employees, they can be discharged for just cause.

10. Where possible, organizations should perform a job analysis to determine the criteria upon which a job can be measured.

Too many personnel professionals and managers miss 50 percent or more of these rather simple, straightforward questions. Here are the answers to the quiz.

1. True.[1]

2. False. These terms cannot be evaluated fairly or objectively. Other terms to be avoided are honesty, integrity, appearance, and initiative.

3. True. The organization must be able to prove that there is no other means of obtaining this data.

4. False. See a more detailed explanation in chapter 7, but all aspects of the employment process are covered, including promotion, transfer, training, and discharge.

5. True. Organizations must be able to establish a "business necessity" based upon the safe and efficient conduct of business. The organization has "to establish that there is no method for achieving this necessary business purpose that would be less discriminatory in its effects and that none can be developed. Otherwise, the less discriminatory method would have to be substituted."[2]

6. True. Unless this is done, it could be interpreted as a difference in the work being measured rather than in the actual performance of the work itself. This does not mean that we cannot have separate systems for salaried exempt (SE) and salaried nonexempted. But whatever the system, it must be applied equally to all classes of employees.

7. False. Not necessarily, but jobs that require the same skills, effort, responsibility, and working conditions (see chapter 7) should receive equal pay. If the organization defends its compensation program on the basis that it pays for performance, then the answer would be true. Bonuses and other forms of compensation may and often do vary from level to level and from job to job.

8. True. Not only have serious legal questions been raised about the validity and reliability of performance appraisal processes, but without a direct relationship to the job, a serious question could be raised: What is really being measured? This job relatedness is usually done through a job analysis.

9. True. Just as hiring need not be done because of race, color, creed, handicap, or Vietnam service, neither are we required to keep someone for these reasons. By the same rule, however, hiring or firing on a whim is no longer defensible. It is important that people who can no longer do a job be removed from that job.

10. True. A job analysis can establish if a person is being evaluated and compensated for the job to which he or she has been assigned.

Some of these questions and answers seem obvious, but we must remember that organizations and their representatives are expected to comply with these laws. The more we know about the employment process, the greater the chance that we will not get ourselves or our organizations into difficulty.

A History of Performance Appraisal

Performance appraisal was taken more lightly than the hiring process in the 1950s, 1960s, and even the 1970s. Organizations used one process for most performance appraisals. A form, similar to the one in figure 8.1, was often kept secret from employees, and it listed a series of characteristics the supervisor was to evaluate. *

The process evolved from a list of characteristics that served as guides for a supervisor's comments to the use of a five-point rating scale: 1 = poor, 2 = below average, 3 = average, 4 = above average, and 5 = excellent. Somehow the adding up of numbers was to make this process more "scientific." Some organizations used secret forms for specific levels of employees, and employees seldom saw such appraisals or knew that they were being done. There were obvious problems with this approach. Each supervisor had a different definition for each characteristic; one supervisor's opinion of an employee might be quite different from another supervisor's; and the rating process was often irrelevant to the job itself.

Performance Appraisal Form	
Name: _____ Department _____	
Appraisal Date _____ Length of Employment _____	
1. Character	
2. Integrity	
3. Attitude	
4. Willingness to work with others	
5. Creativity	
6. Cooperativeness	
7. Appearance	
8. Stability (Emotional)	
Total	

Figure 8.1   *Traditional Performance Appraisal Form*

*This form is a composite of many forms and does not represent any particular organization's appraisal method.

Some organizations still use this approach. They argue that the qualities and characteristics listed are important. No one can argue with this point, but what do they have to do with an employee's ability to get a job done? We should avoid "trait" or "characteristic" ratings in order to prevent troubles with employees and the law.

There have been two basic movements in the performance appraisal process during the last ten to twelve years. The behavior anchoring approach and the management by objectives (MBO) system are beginning to be used widely. Because most of our discussion will deal with the MBO process and performance measurement, let's examine first the behavior anchoring method.

Skills that are used on a specific job are identified through a job analysis, and standards are set for that job. Industrial engineers, who may also be involved in setting standards, often conduct the job analysis. Some sophisticated personnel departments are developing expertise in conducting job analysis studies. Typical jobs for which specific behaviors have been identified and standards set include key-punch operators (at so many strokes per minute), meter readers for utility companies (at reading so many meters per hour), and data entry clerks or programmers (at so many lines of code per hour). Usually job analysts identify specific skills and weigh their relative worth or usage. With this approach, each job can have specific measurable skills that eliminate game playing or interpretation by supervisors.

The major problems with this approach to performance appraisal are (1) it is extremely time-consuming, (2) not every job has measurable or easily identifiable skills, and (3) arguments arise when specific standards are set. There is an old saying that any motivated employee can beat any standard. This performance appraisal approach can determine reliably what a reasonable standard of performance is; however, even experts have difficulty answering the question, Who should decide the standards? Major advantages of this approach are that once a study has been completed, employees know what skills they are expected to have, their relative worth to the organization, and how their performance will be measured. The system passes the tests of job relatedness and equal treatment of employees. There are many jobs, however, that defy this approach. Such abilities as decision making, problem solving, and leadership must be judged by other approaches. Standardization of these characteristics is impossible. *

Why Use Objectives to Measure Performance?

When we consider the obvious weaknesses of the checklist system and the time-consuming nature and frequent impossibility of using the behavior anchoring approach, the most easily established system is the objective, goal, or target-setting system. Probably the most widely used method today is called management by objectives.[3] This approach not only meets all of the tests for a good

---

* Development Dimensions, Inc., the American Management Association, and other organizations conduct assessment centers that can be used to identify these abilities.

performance appraisal system, but most organizations who use it employ it as a good business planning tool, compensation indicator, and method for career pathing and planning.

Ideally, a MBO system should operate from the top down. The chief executive or operating officer should issue the basic corporate or organizational objectives to the officers, and these should be the bases for the objectives for the remainder of the organization.* This system enables the organization below the officers to understand the goals and direction of the organization and to plan accordingly. Here are some important guidelines for an MBO appraisal approach.

1. The total process should be valid and reliable. Although statistically not as sound as the behavior anchoring approach, a face or content validity can be established.**

2. Any system must meet the test of job relatedness. An objective setting approach can allow for the kind of flexibility that is needed by many managers to adapt the goals and objectives to a variety of jobs.

3. This process can be standardized but not applied rigidly to everyone.

4. It should be an open, nonsecretive process. With agreement and sign-off at the beginning and end of the appraisal process, both parties should understand what is expected of them and how measurement is to be achieved.

5. The goals, targets, or objectives should be measurable. Unless there are some means of measurement, no one will know what has been accomplished and why. If it is not measurable, it should not be an objective.

6. The goals, targets, or objectives must be set in a mutual top-down environment. Unless the persons being appraised participate in the goal-setting, there will be no commitment to accomplishing these goals.

7. The goals, targets, or objectives must not be too easy to meet or too difficult to reach. The goals must require the performer to stretch to complete them. If any system has built-in evils, this is certainly one of them. If we want to beat the system, we set a number of easy or difficult goals and then say, "See, I told you this would not work."

8. Goals, targets, or objectives must be few, well defined, and practical. Another evil of this approach is to list thirty-three objectives with subpoints for each employee. This discourages employees and the supervisor and gives rise to the criticism that such a system won't work. It may be the *use* of the system that is at fault, not the *system.*

9. In setting the goals and objectives, we must not attempt to measure everything and end up measuring nothing.

10. In setting goals, targets, and objectives, do not make the measures too precise.

*Most performance appraisal systems use a form of negotiated objectives so, in the strictest sense of the word, we are talking about general guidelines to be issued and the formulation of the specific objectives to be negotiated between supervisor and subordinate.

**Content or face validity is nothing more than being able to look at the content and, with our expertise, to judge it as valid.

Books on objective setting will give us additional guidelines, but these ten can insure that the targets we set are reasonable. An understanding of the performance appraisal process will enable us to gear our interviewing techniques to assist in such a process. The objective-setting stage and the evaluation of the performance toward these objectives, while distinct units, are tied together. The knowledge of this process is critical to insuring that the performance review is fair.

The Performance Appraisal Process

The performance appraisal process should begin with the setting of mutual objectives. This part of the process is the most difficult and time-consuming. If a top-down process is followed in our organization, our subordinates will meet with us in carrying out our objectives. But unless our subordinates have some objectives that are specific to their jobs, one of us isn't necessary to the organization. A reasonable proportion of our objectives to their objectives is about 50–50 or certainly no more than 60–40 in favor of our objectives.

There are several approaches that we can use in setting our objectives. The first is a group process through which we share our goals with our subordinates and then help them to establish theirs. This allows us to integrate the goals as well as to keep the group mindful of overlapping or interrelated goals. The knowledge of goal interdependency among our employees can go a long way toward creating the desired team spirit that will assure that work gets done in a cooperative fashion. The second method is to send out a notice and ask our subordinates to prepare goals for the coming year. Other methods include using the responsibility statements from their job descriptions, developing special surveys, or using a responsibility and authority chart to determine major objectives.

If we use the one-on-one approach that is the most popular setting, it may take as many as three meetings with our subordinates before we reach agreement on objectives and their accompanying measures and are able to ''sign them off.'' Most organizations that employ an objective format use a three-level sign-off to prevent the manager from being dictatorial. The interviews or discussions require both participants to have open minds. The biggest point of contention is how to make sure that the measurements are fair.

Measuring Performance

There are a number of sophisticated techniques in work measurement, so this discussion will focus on setting objectives. Let's begin by looking at the four basic areas of a person's work. (1) If employees are to accomplish anything on the job, they must have the **inputs** (equipment, tools, materials, money, staff). (2) To accomplish anything, they must do something with the inputs, and this is usually called **activities.** (3) Once employees have done something with or to the inputs and have performed tasks, there is an **output** in terms of results, outcomes, end products, dollars, reports typed, or some service that is rendered such as answering complaints or giving out information. (4) Something must happen to these outputs, and the reaction or lack of it is called **feedback.** The four major elements of work, then, are:

> **Inputs:** all those things an employee needs to do the assigned work.
> **Activities:** all those things done by an employee in order to accomplish the assigned task.
> **Output:** the end products of an employee's activities.
> **Feedback:** the reaction(s) to the end product ($+$), ($-$), or (0). No feedback is feedback because, unless we hear something, we must assume that the employee has performed at a competent level (CP = competent performance).

The model in figure 8.2 is an attempt to show how the four major work elements relate in order to measure the work of an individual regardless of the type of organization or work that is being done.[4] It works best in nonhourly jobs where rates and standards are not easily established.

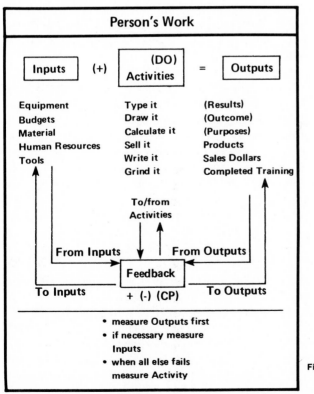

Figure 8.2   *MBO Performance Appraisal Model*

When employees come to work, they must have things to work with, and this area is easily measured. When employees do what they are supposed to do with these inputs, these activities produce end products that can be measured. We can measure how long it takes for someone to perform a task and we can count the quantity, quality, and cost. Feedback may cause us to adjust the inputs or make appropriate adjustments in the work being done.

Perhaps the most accurate and important measure to begin with in understanding performance is output. The second most accurate measure of performance is input, and we may subtract input from output. Finally, when all else fails, we can measure the activities people engage in. This may give us an indicator of how people have spent their time but not what they were able to accomplish with it.

This approach can be supported and supplemented if we keep in mind the following principles of measuring human performance.

1. *Always consider quality, quantity, time, and cost.* Almost any job can be measured by using these four criteria. The more of these goals we can use, the greater the chances that the measurement will be accurate. If we wanted to measure the effectiveness of a recruiter, for example, we might count the number of interviews conducted by that recruiter per hire. If we compare the number of interviews per hire, we might obtain the quantity and quality measure we need. We could calculate cost in terms of the time it takes to fill a position. A measure of quality might be the number of people hired by a recruiter that received outstanding performance ratings at the end of the first year. Whenever we can use quantity, quality, time, and cost, we stand a good chance of assessing accurately a person's performance.

2. *State results in terms of ranges rather than in absolutes.* Whether we use the terms minimum, maximum, or achievable or five-point or seven-point scales, it is best to measure human performance in terms that allow for freedom of movement and adjustment. Human performance is difficult enough to measure without trying to calibrate or fine-tune the measure at the start. If past history gives us some knowledge as to how to set the measure, we may want to tighten the range, but our recommendation is to begin with a broad range of performance that we can adjust as the performance period continues.

3. *Keep the number of objectives small and set them in a mutual environment.* If we are measuring a year's performance with quarterly or semiannual reviews, we should measure only the major or critical aspects of performance, which should number no more than six to eight. In some positions such as research or experimental engineering, we may have only one objective. If we are setting a half-dozen objectives and there is at least one major piece of work every two months along with work necessities such as correspondence, reading reports, and routine assignments, we have more than enough to judge a person's performance. We must allow for routine items such as attendance, staying within the budget, filling open positions on time, and other measurables that come up during the performance measurement period. The agreed-upon objectives should

comprise about two-thirds or 70 percent of the work, with other assignments that we can measure objectively comprising the other one-third or 30 percent. Obviously the employee should be aware of what we are measuring. This relationship between planned objectives and the ability to adapt to a manager's request is realistic and should not present a problem for most employees. The rater should not keep the 30 percent in reserve for punishment but rather to use it to measure an employee's performance of assignments that come up unexpectedly.

4. *Try for "trade-offs" between mutually exclusive aims or measures.* Suppose we receive this request: "I want you to increase production, improve quality, reduce labor, and decrease cost." A natural reaction would be, "If we are going to increase production, quality should not only stay the same but improve." However, when we attempt to reduce labor and decrease cost at the same time, we may create more problems than we solve. An objective that is too complex may be self-defeating, so we need to ask questions such as: What am I giving up to get what? What is the trade-off? Is the trade-off worth it? What are my performance priorities? What remaining aspects of performance may deteriorate by focusing improvement on one? Performance in the work-setting is a lot like performance in sports. Often when we concentrate on one aspect of our game, the remainder deteriorates. The best action might be to break down the goal step-by-step until we have achieved the objective.

5. *Where the value of the performance is abstract, initiate practices that make it measurable.* All departments, managers, staff members, plants, and so on believe that they are different, special, and cannot be measured. Measuring is often difficult, but anyone or anything that works can be measured. In a legal department, we might measure the number of cases won or lost and the amount in terms of dollars lost to the company. In graphic arts, we might measure the response time, cost, and customer satisfaction with the product. Some departments are more difficult to measure than others, but if we try, we can develop a measure that makes sense to both parties.

6. *If we cannot predict conditions upon which performance success depends, we should use a floating or gliding goal.* This means that as one part of the target grows or moves, the other part does the same. This comparative measure works, for example, with production changes when people say, "You can't measure us because the production schedules change so often." We simply measure the amount produced versus the amount scheduled. Our measure is comparative between what was scheduled to be produced and what was actually produced. Another example would be collections versus sales. It would not matter how fast or slow sales increased because we would compare the collections with the dollars sold.

Setting the Objectives

Almost every book on setting objectives begins with the statement, "begin with *to,* followed by an action verb that points the direction in which you want the objective to move." The measure can be a part of the objective or separate from it. Attitudes and feelings should not be parts of a well-written objective. We should avoid glowing language that tells us or the employee nothing about what is expected in terms of performance. Here is an example of how *not* to phrase an objective: To communicate a sense of teamwork and unity in order to insure a sense of cooperation and group effectiveness, which transcends the common daily work environs and eschews parochial interests. This statement says nothing and it cannot be measured. Objectives should state (1) the behavior or performance expectations and (2) the method of measuring the degree to which the objective has been accomplished.

Here are some words that we can use in formulating objective statements:

Achieve	Complete	Increase
Decrease	Obtain	Operate
Develop	Train	Review
Reduce	Lower	Gain
Establish	Maintain	Evaluate

Here are a few sample statements that would be good objectives. Notice that some of them have the measure contained within the objective.

1. Reduce the scrap rate on lines 1 and 2 by 3–5 percent before the second quarter is completed.

2. Establish a performance appraisal system for the corporation by year-end.

Outstanding performance:	completed on time, within budget, with 80 percent compliance
Average performance:	complete in fifteen months, plus or minus 5 percent on the budget, 60 percent compliance
Marginal performance:	no targets completed by year-end

3. Develop one subordinate to take my place by 1983.

The form for preparing objectives can be a blank sheet of paper or a simple form such as in figure 8.3. The back side of the form may be used to lay out developmental plans for the appraisee after the final review. It is critical that we review, change, or update objectives at least semiannually; we prefer quarterly. Now let's explore the process of providing feedback to employees about their performance.

```
┌─────────────────────────────────────────────────────────────────┐
│  Name: _____ Date of Appraisal: _____   │
│  Performance Expectations          Performance Accomplishments    │
│                                                                   │
│                                                                   │
│                                                                   │
│                                                                   │
│                                                                   │
│                                                                   │
│                                                                   │
│                                                                   │
│  Employee                        Employee                         │
│  Signature_____    Signature_____     │
│  Supervisor                      Supervisor                       │
│  Signature_____    Signature_____     │
│  Manager                         Manager                          │
│  Review _____    Review _____     │
└─────────────────────────────────────────────────────────────────┘
```

Figure 8.3 *Performance Appraisal Review Form*

Conducting Appraisal Interviews

Rapport between the supervisor and the subordinate, plus a fair and equitable system, will do much to make the appraisal interview easier for all concerned. Knowing what we are getting into aids us in preparing psychologically as well as factually. Earlier we suggested that we could not make you sensitive or give you good judgment. This is particularly true with the appraisal interview. Our knowledge of an employee's needs and a feeling for the individual can make a difference.

To prepare for appraisal interviewing, be sure that we and the interviewee are well informed on what the appraisal will and will not include. Be sure that we have checked all available information on the employee well in advance of the interview and split the interview into a salary discussion and a job improvement discussion focused on the future. This means more work for us, the interviewer, but it will probably result in more employee improvement on the job. Do not get so wrapped up in company forms that we lose sight of the individual. Give the employee a copy of the evaluation form prior to the interview.

For some reason, usually because personnel matters are low in priority or because the supervisor dreads the appraisal part of the job, performance appraisals are held on a once-a-year basis. This may be one reason for the negative attitude associated with them. Do not make the evaluation and self-improvement process a once-a-year tooth pulling. If we create opportunities for employees to communicate their thoughts, feelings, and reactions immediately, we will have gone a long way toward removing the once-a-year stigma from the appraisal process. Some people are self-evaluators and are constantly trying to improve themselves; they may not need as much evaluation as other employees. One employee may require a quarterly evaluation, another one every eighteen months. The point is, do not treat all employees exactly alike. Adapt the appraisal process to fit the employee.

Do not let the past hold a mortgage on the future. Remember, this session (some evaluations may require several sessions) is designed to enable the individual to improve and to advance as far in the organization as abilities will allow. While past performance is certainly a guide to how well a person is doing, this does not mean that the person will continue to stay at one level. Do not

Supervisors at all levels have found it useful to talk over the work periodically with each of their subordinates.

Performance Appraisal and Discipline Interviewing

become alarmed if an employee seems to have hit a plateau and has not improved since the last formal evaluation. Use the past as a yardstick to measure the future. If we go into the interview situation with the assumption that the interviewee cannot and will not improve, we are asking the employee to live down to our expectations. This is neither fair nor wise. There may be hundreds of reasons why the interviewee has not improved. Perhaps we can discover these reasons and help the person to solve them. If so, we will contribute to the individual's and the company's growth. Enter the interview with a positive attitude, an attitude that will probably transfer to the interviewee.

While a positive attitude and mutually agreed-upon objectives will help to make the performance appraisal interview a constructive process, there are additional guidelines for preserving an employee's self-esteem or self-image and making the appraisal interview a positive growth experience. We can damage employee self-esteem if we offer nothing but criticism that arouses anxiety, defensiveness, and resentment. When presenting criticisms, we should mention no more than two major areas of improvement. If an employee has six objectives, this is a considerable amount of improvement to expect in performance. Remember, performance appraisal should result in behavioral change. We can compound the problem by criticizing the highly important aspects of an employee's performance. If an employee takes special pride in an accomplishment and this is the one we want to improve, then we will have problems in improving performance. If employees believe that we are attacking their personality, character, or integrity, there may be no bases upon which to assist them in improving performance.

Employees may be frustrated when they receive no suggestions for improving performance. If we as supervisors do not have suggestions or counseling to give employees, where are they to get help? The aim of a performance appraisal should be to help the performer to increase effectiveness or to improve performance. Employees who receive no feedback that suggests ways to improve (with our help) will not change their behavior. The counseling or coaching role is critical, especially if we are to turn around bad performers and to assist our superstars in the learning-growing process. Some managers are natural coaches and have the ability to bring along subordinates and to teach them the tricks of the trade. More companies are beginning to offer internal courses in counseling and coaching skills.

Organizations expect supervisors and managers to evaluate performance. But the way they conduct evaluations can make or break future relationships. When the appraisal interview is over, supervisors and employees will have to work together; both interview parties should keep this fact in mind. Unfortunately our perception of our performance (as employee or supervisor) is not the best yardstick. It is not what we intended that counts, but what an employee believes we meant by a comment or suggestion—especially criticisms.

When presenting feedback about performance, phrase the feedback in terms of more or less rather than either-or. Making demands or issuing ultimatums may force employees to continue their behavior or reinforce the wrong behavior, resulting in what psychologists call "retrenchment effect." For instance, if an employee is told not to charge dry cleaning on the expense report one more time or he or she will be fired, the person may react, "If you think my dry cleaning charges were excessive, watch me get you on the next trip I take." An employee may get worse just to show that he or she cannot be pushed around. Try, "I'd like to see you become more involved in the budgeting process by (1) reviewing the old budgets for the past three years and noting the variances, (2) taking the new budget guidelines and preparing a preliminary draft excluding salaries, and (3) preparing to discuss the draft with me in two weeks." This kind of coaching enables employees to see, from our behavior, that we are interested in performance improvement. We have given more than generalized feedback about their involvement in budgeting, which would be meaningless without exact directions. Employees will seldom become defensive with a "more or less" approach. Suppose we have an employee who is involved in too many details. We may want to suggest that he or she need no longer be involved in the "day-to-day" operations. Be sure to specify what "more" and "less" mean in terms of on-the-job behavior.

Focus performance feedback on the exploration of alternatives for improvement, *not* on fixed answers or solutions. There are performance problems that the manager can solve by saying, "Don't do it," but today's employees often want to know what needs to be done and they want to select the method for getting it done. Ask the appraisee for suggestions. It is good communication, and the employee closest to the job probably has a number of good ideas for doing the job better. For example, we may be having trouble filling back orders and responding quickly to orders that come in from the field. We ask the employee, "What suggestions do you have for improving our order filling system?" This approach tells the employee that we do not think that we have the best system and shows that we are willing to work with individuals in order to solve mutual problems. If the employee has no suggestions, we might mention several solutions and ask the employee to comment on each. Solutions to performance problems are seldom cast in concrete or appear only in the minds of supervisors.

Focus on performance feedback that is of value to the *recipient*. Old style managers and performance appraisal processes encouraged the "boss" to feel that the once-a-year appraisal was an opportunity to unload on employees. The manager would play "dump truck" and, when an employee pulled up a chair, unload all the things perceived to be wrong with the employee. Not much improvement in job behavior took place under this system. The performance appraisal is not the time to take out our frustrations on employees.

Most supervisors and managers have favorite employees who they believe have the most potential. This is natural. However, we must evaluate employees not on a likeability scale but on objectives and measurable performance over a period of time. Playing favorites or games with the appraisal process can cause legal problems and cost the supervisor the credibility needed to continue to assist people in improving their job performances. When we are faced with an employee that we would like to "rip to shreds" verbally, remember that emotions go both ways. The employee may harbor the same feelings about us. We can gain nothing from verbal brawls.

The appraiser is responsible for controlling the environment of the appraisal process. If we lose control, we cannot expect the employee to sit and take it. In today's work environment, we need not like certain employees, but we must treat them in a fair and equal manner. This is, after all, what employees expect from supervisors; not love but a fair and just hearing concerning job performance.

Focus feedback on time, place, what, when, where, who, and how so that we can outline specific steps for improvement. Take as an example the employee whose work is always excellent but never on time or within budget. We have tried kidding and mentioning problems when they happen. Now we must confront the employee because the problems are barriers to the person's future advancement. We can use two basic approaches. The first is to confront the person with data in hand: "You were given project Q, due on X date for Y amount, and you turned it in on. . . ." Second, if we believe that the poor work habit is partially our fault, we may use a softer approach. The opening may be as important as the questions we ask: "I've got to admit, Bob, that whenever you turn in work it is always first-rate and with a certain creative touch. So I have no quarrel with the end product. But, as you know, if you are going to move into supervision, you must be able to respond to deadlines and to stay within budgets. Now let's talk about the last three projects. I'd like to know why, on three separate occasions, you failed to get the projects done on time and within budget?"

A textbook cannot give us good timing, good judgment, and sensitivity. It can only suggest that we provide a climate and approach that are appropriate to the employee's offense or performance error, the organization, and ourselves. Talk about what has been done in the past and what must be corrected in the future. Look toward how employees can improve performance for the benefit of the company and for themselves. Do not get caught in the trap of talking about *why* we think someone did something. Speculating about motivation, especially if it is negative, can do no good and much harm. Take as an example an employee who never gets anything done on time. We might begin to speculate about why the work isn't being turned in on time: "You're trying to make me look bad, aren't you?" or "You think I'm stupid and won't remember that I set X deadline!" or "You just want to show who is really in control, and I won't have it!" Some or all of these suppositions may be true, but what if they are not? We have gotten the interview onto a wrong track, and we may have difficulty bringing it back to a meaningful discussion of performance or reestablishing a working relationship with the employee.

Performance appraisals, like discipline interviews, must be conversations held in confidence. Do not allow the interview to get into ruts, such as "Well, I hear you said this about me," or "Someone said you made this comment about my last sale," or "If you don't like my work, come to me about it." Refuse to talk about gossip; bury it. We will lose if we engage in defenses or attacks on statements that may or may not have been made. The objective is to discuss performance and how it can be enhanced or improved.

Beginning the Interview

Suggestions for rapport building in employee selection interviews apply to the appraisal interview. Both parties know why they are meeting, so they should get down to business. As interviewer, we may want to begin the interview with a brief outline of how we want to conduct the interview. Remember, this is the employee's interview, so if there is something on a person's mind, let the person say it. If an employee says, "Why don't we talk about my production standards first?" what have we got to lose? It may disturb our interview organization, but it may create a more viable communication climate.

Suppose that we begin with the production record, which includes attendance, waste, and productivity figures. We have a production standard that rates anything below 90 percent of standard as below average, 100 percent of standard as good, and 110 percent or more as excellent. Have documentation rather than vague generalizations to support the ratings. This employee has an average production standard of 85 percent for the past six months. While this person will probably not dispute the figures, he or she may want to discuss why the standard is at that level. The way we approach the discussion of this problem will set the tone for the remainder of the interview.

Obviously, we should not begin by putting the person on the defensive. Take a positive approach and simply ask for a reaction to the rating: "Jim, how do you react to this rating?" Another approach might be to ask about problems encountered during the last rating period that might account for the below average rating. One supervisor we know believes that if a person has not attained an average rating, it is because the supervisor has not done enough to help. He would probably say, "Kim, what problems can I help you solve that will get us back to standard?" He believes that an employee's problems are his problems, and the sooner he can help them solve them, the better for all concerned. Furthermore, he believes that by genuinely sharing the responsibility with the person, the person will be motivated to do better. It is impossible to know all about any person we work with, and it is impossible to know all of the factors that create a below-average production level. By discovering a person's problems and counseling, we may produce a more productive individual. A person is innocent of laziness or wrongdoing until proven guilty, so do not let poor ratings influence our attitude toward or treatment of a person.

Organization of the Interview

Make our organization compatible with the interviewee. We may wish to begin with objective ratings or the employee's attitudes toward a job, supervisor, or coworker. Do not get into a lockstep pattern that prevents us from being flexible. The central focus of any appraisal should be the discovery of *why* things are as they are and *how* they can be improved in the future. In advising an employee, never *tell* him or her how to act or change until we have exhausted all other approaches.

Do not move to a new area without summarizing ("As I see it, you are going to. . . .") and making sure that all of the employee's questions are answered to the best of our ability. Try not to overload employees with criticism, suggestions, or praise. Do not give them all the information we think they need, but only the information they can process and translate into behavior on the job. Offer practical help. Be acutely attuned to nonverbal responses and, before changing the focus of an interview, ask if there are any questions or comments. Reassure appraisees that we are concerned that both parties in the interview reach a level of understanding.

Human Relations Factors

Now comes the most delicate problem facing the appraiser: how to handle the human relations factors that are so important in the appraisal setting. When we discuss personalities, attitudes toward co-workers, and attitudes toward the company, we are treading on potentially dangerous territory. We must decide the best method to use in activating changes within each employee. For example, we can be indirect with some employees but may find it necessary to be extremely direct with others. We can usually break attitudes down into two categories.

Job knowledge
Does the person seem to know the job?
Does the person seem to recognize and solve job problems?
Does the person view the job as important?
Attitudes toward others on the job
How does the person respond to the supervisor?
How does the person get along with co-workers?
How does the person view the company in general?

Remember that these questions are reviewed and answered from the observations and through the perceptions of the supervisor. The argument is often made that a supervisor should not rate an employee on anything he or she cannot observe or quantify because it is a matter of the supervisor's word or inference against the employee's word or inference. Naturally both supervisor and employee believe they are correct. Too many evaluations or appraisal procedures require supervisors to make judgments in attitudinal areas. Some organizations have a category "progress toward management," and the appraiser is asked to assign a percentage evaluation to the candidate.

Whether the employee's problem is bad breath, bad manners, or a bad temper, keep in mind that perceptions are individual and that defensiveness is easily aroused in the appraisal interview. Keep a sense of proportion about the task. A woman who worked as a secretary/receptionist had the habit of kicking off her shoes the moment she got to work and not putting them on until she had to leave the office for errands, lunch, or going home. Her supervisor said, in a very businesslike manner, that she was the first-line impression-maker for the company and that her "barefoot contessa" act did not make the kind of initial impression on visitors that the company would like. Therefore, she would wear shoes from this point on. Tact and face-saving are vital in such situations, but we as employers have a right to make reasonable demands on employees. Some circumstances require that we not beat around the bush.

Establish a sense of priorities about attitudinal items. Some attitude and personality problems can be taken care of by peer group pressure, others simply by pointing them out, and others require cultivation before curing. We must decide how important these attitudes, feelings, thoughts, and behaviors are to the progress of the individual and our organization.

If we are going to indicate that an individual is lacking in some area, we should have persons, places, and dates if possible. Make sure the factors upon which we are rating the individual are job related. Appraisal is not a chance to pry into personal lives or to chase down idle gossip. Discuss only items that relate directly to performance on the job or relationships with other employees.

Suppose an employee loves to break rules. The person never breaks any serious ones, but smokes in the wrong places, will not wear safety shoes, and has a chip on the shoulder toward people in authority. A declarative sentence backed up by our authority will probably not solve the problem. Be concerned about how our approach may affect the employee. Too often the tendency is to cite rules or laws to force the employee to behave. This passing the buck is likely to harm our own rapport with the employee. Do not ignore rules, but do not use them as a crutch. We may be tempted to use other employees to help us in working on this problem child. Do not yield to this temptation. The problem is between us and the employee. Seek advice if desired, but do not run the risk of making it worse by involving other employees.

When we have completed most of the interview, do not be in a hurry to finish.

1. Look toward the future and emphasize the employee's approach to self-improvement.

2. Try not to do too much in a single sitting. It is better to have two moderately lengthy sessions than one marathon session.

3. Be of whatever practical help you can. Make suggestions; give addresses of referral help (doctors, bankers, ministers) when necessary and asked for by the interviewee.

4. Close the session with an open door.

Closing the Interview

Suggestions in chapter 3, "Structuring the Interview," will help us to conduct and close appraisal interviews. The closing is as important as the opening. Be sure to leave an impression that enhances a sense of trust and open communication.

Do not leave the impression that we are "Glad this is over until next year," or "Well, now I can get on to some really important work." If possible (depending on company policy) allow the interviewee to change, alter, or put a note next to those items in our report that he or she feels strongly about. Employees have a right to believe that we are wrong. Give them copies of the rating forms and together summarize in writing a plan for the coming time period. If we must fill out an additional report, do so with care. Do not let the form force us into a mold.

Taking Part in Appraisal Interviews

It is natural and even expected that if we are attacked or perceive ourselves in danger, we will become defensive. Few interviewers would expect us to play doormats for unjustified criticism. However, we cannot all be boss, and perhaps we deserve some criticism. Self-improvement is a fine goal and, if we look at the appraisal interview as an opportunity for us to obtain information that can help us to improve, we will make the appraisal process more enjoyable for all concerned. The biggest advancement barrier to many individuals is themselves. If we are looking for a fight, are sure our supervisor is unfair, or think the appraisal process is a waste of time, we are heading for trouble. Psychological preparation is very important for appraisal interviews and here are some suggestions for preparation.

1. Study production, attendance, and other records. Self-criticism often helps to soften criticism from others.

2. Do not be too eager to defend ourselves until we have something to be defensive about. Review the listening principles in chapter 2.

3. Enter the interview with a feeling of cooperation that will enable both parties to reach fair and honest decisions.

4. Enter this experience with a desire to preserve our dignity but also to come out of the experience with information about ourselves that we can use.

5. Begin to think about things we could do on our own to improve ourselves.

6. Be willing to admit that we may be wrong.

7. Do not be in a hurry to get the interview over with.

8. If possible, try to check out our supervisor's mood prior to the interview.

9. Each of us has our blind spots and reasonable assessments of our abilities. Be honest.

10. What we are, what we think we are, what others think we are, and what we would like to be may be several different people.

11. Our supervisors will not see us through the eyes of our spouses, children, or parents. Do not expect them to.

12. The interviewer is not out to humiliate us but to help us grow for our sake and the company's sake.

Here are some suggestions to make the interview a productive session once it has started.

1. Answer all questions as completely as possible.

2. Offer explanations but do not engage in excessive excuse making or blame fixing.

3. Ask for clarification if we do not understand a rating comment.

4. Push for a resolution of our difficulties by asking for specific suggestions for improvements.

5. Do not be afraid to ask for help: Who can we see about our problems? Where can we go for additional aid? Can and will the company help us?

6. If we are confronted with a serious problem, how long do we have to get this problem solved?

7. Do not try to improve everything at once. Set priorities—first things first. Establish short- and long-range goals.

8. Keep our tempers cool. Telling the supervisor where to go may give us a great sense of self-satisfaction, but the person is still likely to be our supervisor after the verbal blast and the problem remains—or is worsened.

9. Summarize and state the problem or solution in our own words.

10. Put the best foot forward and try to maintain an ongoing relationship with the supervisor.

11. Be sure to correct any false impressions or assumptions the supervisor may have of us. If we can remove some misgivings about ourselves, the supervisor may see us in an entirely different light.

12. Close the interview with an open mind.

Much of this advice may sound like sermonizing, but it does work to make the appraisal interview profitable for both parties. When the interview ends, get down to work and start being a better person.

What We Know about the Appraisal Process

A number of researchers during the past decade have conducted studies into the nature of appraisal interviewing and the styles or types suggested by Gibb, Kindall and Gatza, Maier, and others. These researchers have assumed that if styles of appraisal interviewing can be isolated, if interviewers know which style creates anxiety and defensiveness, and (assuming they want to avoid these effects) if they know the style the interviewees prefer and why, they can alter their interviewing behavior to avoid anxiety and defensiveness. What, then, do we know about appraisal interviewing from recent research that should enable us to perform better in appraisal situations?[5]

1. Sometimes it is not so much what is said in an appraisal interview as how the interview is handled by the interviewer.

2. What an interviewer thinks about the interviewee, and vice versa, influences the climate of the interview.

3. The more an interviewer points out areas of needed improvement to an employee, the more threatened and, therefore, the more defensive the employee becomes.

4. The greater the threat the more negative is interviewee attitude toward the appraisal process.

5. An annual performance appraisal has little value in terms of actually improving the interviewee's on-the-job performance; appraisals should occur at least semiannually.

6. Separating money from job improvement seems to have a positive effect on the employee.

7. Subordinates perform best when asked to set their own goals.

8. Increased participation in the appraisal process tends to improve the worker/boss relationship.

9. The greater the criticism, the greater the anxiety.

10. Praise can create anxiety and defensiveness.

11. Interviewees in general seem to have no specific interviewing style preference.

12. A problem-solving style of interviewing creates the least anxiety and defensiveness.

13. Regardless of the style employed by the interviewer, criticism appears to be the key factor in creating defensiveness.

14. Interviewees accept and desire discussion of performance weaknesses.

15. Women rate achievements of other women less favorably than similar ones achieved by men unless evidence of outside recognition is available.

16. Male administrators tend to discriminate against women in promotions, development, and supervision.

17. Administrators tend to find males more acceptable for management positions than equally qualified females.

18. When raters evaluate performances using objective criteria, they rate (a) high-performing blacks and whites equally, (b) low-performing males and females the same, (c) high-performing females significantly higher than high-performing males, and (d) low-performing blacks significantly higher than low-performing whites.

19. Stereotypes held prior to the appraisal interview are usually confirmed during the interview.

20. The more prejudicial the information against the candidate the greater the stereotype.

The Disciplinary Interview

The disciplinary interview is a cross between appraising an employee's performance and counseling an employee to improve performance. It is probably the supervisor's most distasteful task. The good supervisor must separate the working world from what goes on before and after work. When the standards of performance are not met or the employee's conduct endangers other employees or herself or himself, the supervisor must take action. (The "disciplinarian" would be wise to review the information in this chapter on the appraisal interview and in chapter 9 on the counseling interview before conducting disciplinary interviews.)

It is crucial for performance standards and expectations to be defined and communicated to employees. Without standards we are supervising by whim and guess rather than fact and data. There are two basic reasons for disciplinary action. One includes all the areas called performance problems. When an employee's performance gradually or suddenly slips, the supervisor must confront the person. The problem may be motivational, personal, something in the work, or the supervisor. Drops in performance may be identified by swings in the employee's behavior. Suddenly a friendly employee becomes nasty, aggressive, or uncooperative. A good supervisor keeps an eye on performance indicators — attendance, quantity and quality of production, and willingness to take instructions — to correct a problem before it becomes serious.

A second reason for disciplinary action is the "troubled" employee. He or she may have performance problems, but the reasons are quite different. A troubled employee may have a drinking problem, a drug addiction, a marital problem, or a serious emotional problem such as depression or anxiety. An employee may be stealing from the company to support a gambling habit, drug addiction, alcoholism, or a boyfriend or girlfriend. Most organizations have problems in dealing with troubled employees. These employees need counseling not discipline (except in cases of stealing), but they may not take to counseling. The obvious conclusion, often reached too quickly, is to separate or fire them.

Conducting the Discipline Interview

Suppose we have identified an employee who has a performance problem. This person has been tardy the last three weeks on a regular basis and during the last three months has been absent four days, all Fridays. We have asked the employee to come in to see us. Here are thirteen steps used by a number of organizations in disciplinary interviews that might help in this situation.

1. *Keep ourselves and the situation under control.* We are the supervisor and, while we want to head off a problem before it becomes critical, losing our tempers or allowing a situation to get out of hand will not help. Never conduct a discipline interview when we are angry.

2. *When possible hold the interview in a private location.* Discipline interviews are often ego shattering. Do not worsen the situation by reprimanding an employee in the presence of peers. Discuss the problem in a private location where both parties may feel free to discuss the problem and where neither is encouraged to play to an audience.

3. *When severe discipline problems arise, it may be wise to delay a confrontation with an employee or to obtain assistance.* If two employees are caught fighting on a dock, in the plant, or in another public place, have them report to the office or send them home and have them come in the next day.

Never conduct a discipline interview when you are angry, and when possible, hold the interview in a private location.

Most organizations forbid drinking or carrying firearms on the job. In such cases, call security, the local law enforcement agency, or send the persons home. Have them driven if they are drunk; we do not want lawsuits.

4. *When we are face to face, focus on this specific situation but refer to previous encounters.* Deal with facts such as absence or time reports, witnesses to the event, films made by our security department showing the thefts. If we have taken previous action (for example, a one-day suspension from work), review the record. Do not allow the situation to become a trading contest: "Well look at all of the times I have been on time," or "How come the other guys get away with it?" Talk about *this situation* and *this employee* right *now.*

5. *If necessary, have a witness and perhaps a union representative.* The witness should be another supervisor. Using an employee to testify against another employee can be very dangerous. The union contract may spell out the employee's right to representation, so be sure to follow this procedure. If time permits, have the witness detail the events in writing: names, dates, locations, others involved, weather, and anything else that might be important.

6. *Write down all available facts.* Unions, EEOC, and lawyers make it important that we have complete and accurate records. Take careful notes. Time and date all material because it may be used later.

7. *Do not use accusatory statements or words such as:* "You are lying aren't you?" "Admit you stole those tools," "Cheater," "Thief," "Drunk." We as supervisors cannot make medical diagnoses of drunkenness or drug addiction, so we must eliminate these words from our vocabularies. Point to facts and leave medical judgments to professionals.

8. *Use or preface remarks with phrases such as:* "From what I know
. . . ," "According to your attendance report . . . ," "As I understand it
. . . ," "I have observed . . . ," "The information I have. . . ." These prefaces force us to be factual and do not give an employee the feeling he or she is guilty until proven innocent.

9. *Ask questions that allow the person to express feelings or explain behavior:* "Tell me what happened . . . ," "Why do you feel that way . . . ?" "What was your reaction . . . ?" "When he said that, what did you . . . ?" Open questions allow us to get to the facts with some objectivity. We need and should want the employee's feelings and explanations.

10. *Avoid verbalizing conclusions during the interview.* A flash statement or hastily drawn conclusion may create problems. Some organizations train their supervisors to use standard statements under particular circumstances. If we are sending an employee off the job or ordering the employee home, we may say: "I do not believe you are in condition to work. I am sending you home and I want you to report in my office tomorrow at . . . ," or "I want you to go to medical services and have a test made. When you return, bring a slip from the company doctor," or "I am sending you off the job. Call me tomorrow at nine, and I will tell you what action I plan to take." This last statement gives us time to talk with others about what can and should be done in this situation. It also provides for a cooling-off period for all concerned.

11. *Conclude the interview in neutral.* If discipline is appropriate, give it, but delaying the action may enable us to think more clearly about the entire case. Be sure to follow the requirements of the union contract if the employee is a member of the union.

12. *Be consistent with the union contract, the employee, and other employees.* Organizations usually set up specific disciplinary actions for specific offenses. Theft, except under very unusual circumstances, is usually grounds for automatic dismissal. Employees with alcohol and drug problems are usually counseled the first time and fired the second time. Whatever the rules, be sure they are applied equally to all employees.

13. *Take extensive notes and have them initialed by the witness and the employee.* Some employees will not sign their names to these statements. While it is not necessary to get the employee's statement and signature, it would be a plus if the situation goes to arbitration or a court of law.

Each organization must have ways, just as society does, of dealing with persons who cannot or will not go along with the rules. Establish discipline policies and make them known to all employees. Employees deserve to be protected from an unethical supervisor just as the company must protect itself from uncooperative employees. These thirteen steps are not magic, but they can help us to conduct a discipline interview that will enable us to glean the important facts and make the necessary decisions.

Summary

When making judgments about an employee's performance, base judgments and decisions upon a set of established objectives or standards. Apply the same objectives or standards equally to all employees. Research and good sense tell us to separate appraisal, promotion, salary, and discipline discussions. Effective appraisal interviews should occur at set intervals, at least semiannually. Promotion, salary, and discipline interviews tend to be situational; they occur when there is a need. We should deal with discipline problems before they become serious barriers to an employee's work or association with our organization.

Flexibility or willingness to change our minds in light of new evidence is probably the biggest key to taking part in or conducting performance interviews. This flexibility needs to be tempered with some understanding and tolerance for differences in individuals. The appraisal process must be viewed as an ongoing process with no particular beginning or ending. Employees and supervisors are constantly being judged by the people around them. If they get insights into their behavior and how it affects others, they can modify their behavior and be better persons and employees or supervisors.

An Appraisal Interview for Review and Analysis

The interviewer is the night supervisor for a medium-sized (500-employee) paper products firm and is conducting a performance review with John Xavier. John has been told that he will be moved up to pressman three (on a five-step scale) with an increase of 12 cents per hour above the cost-of-living increase. John is neither an exceptional employee nor below average. He gets the job done. In the last two to three months, however, he has been unpleasant, uncommunicative, and at times belligerent. Beverly Yeoman, the night plant supervisor, is a no-nonsense, undiplomatic person.

Is this appraisal interview closest to the traditional or the MBO approach to appraisals? How would you evaluate the communicative abilities of supervisor and employee? Which of the supervisor's questions "provoke" the employee? How would you alter the supervisor's questions and statements? Does the employee "settle down" and reveal true feelings because of or in spite of the supervisor? Evaluate this employee using both the MBO and the traditional forms included in this chapter. Which did you find most satisfactory and why?

1. Supervisor: Well John, we got the salary stuff taken care of several weeks ago, and now I'm supposed to do the other part of your appraisal. It says on my guide for doing this that I should ask the employee if he has any questions. Well, do you?

2. Employee: (grumpily) No! Not right now.

3. Supervisor: If you do, just let 'em out and we'll talk about 'em. None, uh? Okay. Let's start with your production figures. You started out with a bang and were 10 percent above standard for the first seven pay periods and then you fell down in late September. Why?

4. Employee: Well, I did one hell of a job from the end of July until September, didn't I I! I mean . . . at least it was above average.

5. Supervisor: Yes! But why the drop off?

6. Employee: I don't know. I guess I got that safety award and the raise to pressman two and I wanted to show you I deserved it. See, I was hoping to get to pressman three in six months, and I thought if I hustled my tail that my foreman or you might promote me sooner.

7. Supervisor: Now that can't be the only reason. Come on. Are you having trouble with your wife or something?

8. Employee: No! I think with the kids going back to school and my wife taking a part-time job, I just kind of let things slide. (long pause) No, nothing to speak of . . . I mean . . . no real trouble, just a lot of little things.

9. Supervisor: Now you're sure?

10. Employee: (rather irritably) Yes! Yes, I'm sure. Why?

11. Supervisor: No real reason. But I thought Dan, your foreman, or I might be able to give you a hand.

12. Employee: No. (long pause) No I don't think so. . . .

13. Supervisor: Okay. Then in mid-November you began to pick up your rate of production and by February you were leading everyone on your shift. You want to comment on that?

14. Employee: Why should I?

15. Supervisor: You don't have to, but I was wondering what set you on fire. You really produced between February and April. See here . . . you were 23 percent above standard. That's great.

16. Employee: Yes, I guess it was that good. So . . . ?

17. Supervisor: Well, we'd like to get that kind of production out of you all the time.

18. Employee: (laughing) Yeah, I'll bet you would. The more I make the more you make, or something like that. Why should I kill myself for a once-a-year nothing raise?

19. Supervisor: You think 12 cents above the cost of living is a nothing raise? Maybe that's why you've dropped below standard since April.

20. Employee: Now that's really interesting! If I bust my butt for you, I'm a real champ, but when I fall below standard, I'm a below average man. Did you ever think that some of us are tired of you pushing production all the damn time?

21. Supervisor: Now wait a minute John! I didn't mean to climb all over you about production. But you yourself admitted that you wanted to be promoted earlier, and we sure aren't going to promote the average worker. You've shown us that you can do much better than average work and we'd like to see you be more consistent. Let's face it, the better you do the better the company does . . . for that matter, the better we all do.

Performance Appraisal and Discipline Interviewing

22. Employee: Yeah, sure, and you get the credit for my work.

23. Supervisor: Right! But *only* indirectly. Not only does the company do better, but you do better. Now let me straighten you out on this "who gets the credit" bit. Your production records are yours, and they are what we—Dan and I—look at when we are promoting people to group leaders and foremen. Sure I get the credit for your production, but I also get blamed if you aren't producing. Maybe this is why your attitude has been so bad lately.

24. Employee: Well I'll be damned! If it isn't my production, it's my attitude. Are you through with me? I've got work to do.

25. Supervisor: No! I'm not through with you. Look John, I'm trying to see if I can find out how to help you get that foreman's job. I really would like you to take my job someday. Now let's calm down and see if we can accomplish something from this appraisal.

26. Employee: If you're interested in me, like you say, you sure have a funny way of showing it. No matter what I say, you've got an answer.

27. Supervisor: John you know me well enough to know that I'm not the smartest *&#?/! in the world and maybe I am too blunt, but I've got nothing against you. I just want to know why you've been so grumpy the last month or so. You haven't been yourself.

28. Employee: You tell me I'm not myself. Don't start that snow job on me . . . who do you think you're kidding?

29. Supervisor: (surprised) What do you mean?

30. Employee: First, you don't like my production, then it's my attitude, and now I'm grumpy. And then you say you're really interested in me. You've got a queer way of showing it!

31. Supervisor: John, I think your work might not be as good because you've got something on your mind. If I can help you, I will. Come on John . . . we've known and worked together for several years now and have never gotten mad at each other. How can I help you?

32. Employee: You want to pry into my private life so you can pass it on to that foreman of mine. No thanks.

33. Supervisor: Somewhere we got off the track here, and I really think we need to get this straightened out. You seem to have some problems that are hurting your work. I want to help you with them. Now come on . . . what seems to be the problem?

34. Employee: You only care about production. Why should I tell you my problems?

35. Supervisor: Well, first, I do care because we hate to see a good employee go sour. And I just might be able to give you some help or advice. If I'm being too hard, it's only because I get my butt kicked when production goes down, so I guess I'm too interested in it.

36. Employee: Yeah, if you didn't ride us so much, we might feel like talking to you. But every time you're around my foreman, Dan, is always uptight with us and pushing production. Maybe if you took time to get to know us common folks, we might be able to talk with you.

37. **Supervisor:**	Well, how do you expect me to find the time with everything I need to do? Maybe we need to have these sessions more often.
38. **Employee:**	Yeah, I suppose, but it isn't so much that as it is the production push.
39. **Supervisor:**	Well, I'll make you a deal. You level with me about what is really bothering you, and I'll get off the production kick.
40. **Employee:**	Well, maybe you could help, but I sure don't want Dan to find out about this!
41. **Supervisor:**	Don't worry; I won't tell him. Now what is bothering you?
42. **Employee:**	Well, I've got some money problems; that's why my wife had to take a part-time job. I could really use $3,000, and most of my troubles would be over.
43. **Supervisor:**	Well . . . have you tried to get a loan from the credit union?
44. **Employee:**	No, I'm not a member and, besides, if I borrow from the company, then everyone will know I've got problems. I don't want everybody prying into my business.
45. **Supervisor:**	I can provide you with an application and we can set it up so it will be taken out of your pay. Neither Dan nor anybody else on the night shift will be aware of the loan. No one in the credit union will be spreading the gossip either. Why don't you take this application with you and bring it back tomorrow?
46. **Employee:**	You'll keep this under your hat? I mean it!
47. **Supervisor:**	Sure I will. Why don't we make an appointment for about two weeks from now so we can finish talking about your progress?
48. **Employee:**	Okay, but no one had better find out.
49. **Supervisor:**	Don't worry John; I promise that no one will. See you in two weeks.
50. **Employee:**	Okay Beverly . . . and thanks.

Appraisal and Disciplinary Role-playing Cases

A Recreation Department Assistant

The interviewer, Mac Roberts, is the director of a city recreation department. His assistant director is a young college graduate with a major in recreation. There are eight full-time members on the recreation staff and a large group of part-time or volunteer workers. Mac is in his early forties and has been involved in physical education, recreation, and industrial education most of his life. He has built a good, working relationship with the local high schools and industries. Jim Morrison, his assistant, has been with the department for one year and has been eased into dealing with local industry. Much to Mac's amazement, he has received several phone calls complaining about Jim putting pressure on local industries and retailers to donate equipment. During his job performance review, Mac intends to resolve this problem.

The interviewee would like the recreation department to have better and more up-to-date equipment. He thinks some of the local merchants and industries who make money off the kids should donate some new equipment each year. He has been calling on them to see if they will loosen up their purse strings. He has hinted that kids should support only those merchants and industries that support them. Jim is up for his first performance review and, while not unhappy with the job, feels he could use more help and support.

An Instructor in a Small College

The interviewer, Donna Hoosier, is the chairperson of the history department at a small college. The college prides itself on its outstanding teachers. Donna Hoosier has instituted, with the help and approval of her staff, an annual review of each history staff member and conducts the appraisals herself. The results of each review are noted and placed in the professor's open personnel file. She is interviewing Harry Lackington, who seems to be an extremely weak teacher and to have problems relating to students. Harry has ranked lowest on student evaluations for the entire campus and has flunked more students than the other six members of the History Department combined. He is untenured.

The interviewee, Harry Lackington, is in his mid-thirties and thinks he has found a place where he can teach and enjoy life. He previously taught high school for twelve years and is fed up with spoon-feeding kids. He does his job, and he wants plenty of time to play tennis, read, and take some courses toward his doctorate. He is strongly opposed to the evaluation system but has to remain silent until he gets tenure. He does not like the idea of a performance review and plans to say so during the appraisal interview.

A Secretary in Industry

The interviewer, Max Johnson, is forty-three years old and manager of an office of eight secretaries. The company produces products for office and commercial use. This plant has a dozen salespersons on the road, and each secretary in the office is assigned a salesperson or two and several distributors. Ability to handle the telephone and people is crucial. When an account calls directly to the factory, the salesperson assigned to that territory is given the commission. It is important that the secretary be accurate in recording the order and to whom the commission is to be given. Max is about to interview Sarah Randolph. She has been with the company nearly two years and is above average in performance. Recently, however, she has cost the company money because she is inaccurate in recording phone orders. She is terrible on details, causing the wrong quantities and items to be shipped.

The interviewee, Sarah Randolph, is a college graduate in her early twenties. She turns out twice the volume of most employees, but some of it must be done over. She is pleasant and enjoys her work. She loves to talk to the salespersons on the phone, especially concerning the big accounts. Lately, however, one of the married salespersons has been driving her up the wall. He calls her at least twice a day, mails her funny cards, and gives her silly presents. Quite recently he has been stopping by her apartment unannounced. Her frustration level has been reached. She does not want to be a tell-all to the boss, to get the salesperson in trouble with his wife, or to tell him off. She knows her work has been affected. Should she tell the truth during the appraisal interview?

An Hourly Worker

The interviewer, Marie Pauling, is a salesperson who has just recently been converted to assistant personnel manager. Because of a recent turnover in plant personnel, she has been assigned to conduct performance reviews of several hourly workers. She is interviewing Maud Raston who has just completed her six-month probation period. Her production record is above average, her waste is within the prescribed limits, and her attendance is normal. But she is a chronic bitcher. She complains about the insurance plan, the vending machines, the material handlers, the water fountains, and the supervision. She is constantly throwing suggestions into the suggestion box and is a persistent cloud of gloom.

The interviewee, Maud Raston, had to go to work because of her husband's back trouble. While she does not mind working, she hates being forced into it. Doctors tell her that it will be two or three years before her husband can go back to construction work. Until then she will be the sole support of her family. She dislikes people who do not speak their minds. While this is not a bad place to work, it is not a good one either. She is surprised that some people who work with her have been at the job for ten, fifteen, or twenty years. She complains a lot but does not really mean it. Lately some of the women on her shift have been giving her the cold shoulder.

A Fashion Manager

The interviewer, Mary Alice Tame, is the manager of a large women's department in a major metropolitan department store. She is ambitious, competitive, and hopes to become the head buyer for the entire department store chain. She has forty-three people working for her in three areas. The big turnover is the college shop. The new group leader (her name for manager) of this area is a young college graduate named Linda Wakefield. She is beautiful, efficient, and extremely bossy. She had two years of experience at a competitor and, during the year she has just completed with Tame's store, has improved her area's business by 13 percent. She is an excellent merchandiser, but complaints have reached Tame that she spends considerable company time with the male trainees and is occasionally more than friendly with some members of management. How can Tame correct her without losing her?

The interviewee, Linda Wakefield, is twenty-five but looks nineteen. She is tremendously proud of her figure and tries to dress to show it off. After all, she feels, people in the fashion business should be a picture of fashion. She wants to be a big success in fashion retailing. She spends long hours at night keeping up on the latest fabrics, trends, and designs. During college, sororities,

Performance Appraisal and Discipline Interviewing

classes, and beauty contests kept her too busy for much socializing. Now that she is making a good living she intends to make up for lost time. Her feeling toward her boss is anything but warm, but Tame is her boss. If Tame would order some of the things Linda suggests, she could improve business by 25 percent. Linda plans to let her know this at an appropriate time during the appraisal interview.

Student Activities

1. Utilizing the concepts of "Johari" Window (see Joseph Luft, *Of Human Interaction*, Palo Alto, California: National Press Books), or some other form of self-disclosure, make a list of your strengths and weaknesses as a communicator or interviewer. Trade this list with another member of the class and allow that person to appraise you from his or her perspective. Do not look at each other's lists until you have interviewed each other. Give compliments and praise where appropriate. When you have completed the interviews, read to each other your evaluations of yourselves. Compare perceptions and evaluate one another as appraisers.

2. Obtain a union contract from a local company and examine the section on discipline. What are the steps that must be taken? What are the offenses for which an employee may be fired? What kinds of programs does this company have for the troubled employee? What happens if an employee refuses counseling.

3. Check with several local organizations to see what kinds of appraisal or planning processes are used. What performance indicators, standards, or objectives do they use? How does each organization measure performance? How do they deal with employees who are not performing satisfactorily to get them back on track?

4. Find an organization that uses the merit rating system, one that employs the standard appraisal interview approach, and one that uses the assessment center approach. Interview a member of the personnel staff of each organization to discover the advantages and disadvantages of each system. Discuss with the interviewees where appraisal interviewing can best be used and how.

5. One of the frequent comments about teaching is that there is no way to evaluate good teaching. With this comment as a framework, develop a means of measuring or evaluating your instructor. Use student reaction forms and faculty critiques to develop a statistical means of arriving at a rating and ranking. How could an appraisal interview be used to convey this material to the teacher? Would teachers benefit from appraisal interviews? Who should conduct the interviews?

6. Find an organization that uses a management-by-objectives method of evaluation. Interview members of this organization concerning their feelings about the use of MBO as a means of evaluating their performance. What role does interviewing seem to play in MBO systems?

Notes

1. See Robert Layer, "The Discrimination Danger in Performance Appraisal," *Conference Board Record*, March 1976, pp. 60–64.

2. Robert I. Lazer and Walter S. Wikstrom, *Appraising Managerial Performance: Current Practices and Future Directions* (New York: The Conference Board, 1977), p. 2.

3. George Odiorne, Peter Drucker, S. J. Carroll, and H. L. Tosi, Jr., *Management by Objectives: Application and Research* (New York: Macmillan, 1973).

4. This model and explanation come from a booklet developed by Baxter/Travenol Laboratories entitled *Performance Measurement Guide*. The model and performance appraisal system were developed by William B. Cash, Jr., Chris Janiak, and Sandy Mauch. The model is reprinted with the permission of Baxter/Travenol, Deerfield, Illinois.

5. See, for example, William B. Cash, Jr., "An Experimental Study of the Effects of Five Styles of Appraisal Interviewing Upon Anxiety, Defensiveness, and Interviewee Style Preference," unpublished doctoral dissertation, Purdue University, 1972; Ronald J. Burke and Douglas S. Wilcox, "Characteristics of Effective Employee Performance Review and Development Interviews," *Personnel Psychology* 22 (1969): 291–305; H. H. Meyer and W. B. Walker, "Need for Achievement and Risk Performance as They Relate to Attitudes toward Rewards Systems and Performance Appraisal in an Industrial Setting," *Journal of Applied Psychology* 1961, pp. 251–56; Herbert H. Meyer, E. Kay, and John R. P. French, Jr., "Split Roles in Performance Appraisal," *Harvard Business Review* 43 (January/February 1965): 123–29; John R. P. French, Jr., E. Kay, and Herbert Meyer, "Participation and the Appraisal System," *Human Relations* 19 (1966): 3–20; Richard E. Farson, "Praise Reappraised," *Harvard Business Review* 41 (September/October 1963): 61–66; Michael Z. Sincoff, "An Experimental Study of the Effects of Three 'Interviewing Styles' upon Judgments of Interviewees and Observer-Judges," unpublished doctoral dissertation, Purdue University, 1969; E. Kay, Herbert H. Meyer, and John R. P. French, Jr., "The Effect of Threat in a Performance Appraisal Interview," *Journal of Applied Psychology* 49 (1965): 311–17; Clive A. Fletcher, "Interview Style and the Effectiveness of Appraisal," *Occupational Psychology*, 1973, pp. 225–30; G. I. Peterson, S. B. Kiesler, and P. A. Goldberg, "Evaluation of the Performance of Women as a Function of Their Sex, Achievement, and Personal History," *Journal of Personality and Social Psychology* 57 (1971): 114–18; B. Rosen and T. H. Jerdee, "The Influence of Sex Role Stereotypes on Evaluations of Male and Female Supervisory Behavior," *Journal of Applied Psychology* 57 (1973): 44–54; B. Rosen and T. H. Jerdee, "Effects of Applicant's Sex and Difficulty of Job on Evaluation of Candidates for Managerial Positions," *Journal of Applied Psychology* 59 (1974): 511–12; William J. Giboness, "Effect of Applicant's Sex, Race, and Performance on Employers' Performance Ratings: Some Additional Findings," *Journal of Applied Psychology* 61 (1976): 80–84; Manuel London and John Poplawski, "Effects of Information on Stereotype Development in Performance Appraisal and Interview Content," *Journal of Applied Psychology* 61 (1976): 199–205.

Suggested Readings

Beck, Arthur C., Jr., and Hillmar, Ellis D. *A Practical Approach to Organization Development through MBO.* Reading, Mass.: Addison-Wesley, 1972.

Conley, James H.; Huegli, Jon L.; and Minter, Robert L. *Perspectives on Administrative Communication.* Dubuque, Iowa: Kendall-Hunt, 1976.

Cummings, L. L., and Schwab, D. *Performance in Organizations: Determinants and Appraisals.* Glenview, Ill.: Scott, Foresman, 1973.

Fear, Richard A. *The Evaluation Interview.* New York: McGraw-Hill, 1973.

Fordyce, Jack K., and Weil, Raymond. *Interpersonal Behavior and Administration.* New York: Free Press, 1969.

French, Wendell, and Hellriegel, Don., eds., *Personnel Management and Organizational Development: Fields in Transition.* Boston: Houghton-Mifflin, 1971.

Levinson, Harry. *The Great Jackass Fallacy.* Boston: Graduate School of Business Administration, 1973.

———. "Management by Whose Objectives," *Harvard Business Review* 48 (July/August 1970): 125–34.

Mahler, Walter R. *How Effective Executives Interview.* Homewood, Ill.: Dow Jones-Irwin, 1976.

Maier, Norman R. F. *The Appraisal Interview.* New York: John Wiley & Sons, 1958.

Morrisey, George. *Appraisal and Development through Objectives and Results.* Reading, Mass.: Addison-Wesley, 1972.

Morrisey, George L. *Management by Objectives and Results.* Reading, Mass.: Addison-Wesley, 1970.

Redding, W. Charles. *Communication within the Organization.* New York: Industrial Communication Council, 1972.

Schneider, Katie R., and Hawk, Donald L. *The Performance Appraisal Process: A Selected Bibliography.* Greensboro, N.C.: The Center for Creative Leadership, 1980.

Souerwine, Andrew H. *Career Strategies.* New York: AMACOM, 1978.

Strauss, George, and Sayles, Leonard R. *Personnel: The Human Problems of Management.* Englewood Cliffs, N.J.: Prentice-Hall, 1972.

Winstanley, Nathan B. *Current Readings in Performance Appraisal.* Scottsdale, Ariz.: American Compensation Association, 1974.

Counseling Interviewing $\mathcal{9}$

The counseling interview is perhaps the most sensitive of all interview settings. It usually does not occur unless either a person feels incapable of handling a problem alone and seeks help (often a blow to one's self-concept) or a "counselor" decides that a "counseling" session is needed (visibility of the problem may be another blow to a person's self-concept). In addition, the problem is likely to be a highly personal one involving such matters as finances, sex, emotional stability, physical health, marriage, morals, work performance, or grief over the death of a friend or family member. The counseling interviewer must generate level 3 interactions that require a high degree of trust and openness if the true nature of the problem is to be seen by both parties and a solution found and carried out.

When we think of a counselor, we often think of a highly trained psychiatrist or psychologist sitting in an overstuffed chair with notebook and pen in hand and listening thoughtfully and quietly to a patient who may be lying on a couch. The movies and television have printed this stereotype upon our minds. A remarkable fact is that the majority of counseling interviews—including those that are highly sensitive and critical—are conducted by professional persons (doctors, clergy, lawyers, teachers, supervisors), associates (fellow workers, students, club members), friends, and family members with counseling experience gained only from having given counsel in the past. As Dressel wrote:

It has been said that giving advice is like kissing; it costs nothing and it is a pleasant thing to do. While I do not believe that counseling is synonymous with giving advice, the analogy, nevertheless, has some relevance. Counseling has further similarities to kissing in that (1) everyone feels qualified to practice kissing and most everyone does at some time; (2) the objectives of kissing are usually not clearly stated but are not entirely intangible; (3) kissing itself is apt to be so satisfying that there is little tendency to evaluate it otherwise.[1]

Fortunately, the "lay counselor" has proven to be a remarkably successful counselor in many situations—including urban and campus crisis centers. Counselees often seem to trust someone more like themselves, someone who is not part of the "establishment," someone they perceive to be neutral and objective.

What is this phenomenon called "counseling" that we do so often and enjoy so much and that requires a high degree of sensitivity, trust, and openness? Simply stated, it is the process of helping a person to gain insight into a problem and to discover a way to cope with it. As we can see from this definition, the counseling interview is closely related to the appraisal interview discussed in chapter 8.

Approaches to Counseling

Although types of counseling interviews vary from setting to setting and profession to profession, there are two fundamental approaches to the counseling interview: directive and nondirective. In the directive approach, the *counselor* controls the structure of the interview, the subject matter attended to and avoided, the pace of the interview, and the length of the interview. The counselor collects and supplies information, defines and analyzes problems, suggests and evaluates solutions, and provides guidelines for actions. In short, the directive counselor serves as an "expert" who consults with clients. The directive approach has a number of advantages.

1. It is fairly easy to learn and to conduct.
2. It takes less time.
3. It allows the counselor to focus on specific matters of interest.
4. It allows the counselor to provide necessary information and guidelines.
5. It permits the counselor to serve as an advisor when clients are unwilling or unable to analyze their problems or to assess possible solutions.

The directive approach is based on the *assumption* that the counselor is better suited than the client in analyzing the problem and assessing solutions and is more knowledgeable about both the problem and possible solutions. The accuracy of this assumption, of course, depends upon the counselor, the client, and the particular situation (including the problem and possible solutions). The counselee, for instance, may or may not be "disabled" by a crisis. The counselee may know exactly what kind of solution is needed, or may be undecided about different courses of action, or may be uninformed or misinformed. An academic counselor, for example, may be an expert on courses and majors and a novice when giving advice about careers. A student may know more about medical school than a "preprofessional" counselor.

In the nondirective counseling interview, the *client* controls the structure of the interview; determines what topics will be discussed, when they will be discussed, and how they will be discussed; the pace of the interview; and the length of the interview. The counselor acts as a passive aid and helper during the interview, not as an expert or advisor. The counselor *helps* the client to obtain information, to gain insights, to define and to analyze problems, and to discover and to evaluate solutions. The counselor listens, observes, and encourages but does not *impose* ideas or solutions. Arthur Turner and George Lombard, in their book *Interpersonal Behavior and Administration,* describe the roles of counselor and client in nondirective interviews as follows:

> This method of counseling views the client and the resources within him as the source or focus of changes in his own behavior. The counselor's role is to facilitate those changes which the client—not the counselor— sees as desirable and possible for him. Further, this approach explicitly warns the counselor not to make interpretations of covert and hidden meanings, and to concentrate only on listening to, accepting, and clarifying the feelings which the client himself is expressing.[2]

The nondirective approach has a number of advantages.

1. It allows the client to reveal what is most important to him or her at a given time.

2. It allows the client to volunteer information the counselor might not think to ask for.

3. It gives the client control over his or her decisions and actions.

4. It may encourage the client to give in-depth answers and comments.

5. It provides the counselor with an opportunity to listen to and to encourage the client.

6. It may communicate to the client that the counselor is sincerely interested in him or her and is not in a hurry to get to the next client or task.

The nondirective approach is based on the *assumption* that the client is more capable than the counselor of analyzing problems, assessing solutions, and making correct decisions. In the extreme, this assumption questions the *right* of another person to "meddle" in another's problems or to serve as more than an indirect helper. The accuracy of this assumption, like the directive assumption, depends upon the counselor, the counselee, and the interviewing situation. The counselee may know nothing about the problem or potential solutions or, worse, may be misinformed about both. Are the training and experiences of the counselor worth nothing in the counseling situation? The counselor, however, must be able to distinguish between when he or she is serving as an expert advisor and when, quite subtly perhaps, he or she is imposing personal preferences upon a client. A crisis may make the counselee incapable of expressing or visualizing a problem, of making sound decisions, and of considering all potential ramifications of specific decisions. A counselee may refuse to admit that he or she has a problem. If the counselee party consists of two or more people, the party may be hopelessly divided over what to do and how to do it. At such times, the interviewer may serve as an objective, neutral referee who can present pros and cons of specific courses of action.

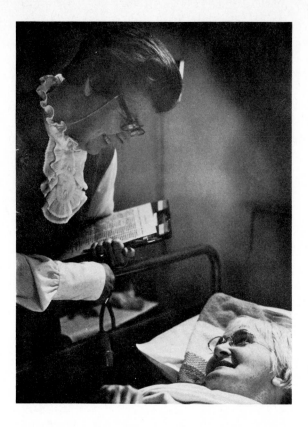

Counselors usually find it necessary to use an appropriate combination of directive and nondirective approaches.

Counselors, such as academic counselors, Social Security counselors, marriage counselors, and medical counselors, usually find it necessary to use an appropriate *combination* of directive and nondirective approaches. For example, during the first part of an interview with a family, a social services counselor may use a directive approach to obtain information on the family such as ages, sexes, incomes, addresses, occupations, physical handicaps, and so on. The counselor may switch to a nondirective approach when attempting to discover the problems a family is encountering, how family members perceive their problems, and what they expect from social services. The difficult task of the counselor is to determine when a particular approach is most appropriate and when to switch from one approach to the other during a counseling interview. Regardless of approach, we must resist the urge to make educated guesses about what is going on in an interviewee's mind, why an interviewee is acting or not acting in a particular manner, or why an interviewee maintains certain ideas or prefers certain practices.

Up to now, we have been trying to understand the general nature of the counseling interview and the fundamental approaches an interviewer might employ. Let's turn now to a review of the counseling interview as a five-step process:

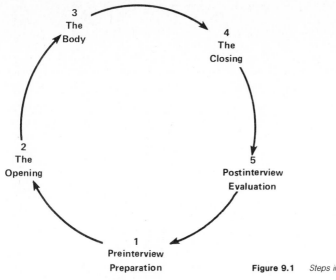

Figure 9.1 *Steps in Counseling Interviews*

preinterview preparation, the opening, the body, the closing, and postinterview evaluation. Each step plays vital functions for the interview (see fig. 9.1). If we, as interviewer or interviewee, fail to take any step seriously in our rush to move ahead or to get to other tasks or clients, succeeding steps and, most likely, the whole counseling interview process will suffer.

Preinterview Preparation

Our preinterview preparation should begin with a detailed and insightful self-analysis. Although self-analysis is not easy, we will have difficulties when trying to understand and help others if we do not know ourselves. What are our personality characteristics? Are we open-minded, optimistic, trusting, serious, self-assured, relaxed, and patient or the opposite of these? Are we argumentative and defensive when there is no real need to be so? Are we willing and able to disclose our motives, feelings, beliefs, attitudes, and values to others? If not, how can we expect interviewees or interviewers to be open with us? Do we tend to dominate our interpersonal interactions with others? Do we have a sincere desire, and perhaps need, to help others? Do we have a strong desire to be liked by others? Are we "people" or "problem" oriented? Most of our education and professional training is geared to solving problems such as slow production rates, poor sales, defective products, customer complaints, and mechanical breakdowns. But in nearly all counseling interviews the problem is attached to one or more people. As interviewers, we must be "client-centered" if we are going to be sensitive to interviewees' needs and communicate understanding, comfort, reassurance, and warmth. As interviewees, we must be "people-centered" if we hope to understand our problems and other persons, including the counselor. In short, we must strive to become empathic with other people.

What are our intellectual, communicative, and professional strengths? Are we imaginative, analytical, organized, and able to learn quickly and to recall accurately and completely? How well do we communicate with others in various settings and situations? Are we good listeners? Are we skilled in receiving and transmitting messages verbally and nonverbally? How adequately are we trained in our profession and are we up to date with changes and trends? What have we learned from our experiences? How do other people, the present counselor or client in particular, view us, our organization, and our profession? As interviewers do we have realistic views of our counseling skills and what can and cannot be accomplished in "typical" counseling interviews? Read each of the following hypothetical counseling situations with the preceding questions in mind, and ask, Should I try to handle it and, if so, how should I try to handle it?

Situation 1: You are in the personnel department at Wazy Manufacturing Company. Paul Schwartz has made an appointment to see you about his progress with the company. He is one of your highest rated production workers and has been with Wazy for seven years. He feels he is going nowhere in the company and that his work is not being recognized.

Situation 2: You are a professor at a large state university. Donna Williams drops by your office to discuss her low grades on your tests. Early in the conversation she tells you about her family problems and says that everyone seems to be against her: her classmates, instructors, sorority sisters, father, and stepmother.

Situation 3: Don Turcain, a junior with a teaching major in your department, stops by to discuss the oversupply of teachers in your field and the difficulty seniors are having getting jobs. He is thinking of changing to a nonteaching program, maybe to another department.

Situation 4: You have a report from one of your supervisors that Margie Peterson has been late for work several times during the past five weeks and that her production rate is the lowest on her shift. She has been with your company for three years and has had a better-than-average employee record until recently. You have called her in to see you.

Situation 5: John Macomb, a close personal friend, feels his marriage is falling apart because his wife is developing a highly successful career in advertising. You have known John and his wife, Elizabeth, for fifteen years and admire both of them. You have felt for some time that their marriage was heading for trouble, and you think you know the cause and solution.

As part of our preinterview preparation as *counselors* we ought to think about how we might respond to various kinds of questions and comments from counselees. How might we respond to the following?

I don't want your help or anyone else's.

How can we get this over with quickly and painlessly?

Why should I discuss my personal finances with you?

I don't want my family involved in this.

Why don't you just tell me what I ought to do?

I don't need your help.

How can you stand being a psychologist and listen to people's problems all day long?

You won't understand.

An operation is out of the question; I can't afford it.

Why are doctors so anxious to cut into people?

You've never been married; how can you help me with a marriage problem?

We can respond to questions such as these in a variety of ways. For instance, we might remain silent, use nudging probes, or repeat questions or comments to urge the counselee to continue and perhaps to explain feelings, attitudes, and reasons or to give us information. We might probe into the cause of feelings, attitudes, or reasons. We might provide information that will allay fears or remove misconceptions. We might allude tactfully to our training or experiences to reveal our ability to help and to understand the counselee's feelings.

As part of our interview preparation as *counselees*, we ought to think about how we might respond to questions, comments, and nonverbal actions such as the ones illustrated in the following exchanges.

1. **Counselee:** I don't need your help.
   Counselor: You don't need my help?
2. **Counselee:** Why are doctors so anxious to cut into people?
   Counselor: What makes you think they are?
3. **Counselee:** I don't want my family involved in this.
   Counselor: (silence)
4. **Counselee:** Why don't you just tell me what I ought to do?
   Counselor: Do you really want *me* to dictate a solution for *your* problem?
5. **Counselee:** Well, at first I thought everything was working out okay.
   Counselor: Um hmm?

If as interviewer or interviewee we formulate answers and think about possible questions or comments *before* the interview, we are less likely to get caught off guard *during* the interview. We should be ready to respond to unusual questions and requests. Above all, we should not become defensive or jump to premature conclusions. Review the question tools discussed in chapter 4. We will discuss a variety of possible interviewer responses and reactions later in this chapter.

The self-analysis guide presented in figure 9.2 is designed to focus attention on specific traits crucial to counseling interviews. The five-level scales between opposite traits allow us to determine, for example, whether we are highly optimistic, highly pessimistic, or somewhere in between. We, of course, are unlikely to be at a specific point on a scale at all times and under all circumstances. However, we should place a check on the scale that represents our usual level with each trait. When we have completed the self-analysis and if we have tried to be candid with ourselves, we should have a profile of ourselves that reveals our strengths and weaknesses as counselors or counselees. The profile should suggest where we have work to do.

1. **Personality traits**

Happy					Sad
Open-minded					Closed-minded
Optimistic					Pessimistic
Trusting					Suspicious
Patient					Impatient
Even-tempered					Emotional
Democratic					Autocratic
Humble					Arrogant

2. **Professionalism**

Ethical					Unethical
Trained					Untrained
Competent					Incompetent
Thorough					Superficial
Trustworthy					Untrustworthy

3. **Intellectual traits**

Imaginative					Unimaginative
Organized					Unorganized
Alert					Slow
Perceptive					Imperceptive
Intelligent					Unintelligent

4. **Communication and human relations skills and traits**

Open					Closed
Sensitive					Insensitive
Tactful					Tactless
Talkative					Reticent
Empathic					Distant
Poised					Nervous
Nondefensive					Defensive
Interested					Disinterested
Dynamic					Energyless
Attentive					Inattentive
Thoughtful					Inconsiderate

Figure 9.2 *A Guide for Self-Analysis*

We should review everything we know about the counselee in order to gain insight into the interviewee and the current problem: education and work histories, family background, test scores, previous counseling sessions, statements from teachers, acquaintances, supervisors, and other counselors, and information about past problems and solutions. What relationships (social, family, professional, religious, political) do we have with this counselee? What situational variables will affect this interview and interviewee? Have we counseled this person before? If so, have we done everything we said we would do? Has the client done what he or she agreed to do?

Frequently an interviewee will come to see us without advance notice or explanation. Teachers and supervisors face such situations often and must rely on training and past experiences to get these interviews underway successfully. Be particularly cautious in handling situations where there is little or no information available on the client. Encourage clients to make appointments so we can do necessary preinterview preparation. An appointment will also prevent our having to rush the client or to close the interview prematurely. Either could be disastrous to the interview.

Provide a climate conducive to good counseling. Too often the climate is directed by company or school policy or by tradition. A great many college students, after experiencing numbers of teachers unwilling to give of their time outside of the classroom, are hesitant to call or to come in for help. We can overcome these obstacles if our personal policy of openness and willingness to help are communicated to employees or students.

When a person comes in with a problem, find a quiet, private, comfortable spot. Too many supervisors and teachers share offices with others or have open partition offices that provide little or no privacy. We cannot expect an interviewee to be open and completely honest if outsiders (fellow employees or students or other clients) can overhear the interview. A coffee lounge is often more private and conducive to good counseling than our office. Avoid interruptions by telephones, secretaries, and other staff. Arrange the seating so that both interviewer and client are at ease and able to communicate freely. (Review the discussion of seating arrangement in chapter 2.) Many students comment that the interviewer behind the desk setting makes them feel ill at ease; they feel the "mighty one" is sitting in judgment. They prefer a chair at the end of the desk—essentially two chairs at right angles—or chairs facing each other. The point to remember is that arrangements of furniture and seating can contribute to (or detract from) the informal, conversational atmosphere so important in counseling interviews. Many counselors are discovering that a round table, similar to a dining room table, is preferred by clients and allows interviewers to take notes and to pass materials around more easily than a setting involving chairs around a desk or a small coffee table. This setting is particularly useful when the client party consists of two or more people. Clients seem to like the arrangement because they often handle family matters around the dining room table and a round table has no "authority" position.

If our preinterview preparation has been thorough, we should now be ready to conduct the counseling interview in a sensitive, organized, communicative, and professional manner.

The Opening

Greet the client by name and in a warm, friendly manner, being natural and sincere. Do not be condescending or patronizing. Accept the interviewee as he or she is. Do not try to second-guess the interviewee with statements such as "I'll bet I know why you are here," "I assume you want to talk about the project," or "No doubt you came about your low test grade." The client may not have come for any of these reasons but may feel pressured into agreeing, to some extent, with our guess. In addition, our opening might ruin a very meaningful opening the interviewee has prepared, one that revealed the central concern. Avoid reactions such as "You look terrible," "You've put on some weight haven't you," "What's on your mind," or "Isn't that dress a bit short?" These openings are not conducive to the kind of relationship needed for successful counseling. We know of a college professor who keeps a long list of student excuses on his desk. When a student begins to explain why a paper is late or why he or she has not been to class lately, the professor hands the excuse list to the student and comments, "Would you care to add your excuse to this list?" This is a clever practice, but it reeks of insincerity, mistrust, and a "mightier than thou attitude."

When the client initiates the interview, allow the client to state the reason for the visit and why and how the client thinks we can be of assistance. When we as interviewers initiate the interview, we should state clearly, precisely, and honestly why we want to see the interviewee. If there is a specific amount of time available for the interview, make this known so both counselor and client can work within the time allotted. The interviewee will be more at ease knowing how much time is available.

The counseling interview, unlike other interviews we have discussed, often consumes considerable time in establishing rapport, a "get acquainted" time during which a working relationship is established. We have found such a time to be necessary even with students from a small class we have been teaching for weeks. There is something very different and more threatening about the intimate, one-to-one interview setting. Students often begin by referring to the number of steps up to the office where the interview is taking place, the size of the office, the view out the window (even though another building may be only fifteen feet away), family pictures on the desk, books along the walls, other students in the class, or incidents in the class. Do not rush this seemingly frivolous process. The client is sizing up us and the setting.

The rapport stage is our chance to begin to establish a reputation for being interested, fair, and able to maintain confidences. We can discover if the client expects too much or too little from the interview and if the client has a negative stereotype of counselors. The interviewer must be comfortable with the interview situation (for example, an embarrassing topic, a crying interviewee, a client talking about everything but the real problem) if the interviewee is to be comfortable with the situation.

When rapport is accomplished, let the client begin with the topic that seems to interest him or her the most. This is the first step toward discovering the precise nature of the client's problem and why the client has been unable to solve it. Remember, do not rush the client. The client will usually tell us *what* he or she wants us to know *when* he or she is ready. Above all, we must not rush in with a solution as soon as we think *we* have discovered the problem. Observe the client's nonverbal actions very carefully because they may reveal inner feelings and the intensity of these feelings.

The Body

The interviewer plays many roles in the typical counseling interview: listener, observer, reacter, questioner, helper, sympathizer, and informant. Listening and observing are perhaps our most important roles. If we do not give undivided attention to what the client is saying, the implications of what is being said, and what might be said and is not, we are unlikely to get to the heart of the problem. Be genuinely interested in the interviewee and what the interviewee is saying. Do not interrupt or take over the conversation. Beware of interjecting personal opinions, experiences, or problems; maintain the focus on the client. If the client pauses or stops for a few moments, do not chatter to fill in the silence. We may use silence for a variety of purposes, an important one being to encourage the interviewee to continue talking. (Review chapter 2 for uses of silence and for listening principles.) Listening will be effective if we—

1. view all topics and comments as potentially important to the success of the counseling interview;

2. avoid paying attention to distractions such as mannerisms in the client's delivery;

3. do not become overstimulated or emotionally involved;

4. listen for attitudes, beliefs, and philosophies—the client's views of self, the world, and the people in it—rather than for facts;

5. do not interpose comments or questions until we fully understand what the client has been saying;

6. do not use emotionally laden language and comments—often used by interviewer or interviewee as defensive tactics—to interfere with listening to what is being said or implied;

7. prevent personal prejudices and convictions from impairing listening comprehension and understanding.

Observe how the interviewee sits, gestures, fidgets, and maintains eye contact; listen to the voice for loudness, timidity, and evidence of tenseness. These observations may give clues as to how disturbed the person is, the seriousness of the problem, how relaxed the client is, and how comfortable the client is with us. If we decide to take notes or to record the interview, we should explain what we are doing and why. Stop either if we detect the procedures are affecting the interview.

Let's focus now on the general phases of counseling interviews, the information potentially available to the counselor, and ways in which the counselor may respond or react.

Interaction Phases

Hartsough's and Echterling's sequential phase model of a crisis call, to a campus or community crisis center, is applicable to most counseling situations.[3] Figure 9.3 illustrates these phases. The *affective*, or emotional, phases, boxes 1 and 3, involve the interviewee's feeling of trust in the counselor and feelings about self and the problem. The *cognitive*, or thinking, phases, boxes 2 and 4, involve thinking about the problem and taking some action.

Affective	Cognitive
1. Establishment of a Helpful Climate (a) making contact (b) defining roles (c) developing a relationship	2. Assessment of Crisis (a) accepting information (b) encouraging information (c) restating information (d) questioning for information
3. Affect Integration (a) accepting feelings (b) encouraging feelings (c) reflecting feelings (d) questioning for feelings (e) relating feelings to consequences or precedents	4. Problem Solving (a) offering information or explanations (b) generating alternatives (c) decision making (d) mobilizing resources

Figure 9.3 *Phases of Counseling Interviews*

The typical counseling interview begins with establishing rapport and a feeling of trust, phase 1; proceeds to discovering the basic nature of the client's problem, phase 2; probes more deeply into the client's feelings, phase 3; and finally comes to some decision about a course of action, phase 4. Except in medical emergencies or when delaying action is life threatening, do not move from phase 1 to phase 4 or omit phase 3 without careful thought. If we do not discover the depth of a client's feelings, we may not truly understand the problem or the range of possible solutions. Do not expect to move through all four phases in every interview or to proceed uninterrupted in 1, 2, 3, 4 order. We may go back and forth between phases 2 and 3, or 3 and 4. Unless the interviewee wants specific information (where to get medical help, how to get birth control information, how to get an emergency monetary loan) we may not get to phase 4 until a second, third, or fourth interview. Be patient!

Information and Responses

Turner and Lombard summarize, in figure 9.4, the information potentially available to the counselor and the general ways the counselor may respond.[4] These types of information and responses may occur in any of Hartsough's and Echterling's four interaction phases. Turner and Lombard say the client is likely to talk about (1) objects, events, ideas, concepts, and so on, (2) other people, or (3) self. With a choice among these kinds of information, the interviewer should respond to what the interviewee is saying about himself or herself. The interviewer may respond by (1) giving opinions, advice, or suggestions, (2) interpreting what the interviewee is saying, or (3) accepting or clarifying "what the client has been saying from the client's own frame of reference." This is a client-centered approach.

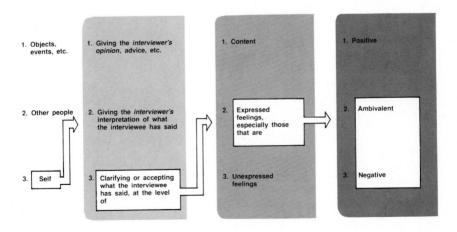

Figure 9.4 *Information and Responses in Counseling Interviews*

With these choices, the interviewer should accept or clarify what the client has been saying about the self. The interviewer may respond to the client's talk about the self at the level of (1) content, (2) expressed feelings, or (3) unexpressed feelings. The client-centered interviewer should respond to expressed feelings.

These expressed feelings provide a fourth interviewer decision, whether to respond to feelings that are (1) positive, (2) ambivalent, or (3) negative. Turner and Lombard say the interviewer should respond to ambivalent and negative feelings rather than to positive feelings in order to gain insight into the client's problem—which is why the interview is taking place.

Turner's and Lombard's suggestions should not be interpreted as fixed rules. The specific interview, the client, and the phase of the interview will determine what kinds of materials become available and which have priority. Phase 4, for example, may require advice rather than clarifying what the interviewee has said. Be flexible, but use Turner's and Lombard's suggestions as guidelines.

Interviewer Responses and Reactions

The counselor may respond or react to the counselee's comments, revelations, questions, and answers in an infinite variety of ways.[5] We may place these responses and reactions along a continuum from highly nondirective to nondirective, directive, and highly directive.

Highly nondirective reactions encourage the interviewee to continue commenting, to analyze ideas and solutions, and to be self-reliant. The interviewer offers no information, assistance, or evaluation of either the client or the client's ideas or of possible courses of action. Highly nondirective reactions and responses are used in phases 1, 2, and 3. The counselor may simply remain silent and thus encourage the counselee to continue or to answer his or her own question.

1. **Counselee:** I don't know what to do.
   Counselor: (silence)
   Counselee: I've thought about going home for a few weeks until I can get things sorted out.
2. **Counselee:** What do you think I should do?
   Counselor: (silence)
   Counselee: Yes, I guess it's my decision to make.

The counselor may encourage the counselee to continue speaking by employing semiverbal phrases, such as in the following.

1. **Counselee:** I'm trying to decide whether to stay on campus or return home for a few days.
   Counselor: Um-hmm.
   Counselee: If I stay here, I'm afraid I'll. . . .

2. Counselee: Well, I think I've decided how to handle my financial problems.
Counselor: Uh, huh?
Counselee: First, I'm going to sell the house that is too big for my needs anyway. Then. . . .

The counselor may encourage the counselee through assurances that specific feelings are normal or that he or she will be able to handle a problem or situation.

1. Counselee: I simply can't face that disciplinary committee.
Counselor: I'm sure it seems like an impossibility now, most people would.
2. Counselee: I can't sleep; I don't have any appetite; and I burst into tears over nothing.
Counselor: These are very normal reactions to the death of a parent.

When reacting and responding in a highly nondirective manner, we must be aware of our nonverbal behaviors. Face, tone of voice, speaking rate, and gestures must express a sincere interest in and reveal a high level of empathy for the interviewee. Interviewees look for signs of approval or disapproval and interest or disinterest. An "um-hmmm!" may signal a positive or a negative reaction by the counselor. Either reaction may adversely affect the interview by making the client wary of expressing true feelings or desires or by encouraging the client to express feelings and desires perceived to be most acceptable to the counselor. Do not permit a silence to become prolonged or awkward. If the client seems unable to continue or to "go it alone" at this point in the interview, switch to more appropriate responses. Avoid clichés, meaningless reassurances, or mini-sermons such as the following.

Every cloud has a silver lining.
You'll laugh about this some day.
We all have to go sometime.
It's always darkest before the dawn.
You're a very lucky person. Why, when I was your age. . . .

A variety of question techniques may serve as highly nondirective responses. For example, the counselor may *restate* or *repeat* the client's question or statement instead of providing answers or volunteering information, ideas, solutions, or evaluations. The attempt is to urge the *client* to elaborate or to come up with answers.

1. Counselee: I don't know what to do.
Counselor: You don't know the options available to you?
2. Counselee: It doesn't seem real.
Counselor: The loss of your job does not seem real?

Restatements and repetitions must be tactful and purposeful. A client may become upset if there seems to be a constant echo during the interview.

The counselor may *return* a question to a client rather than answer it. Once again, the attempt is to encourage the *client* to analyze problems and to select from possible solutions.

1. Counselee: Should I have a business minor?
Counselor: How do *you* feel about a business minor?
2. Counselee: I don't know which minor to take.
Counselor: What minors do you have in mind?

We should not continue to push a decision back to the interviewee if we detect that the interviewee is confused, has little information from which to make a decision, is misinformed, is genuinely undecided, or is unable to make a choice. To continue with a highly nondirective approach would be nonproductive and potentially harmful to the counseling (helping) process and relationship.

The interviewer may *invite* the interviewee to discuss a problem or idea.

1. Counselee: I'm under a lot of pressure from Mary's family.
Counselor: Would you like to discuss these pressures?
2. Counselee: I have some serious reservations about this operation.
Counselor: Care to tell me about them?

In highly nondirective invitations, the client retains the freedom to refrain from elaborating or to keep feelings concealed if so desired. The counselor does not say "Tell me about it" or "Such as" but asks if the client is willing to discuss, to explain, or to reveal.

The *reflective question* is a valuable means of discovering, in a nondirective manner, if the counselor understands what the client has just said. As we discussed in chapter 4, reflective questions are designed to clarify or to verify statements, not to lead the client toward our point of view or preferred solution.

1. Counselee: I think we have decided to put my mother in a home.
Counselor: Such as Lafayette Care?
2. Counselee: We first noticed that Alice was having learning problems in early grade school.
Counselor: That was around first or second grade?

Reflective questions require careful listening and a concerted verbal and non-verbal effort not to lead the interviewee. Counselees are often highly vulnerable and may be swayed rather easily, even when we do not intend to sway them. Highly nondirective responses and reactions are designed to reduce persuasion to a minimum.

Listen perceptively and empathetically to clients. Quite often they are not asking for information or advice or answers. They need to talk to someone who will listen and reassure them by *not* preaching, offering advice, or judging their ideas, actions, or feelings. We should simply let them know that we have "heard" what they have said and that we are available when they need us.

Nondirective reactions tend to inform and to advise counselees. No imposition of either information or advice is intended. It is hoped that clients will interpret either response as an offering of assistance, not as an authoritative utterance. These reactions occur primarily in phase 4, but may appear in phase 2. Clients remain free of pressure to make their own decisions.

1. Counselee: Do I have to have a minor?

Counselor: There is no regulation that requires a minor. However, graduates have often found that a good minor such as business or supervision makes them more attractive to potential employers. I guess the answer is yes and no.

2. Counselee: What kinds of assistance can you give us?

Counselor: We have an Aid to Dependent Children Program, a Food and Shelter Program, and a new Upward Bound program that is aimed at providing training in job skills. You may qualify for one or more of these.

We should try to be specific in answers and must not hesitate to refer counselees to sources better qualified than ourselves. We need not have all of the answers. We may have to work at being nondefensive. Clients may be blunt, even abusive, on occasion, but replying in kind will gain nothing beyond a little short-lived satisfaction and may harm both the client and us. Counselees who ask why are usually not trying to put us on the spot.

Some interviewee comments and questions ask us to evaluate or to rate courses of action. One type of nondirective response provides information and minimal evaluation, but it does not make recommendations. The interviewer attempts to keep personal preferences out of the decision.

1. Counselee: What would you do if you were me?

Counselor: That's a decision you'll have to make and live with. A number of students have been successful in dropping out of school for a few semesters and returning when they feel they are ready to settle down.

2. Counselee: Should I consider changing jobs when the economy is so depressed?

Counselor: I have seen a lot of people change jobs lately. It seems to depend a great deal on the job being selected.

A second type of response does give personal preferences when asked. It is wise to explain our preferences because our reasons for selection may not be appropriate for a particular client.

1. Counselee: Would you have an abortion?

Counselor: No, I would not, but I am Catholic and my religion prohibits abortion. In addition, I have an adopted daughter and know that she would probably not exist if abortion had been legalized ten years ago.

2. Counselee: Should we try to explain my mother's death to our young children?

Counselor: I agree with a number of writers on death and dying who state that we should try to explain death to children in their language and at their level of maturity. These sources urge us to avoid telling children that a grandparent has "gone on a long trip."

Directive interviewer reactions go beyond encouragement, information, and mild advice. They often give the client a gentle push toward accepting information or advice or acting upon information received during the counseling interview. Directive reactions are used in phases 2 and 4 and sometimes in 3. In the following interchanges, the counselor supports a counselee's ideas and urges action or acceptance.

1. Counselee: I have been thinking about going back to school to work on an MBA. What do you think of this idea?

Counselor: I think that's an excellent idea. Why don't you contact some good schools right away about their programs and financial support.

2. Counselee: I don't know if Frank will go along with taking Billy to a child psychologist.

Counselor: Why don't you talk to him about it and find out?

A second form of directive response actually questions the client's comments or ideas. Naturally we must be tactful and cautious when employing this technique in counseling interviews.

1. Counselee: I don't think I'm going to tell Aunt Elizabeth in New Orleans that Mom has died. She said she didn't care if Mom lived or died.

Counselor: Do you really think she meant that?

2. Counselee: I'm not going to tell Mom that Dad has terminal cancer.

Counselor: Don't you think she has a *right* to know that her own husband is dying of cancer?

Directive responses and reactions may challenge a client's actions, ideas, or judgments or they may urge a client to pursue a specific course of action or to accept information or ideas. We are usually wise to employ directive responses only if nondirective responses do not appear to work.

Highly directive interviewer reactions should be held in reserve for special circumstances—when all less directive means of counseling have been exhausted. Suggestions are replaced with ultimatums, advice with threats. These reactions should be reserved for phase 4. The following are examples of highly directive responses:

1. Counselee: I would like to have an extension of time in preparing my sales report on the model 325 calculator.

Counselor: I'm sorry, but we need your report on time if we are to make the production changeover. You were told of the deadline nearly two months ago.

2. Counselee: I don't think I can work on Saturday because of family problems.
   Counselor: If you can't work on Saturday, we'll have to replace you permanently.
3. Counselee: What do you suggest?
   Counselor: Here is exactly what you must do. Your production rate will increase by 20 percent and you will not miss work or be late for any reason.

We should have few opportunities to use highly directive reactions and responses. First, few counselees will push us to the point where such extreme reactions are necessary. Second, counselees usually have a number of options and a number of counselors from whom to choose and are likely to avoid ones that would not seem reasonably compatible with their desires. And third, counselors often have little authority with which to impose ideas or solutions on clients, even if they are inclined to do so.

When reacting to an interviewee's remarks, we must not be shocked by what we hear, or at least should not reveal our shock. Extensive reading in counseling and thorough preparation for each interview will reduce the number of "surprises" we encounter in counseling interviews. If we know, for example, how people have reacted to divorces, failing grades, deaths of family members, or losses of jobs, we are less likely to be shocked by extreme or unusual reactions or comments during interviews. We must not try to dodge unpleasant facts. Be honest, but be tactful, if possible. Our tone of voice, inflections, and gestures should communicate a relaxed, unhurried, confident image to the client. If we are nervous and show it in our reactions, we cannot expect the client to be relaxed. Avoid appearing brusque or overbearing, too cold, polite, or formal. The client may lose confidence in us as counselors, terminate the interview, and not subject himself or herself to other counselors. A number of studies have discovered the following about interviewee disclosure during counseling interviews.[6]

1. Data is more extensive and authentic when the interviewer is highly disclosing rather than impersonal—shows interest, acceptance, and understanding.

2. The interviewee's perception of the risk and utility of providing information affects disclosure.

3. The interviewee's disclosure history affects disclosure in counseling interviews.

4. Female interviewees respond longer to female interviewers but do not reveal more information to females than to males.

5. An interviewer's reflection or restatement of the interviewee's statements are effective with negative but not positive self-reference.

6. Interviewee's responses are more disclosing when they perceive greater personal contact.

Each of these findings tells us something important to do or to avoid in interviews, or tells us what to expect in interviews.

Questions

Questioning can play an important role in counseling interviews, but we often ask too many questions and interrupt the interviewee with questions that are unclear, unimportant, and meaningless. Beware of asking so many questions that the interviewee stops communicating feelings and ideas and becomes content with (or resigned to) answering our questions. We may stifle a client's questions by flooding him or her with ours. Avoid closed questions, especially leading or loaded questions and ones that can be answered yes or no. Counseling interviews are not cross-examinations, so a machine-gun method of questioning is out of place. Since client-centered interviews tend to be nondirective in nature and controlled by the interviewee, the counselor rarely prepares more than a nonscheduled interview structure. Few questions can be planned in advance, so think about questions carefully before asking them. Ask questions that encourage the client to verbalize emotions, to look deeper into a problem, or to examine possible solutions.

> Why do you think your supervisor reacted that way?
> What events led up to this confrontation?
> How did you react to your supervisor's threats?
> What solutions would you suggest we consider?
> What ideas do you have in mind?
> What solutions have you tried?

Use encouragement probes such as:

> What else would you like to say?
> Uh-huh?
> What happened next?
> I see.
> Go ahead with your story.

Encouragement in all facets of the counseling interview is vitally important to the counseling process. Avoid curious probing into feelings and embarrassing incidents, especially if the client seems hesitant or unwilling to elaborate. Beware of questions that may communicate disapproval, displeasure, or mistrust. The common "why" question, for example, may connote any or all of these interviewer attitudes and provoke a negative or defensive reaction from the interviewee.[7] How might a worker react to questions such as the following?

> *Why* didn't you report sooner?
> *Why* didn't you give to the United Fund?
> *Why* don't you do what your supervisor tells you to do?
> *Why* did your production rate decrease by 2 percent?

Helping and Information Giving

Helping the interviewee should usually be an indirect process in tune with the climate of the client-centered interview. Avoid sermonizing to the interviewee. Be a helper, not an oracle. Comments that begin with phrases such as "Now when I was your age . . . ," "Now if I were in your shoes . . . ," "I know just how you feel . . . ," and "We all go through that," are likely to be detrimental to the counseling interview. Do not argue with the client. Yield as much as possible without imposing a decision, and guard against our own ego involvement in the situation or solution. Encourage the client to think and to develop plans or solutions. The client may reject a solution because it is *our* solution.

Give information rather than advice. Suggest a range of possible solutions. Serve as a stimulator, a director, a motivator, a mirror reflecting the interviewee's ideas and feelings. Above all, be honest. Admit that we do not have all the answers or the answer. Refer the client to someone with more expertise in an area of concern or with counseling experience and training capable of handling a serious psychological problem. Research studies have stressed the importance of expertise in counseling interviews. Some conclusions are that—[8]

1. clients perceive accurately a counselor's expertness or lack of it;

2. expert interviewers tend to be more effective in satisfying client's needs;

3. expert interviewers tend to be less directive than inexpert interviewers;

4. expert interviewers limit their responses to a few important areas in the interview;

5. expert interviewers have clients with more favorable attitudes.

The counselor is an information giver when explaining the counseling process, an agency or department, and his or her position or background. This information should be brief and to the point. Introducing and using tests (intelligence, aptitude, etc.) are parts of both gathering and giving information. Explain tests, their uses, and strengths and weaknesses very carefully because they can ruin all that has been accomplished during an interview. Reveal results even more carefully. Explain them and do not blast the client's dreams with comments such as "I'm afraid you're in the wrong field," "Have you ever thought of doing something else?" or "You ought to get out of teaching." Unnecessary emotional shocks should be avoided at all costs.

Any of several factors may prevent a counselee from retaining or being able to repeat information accurately and completely. (1) The physical setting (noise, seating arrangement, interruptions) may distract a person and make it difficult to listen and to hear a message. (2) Personal restrictions (ability to listen, nervousness, lack of concentration) may affect comprehension and retention. (3) The relationship between counselor and counselee (degree of trust, credibility, previous contacts) may affect the way a person *perceives* information and ultimately both retention and how the information is retransmitted. (4) The way we transmit information may aid retention and understanding or detract from both. (5) We may be guilty of information overload. The human circuitry, even

Give information rather than advice. Serve as a stimulator, a director, a motivator, a mirror reflecting the interviewee's idea and feelings.

under the best of circumstances, is prone to breakdown under an avalanche of figures, dates, times, places, laws, procedures, options, agreements, and so on. The counseling situation may drastically affect a person's ability to listen and to comprehend. Counselors may employ a variety of communication techniques to enhance a counselee's ability to receive, to comprehend, to retain, and to repeat information. For example, we might use a variety of visual aids (pictures, slides, models, charts), vocal punctuation (pauses, emphasis, change of volume), questions (from both interviewer and interviewee), strategic repetitions, systematic presentation of information, definitions and explanations (of terms, procedures, processes, actions), elimination of all but necessary detail, and reduction of the number of times a counselee will have to retransmit information.

Many counselors employ interview guides or have forms to fill out during the interview. People tend to be suspicious of forms and are curious about what interviewers are writing. We can lessen these problems by explaining what we are doing, what the forms are, and how we will use the information we are gathering. Do everything in the open. Alfred Benjamin, in his book *The Helping Interview*, warns that we should never write notes that we are unwilling to show a client. After all, the client may be able to read what we are writing. *Do not* take more notes than are needed and *do* maintain effective communication (listening, eye contact, feedback) with the counselee. We may miss important information and clues about feelings and desires while we are engrossed in extensive note taking.

The Closing

The closing of the counseling interview—as with all sensitive interview settings—is vital to success of the entire interview. If the client feels pushed out the door, hurried along on a communications assembly line, or that he or she has imposed on the interviewer, much of the progress made during the interview may be erased, especially the interpersonal relationship established so carefully. The client may be reluctant to come back for further counseling.

The verbal and nonverbal leave-taking actions listed in chapter 3 will help us to understand how we, as counselors and counselees, close interviews—consciously or unconsciously. Decide which means or combination of means best suits us and the other party in each interview. There are a number of guidelines for choosing the proper closing for counseling interviews. For instance, both interviewer and interviewee should be able to tell when the real closing is taking place—avoid false finishes. Do not begin new topics when the interview has in fact or psychologically come to a close. Do not expect to finish with a neatly wrapped package with a solution all worked out. Be content that thought has been stirred or that the interviewee was able and willing to discuss the problem with us. Do not be overconcerned with meeting all expectations—remember that both parties are human beings with failings. Leave the door open for further conversation. We should be sincere and honest in the way we close interviews. The way we close an interview can enhance or ruin all that we accomplished during the interview.

Postinterview Evaluation

We should think carefully and critically about the counseling interviews we take part in. Only through perceptive self-analysis will we begin to improve our interactions with others. We must be realistic, however. We cannot expect *all* counseling interviews to be complete successes because they are interactions between complex human beings, at least one of whom has a serious problem. Remember that *our perceptions* of how the interview went and how the counselor or counselee reacted and related to us may be exaggerated or totally incorrect.

The following questions may serve as guides for our postinterview evaluations, whether we are counselors or counselees.

Preinterview Preparation
1. Did I review available materials concerning the interviewee or interviewer before the interview?

2. Did I make an effort to know myself and my level of counseling expertise or ability to solve my problem?

3. Did I assess how I communicate and "come across" with others, particularly with *this* party?

4. Did I evaluate how others, *this* party in particular, view me or groups to which I belong?

5. Did I review questions I might ask to get necessary information and to make informed decisions?

6. Did I review questions the client or counselor might ask and think about how I might respond helpfully and nondefensively?

7. Did I prepare a climate and setting in which openness and willingness to communicate would be fostered?

Interviewing Skills

1. How effective and complete was the opening?

2. How skillful were my questioning techniques?

3. Did I use an appropriate blend of directive and nondirective approaches?

4. Did I take adequate notes without disturbing the interview process?

5. Did I set a good pace for the interview—neither too fast nor too slow?

6. Did I employ visual aids to help the other party to remember and to comprehend discussions, explanations, and options?

7. If the party consisted of two or more persons, was I able to involve all members of the party in the interview?

8. How effective was I in motivating the counselee or counselor to communicate at levels 2 and 3?

9. How tolerant was I of silent moments during the interview?

10. How prepared was I to deal with questions and comments, especially negative questions and comments?

11. How effective and complete was my closing?

Counseling Skills

1. How well did I adapt to this party and to this situation?

2. Did I explain all options clearly, thoroughly, and objectively?

3. Did I "help" the other party to gain insights and to make decisions without dominating the interview or applying real or subtle pressures?

4. In my attempt to remain *neutral*, did I fail to be an effective counselor, to be a concerned human being?

5. Did I discover the real problem or problems bothering the counselee or merely the surface problem or problems suggested by the counselee or the situation?

6. Did I listen carefully to what the client or counselor was saying, implying, and not saying?

7. Did I try to handle a problem too difficult for my frame of mind or for my level of counseling experience and expertise?

8. Was I too anxious to be liked by the other party?
9. What promises and agreements did I make, and can I satisfy them?
10. How well did I relate to each member of the other party?
11. Did I agree with the client or counselor when I should have disagreed?

Our experiences and counseling situations may add to or subtract from these lists of postinterview questions. The important point is that we should evaluate what we do with an ever-present willingness to change for the better.

Summary

The counseling interview is best thought of as a series of interlocking stages or steps. The series begins with preinterview preparation, proceeds to the opening, the body, and the closing, and ends with a careful postinterview evaluation. When the circle is completed, we should be ready—and better prepared—to handle our next counseling interview. *Preparation* is the keystone to the whole counseling interview process. Our abilities to listen, to question, to respond, to inform, to explain, and to relate as concerned persons depend upon our training, experiences, and preparation prior to each interview. No two interviews are identical because no two counselees and situations are identical. Therefore, we can develop guidelines but not rules. We must adapt to each counselee, situation, and problem.

A Counseling Interview for Review and Analysis

This counseling interview is between a graduate student counselor in a women's dormitory and a first-year college student. The Dean of Students has sent the counselor a note about the student because she has not been attending one of her classes. The counselor is to discover the student's reason(s) for not attending class.[9]

How does the counselor provide a "supportive" climate during the interview? How well do client and counselor follow the guidelines for good listeners? Does the counselor use a directive, a nondirective, or a combination approach? How appropriate is the counselor's approach? How would you evaluate the counselor's use of questions? How well does the counselor follow the suggestions of Turner and Lombard and the phases developed by Hartsough and Echterling? How well does the counselor achieve an acceptable level of self-disclosure?

1. Counselor: Hi Karen! Do you have a few minutes just to talk?
2. Counselee: Sure, Miss Potter.
3. Counselor: Just call me Barbara, okay? After all, I'm not that much older than you are, Karen.

4. Counselee: I know that Miss Pot- . . . I mean Barbara.

5. Counselor: So what do you think of our university?

6. Counselee: Wow! I think it's great!

7. Counselor: I like it too. What do you like most about it?

8. Counselee: Just about everything! I think it's really great to be able to do whatever I want, whenever I want to do it. No parents, you know, keeping the noose around my neck.

9. Counselor: (smiling) Sure, I know the feeling very well.

10. Counselee: (encouraged) Yeah, and my boyfriend lives in this dorm, too. That's really nice.

11. Counselor: His name is Roger, isn't it? He is really handsome, Karen. You seem to be doing real well for yourself.

12. Counselee: Uh huh!

13. Counselor: It's easy to meet boys here. There's the library, the union, and lots of boys in your classes. Where did you meet Roger?

14. Counselee: I met him at Mary's apartment about a month ago. He sure likes to have fun. And, boy, does he love beer!

15. Counselor: We all like to do that in our free time. Your social life seems to be developing fine for you. How are your classes coming along so far?

16. Counselee: (vaguely) Okay, I guess.

17. Counselor: (pausing) Just okay, Karen?

18. Counselee: Well, things could be a little better, I guess.

19. Counselor: (probing gently) In what way, for instance?

20. Counselee: They're all going fine except for one class. I just can't seem to. . . . Listen, Miss Potter. . . .

21. Counselor: Barbara.

22. Counselee: Barbara. It's awfully hard to explain so that you'd understand.

23. Counselor: Try me.

24. Counselee: Okay. It's my math class. I can hardly understand what he says, let alone the stuff he puts on the board.

25. Counselor: Um hmmm?

26. Counselee: We had a test after the first two weeks of class. I was real scared, but I got a B.

27. Counselor: Great! And then?

28. Counselee: (embarrassed) Well . . . I guess I got overconfident. I cut the class for a whole week after the test.

29. Counselor: I can see how that might happen.

30. Counselee: Well . . . when I did go back, I was really lost. I failed a couple of quizzes, too.

31. Counselor: (silent probe)

32. Counselee: I suppose the first couple of weeks was a review. After that test, he must have started the new stuff. I never had it before and I'm really swamped now!

33. Counselor: What did you do after you failed those quizzes?

34. Counselee: I can't tell you Barbara; you'll think I'm stupid or something.

35. Counselor: Karen, I'm not here to judge you, only to see if there's something I can do to help.

36. **Counselee:**	Well . . . I quit going to the class. I'm so far behind now, it's too late to catch up.
37. **Counselor:**	Do you really think it's too late?
38. **Counselee:**	No . . . probably not, but it sure would take an awful lot of extra work. What's the answer, Barbara?
39. **Counselor:**	I think you know the answer.
40. **Counselee:**	You're right. . . . How should I go about catching up?
41. **Counselor:**	What do *you* think?
42. **Counselee:**	There are tutors in the math department. I suppose they could help me.
43. **Counselor:**	Seems to me that you have the right idea.
44. **Counselee:**	Thanks to you!
45. **Counselor:**	No, Karen, you're the one who decided what to do.
46. **Counselee:**	I think I'll go and see one of those tutors. I sure hope it works.
47. **Counselor:**	It's a step in the right direction. Keep me posted on how things are going, okay? I'm always around in case you want to talk—or maybe even play some tennis sometime. I've seen you play, Karen; pretty mean serve you have.
48. **Counselee:**	You really think so? Why thanks. I'll be seeing you in a few days. Thanks again, Barbara.

Counseling Role-playing Cases

Cheating on a Test

The counselee, John Williams, is a sophomore in college and has never cheated. He recently had been having trouble with grades and needed an A in a certain course to keep from going on probation. The professor of this course, Dr. Ed Johnson, was talking to him one day in his office and left the room for a few minutes. John took a copy of the final exam from Dr. Johnson's desk, knowing that he would never miss it since he cannot keep track of his papers. But before John took the test, his conscience began to bother him. He decided to see Mr. Steve Hansen, an instructor he knows very well, to decide whether he should return the final to Dr. Johnson and apologize to him or never return it since Dr. Johnson probably will never miss it.

The counselor, Mr. Steve Hansen, is an instructor at the college which John attends. He has a good reputation for being a good counselor. He knows John very well. When John comes in to tell him what he has done, he finds it hard to believe. He has never had anyone come to him with such a problem. John explains the situation and asks what he should do.

An Employee/Employer Relationship

The counselee, Karen Goety, is a legal secretary in her early twenties. She has been working for Gordon Mayfield, a well-known lawyer. Gordon is married and has two children, but he has repeatedly asked Karen to go out with him. She has told him no, but he keeps asking her. Karen has decided to quit working for him because she does not want to get involved in his personal life. Gordon is a nice person, an excellent employer, and pays Karen well. When she tells him she is quitting, should she tell him the truth or make up a story? Karen decides to talk the matter over with Evelyn Ward, a long-time friend who is in personnel relations with a department store.

The counselor, Evelyn Ward, is thirty-two years old and personnel manager at Hicks Department Store. Karen Goety has asked to discuss a problem with her over lunch. Evelyn has a vague idea that the problem pertains to Karen's job, but she knows that Karen has enjoyed the job very much.

A Theft and Personal Involvements

The counselor, Judy Ray, is a member of a medium-sized English Department and one of the youngest teachers in the high school. Even though she teaches English only to freshmen and sophomores, she is liked and respected by the seniors. Several days ago someone broke into six vending machines in the basement of the school. The merchandise and over $70 in coins were taken. The principal has made a number of announcements over the public address system that if the money is returned, no charges will be pressed—but the guilty person must apologize to the entire school and pay for the merchandise and the damage to the machines. One of the better known seniors, Bob Mitchell, has confessed to Judy that he stole the money to buy his girl a watch. He wants to know what to do.

The counselee, Bob Mitchell, is the son of a widow and has never been in any kind of trouble. He met Becky several weeks ago, and since then has been seeing her every day. His mother does not want him to date Becky because she feels that Becky is not a respectable companion for Bob. The counselor knows that Becky is from a poor family. She is extremely good-looking, and the guys think she is the greatest. The competition for Becky was pretty stiff, but by picking her up from school in his mother's car and taking her home, Bob apparently won her over. She was waiting for him one night after basketball practice, and before they started home she asked him to buy her a pack of cigarettes. Both went downstairs to the vending machines and she kept talking about how much money was in the machines and how nice a watch would look on her wrist. Before Bob realized what he had done, he and Becky were carrying cigarettes, candy, gum, and money out to his car. He does not want his mother to find out, but—more important—Becky will drop him flat if she is implicated.

Dating and Religion

Cathy McNamara, the counselee, is twenty-two years old and has been dating Richard Brooks, who is twenty-four, for almost a month. She cares very much for him, and feels there could be a future to their relationship. She is a strong Catholic and recently learned that Richard is studying to be a Presbyterian minister. He is coming to Cathy's home for dinner on Friday evening, and he does not know she is Catholic. Should she tell him before he comes to meet her family? What should she do about the entire situation? She has decided to talk to Father Collins, whom she has known all of her life, about her problem.

The counselor, Father Patrick Collins, has been the priest at St. Mary's Church for nearly twenty-five years. Cathy McNamara, whom he has known during all of her twenty-two years, is coming to see him. She sounded upset when she phoned him in the morning. He knows she has recently been dating a non-Catholic and that perhaps this could be the reason she is troubled.

Class Attendance

The counselor, John Hollstein, is a twenty-three-year-old graduate counselor in a men's dormitory where he has worked for nearly a year. Norman Pilliwaski is one of 110 freshmen on the floor where John lives. Norman shows the normal tendencies of a college freshman. He is girl-crazy, does not like to study, loves beer, and is thoroughly enjoying the freedom he gets from not living at home. The dorm where he lives is a coed unit that suits Norman just fine, since his latest girl lives in the same building. About the middle of the quarter, John received a note from the Dean of Student's office that Norman has not been attending one of his classes for three weeks. He would like the counselor, John, to investigate the situation.

The counselee, Norman Pilliwaski, is eighteen years old. He has recently been let loose for the first time in his life. The thrill of finally being able to do what he wishes and to go whenever he chooses is almost too much for him. He is finally out of the clutches of his parents, who were very strict throughout high school. Norman's mother was hesitant to let him go away to college, but his father convinced her it was the best thing for Norman. Since his arrival at school, he has found many new friends and activities. In high school his academic record was about average because he never put forth much effort. He is now in his sixth week of college. For some reason he just could not get through his math class, so he stopped going to it. John Hollstein stops him in the lounge and asks to talk to him.

Student Activities

1. Analyze the sample counseling interview. What are its strengths and weaknesses? How is the counselor following the suggestions made in this chapter? How much information does the counselor obtain about the problem of the counselee?

2. Visit a crisis center in your community or on your campus. Observe how volunteer counselors handle telephone counseling. Talk with several counselors about their training and techniques. How does telephone counseling differ from face-to-face counseling?

3. Interview three kinds of counselors: a marriage counselor, a student counselor, and a financial counselor. How are their approaches and techniques similar and different? What kinds of training do they have and recommend for counselors? What is a "successful" counselor in their estimation?

4. Pick one of the counseling role-playing cases and develop a complete approach to this case, beginning with setting and furniture arrangement. How would you begin the interview? What questions would you ask? How much would you disclose about yourself—your training, background, experiences, and so on? What kind of solution would you offer, if any? How would you close the interview?

5. Make arrangements to observe a counseling interview between a student and teacher, an employer and employee, a parent and child, or a professional counselor and client. Try not to be an obvious third party if possible. Observe the opening, questions and responses, nonverbal behavior of both parties, self-disclosures, effect of interruptions, suggestions, directive and nondirective techniques, and the closing. Write a detailed criticism of this interview with suggestions for improvement.

Notes

1. P. Dressel, "The Evaluation of Counseling," *Concepts and Problems of Counseling*, R. Berdie, ed. (Minneapolis: University of Minnesota Press, 1951), p. 70.

2. Reprinted with permission of Macmillan Publishing Co., Inc. from *Interpersonal Behavior and Administration* by Arthur N. Turner and George F. F. Lombard. Copyright © 1969 by Arthur N. Turner and George F. F. Lombard.

3. Echterling, Lennis G.; Hartsough, Don M.; and Zarle, H. "Testing a Model for the Process of Telephone Crisis Intervention,"*American Journal of Community Psychiatrists*, vol. 8 (1980): 715–25.

4. Turner and Lombard, *Interpersonal Behavior and Administration*, pp. 305–6.

5. For another discussion of interviewer reactions, see William U. Snyder, "An Investigation of the Nature of Nondirective Psychotherapy," *Journal of General Psychology* 33 (1945): 193–223.

6. Sidney M. Jourard and Peggy E. Jaffe, "Influence of an Interviewer's Disclosure on the Self-Disclosing Behavior of Interviewees," *Journal of Counseling Psychology* 17 (1970): 252 and 254; Joseph Doster and Bonnie R. Strickland, "Disclosure of Verbal Material as a Function of Information Requested, Information about the Interviewer, and Interviewee Differences," *Journal of Consulting and Clinical Psychology* 37 (1971): 187; Alexis A. Spiritas and David S. Holmes, "Effects of Models on Interview Responses," *Journal of Counseling Psychology* 8 (1971): 217; W. J. Powell, Jr., "Differential Effectiveness of Interviewer Interventions in an Experimental Interview" *Journal of Consulting and Clinical Psychology* 32 (1968): 213–14; Benjamin Pope and Aaron W. Siegman, "Interviewer Warmth in Relation to Interviewee Verbal Behavior," *Journal of Consulting and Clinical Psychology* 32 (1968): 589–90.

7. Stanley L. Payne, *The Art of Asking Questions* (Princeton, N.J.: Princeton University Press, 1951), p. 204; Alfred Benjamin, *The Helping Interview* (Boston: Houghton-Mifflin, 1969), pp. 77–84.

8. Stanley R. Strong and Lyle D. Schmidt, "Expertness and Influence in Counseling," *Journal of Counseling Psychology* 17 (1970): 81–87; Martin J. Bohn, Jr., "Counseling Behavior as a Function of Counselor Dominance, Counselor Experience, and Client Type," *Journal of Counseling Psychology* 12 (1965): 346–51; Allen E. Ivey, C. Dean Miller, and Karen H. Gabbert, "Counseling Assignment and Client Attitude: A Systematic Replication," *Journal of Counseling Psychology* 15 (1968): 194–95.

9. This interview is reprinted with permission of Randall Owen and Barbara Rassel, two former students at Eastern Illinois University.

Suggested Readings

Arbuckle, Dugald S. *Counseling: Philosophy, Theory, and Practice*. Boston: Allyn and Bacon, 1970.
Beck, C. F. *Guidelines for Guidance*. Dubuque, Iowa: Wm. C. Brown Company Publishers, 1966.
Benjamin, Alfred. *The Helping Interview*. Boston: Houghton-Mifflin, 1980.
Evariff, William, *Helping Counselors Grow Professionally*. Englewood Cliffs, N.J.: Prentice-Hall, 1965.
Hackney, Harold, and Cormier, Sherilyn N. *Counseling Strategies and Objectives*. Englewood Cliffs, N.J.: Prentice-Hall, 1973.
Jourard, Sidney M. *The Transparent Self*. New York: Van Nostrand Reinhold, 1971.
Kennedy, Eugene. *On Becoming a Counselor: A Basic Guide for Nonprofessional Counselors*. New York: The Seabury Press, 1977.

McGowan, John F., and Schmidt, L. D. *Counseling: Readings in Theory and Practice.* New York: Holt, Rinehart and Winston, 1962.
Parker, Clyde R., ed. *Counseling Theories and Counselor Education.* Boston: Houghton-Mifflin, 1968.
Rogers, Carl R. *Counseling and Psychotherapy.* Boston: Houghton-Mifflin, 1942.
———. *Client-Centered Therapy.* Boston: Houghton-Mifflin, 1951.
Schubert, Margaret. *Interviewing in Social Work Practice: An Introduction.* New York: Council on Social Work Education, 1971.
Sullivan, Harry S. *The Psychiatric Interview.* Edited by Helen S. Perry and Mary L. Gawel. New York: W.W. Norton, 1970.
Truax, Charles B., and Carkhuff, Robert R. *Toward Effective Counseling and Psychotherapy.* Chicago: Aldine, 1967.

Persuasive Interviewing 10

We are and we encounter persuasive interviewers in a variety of settings nearly everyday: the "sales rep" who wants to sell a product or service, the "recruiter" who wants people to join an organization, the "activist" who urges people to vote, to protest, or to write in behalf of a person or cause, the "PR" person who seeks to enhance the image of a person or organization, the "true believer" who wants to alter beliefs, the "campaigner" who wants support for a candidate or a referendum, and the "socializer" who urges people to go to a particular movie, game, or restaurant. In each of these settings, the *interviewer seeks through the manipulation of verbal and nonverbal symbols to affect the interviewee's perceptions and thus to bring about desired changes in ways of thinking, feeling, and/or acting.*[1]

Note that not all persuasive efforts are aimed at securing an immediate *decision* or *action* such as buying a pair of shoes, giving to the missions, or voting for Marilyn Goodperson. An interviewer may wish to instill feelings of pride in a person, place, or thing and not to urge any action. An insurance representative, for example, may strive in an initial interview to get a person to *think* about life insurance and to develop or call upon strong *feelings* of responsibility for loved ones; the action step may not occur until a second or third interview.

This chapter addresses situations in which both parties perceive the freedom to choose among reasonable alternatives. Parents, teachers, employers, supervisors, and even some sales representatives may employ threats and "arm-twisting" tactics because they do not want to expend the time and effort required to persuade a person to respond positively. After all, we do not normally change our behavior (thinking, feeling, or acting) unless there is a *reason* to do so, an apparent *need,* and the more we oppose a change the less probability there is for change in our actions. A modification in thinking or feeling about an issue or a proposal may be achieved in a single persuasive interview, but often a series of interviews is necessary before a persuadee will buy a product, work more efficiently, support a project, or alter beliefs. "Coercion" may appear to be the quick and easy way to bring about change—and it is under certain

The persuasive interviewer may tailor the message to suit the individual.

circumstances—but this strategy may precipitate conflicts between the interview parties and assure the failure of this and future interview interactions between these parties.

The persuasive interview, when compared to public speaking and mass persuasion (radio, television, newspapers), has several unique characteristics and advantages.

1. We may tailor a persuasive message to fit a particular person.

2. We may demonstrate a sincere interest in a particular person and that person's needs.

3. We may alter our persuasive effort as the interview progresses to adapt more effectively to the situation and the interviewee.

4. The roles of persuader and persuadee may switch during the interview and permit us to hear the interviewee's counterarguments and evidence.

5. We get immediate verbal and nonverbal feedback as the persuasive effort unfolds.

6. We can see and hear the other party with little or no difficulty.

7. We may select the best time and place for the interview: the interviewee's home or place of business or after a fine meal in a restaurant or a game of golf.

8. It is easier to maintain the attention and interest of the persuadee.

9. We may control distractions or interruptions by the situation and other persons.

10. There are no third parties present to counteract the persuasive effort.

11. The persuadee has more difficulty terminating a face-to-face encounter than a mass media encounter.

12. The interview makes the persuadee an active participant in the persuasive process.

A television effort, for instance, may reach millions of persons in a few seconds and, if 75 to 85 percent ignore the message, we still may affect the behavior of millions of viewers. However, the mass media cannot handle many daily persuasive efforts (in families, neighborhoods, schools, and businesses), and often the mass media message urges viewers, listeners, or readers to see a Ford dealer, a Prudential representative, or a doctor. The ultimate success of the media effort, then, often relies upon the person-to-person interview.

Ethics and Persuasion

Before we move into a discussion of the persuasive interview, let's talk about the responsibilities we have as persuaders—as persons intent upon influencing fellow human beings. If we accept the skills, we must accept the responsibilities.

If an interviewee dislikes Jews, blacks, Catholics, Republicans, or "foreigners," is it ethical to appeal to this prejudice or to pretend to dislike Jews, blacks, Catholics, Republicans, or foreigners? If an interviewee does not ask for the source of "facts," is it ethical to keep the source secret? Is it ethical to quote a person in *our* words and to keep this "paraphrasing" secret? Is it ethical to present a proposal we know is inferior to others? Is it ethical to sell a product to a person who does not need it and cannot afford it? Does the end or goal justify the means? Does social context determine the application of any code of ethics?

Some writers have argued that we should judge the ethics of persuasion by the end or goal sought by the persuader.[2] But who will judge the rightness or wrongness of an end or goal? Other writers argue that we should judge the means used to achieve the end or goal. But there seem to be exceptions to every rule. Withholding evidence may be bad in determining which school to attend or which house to buy and may be good when a person's health or security is at stake. Virtually every strategy and tactic discussed in this chapter, even careful analysis and adaptation to the persuadee, may be classed as good or bad, ethical or unethical, depending upon the persuader, the situation, or the persuasive goal.

We could simply conclude, as many writers have, that a generally acceptable code of ethics is unattainable and offer none. But surely there are some guidelines that might help us as persuaders and persuadees. Perhaps we can start with this rule: "Do unto others as you would have them do unto you" and suggest answers to two questions. First, what are some of the things we would like to have done to us? Karl R. Wallace has suggested four moralities that should govern our persuasive efforts: the duty of search and inquiry; allegiance to accuracy, fairness, and justice in selection of ideas and arguments; willingness to submit private motivations to public scrutiny; and toleration of dissent.[3] And second, what would we not like to have done to us? Wayne C. Minnick has listed four things we surely can classify as unethical: falsifying or fabricating evidence; distorting evidence; conscious use of specious reasoning; and deceiving the persuadee about the intent of the communication.[4] These eight moralities and immoralities of persuasion can serve as broad ethical guidelines in our persuasive interviews. As Andersen wrote in *Persuasion: Theory and Practice,* "although we do not wish to force a given system of values or ethical code upon the reader, we do argue that he has a responsibility to form one. We believe that it is desirable both for immediate practical reasons of self-interest and for more altruistic reasons that a person accept responsibility for what he does in persuasion both as receiver and as source."[5]

With these guidelines in mind, let's proceed to a systematic development of the persuasive interview.

Stages in Persuasion

There is no assurance of success in any persuasive interview. However, we know that the possibility of success is enhanced if a proposal *seems to the persuadee* to meet the following criteria.[6]

1. The proposal appears to satisfy an urgent need or one or more desires or motives, *and*

2. the *proposal* and the *persuader* appear to be congruent (consistent) with the persuadee's beliefs, attitudes, values, ethical and moral standards, cultural background, stereotypes, *and*

3. the proposal appears to be feasible, workable, practical, *and*

4. objections to the proposal seem to be outweighed by the benefits, *and*

5. no better alternative course of action seems to be available.

The "ands" between the criteria signify that they are interrelated and not separate concerns. All are vital to success, but the key criterion is establishment of need or desire. If, for instance, an insurance client sees no need and has no desire for increased life insurance coverage, it would be a waste of time demonstrating that the client can afford a larger policy or that it is the best policy available. A common error of interviewers is the assumption that interviewees perceive a need or have a desire for change. The result is premature introduction of solutions to uninterested interviewees.

The persuasive interview is a complex process and is best approached in a systematic manner that satisfies these five essential criteria outlined. Like other interviews, the persuasive interview process tends to be circular (see fig. 10.1).[7] It begins with determination of a general purpose and ends with analysis of results.

Stage 1: General Purpose

The first stage of the persuasive interview process is to determine our general purpose, the ultimate goal we wish to attain. It may be to obtain a $50,000 contribution for a college building fund, to get a signature on a petition, to change

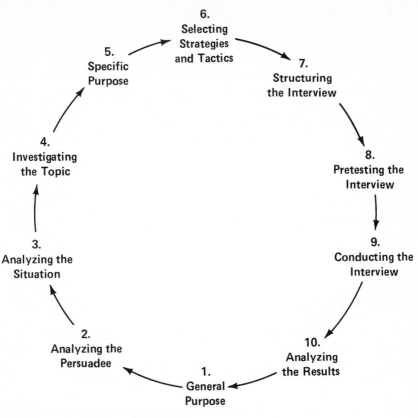

6.
Selecting
Strategies
and Tactics

5.
Specific
Purpose

7.
Structuring
the Interview

4.
Investigating
the Topic

8.
Pretesting the
Interview

3.
Analyzing the
Situation

9.
Conducting the
Interview

2.
Analyzing the
Persuadee

10.
Analyzing
the Results

1.
General
Purpose

Figure 10.1   *Stages in Persuasive Interviewing*

a person's attitudes toward nuclear power plants, or to sell a house. A clear understanding of our general purpose is essential for each succeeding stage because it will determine, for example, what we need to know about the persuadee and the situation, how we will investigate the topic, and the strategies and tactics we will select for a particular interview. We must be realistic and patient. A goal may require a series of interviews or prove unattainable regardless of the sophistication of our persuasive efforts.

Stage 2: Analyzing the Persuadee

With a general purpose in mind, we should search for all available and potentially relevant data about the persuadee so we may tailor the interview to this person. A proposal shaped to appeal to one person's needs, desires, values, standards, or capabilities might be totally unattractive to a second person.

Do not overlook any source of information. For instance, what do we know about the persuadee from previous interviews and other contacts? Search personal or company files for information about the interviewee's current and past activities and actions. Talk with the persuadee's acquaintances, coworkers, neighbors, and friends. Search biographical sources such as *Who's Who in America, Who's Who in the Midwest, Current Biography, Dictionary of American Biography,* and directories of professional organizations to which the persuadee belongs. Has the person expressed an interest in a particular proposal? If so, when and under what circumstances? If there is little or no opportunity to analyze the interviewee prior to the interview, use the first few minutes of the interview to discover important information about the persuadee.

Physical and Mental Characteristics   Physical and mental characteristics include age, sex, race, physical size, physical health, physical appearance, and intelligence. Studies have indicated, for example, that women appear to be more easily persuaded than men.[8] Race might be important in an interview dealing with school busing or school funds for the inner-city. In a life insurance sales interview, age, size (for example, overweight), and health would be critical pieces of information. A persuadee's limited intelligence and education or vocabulary may require that we develop a simple presentation of our proposal. Our task is to determine which characteristics are relevant and then to shape our interview to fit these traits.

Socioeconomic Background   Socioeconomic data includes the interviewee's group memberships (churches, social and service clubs, professional societies, labor unions, sororities or fraternities, political parties, and social action groups), occupations, avocations and hobbies, superior/subordinate relationships, formal and informal education, marital status, dependents (children, wife or husband, parents), work experiences, war or military experiences, and geographical background (large city, small town, farm, the South, the Midwest, and so on). As a life insurance sales representative, for example, we might shy away from or develop a unique proposal for a person with a dangerous occupation (deep-sea diver, law enforcement officer, coal miner) or a dangerous hobby (sky diving, mountain climbing, auto racing).

Frames of reference—ways of viewing people, places, things, ideas, and issues—are created and altered by a person's experiences, associations, and surroundings. If we want to convince a neighbor to sign a petition against an adult bookstore that has moved into the neighborhood, we would be wise to know the person's marital status, dependents (especially children or grandchildren), religious and political affiliations, social memberships (such as Playboy Club), geographical background (from a small town), and occupation (a small business owner who fears petitions against neighborhood businesses). In addition, we might consider the interviewee's past reactions to and experiences with petitions and past events (such as a rape in the area or a recent instance when small children obtained pornographic literature from another bookstore) that might trigger a favorable or unfavorable response to our proposal.

Psychological Makeup   We might want to consider the interviewee's usual temperament: serious, happy-go-lucky, moody, optimistic, pessimistic, suspicious. Does the person's temperament vary or change rapidly or unexpectedly because of health, the weather, personal involvements, certain topics, work load, time of day, and so on? What about the interviewee's personality?[9] Is he or she a fearful, anxious type? To what extent does the person rationalize — attempt to find socially acceptable reasons — for feelings, beliefs, or actions? Is the person open- or closed-minded, especially toward us, our proposal, or our topic?[10] Closed-minded individuals tend to have strong, unchangeable central beliefs, to rely on *trusted* authorities, and to be more concerned with *who* supports the proposal than with the proposal itself. Open-minded people tend to be more willing to change, to hold fewer central beliefs, to rely on the nature of the persuasive message, and to be concerned with the merits of the proposal. The likelihood of changing the behavior of a closed-minded, fearful persuadee who rationalizes to excess is slight. A degree of success would be possible only after we had established ourselves as trusted authorities, associated ourselves with the persuadee's central beliefs, and reduced the persuadee's fear and anxiety levels. Obviously these accomplishments would require a series of interviews, not a one-shot persuasive effort.

Motives and Values   A *motive* is that something that prompts an interviewee to think, to feel, or to act in a particular manner. The "something" may be a physical drive such as hunger, thirst, or sexual satisfaction, but it is frequently one or more *values*. Values are "the things of social life toward which the people of a group have an affective regard," "a type of belief . . . about how one ought or ought not to behave, or about some end state of existence worth or not worth attaining. Values are thus abstract ideals, positive or negative, not tied to any specific attitude, object, or situation, representing a person's beliefs about ideal modes of conduct and ideal terminal goals."[11]

Lists of values often run into the dozens with many apparent overlappings. The ones listed here seem to be the most common values in American society, ones we are likely to appeal to in our persuasive efforts or ones to which we will respond as persuadees.[12]

1. Comfort and convenience (striving for a comfortable, pleasant life).

2. Health, safety, and security (for self, family, friends, "others," the nation).

3. Pride, prestige, and social recognition (for being the best, for being fair, for personal achievements).

4. Affection and popularity (among family, friends, workers, "others").

5. Happiness (an exciting, stimulating life with pleasures, leisure time, a feeling of contentment).

6. Ambition (to be successful through hard work, to get ahead).

7. Cleanliness (of self, home, environment).

8. Companionship (friends and close relationships, a sense of belonging).

9. Competition (striving to be number 1 in work and avocations).

10. Conformity and imitation (externally being the same as others).

11. Accumulation and ownership (of things, records, achievements).

12. Power and authority (while resisting other's authority).

13. Freedom from authority or restraint (independence, free choice, freedom of movement and action).

14. Sexual satisfaction (mature love and affection).
15. Sense of accomplishment (a lasting contribution).
16. Peace and tranquility (in home, neighborhood, nation, the world).
17. Education and knowledge (to be well trained and knowledgeable).
18. Sense of humor (even in time of crisis).
19. Equality and value of the individual (equal opportunity for all).
20. Change and progress (to improve, to advance, to reach new goals).
21. Optimism (things will always get better, setbacks are temporary).
22. Efficiency and practicality (things must be efficient and produce practical, useable benefits).
23. Generosity and considerateness (to help others, to give help to the less fortunate).
24. Patriotism and loyalty (to home, employer, community, the nation).

Our task as persuader is, first, to determine which values might be relevant to our persuasive effort, situation, and interviewee and, second, to decide when and how to appeal to them in our interview. For example, a life insurance sales representative might appeal to values 1 (a comfortable life from the dividends), 2 (security for family), 3 (pride in taking care of the family's future), and 10 (doing what others are doing). A United Way campaign worker might appeal to 3 (social recognition for giving to the fund), 9 (competition with other retail stores who are striving to have 100 percent of their workers give to this year's campaign), and 23 (generosity in helping others).

Which values are appealed to in the following interview excerpt?

Air Force recruiter: The Air Force has many more high-level career fields than the other military services. We need computer specialists, pilots, communications experts, medical technicians. . . .

Potential recruit: Do I have my choice among these areas?

Air Force recruiter: You sure do! Of course you must pass an aptitude test for the career field you select, but with your educational background, I don't see any problems.

Potential recruit: I'm black. What effect would that have on my choice?

Air Force recruiter: None whatever! We have no racial problems in the Air Force. Black airmen and officers are serving their country in every career field and American base of operations throughout the world. If you decide to leave the Air Force at the end of your enlistment, you are certain to get a good paying job with real security.

Beliefs Seek out the interviewee's relevant political, economic, social, and religious beliefs. These are likely to be closely associated with the interviewee's value system. For instance, if the value of equality is important, a persuadee is likely to believe in civil rights and equal opportunities for women, blacks, Chicanos, and other minorities. If freedom from authority and restraint is an important value, the person is likely to have conservative political and economic beliefs—for small government with few controls and regulations of citizens and a "free" economy. The interviewee's group affiliations and occupation often provide clues about values and beliefs.

We tend to view ourselves as paragons of consistency in *beliefs* when in reality we are often consistently inconsistent. We decry excessive taxes and government spending, but demand billion-dollar superhighways to every point on the map. We preach law and order, place bumper stickers on our cars pleading for support of the local police, and then try to complain or bribe our way out of speeding tickets. We worry about permissiveness in our society and deny schools any right to punish our children. We are for integrated schools and neighborhoods until ours are affected. We attend churches and synagogues and are proud of our faith, but declare off limits sermons on political corruption, shady business practices, war and peace, or equal rights. We must try to discover the persuadee's beliefs and attitudes and look for apparent conflicts and contradictions that might affect the interview. How might we respond to this statement that was made during a "call in your opinion" radio program: "I hope you will do everything you can to restore Sunday closing laws. My employer says that I will have to begin working on Sundays if the laws are not restored. Sundays have always been sacred to me and, besides, Sunday is the only day I have to shop."

Attitude toward the Persuader   No attitude is more important than the one toward the persuader, the interviewer's image and credibility in the interviewee's mind.[13] If the interviewee dislikes or distrusts us (or the organization we represent), there is little chance of success unless we can alter our image during the interview.

Credibility is created first by the persuadee's knowledge and impression of our reputation, attainments, and personality, prior to the interview. When we are unknown before the interview, stereotypes—fixed, conventional images—may play a significant role in creating image and in the outcome of the interview. If, for instance, an instructor views all athletes as big, dumb, and seekers of easy grades, a football player might start an interview on a test grade with an immovable handicap. Modern society is so complex and moving at such a fast pace that stereotypes have become a necessity for imposing some order in our thinking. We have definite images of a medical doctor, truck driver, college professor, politician, corporate executive, physical education major, and others. Stereotypes are not inherently evil *if* we realize that they are highly simplified generalizations to be held lightly and changed easily. However, they often become so instilled in our minds that the mere mention or appearance of such a person produces a knee-jerk reaction. We refuse to accept a stereotype for what it is and insist that it applies equally to all members of a given class. A few summers ago a young female Fuller Brush salesperson dressed in a tee shirt, blue jeans, and tennis shoes found it difficult to gain entry into homes or to make sales. Residents felt she did not "look like a Fuller Brush representative." She could gain entry into homes or give her sales pitch only after presenting her credentials proving that she was a "real" Fuller Brush salesperson. A great many people believe we are what we look like we are.

A favorable image may play a significant role in the outcome of the persuasive interview.

Researchers have tried to identify the dimensions of credibility. Lists include competence, trustworthiness, dynamism, authoritativeness, character, reliability/ logicalness, morality, bodily skill, data evaluation, speed, extroversion, sociality, and composure.[14] Agreement on a single list of dimensions is unlikely, but we can generalize that, to create and to maintain a favorable image, our appearance, reputation, attainments, personality, and character should reveal to the persuadee a confident, poised person who is restrained and even-tempered, who exhibits physical energy, mental alertness, and knowledge, who is sincere in convictions, and who is fair, honest, sympathetic, and decisive in actions.

If we feel our credibility will be low with a prospective persuadee, we should determine the probable causes and the best strategy for changing our image. For instance, if the persuadee perceives us to be inexperienced, we might allude *tactfully* to qualifications, experiences, and special study, and introduce substantial authoritative evidence. If the persuadee perceives us to be too young, we could employ these methods while avoiding undue informality, the impression of cockiness, and the I . . . , I . . . , I . . . complex. If the persuadee perceives us to be argumentative or a know-it-all, we should be particularly careful in referring to qualifications, experiences, and achievements. Try to avoid a confrontation, direct attacks on the persuadee's position on the issue, and categorical demands and statements. If image problems are insurmountable, we should not do the persuading but have a person with higher credibility act as persuader.

Attitude toward the Proposal   In addition to discovering the persuadee's attitude toward us, the persuader, we must determine the probable attitude toward our proposal. An imaginary linear scale such as the following can aid in this analysis.

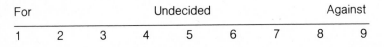

For			Undecided				Against	
1	2	3	4	5	6	7	8	9

From all that we know about the interviewee, and attitudes toward us, our organization, and the setting, where along the scale is his or her attitude likely to rest? If it is on positions 1 or 2, little persuasion will be required. If it is on positions 8 or 9, persuasion is probably impossible, except perhaps for a small shift in feeling or thinking. If the attitude is on positions 4, 5, or 6, we should be able to alter behavior with a good persuasive effort. However, we need to consider two additional factors: degree of commitment to a position and ego involvement. If an interviewee is highly committed to an undecided position such as 5, persuasion may be as difficult as a 9 position. If a proposed behavioral change clashes with the persuadee's ego involvement, any persuasive effort may be fruitless unless we can remove the perceived ego threat.

There are many reasons why a person might oppose our proposal, and we must discover which one or ones are operating at the moment. The persuadee may perceive us, our ideas, or both (rightly or wrongly) as threatening in some way. The persuadee might perceive us as shaking up his or her established (and perhaps cherished) habits, routines, rules, or traditions. The persuadee might perceive our proposal or us as being incongruent with beliefs, values, or stereotypes. The persuadee might prefer to do something else, and may have a counterproposal in mind. He or she may not know the facts or may be misinformed. His or her temperament—against everything, suspicious, overly cautious, or hypercritical—may create opposition. Or the persuadee may identify us, our organization, or our proposal with alien beliefs, ideas, or groups. Key phrases during the interview often tip off the persuadee's position, motives, or defensive tactics. How might we handle the following statements and what might they tell us about the persuadee?

> I've tried that before.
> We don't have the time.
> The students will never buy it.
> It's against company policy.
> Let's give it more thought.
> We did okay without it.
> Let's form a committee.
> Has anyone else tried it?

Why? It's still working.
You're right, but. . . .
You're two years ahead of time.
Let's all sleep on it.
That's good in theory, but. . . .
Maybe that will work in your department, but not in mine.

Stage 3: Analyzing the Situation

Consider carefully the physical and situational atmosphere in which the interview will take place. The size of the room (assuming the interview takes place indoors), furniture arrangement, seating for persuader and persuadee, noise level, heat, and lighting are important physical considerations.[15] Can we provide or obtain privacy and control interruptions, especially telephone calls? Have we made an appointment? Have we allowed for enough time? Will the setting be formal or informal? As persuader, are we the host (the interview is in our office or residence); are we a guest (the interview is in the persuadee's place of business or residence); or are we on neutral ground (a conference room, restaurant, hotel, club, out-of-doors)? Will we be in a superior or subordinate setting, for example sitting behind a desk or in a chair facing the desk? For instance, if we were selling life insurance, we might want to meet in the persuadee's home where he or she is surrounded by family. If we were selling business insurance we might prefer to meet at the customer's place of business. (See chapter 2 for further discussion of situational variables.)

What kind of atmosphere is likely to prevail—trust, suspicion, cooperation, anger, apathy, interest?[16] What events have preceded the interview that might color its atmosphere: earlier interviews, experiences with other members of our company or group, news stories, competition from other groups or fellow employees? Encyclopedia sales representatives, for instance, have found sales to be brisk wherever a major labor strike is underway. The striking workers want a better life for their children, and the encyclopedia sales representative seems to offer a step in that direction with an educational product. Are there forces beyond the persuadee working to mitigate our persuasive effort: company policy, the persuadee's superior, or financial affairs?

Timing and correct setting are very important in persuasive interviews. A husband or wife brings flowers home, takes the spouse to dinner and a movie, and then announces that he or she is thinking of taking a job in Outer Mongolia. A wife or husband may prepare a favorite dinner and provide a comfortable, relaxed atmosphere before mentioning little Mary's need for a fortune in dental work. What worker would choose to be the fourth employee of the day to ask for a raise? Who would present a case for a raise thirty minutes after the boss has discovered the previous quarter has been the least profitable in the company's history? Select the timing and setting that complement the persuasive effort or at least try to neutralize the setting so it will not hamper the interview.

What is the role relationship between interviewer and interviewee? Are we superior to, equal to, or subordinate to the person we are going to persuade? Each relationship has unique advantages and disadvantages (see chapter 5) and affects choices of persuasive approaches and perhaps the persuasability of the interviewee.

Stage 4: Investigating the Topic

With the analysis of the persuadee and the setting completed and this information fixed firmly in mind, the next step is an exhaustive investigation of all aspects of the issue under consideration: events that may have created the issue, reasons for and against a change, evidence for all sides of the issue, and possible solutions.

Sources of Information   Do not overlook any potentially relevant source of information: interviews, personal experiences, letters, questionnaires, unpublished studies (mimeographed documents, newsletters, graduate theses, and dissertations), pamphlets, newspapers, periodicals, professional journals, books, reference works, government documents, and special libraries. Periodicals might include *U.S. News and World Report, Time, Newsweek, Atlantic, Fortune, Nation, New Republic, Reporter, Saturday Review,* and *Vital Speeches.* Newspapers might include (in addition to local newspapers) the *New York Times, St. Louis Post-Dispatch, Christian Science Monitor, National Observer,* and *Wall Street Journal.* Reference works can be divided into four types.

Encyclopedias
Encyclopaedia Britannica
Encyclopedia Americana
Collier's Encyclopedia
Biographies
Who's Who
Who's Who in America
Dictionary of American Biography
Current Biography
Special Reference Works
The Public Affairs Information Service
Congressional Record
The Monthly Catalogue of United States Government Publications
Sources of Fact
The Statesman Yearbook
World Almanac and Book of Facts
Information Please Almanac
Facts on File
Monthly Labor Review
Statistical Abstract of the United States

A number of indexes can aid in finding available materials: *New York Times Index, International Index to Periodicals, Reader's Guide to Periodical Literature, Industrial Arts Index, Agricultural Index, Education Index, Business Periodicals Index, Index to Legal Periodicals,* and *Engineering Index.*

Types of Supporting Materials   Search for a variety of supporting materials (facts and opinions) pertaining to the topic. Remember, whatever we assert without proof can be denied without proof. The nature of the interview requires that we have materials to support our ideas and solutions. The persuadee may stop the interview at any moment to demand evidence to support generalizations or to ask for the source of evidence given. We cannot afford to fail either request. Note the blow to the persuader's efforts in the following excerpt from a classroom interview.

Persuader: Football players are too dumb to learn and are not here to get an education.

Persuadee: That is not my experience at all. Several football players have been in my classes in the School of Economics, and they can hold their own with anyone. Bill Block is an A student. Jim Smith is a solid B student, and so are Rick Rogers, Dan Williams, and Roy Smelzer.

Persuader: Well, don't get me wrong; our players aren't too bad. But in other conferences a student can get a scholarship even if he can't write his own name.

Persuadee: Doesn't the NCAA have minimum scholastic requirements for all athletes, both to get into college and to stay there?

There are four general types of supporting materials with several sub-types.[17] These are illustrated here from an interview in which a building contractor employs these to persuade a city zoning official to rezone a plot of land from R1 limited to single-family structures to R2, which would allow construction of a condominium complex.

1. **Example:** the use of a particular instance or happening to clarify or vivify a statement.

Specific Instance: a nondetailed example. (Examples of condominiums designed by this Atlanta firm are Westwood in Chicago, Deer Creek in Minneapolis, The Shores in Miami, and The Pines in Atlanta.)

Factual Illustration: a highly detailed example. (An excellent example of a condominium designed by this Atlanta firm is Deer Creek in Minneapolis. It consists of eighty-five units, each with its own yard space, garage or carport, and distinct frontal design. The units vary from one to four bedrooms and contain from one to three baths. As you can see from these photographs, the entire condominium is designed to fit into the natural surroundings, not to dominate them.)

Hypothetical Illustration: a highly detailed but mythical example. (Imagine what might happen to this property if it is not rezoned. Since it borders on the businesses along Sagamore Parkway, no one will want to build an expensive home there. The result will be a string of low-cost, low-quality houses with heavy turnover in owners and tenants. This will adversely affect the value of the nice homes nearby. The strip of houses could become a slum area in less than fifteen years.)

2. **Comparison or Analogy:** putting two or more things together and studying how they are alike and how they differ.

Literal Analogy: comparing or contrasting things of the same class. (Let's compare the condominium with the apartment complex. Apartments are usually built by persons interested in a quick profit [less than ten years] and in building as cheaply as possible. There is little incentive for the apartment owner or renter to keep the apartment in excellent condition. Neither gains from the money spent. The condominium builder, on the other hand, is going to sell each condominium to a buyer, to a person who is investing in a home. High-quality condominiums sell faster and at a larger profit. Owners have an incentive to keep condominiums in good condition because the condominiums are their's and they may have to sell them some day.)

Figurative Analogy: comparing and contrasting things of different classes. (You know, buildings can be like the proverbial rotten apple. A poor-quality building can turn rotten in a short time and ruin the whole barrel, the neighborhood it's in. We don't want that to happen to the neighborhood north of Sagamore Parkway.)

3. **Statistics:** drawing of conclusions from numerical evidence or figures that aim to show the proportion of "instances of a certain kind, to show how many or few or great or small they are." (A recent survey by the State Housing Authority found that 64 percent of citizens over sixty years of age prefer to live in an apartment or condominium rather than a house with the cost and difficulty of upkeep. Nearly 85 percent of these citizens would prefer to purchase a condominium rather than pay rent for an apartment. The Housing Authority pointed out that existing condominiums can take care of less than 4 percent of the demand.)

4. **Testimony:** words of a recognized authority in a particular field. (A recent issue of the *National Home Builder's Journal* contained an article by the Secretary of HUD. She said, "With rising building and land costs and with a larger proportion of our population in the fifty- to sixty-five-year age range, we must turn our attention and resources to apartments and condominiums. Greatest demand in the next ten to fifteen years will be for condominiums in which a person owns his or her own apartment.")

Tests for Supporting Materials When perusing evidence that we might use in a persuasive interview, keep four tests in mind: (1) *Is the source of evidence reliable?* Is the observer an authority? Is the observer biased or prejudiced? Does the opinion run counter to natural bias or interests? (2) *Is the evidence communicated accurately?* Are words or specifics altered? Is the material reported out of context? Are statistics "rounded out?" Is the source documented sufficiently? (3) *Is the evidence sufficient in scope?* Are enough authorities or examples cited? Do statistics cover a careful and adequate sample? Does "proof" evidence (statistics and testimony) outweigh "clarifying" evidence (examples and comparisons)? (4) *Is the evidence recent?* Is more recent evidence available? Has an authority changed his or her mind since making the statement? Have changing circumstances made the evidence irrelevant or meaningless?

Answers to these questions can reveal the strength of an interview and the strategies we should employ. These same test questions can aid the persuadee in evaluating the interview and ultimately deciding whether to change behavior because of it.

The following portion of an interview between a building contractor (the persuader) and a city zoning official (the persuadee) illustrates how seemingly convincing arguments and evidence may be challenged by an alert and critical persuadee. Notice that the persuadee asks most of the questions, and the questions reveal weaknesses in the persuader's preparation.[18]

Persuader: We have a real shortage of multiple-family housing in this community.
Persuadee: How can we have a shortage of multiple-family housing when the *Daily Tribune* has long lists of apartment vacancies every evening?
Persuader: Well, there's always a turnover rate in rental housing and this gives the impression of a renter's market. Did you see the article in a recent issue of the *National Homebuilder's Journal* by the secretary of HUD? She said, "The greatest demand in the next ten to fifteen years will be for condominiums in which a person owns his or her own apartment."
Persuadee: Yes, I saw the article. It appeared more than a year ago and reported a study conducted nearly three years ago. The HUD secretary was talking about geographical areas with large populations of fifty- to sixty-five-year-olds. We have a very small senior citizen population in this county.
Persuader: But there is a growing demand for multiple-family housing, especially condominiums. We get inquiries nearly every day.
Persuadee: I have detected no such demand in this city, especially for condominiums. How many serious contacts have you received in the past six months?
Persuader: I can't give you exact figures, but. . . .
Persuadee: I hate to see nice neighborhoods invaded by hordes of apartment dwellers. The need would have to be very obvious before I would support a rezoning petition.

Stage 5: Specific Purpose
Only after discovering everything we can about the interviewee, the situation, and the materials available are we ready to decide upon the *specific purpose* of our interview. Our purpose should be a realistic goal based upon careful analysis, not unsupported assumptions or guesses. For example, if the general purpose (ultimate goal) is to sell a life insurance policy to a person who sees no need for more insurance, the specific purpose might be to get the interviewee

thinking about life insurance. If our general purpose is to get a substantial donation for the college scholarship fund and the interviewee sees no need, our specific purpose might be to make the interviewee aware of student financial problems.

In each of these situations, our analysis has revealed the "crucial issue" of the interview. In other interviews, the crucial issue might be the interviewee's unwillingness to face up to a problem or need, or disagreement with the solution we are proposing, or a negative attitude toward us, the organization we represent, or both, or a preference for another solution or course of action. Our analysis should have also revealed the foundation for the crucial issue: fact, past experiences, apathy, fear, suspicion, ignorance, prejudice, emotional involvement, and so on.

Stage 6: Selecting Strategies and Tactics

With the analysis steps completed, a specific purpose in mind, and the potentially crucial issue located, we are ready to select the strategies and tactics best suited to our interview. We still have many choices to make. Remember our personal and professional code of ethics as we proceed to develop the persuasive interview.

Strategic Ordering of Materials and Reasons   Some strategies pertain to the overall "approach" of the interview and are particularly applicable with a potentially hostile interviewee. For instance, we employ a *common ground* approach when we stress throughout the interview the beliefs, attitudes, feelings, and goals we and the interviewee have in common. Avoid, whenever possible, areas of disagreement or conflict.

In the *yes-but* approach, we begin the interview with areas of agreement and gradually lead to the point where we must say, "But here is where we disagree." The persuader hopes that early agreements will soften the persuadee's opposition when disagreements are broached.

The *yes-yes* approach is used in many sales situations. The sales representative hopes that a series of agreements or yes answers will lead the customer to further favorable replies through sheer habit of saying yes. Studies show that effectiveness increases when a persuader expresses initially some views held by the persuadee.[19] The common ground, yes-but, and yes-yes approaches all take advantage of this finding.

In the *implicative* approach, the persuader wants the persuadee to get the implication of the message without explicitly stating it. This approach is applicable when reasons or solutions presented explicitly are likely to meet with instant negative response. The persuadee in perceiving the implication may feel *he* or *she* thought of the solution or discovered the reasons for a change. Only highly skilled persuaders should use the implicative approach because the persuadee may miss the implication and see the interview as a pointless waste of time. In addition, some studies suggest that people are more likely to change attitudes when the persuader states conclusions explicitly. All of these approaches get the interviewee involved in the interview, and active participation tends to overcome resistance.

Other strategies involve the order of reasons and when to treat both sides of an issue. For example, if we have three reasons for a change, which do we present first, second, or third? Researchers generally agree that the strongest point should not be lost in the middle of the interview, that either of two approaches are persuasive: strongest point last (climax order), or strongest point first (anticlimax order).[20] The climax order seems to have a slight edge in persuasability. However, writers have usually studied public speaking situations in which the speaker is certain to present the entire message. The interviewer has no such guarantee since the interviewee may decide to terminate the interview. In using a climax order, we may never get to our strongest point. Some researchers have suggested that the interest of the interviewee is an important factor. If the persuadee is interested, start with a weaker point so we will finish strong. If the persuadee is disinterested, start strong to build interest in the interview. All of this theory rests, of course, on our ability to determine which is our strongest point, next strongest, and so on. Only extensive knowledge of the persuadee, the setting, and the topic can give us this information.

When should we present both sides of an issue or recognize opposing solutions during an interview?[21] A one-sided approach seems best when the persuadee is generally favorable to our position, is not highly intelligent or well educated, and will not face counterpersuasion from another source. A two-sided approach seems best when the persuadee is neutral or unfavorable to our position, is intelligent or well educated, and will face counterpersuasion. A two-sided approach has the added advantage of enhancing a persuader's credibility, making us appear unbiased, fair, and open-minded. Again, analysis of the persuadee is vital to our decision.

Patterns of Reasoning Knowing which reason to place first or last or whether to present reasons on both sides of an issue is the first step. The second step is knowing how to develop these reasons into valid, acceptable patterns. Once again, we have choices to make.[22]

Reasoning from an accepted belief, assumption, or proposition may involve three steps: (1) Salk vaccine prevents polio; (2) Mary has been vaccinated with Salk vaccine; (3) therefore, Mary will not get polio. The strength of this pattern rests on the strength and acceptance of the belief, assumption, or proposition upon which it is founded. If Salk vaccine does not prevent polio or if the interviewee refuses to believe that Salk vaccine prevents polio, the reasoning is a failure.

In actual interviews, the interviewer seldom states explicitly all three parts of this pattern but allows the interviewee to supply one or more parts. For instance, a doctor may simply say, "Mary was vaccinated last spring, so she is safe from polio," or "Mary should be vaccinated again." The parent will supply the reasons or the conclusion. A salesperson might remark, "This G.E. refrigerator is a brand name product," and hope that the customer will add (in mind at least), "Brand name products are of high quality; this refrigerator must be high quality."

It may be wise to allow the interviewee to provide parts of this pattern of reasoning, to draw his or her own conclusions. For instance, if we were trying to sell a refrigerator with an unusually large freezing unit, we might say, "This is a very practical appliance because you could shop only once a month." This reasoning would appeal to a person who is paid and shops once a month. It might not appeal to a farmer, a hunter, an unmarried student, or a weekly shopper for a family of five. A simple, "This is a very practical appliance," allows the farmer to add, "Yes, we could freeze our garden vegetables"; the hunter to add, "Yes, it would hold a lot of game"; an unmarried student to add, "Yes, I could cook family size recipes and freeze the leftovers"; and the family shopper to add, "Yes, I could buy large quantities of sale items and freeze them."

As interviewer or interviewee, think about the belief, assumption, or proposition upon which the reasoning is based. Do we accept it or should we accept it? If not, don't accept the conclusion. Not many patterns based on a particular belief are as strange as the ones following, offered seriously by an entertainer on a talk show, but many are just as weak.

The moon controls water, and man is 80 percent water, so the moon controls man.

To be beautiful you must eat beautiful food. Flowers are beautiful food, so you must eat flowers.

Reasoning from condition is based upon the assertion that if something does or does not happen, something else will or will not happen. A person might reason, "Look, if I can afford $50,000 in life insurance, you can afford such coverage. I can afford it, so you can too." The stated or implied condition is highly important to the strength of conditional reasoning. If, for instance, the interviewee thinks our financial status is significantly above his or her's, the interviewee will probably deny our point. We must be able to show that the persuadee's financial status is above or equal to ours. As interviewer or interviewee, weigh conditions carefully. For example, the conditional statement "If we build the house east of the creek we will have a dry basement," may ignore the water table or an underground spring east of the creek. A lobbyist who states, "If you raise the sales tax, we can have property tax relief," may be ignoring the propensity of governments to spend what they take in and rarely to lower taxes.

Reasoning from two choices is based on the assertion that there are only two possible proposals. The persuader then removes one proposal and concludes the obvious. For example, "Look John, either our company will conform to federal civil rights regulations or federal contracts will be withheld. You and I know it will not conform, so it will lose the federal contracts." The interviewer's task is, first, to convince the persuadee that only two possibilities exist and, second, to remove successfully one of the possibilities so the preferred point or solution remains. The persuadee's task is, first, to decide whether to accept the two-possibility, either/or situation and second, whether to agree with the discarding of one possibility by the persuader. Two-choice reasoning is very common in persuasive interviews. Beware of interviewers and interviewees (in counterreasoning) who try to oversimplify complex problems or solutions.

Reasoning from example is a generalization about a whole class of people, places, or things based upon a sampling from that class. For instance, a doctor might try to convince a reluctant parent to have a child vaccinated for mumps by stating: "A study of 50,000 children vaccinated for mumps showed that only one percent of vaccinated children got the mumps. It's evident that the vaccination works." The doctor is reasoning that the results of this sampling can be generalized to all other children who will be vaccinated. The strength of reasoning from example lies in the sample and sampling procedure. Was enough of a given class included in the sample? How was the sample selected? Is the class under investigation clearly delineated? Too frequently a person will argue, "Don't buy a Ford; I had one and it was terrible"; or "You ought to eat at Fossil Shores; I had a great meal there last evening." All future Fords and meals at Fossil's are condemned or praised from a sample of one—a "hasty generalization."

Reasoning from cause-effect is related to reasoning from example because we frequently use a sample as proof of a causal relationship. For instance, a person might argue, "A study of fifty fatal accidents showed that thirty-five drivers involved had been drinking. It's clear that drinking causes most fatal accidents." The persuader or persuadee should question the sampling of accidents used and inquire into other possible causes: excessive speed, faulty automobiles, weather, road, or traffic conditions. An interviewer using cause-effect reasoning is asserting that since B followed A, A caused B. We are often too hasty in citing such relationships. Most of us have heard a person declare, "I got a flu shot last week and came down with the flu the next day. That shot gave me the flu." How sound is this reasoning?

Reasoning from facts is selecting the conclusion that seems to explain best the evidence that is available—the best accounting for a body of facts. For instance, a campaign manager might reason, "Campaign workers are sending in confident reports; our candidate is getting good turnouts for speeches; there is general discontent about cost of living and unemployment; and the polls show us five points ahead. Therefore, I am sure our candidate will win." This was the kind of reasoning used after President John F. Kennedy was assassinated: "Lee Harvey Oswald owned such a rifle, worked in the Texas book depository, ran after the shooting, shot a policeman, and tried to shoot his way out of a theatre. Therefore, Oswald killed President Kennedy." The strength of our conclusion can best be determined by asking a series of questions: What is the frequency of this conclusion with similar facts? How simple is the conclusion? Is the conclusion farfetched? What further evidence would make the conclusion more or less convincing?

Reasoning from analogy occurs when a persuader points out that two things have a number of characteristics in common and then draws a conclusion about one of the two things. For instance, a minister trying to convince a parishioner that the United States is in grave danger might reason, "Ancient Rome and the United States share many characteristics. Both controlled birthrate, had serious political corruption, were overly affluent, and suffered disintegrating morality. It is evident that the United States is destined to fall if it does not change." Analogical reasoning is based on the assumption that if two things have a great deal in common, they will have more in common. The danger of this assumption can be seen in the following: Volkswagen and Rolls Royce automobiles have four wheels, one steering wheel, two seats, a piston engine, reputation for reliability, and are foreign made. Therefore, they look alike; they cost the same; or they are the same size. Analogies can be quite persuasive, and both persuader and persuadee should view them carefully and cautiously.

Persuasive Tactics   While patterns of reasoning appeal primarily to the rational side of the interviewee, persuasive tactics appeal to the emotional side as well. There is nothing evil about appealing to both the head and the heart; tactics are unethical only when they are abused and when they are used for devious purposes.

Interviewers and interviewees should be able to recognize the following common persuasive tactics and to determine when to use them and when to accept them.[23] They are best used in conjunction with patterns of reasoning, evidence, appeals to values, and the needs and desires of the interviewee.

1. **Identification:** to identify ourselves with the persuadee and the persuadee's interests. (I live in this neighborhood and have made the same investment you have made, so I would not be supporting a rezoning petition that would lower the values of our homes.)

2. **Association:** to establish a connection between us or our proposal and some object, person, party, cause, or idea the persuadee respects, reveres, or cherishes. (This rezoning petition has the support of the Barberry Heights Homeowners Association and the City Planning Commission.)

3. **Disassociation:** to remove any connection between us or our proposal and some object, person, party, cause, or idea the persuadee fears, distrusts, or dislikes. (This rezoning petition was not developed and is not supported by the Overnight Homebuilders group that has been trying to get a toehold in this area.)

4. **Bandwagon:** to get the persuadee to "follow the crowd." (Over half of the homeowners have signed this rezoning petition already, and we hope to reach 100 percent.)

5. **Testimonial:** to use an authority, person, or party to support our proposal. (Wilma Rogers, president of the Homeowners Association, was the first to sign the petition and said, "This rezoning should enhance our property values and prevent commercial development in our neighborhood.")

6. **Bifurcation:** to polarize a situation into only two possibilities or eventualities. (It's either rezoning or commercial development; we have no real choice but to rezone to protect our neighborhood.)

7. **Glittering generalities:** to use vague, high sounding words or words with many meanings. (This rezoning petition is a move toward neighborhood independence and integrity and is for real progress.)

8. **Tabloid thinking:** to use generalities and slogans. (We did it before [stopped neighborhood development], we can do it again. Together we stand; divided we fall.)

9. **Suggestion:** to allow words and voice to suggest a point instead of saying it explicitly. (Every loyal member of this neighborhood [suggesting nonsigners are disloyal] is signing the rezoning petition.)

10. **Name-calling:** to use language that degrades an opponent's person, actions, or ideas—*caution,* many interviewees react negatively to interviewers who openly attack the opposition. (Only the slumlords and the "progress for profit" pack of builders are opposing this petition.)

11. **Unification:** to develop a sense of group identity and togetherness. (This zoning controversy and petition is bringing us together as a real neighborhood, as a community in the best sense of the word.)

12. **Activation:** to insult the interviewee to get action—be careful. (John, don't be a fool! These builders are using you for a chump while you wander around thinking you're for progress.)

13. **Rhetorical question:** to pose a question and then to answer it. (Why should you sign this petition? To protect your home and property, that's why.)

14. **Projection:** to portray the outcome if something is or is not done. (Think about what this neighborhood might be like in five years if this rezoning fails: gas stations on corner lots, fast food outlets here and there, houses turned into apartments, and businesses being run from living rooms.)

15. **Panegyric:** to praise the interviewee with explicit labels. (Maggie, you've always kept your property in great shape; you're looked up to as a leading citizen, as a true neighbor, as a person who thinks for herself and then acts intelligently.)

16. **Metaphor:** to use a figure of speech in which a word or phrase literally denoting one kind of object or idea is used in place of another to suggest a likeness. (You know, Paul, this rezoning business is like a war. The builders and speculators are constantly trying to gain control in one battle after another.)

17. **Maximization:** to demonstrate the superiority of a proposal or idea over competing proposals or ideas. (Rezoning this neighborhood stops, once and for all, the attempts at commercial development. It's the only way.)

18. **Minimization:** to demonstrate the inferiority of opposing proposals or ideas. (The idea of each homeowner acting alone to defeat commercialism is sheer folly. What if a few fail or grow tired of the fight? Only by working together can we achieve our goal.)

19. **Comparison:** to point out the similarities between that which is known and that which is not. (Our problem is just like the one faced by the Knox Hill area a few years ago. That area was rezoned and commercial development was stopped cold.)

Use of Questions   Questions usually do not play the major role in persuasive interviews that they do in surveys, journalistic interviews, employment interviews, and counseling; and the persuadee, not the persuader, may ask most of the questions. However, questions may serve several strategic functions for both persuader and persuadee.[24]

1. The persuader may ask questions early in an interview to discover a person's needs, desires, interests, values, attitudes, and general background when adequate preinterview analysis is impossible. For example, a furniture salesperson, after an initial greeting, is likely to ask about a customer's needs (living room, kitchen, bedroom, family room furniture), specific pieces desired, preference for brand names, style, and price range before beginning the sales effort. Nearly every election year produces a news story in which a campaign worker has presented reasons why a homeowner should display a sign for a candidate, only to discover that he or she is in the home of the opposition candidate. A few questions could have prevented this embarrassment.

2. The persuader may ask a series of questions as the opening or lead into a major point in the interview. The following opening is taking place in an interview between two students; notice how the questions lead to the point of the interview.

Persuader: You have an electric typewriter, don't you Jane?
Persuadee: Yes I do; it's an old Smith-Corona.
Persuader: How's it working?
Persuadee: It's working pretty well. I need to have it cleaned and adjusted.
Persuader: What if you could get a good trade-in on a new typewriter and not have to pay the $35 to $40 repair bill? Would you consider buying a new typewriter?
Persuadee: Perhaps. It would depend on cost, trade-in, features of the new typewriter, and of course the brand.
Persuader: Okay. Let me tell you about the college sales program Eberhoff has on the new Sk-1.

3. The persuader may use questions to encourage interaction with the persuadee, to prevent the interview from becoming a monologue. The persuadee may feel freer to ask questions and to provide feedback if he or she has answered questions. Remember, persons tend to be more easily persuaded when they take an active part in the process.

4. The persuader may recapture attention and interest by posing interesting, challenging, and thought-provoking questions. Questions keep the persuadee alert and tuned into the persuasive effort.

5. The persuader may use questions to discover how a nonresponsive or noncommittal persuader is reacting or what the persuadee is thinking. A "poker-faced" persuader may give no feedback except in answers to direct questions. The answers may be revealing even if they are incomplete or inaccurate. This persuader is probing for feedback.

Persuader: How do you feel about this idea so far?
Persuadee: Well, I'm a bit skeptical.
Persuader: Why are you a bit skeptical?
Persuadee: The completion date seems a bit early.
Persuader: What date would you propose?

6. The persuader may use questions to obtain overt agreements during the interview. Be careful of asking for agreements without adequate buildup or precautions. It's tempting, especially if we are nervous, to launch a question such as "Don't you agree that medical doctors charge too much?" What if the answer is a resounding "No!" We look foolish and must operate from a point of overt disagreement. The following exchange should occur only after we have presented a point, supported it, and discussed it with the interviewee.

Persuader: You agree, then, that one truck is inadequate for the weekend business?
Persuadee: Yes, I think so.
Persuader: Okay, let's move to the second problem of our delivery service.

7. The persuader or persuadee may use questions to challenge generalizations, evidence, reasoning, and lack of documentation or to clarify ideas or terms. Note these uses by the persuader in the following interaction.

Persuader: Another way criminals are able to repeat is that even when they are convicted, the penalties are not severe enough. Charges are reduced sometimes, for example, from felonies to misdemeanors.
Persuadee: How are you defining felonies and misdemeanors?
Persuader: Felonies are crimes like burglary, rape, and murder and carry more than a year sentence. Misdemeanors are crimes like petty theft, trespassing, and maybe shoplifting of inexpensive items.
Persuadee: What evidence do you have of widespread reduction?

8. The persuader or persuadee may use mirror and reflective probing questions to be certain that he or she understands what is being said or agreed to. For example, in an interview between a customer and a mechanic, the customer might ask, "If this new muffler wears out within the life of this car, you will replace it free of charge. Is this correct?" The mechanic might reply "Yes," and ask, "You understand that this guarantee is not transferable if you trade or sell your car?"

Failure to ask for clarification or for the exact nature of a commitment can lead to unpleasant results. When should the persuadee have asked questions in the following interview that took place over the telephone a few years ago?

Persuader:	Hello, is this Mr. McCarty of 321 Ronda Lane?
Persuadee:	Yes it is.
Persuader:	This is NBC in Fort Wayne calling, and I have a question to ask you. If you answer it correctly, you will receive a Webster's unabridged dictionary. Would you like to try?
Persuadee:	I guess so; what's the question?
Persuader:	Was Hawaii or Alaska admitted to the Union first?
Persuadee:	Hawaii.
Persuader:	No, I'm sorry; Alaska was admitted before Hawaii. But, as a consolation prize for playing the game, we would like to send you three free magazines. All you have to pay is the postage and a small handling charge. How does this sound to you?
Persuadee:	Okay, I guess.
Persuader:	Fine! Thanks again for playing the game. We will be in touch with you soon. It was nice talking with you.

The interviewee in this case was actually the persuadee in a very slick sales effort and *assumed* that NBC meant National Broadcasting Company and that the call was from a radio or television game show. The initials actually stood for a magazine sales firm. The persuadee could not "lose" this name-the-state game because he or she would receive the "free" magazines for sixty months regardless of the answer. A few probing or mirror questions would have unveiled the interview for what it was.

These, then, are important uses of questions in persuasive interviews. Review chapter 4 on types and uses of questions for guidelines in phrasing and asking questions.

Stage 7: Structuring the Interview

The persuader should select a structure for the interview that corresponds to what is known about the persuadee, topic, setting, and strategies and tactics. The following outline of a standard pattern of organization will fit a great many situations and is designed to satisfy the five criteria discussed at the beginning of this chapter: the proposal satisfies a need; the proposal and persuader are congruent with the persuadee; the proposal is feasible; objections are outweighed by benefits; and no better alternative is available. The persuader must remain flexible, ready for the unexpected, and cautious about assumptions concerning the persuadee's attitudes, possible objections, counter solutions, and so on. Let us look first at the overall structure of a problem/solution interview; second, at a sample interview outline; and third, at modifications of structure to meet specific situations and persuadees.[25]

Opening:
Best choice(s) of openings are discussed in chapter 3 and designed to get the persuadee's attention and interest.
Establish rapport depending on the persuadee and the setting.

Body:

Problem or Need:

Perhaps a clear, concise statement of purpose, need, or problem if this is appropriate and not included in the opening. Point-by-point development of the reasons, causes, or aspects of the need or problem.

Always point out how the reason, cause, or aspect concerns the persuadee.

Employ a variety of evidence and appeals to motives, beliefs, values, and frames of reference.

Summarize and get agreement (at least tentative) before moving to a new reason, cause, or aspect of the need or problem.

Summarize the need or problem and get overt agreement from the persuadee before proceeding further.

Criteria: standards, requirements, norms any solution should meet. Present criteria you have in mind while avoiding the mechanical or dictatorial.

Discuss briefly why each criterion is important in evaluating solutions to this need or problem.

Encourage the persuadee to add criteria to the list.

Summarize and get agreement on all criteria to be used.

Evaluation of Solutions:

Deal with one solution at a time.

Explain the solution in detail.

Evaluate the solution criterion by criterion.

Handle objections before they arise if possible.

Get agreement on how well the solution meets the criteria.

Move to the next solution if more than one is to be considered.

Closing:

Summarize what has been discussed in the interview and the agreements reached.

Obtain a commitment from the persuadee if at all possible.

Arrange for the next interview or for the first step in implementing the solution.

The establishment of criteria for evaluating all possible solutions to the problem is an important part of the organizational pattern outlined. "It presupposes that, consciously or unconsciously, any persuadee evaluates a persuasive proposal in terms of the degree to which that proposal appears to meet various kinds of criteria."[26] Criteria are present in most of our decisions, especially between two choices, even if we never formalize them. In selecting a college, we may consider size, areas of study, geographical location, cost, housing, reputation, and athletic programs. In selecting a job, we probably consider type of work, salary, hours, job security, advancement potential, and fellow workers. Even when choosing a movie, we might consider reviews, plot, actors and actresses, rating, awards won, and whether we are in the mood for drama, comedy, or science fiction. The persuader should try to establish criteria, with the aid of the persuadee, that are most important for persuader and persuadee. Once we are successful in setting up such a list, we have a clear, structured means of evaluating solutions. The following sample outline follows the need, criteria, solutions format.[27]

Opening:
1. Allude to high percentage of marriages ending in divorce and the animosities created in many divorces.
2. Refer to own recent divorce and its problems.

Body:
1. Problem: Divorce laws are creating many problems in divorces.
   a. Divorce laws require the establishment of guilt.
   b. Divorce laws are not constructive in nature.
   c. Children's needs are not properly considered.
2. Criteria:
   a. Divorce laws must maintain our society's structural solidarity.
   b. Divorce laws should be constructive and positive for all involved.
   c. Divorce laws should be based on modern standards and theories.
3. Solution:
   a. Eliminate the issue of guilt by establishing a nonguilt issue such as irreconcilable differences or irretrievable breakdown.
   b. Require counseling for possible reconciliation before divorce hearing and voluntary counseling therapy to help in adjustment if divorce takes place.
   c. Independent representation of children to eliminate their being used by either side in the divorce.
4. Evaluation of Solution:
   a. Counseling and elimination of guilt would greatly aid in maintaining society's structural solidarity.
   b. Elimination of guilt, counseling, and independent representation of children are constructive, positive approaches aimed at helping husband, wife, and children.
   c. Elimination of guilt is in line with modern standards and theories.

Closing:
1. Brief summary of need and solution.
2. Encourage persuadee to express his or her views in writing to local members of the state legislature.

What we as persuader want to accomplish and what we can accomplish realistically will determine how much of the standard organizational pattern we will employ and the proportion of time we will devote to each part. For example, if the persuadee agrees with the need or problem before the interview, we may summarize the need in the opening and move directly to establishment of criteria in the body of the interview. The following outline was sufficient for selling skis to a woman who announced at the beginning of the interview that she wanted to purchase skis for the season rather than renting them as in the past.[28]

Opening:
1. Greeting to an old customer.
2. Determine her seriousness in purchasing rather than renting skis.

Body:
1. Criteria:
   a. Performance.
   b. Price.
   c. Durability.
   d. Resale value.
2. Solution: Blue Star Superlight Skis.
   a. Excellent recreational ski, stable, steady, and easy turning.
   b. A low price for a quality ski.
   c. Strong fiberglass with double layered base to increase life of the ski.
   d. Great demand for quality secondhand skis.

Closing:
1. Offer a free tryout before purchase.
2. Urge to buy while a wide selection is still available.

In other persuasive situations, the persuadee may like the solution but see no need to take action. For example, the persuadee likes electric typewriters but the old standard is still working. We might devote all or nearly all of the body to establishing need or desire for an electric typewriter. If the persuadee is apathetic rather than opposed to the need or solution, we should probably outline both need and solution while stressing throughout the interview how the persuadee is involved or why he or she should be concerned. If the persuadee is generally favorable to need and solution but does not like us, a longer opening with careful establishment of rapport would be in order. The remainder of the interview should contain special efforts designed to enhance our image. If the persuadee's view of the need or solution or both is very different from ours, we might devote all of the interview to need and hope to arrange for a subsequent interview to deal with solutions. The point is, know the situation well and design the interview accordingly—be flexible and realistic. Above all, we should know what we want to accomplish and what we can accomplish in this interview. For example, in discussing sororities with a friend, do we want to convince her that sororities are good places in which to live on campus, or that she should join *a* sorority, or that she should join *our* sorority? Each of these purposes may require a different interview approach, perhaps even a number of interviews.

Stage 8: Pretesting the Interview

Pretest the interview when time is available and the purpose requires one or more major persuasive efforts. Find a person who will play the role of the persuadee as realistically as possible and be critical of the effort. We don't need praise; we need good advice.

Go through the entire interview one or more times. Try out the opening, including possible rapport building and orientation. Tinker with the opening until it is right for us, the interviewee, and the situation.

Develop each of our reasons for a change; obtain agreements; ask and answer questions; and summarize the need. Present criteria and invite the interviewee to add to or to modify the criteria. Explain the solution in detail, not generalities. Show how the solution meets the criteria. Handle potential objections and answer ones raised by the interviewee.[29]

Close the interview as planned. If a further interview will be necessary, set the stage for the next interaction.

After the pretest is completed, ask such questions as:

1. Did the opening establish a friendly relationship and lead smoothly into the body of the interview?
2. Were the reasons for a change clear and developed effectively?
3. Did I obtain agreements after each major point and at the end of the need stage?
4. How did the interviewee react to the criteria for solutions?
5. How did the interviewee react to the solution?
6. How effectively did I handle potential or stated objections?
7. How effectively did I ask and answer questions?
8. How effective was the closing?
9. How well were need and solution adapted to this interviewee?
10. How well did I maintain the interest and attention of the interviewee?
11. Did I use appropriate visual and audio aids when presenting need and solution?

Make necessary adjustments based on the outcome of this pretest and then proceed to conduct the interview.

Stage 9: Conducting the Interview

By now we should have structured and refined the persuasive interview to suit a specific persuadee, situation, topic, and purpose. The following do's and don'ts may serve as guidelines for conducting the interview.

Do's

1. Treat the interviewee as we would want to be treated.
2. Be honest and follow a code of ethics we would be willing to advertise.
3. Be flexible and adaptable.
4. Listen carefully and sympathetically to the interviewee's ideas, objections, and concerns.
5. Maintain control of the interview.
6. Answer questions and meet objections truthfully, fairly, and completely.
7. Be very cautious about criticizing the opposition or competitors.
8. Be thoroughly prepared.
9. Maintain a two-way communication process.
10. Remember that we are dealing with another human being.
11. Select a suitable time and place for the interview.
12. Strive for effective verbal and nonverbal communication.
13. Use audio and visual aids.

Don'ts

1. Talk too much or too long.
2. Attempt a high-pressure sales approach.
3. Pretend the interview is something it is not.
4. Pretend we are someone we are not.
5. Be argumentative, pompous, or sarcastic.
6. Be apologetic.
7. Give speeches.
8. Prolong the interview unnecessarily.
9. Resort to open or implied threats.
10. Make promises we cannot or do not intend to keep.
11. Expect unrealistic outcomes from a single interview.
12. Read too much into nonverbal feedback.
13. Attempt to offer a solution before a need or desire has been established.

Stage 10: Analyzing the Results

When the interview comes to a close, it is time to assess results. Did we achieve our specific purpose? Did we progress beyond our specific purpose? If so, how far? How close are we to our general purpose? If we did not achieve our specific purpose, how far did we get? Why did we fail to achieve our specific purpose? Ask many of the same questions asked at the end of the pretest to assess reasons for success and failure. What was the relationship between us and the interviewee? How can it be improved?

What is our next action? Should we terminate efforts to change the behavior of this interviewee? If not, what should be the purpose and strategy of our next interaction? Should another persuader conduct the next interview?

The Persuadee in the Persuasive Interview

Persuadees cannot afford to be passive recipients during persuasive interviews because the results usually affect their or their associates' social, physical, emotional, or economic well-being in some way. A good offense is often the best defense against unwanted or undesirable persuasive efforts and the best means of choosing between competing proposals.

We should review the materials in this chapter. If we are aware of the types of strategies, tactics, evidence, questions, and patterns of reasoning, we will be better able not only to recognize them during interviews but also to determine their strengths and weaknesses. For instance, we can detect lack of adequate documentation, questionable tactics, and faulty reasoning. We will know the tests to apply to the persuader's evidence. Some persuaders may prefer an "impulse" buyer to a "thinking" buyer—one who thinks, listens, and questions—because their approach or proposal is weak or unacceptable.

We should be active participants during persuasive interviews. Carefully phrased questions can expose a persuader's "real" purpose, reveal a persuader's qualifications, or unravel a complicated or vague idea or proposal. Don't be rushed into making a decision. We may have nothing to gain and much to lose in a hasty decision. Insist on developing criteria for solutions and on applying them equally to *all* solutions. Don't tolerate "smears" or innuendos aimed at a persuader's competitors. Remember the ultimate defenses, termination of the interview or a simple, emphatic no.

Summary

Good persuasive interviews are not debates or confrontations with categorical demands and statements from which retreat is difficult or impossible; they are efforts to establish a common ground between persuader and persuadee during which both parties recognize the necessity of compromise and the virtue of aiming at realistic goals. Good persuasive interviews are not "canned" efforts designed to fit all persuadees and similar situations; they are carefully planned, carefully adapted to the persuadee and situation, and flexible enough to meet unforeseen disruptions or reactions of the persuadee. Good persuasive interviews are not speeches to an audience of one; they are conversations involving the persuadee as an active participant and characterized by all the qualities of good communication, including listening and efforts to understand the persuadee and to protect the persuadee's ego. Good persuasive interviews are not aimed either at the emotions or the "rational" side of people; they include appeals to both emotions and reasoning. Good persuasive interviews are not efforts in which anything goes as long as the persuadee does not catch on; they are honest endeavors following basic ethical guidelines and during which the persuader may admit weaknesses in a proposal.

A Persuasive Interview for Review and Analysis

This persuasive interview is between an inspector-sales representative of Franklin Fire Equipment Company and the director of public safety for a city of 24,000 people located in an area where brush fires are a common hazzard. The persuader was called in to inspect the major pieces of fire equipment. He has decided to persuade the director of public safety that an old pumper, used primarily to fight brush fires, ought to be replaced. This interview with Lisa Barker, Director of Public Safety, is a necessary first step. Eventually the Public Safety Board, the fire chief, and the city council will have to approve any replacement of fire equipment. The interview is taking place in the office of public safety.[30]

Notice the structure of this interview, including need, development of criteria for evaluating solutions, and presentation of solution. How well does this interview satisfy the five criteria necessary for successful persuasive interviews. How well does the interviewer adapt to this persuadee and situation? Which values does he appeal to? Is the persuadee critical enough? Which strategies and tactics does the persuader employ? How effective are the questions asked by each party. Notice that most questions come from the persuadee. How acceptable are the persuader's patterns of reasoning? How does the credibility of the persuader and his organization enhance this persuasive effort?

1. Persuader: Good morning. I'm Dan Shaeffer, the representative from the Franklin Fire Equipment Company who has been inspecting several pieces of your fire equipment, the 1949 La France pumper in particular.

2. Persuadee: Oh yes Mr. Shaeffer. I'm Lisa Barker, Director of Public Safety; won't you please sit down? I've been looking forward to receiving your report.

3. Persuader: Nice to meet you Ms. Barker. This is my first visit here, and I've found your chief and his men to be most hospitable.

4. Persuadee: I'm very glad to hear that. We're proud of our fire department and its record.

5. Persuader: Here is a copy of my report on several pieces of your equipment. Most pieces are in good condition and maintained well.

6. Persuadee: Good! I'm very glad to hear that. I'll look over your report carefully and discuss it with Chief Watkins.

7. Persuader: The report on the 1949 LaFrance pumper is not very hopeful, I'm afraid.

8. Persuadee: Oh?

9. Persuader: Yes, I discovered several problems. First, the water pump needs a complete overhaul. It's pumping at the rate of 550 gallons per minute, well below the 900 to 1,000 gallons per minute level that is needed to fight brush fires or serious house fires. Unfortunately, the necessary gaskets, valves, and bearings are no longer being made. La France stopped making these parts in 1979.

Persuasive Interviewing

10. **Persuadee:**	What about the possibility of used parts?
11. **Persuader:**	Valves and bearings are likely to be worn out on any used pumper available for salvage, and gaskets cannot be removed without severe damage.
12. **Persuadee:**	I see. . . . You said there were *several* problems?
13. **Persuader:**	Yes I did. A second problem is reliability. Chief Watkins said that this pumper averages only a trip and-a-half without requiring some sort of maintenance work.
14. **Persuadee:**	A trip and-a-half?
15. **Persuader:**	This means that there is likely to be a malfunction of some kind during every second call. For instance, during the last brush fire season, this truck had engine problems on the way to a fire on September 15, transmission problems while returning from a false alarm on September 24, water pump failure during a grass fire on September 30, and fuel pump problems during a house fire on October 14. The records go on and on.
16. **Persuadee:**	Um hmm.
17. **Persuader:**	As you can imagine, maintenance costs and down-time are becoming critical. In addition, maintenance is very difficult on these old pumpers with a behind-the-cab engine compartment. Mechanics find it extremely difficult and very time-consuming trying to do simple maintenance tasks such as replacing sparkplugs and adjusting engine timing . . . let alone major tasks such as valve or transmission work.
18. **Persuadee:**	Could you be more specific?
19. **Persuader:**	Well, estimated time to perform a tuneup on a modern truck is one-and-a-half hours. This 1949 LaFrance requires nearly five hours, partly because it has two sets of points and plugs. Old trucks were designed with dual ignition systems—a backup if one failed. These systems are bears to work on.
20. **Persuadee:**	I hoped we would be able to get along for another few years before having to replace a truck.
21. **Persuader:**	I can understand your feelings, but I think you are living dangerously with such an unreliable truck as a key part of your equipment. An untimely breakdown could prove fatal. There is another problem I'd like to discuss with you.
22. **Persuadee:**	What's that?
23. **Persuader:**	Chief Watkins tells me that the two of you have been talking about replacing the small emergency truck purchased nine years ago.
24. **Persuadee:**	Yes, that's correct. It's no longer large enough to carry all of the emergency equipment we have and need. The popularity of small cars has quadrupled our PI (personal injury) calls during the last three years.
25. **Persuader:**	I noticed that in your records along with another interesting figure.
26. **Persuadee:**	What was that?
27. **Persuader:**	A pumper was called to the scene on 56 percent of all PI emergency calls. This meant that you had two units and two crews tied up at each accident at double fuel cost.

28. Persuadee: That's an interesting point I'd not thought about. What's your recommendation?

29. Persuader: I have a particular proposal in mind but, before I present it to you, I'd like to get agreement on a clear set of requirements or criteria that any new unit should meet.

30. Persuadee: Okay.

31. Persuader: First, it should be easy to maintain. Second, it should be compatible with your other equipment. Third, it should be suitable for fighting brush fires away from hydrants. And fourth, it should be large enough and strong enough to carry all necessary fire and emergency equipment. What do you think?

32. Persuadee: I would add three criteria. The unit must meet *all* of *our* specifications, some of which may be unique to a small department such as ours. A sample unit must be available for our inspection. And last, it must be financially feasible for us.

33. Persuader: Fine! I think Franklin has the perfect piece of equipment to suit your needs. It is a pumper-emergency vehicle combination, a single unit that will do it all. It is all aluminum—no wood to rot and no steel to rust. And . . .

34. Persuadee: It is strong enough to hold everything that we want it to hold?

35. Persuader: Oh yes! We make it out of the strongest aluminum alloys, the kinds used in giant commercial and military aircraft. The unit has a tilt cab so mechanics can get to the engine and transmission with ease. A V8, 210 horsepower diesel engine is standard equipment. The diesel is tougher and more dependable than comparable gasoline engines, and diesel fuel is much cheaper than gasoline.

36. Persuadee: That sounds good, but what about compatibility with our present equipment?

37. Persuader: Franklin representatives would work closely with Chief Watkins and his crews to be certain that water valves, electrical connections, and even engine types are matched for maximum compatibility. Franklin will design the unit to meet *every one* of *your* specifications. We are quite flexible.

38. Persuadee: Okay. What about a combination unit's ability to handle brush fires?

39. Persuader: This unit can carry 500 gallons of water aboard, and the Hale pump will put out 1,000 gallons of water a minute. We can install two booster reels with 250 feet of one-inch hose a piece and the truck is designed to carry one thousand feet of two-inch hose. The control panel and valves, as you can see from this picture, are simple to see and to operate so that chances of injuries from improper pressures on lines are greatly reduced.

40. Persuadee: That would seem to be quite adequate for fighting fires; what about its emergency capabilities?

41. Persuader: Here are three views of the unit, the rear and both sides. As you can see, there are very large compartments all the way around. In fact, its storage space is nearly three times as much as the space in your present emergency vehicle. It will hold all of your current equipment and have space left over for future additions.

42. Persuadee: I would like to see one of these units in operation.

43. Persuader: Good. One of our combination units has just come on duty in Westminster. That's only about 120 miles from here. I'm sure I could arrange a demonstration for you. The Westminster chief is very proud of his new unit.

44. Persuadee: We've not talked about cost. What did Westminster pay for its unit?

45. Persuader: The total cost was a little over $84,000. . . .

46. Persaudee: Wow!

47. Persuader: I know that sounds like a lot of money, but this was a completely equiped unit—jaws of life, radio system, automatic transmission, foam guns, the works. Think what two separate units would have cost. A stripped down version of a pumper would run at least $32,000. Some necessary pieces of equipment when purchased separately are double the cost of the same equipment that comes on a new unit. A good, fully equiped pumper will run at least $60,000, and you still face the problem of an inadequate emergency vehicle. A separate emergency unit, fully equiped, will run another $35,000 or $40,000.

48. Persuadee: I guess when you look at the cost of two trucks, the cost of the combination truck is not so bad.

49. Persuader: That's right! And remember the number of two-truck runs you are experiencing! When the combination unit arrives on the scene of an auto accident, for example, it can handle life-saving chores as well as fires and gasoline spills. You can avoid the cost and delay of calling out a second unit and crew.

50. Persuadee: It does appear to be a good solution for us. I'll ask Chief Watkins to draw up a complete list of specifications, and then we'll take this proposal to the board of safety and the city council. If they approve our proposal and provide the funds, in the neighborhood of $85,000, I'll get back in touch with you.

51. Persuader: Very good. Would you like for me to contact the Westminster department for a possible demonstration?

52. Persuadee: Yes, please do. Anytime after the fifteenth would be good for us. It's been good talking with you Mr. Shaeffer. We'll be in touch. (shakes persuader's hand)

53. Persuader: Thank you Ms. Barker for inviting Franklin to review your equipment and for listening to my proposal. If you have any questions about either my report or my proposal, please do not hesitate to contact me.

Persuasion Role-playing Cases

Rezoning Petition for an Apartment Complex

The persuader, Martin Webster, has been active in Citizens for Development and Progress, a group of people pushing for housing and industrial developments in and near Rockland. There is a seventy-five-acre piece of ground in northern Rockland that the persuader and others want to see turned into an apartment complex. The persuader is trying to get property owners to sign a petition in favor of rezoning the seventy-five acres for the apartment complex. He has made an appointment to meet with the persuadee, Joe O'Leary, a very influential member of the community and opposed to using the land for commercial development. Martin wants to convince the persuadee to sign the petition. The interview is in Joe O'Leary's home at 8:00 P.M.

Joe O'Leary, the persuadee, is thirty-one years old with above average intelligence. He belongs to local and national ecology groups, including the Sierra Club. He likes to travel, goes camping frequently, and enjoys all forms of sports. He is a high school science teacher in Rockland, a city of 85,000. Joe is married and has two children. He tends to be optimistic, open-minded—a typical American in values—but is beginning to question "progress." He believes urban-industrial sprawl must be stopped. Joe sees Martin Webster as overly progress-minded, a petition carrier for any cause that might "develop" the area, and one who would do anything for money. Joe would prefer to turn the seventy-five acres into a public park. He views the apartment complex as another move by the Citizens for Development and Progress and has been unhappy with several of the group's past actions.

Reluctant Interviewee for a Journalistic Interview

Melissa Wright, the persuader, is twenty-nine years old and a reporter for the *West Franklin Daily Eagle.* She wants to interview the head of the County Welfare Department concerning the custody of triplets born prematurely to poor parents six weeks ago. The case has angered the community, and all groups involved in keeping the babies from their parents—the courts, the hospital, the doctor, and the County Welfare Department—have come under attack. The head of welfare does not want to talk to anyone about the case, especially not a representative of the *Daily Eagle,* which first reported the story. Final custody of the children is still undecided. The persuader must convince the head of welfare to submit to an interview. She has an appointment for 3:00 P.M. at the County Welfare Department.

The persuadee, Jan Murray, is thirty-five years old and highly intelligent. She belongs to NOW, a number of professional societies, the Democratic Party, and the Catholic Church. She is used to being the boss. Jan grew up in Chicago and moved to West Franklin, a town of 45,000, after receiving her B.A. and M.A. in sociology ten years ago. She is married, but has no children. The controversy created over the triplet case as reported in the *Daily Eagle* has angered her and made her resentful toward the press. She tends to be serious and moody, but open-minded, except on the subject of the triplets. As a welfare worker, she usually believes that children should remain with their parents if possible. She sees the persuader, Melissa Wright, as young, wanting to make a name for herself, and willing to do anything for a story. Jan's ego is highly involved in this controversy, and she is strongly committed to not being interviewed.

Vacancy in the Public Relations/Personnel Department

The persuader, Pat Kremer, works for the J. B. Cunningham Electrical Wire Company. John Williams, one of five employees in Public Relations/Personnel, is leaving the company in two weeks. Pat is the only woman (except for secretaries) on the PR/Personnel staff and wants the vacancy filled with a woman. She has made an appointment with Michael Grable, head of PR/Personnel, to convince him to hire a woman. She is meeting with Grable in his office at 8:30 A.M.; interviewing for the opening will begin at 10:00 A.M.

The persuadee, Michael Grable, is forty-two years old with an above average intelligence. He belongs to the men's club at his church, the Republican Party, and the Elks Club. He enjoys camping, canoeing, and hunting as hobbies. Grable makes $20,000 a year and is Pat's boss. He grew up in a small town, is married, has three children, and his wife does not work outside the home. He was very upset last fall when a female boycott disrupted the annual meeting of the National Association of Personnel Directors. He tends to be suspicious and closed-minded. He adheres strongly to traditional American values and believes in equality of opportunity, usually. He sees Pat as bright, poised, and capable, but does not think she goes all out as much as the males in PR/Personnel. He thinks she is ready to fight for any cause. Grable's ego involvement is moderately high because Pat is questioning his decision on replacing John Williams. He is likely to identify Pat's proposal with that "women's lib stuff."

Installation of a National Credit System in a Farm and Garden Store

The persuader, Ann Harrison, is a partner in Westlake Farm and Garden, a store she started ten years ago with the persuadee. Net profits have grown to nearly $50,000 a year, divided equally between the partners. Westlake Farm and Garden has always extended credit to its customers on a very informal basis. Volume of credit business (about 50 percent of all sales) has grown to the point where a full-time accountant is becoming necessary. There is nearly $10,000 in credit purchases not being paid back on a regular basis. The persuader has decided to convince her partner to install VISA bank card as the only credit card extended. The interview takes place in the office area at 7:30 A.M. The store will open at 8:00 A.M.

The persuadee, Will Smithson, is thirty-three years old, with above average intelligence. He belongs to the Westlake Optimist Club, Small Businessman's Club, and is a Scout leader. His hobbies are gardening and traveling. Will came from a small town in Missouri. Westlake is a town of 25,000 in north central Minnesota. Will completed two years of college in horticulture, is married, and has two children. He is very optimistic, fairly open-minded, likes to help people, and likes to get along with people. His values are clearly small town, middle-American, and conservative. Will believes in national credit for other kinds of stores and has a VISA bank card for his personal use. He sees Ann as too "business" -minded and not "people" -minded. He thinks Ann's M.S. in Agricultural Economics gets in her way in a small-town, personal business like Westlake Farm and Garden. However, he feels Ann is intelligent, well-trained, and honest. Ann's proposal poses an ego threat because it questions a central belief. It is identified with a move toward "impersonal" business practices.

Proposal for Additional Funds for the Next Fiscal Year

The persuader, Tom Rickles, at thirty-three is manager of the Research and Development Division of Smith Tools, a manufacturer of home and commercial power tools. Three years ago, during an economic recession, budgets of all departments were cut severely to meet the financial situation. Only the production division came out fairly well. Budgets and staff allotments are now being considered for the next fiscal year, and the proposed budget for research and development is $277,000 or a 2 percent increase. Tom has made an appointment with the vice-president in charge of budget to convince him that a 15.5 percent increase is the bare minimum needed. The interview is in the vice-president's office at 4:00 P.M.

The persuadee, David Scott, is forty-five years old and highly intelligent. He is a Presbyterian, a Republican, and a Mason. His hobby is sailing, aided by his $63,000 annual salary. Scott is one of three vice-presidents answerable only to the president and board of directors. He has a B.S. and M.B.A. from Harvard. Three division heads (personnel, public relations, and sales) met with him earlier in the day with requests for additional staff and funds. He is serious, somewhat moody, suspicious, a bit closed-minded, and ultraconservative. Scott wants to forge ahead financially, but he wants to maintain an austere budget and is highly motivated to stay within the budget. He sees Tom as a bright young climber, an empire builder, and a bit too pushy. Tom has an excellent record in research and development. Scott basically sees some need, but not how it can be done within the proposed overall fiscal budget. His ego involvement is fairly high since he and his staff created the budget.

Additional Funds for the Welfare Department

The persuader, Scott Brock, is thirty years old and is head of the County Welfare Department. The county council will meet in two days to vote on the proposed fiscal budgets for all county departments and divisions of departments for the next year. The proposed budget for Social Services (caseworkers for families and children) in the Welfare Department is $203,000, the same as this year. Scott Brock wants to convince the president of the county council, Diana Hubbard, to propose a 5.5 percent increase for social services. The interview is taking place in the county council president's office at 11:00 in the morning.

The persuadee, Diana Hubbard, is forty years old and has above average intelligence. She belongs to Citizens against Higher Taxes, the Republican Party, and is a CPA with an upper-middle-class economic status. She is a community, business, and political leader, has a B.S. and an M.S. in business, and is unmarried. Diana tends to be serious, optimistic, friendly, outgoing, fairly open-minded (except perhaps on taxes), and adheres to standard American values, especially desire to work, to advance, and to achieve tangible benefits for hard work. She sees the persuader as a typical social worker who always wants to do more for people, as a good administrator, and as a bit argumentative. Diana disagrees moderately with the proposal, feels we must draw the line on taxes by cutting government spending and handouts, and thinks the welfare budget may be too high now.

Adoption of a New Line of Clothing

The persuader, Mike Knapp, is twenty-six years old and is the assistant manager of the College Shop, a clothing store for men and women near the state university campus. He is unhappy with one of three brands of clothing sold in the College Shop and has decided to try to convince the manager to drop one brand and adopt another. The interview takes place in the manager's office after the shop closes at 6:00 P.M.

The persuadee, Martha McBride, is fifty years old and is highly intelligent. She belongs to the Methodist Church, the Retail Managers Association, and the Chamber of Commerce. She enjoys spectator sports and plays chess. She is in her twenty-fifth year with the College Shop, is upper middle class, lives alone since a divorce five years ago, and never forgets who is manager. She is serious, often optimistic, generally open-minded, a bit suspicious in business matters, and adheres to standard American values. She likes things to stay the same and moderately disagrees with the proposal. Martha has high ego involvement because she personally selected the three brands of clothing several years ago. She perceives Mike to be intelligent, inexperienced, and as a person anxious to become a manager.

A New Home in the Country

The persuader, Cathy O'Brien, is a real estate sales representative for Oaks Realty. She knows that Bill and Jane Peterson have been looking at a variety of homes, new and used, in town and in the country, and building plans for constructing a new home. Cathy O'Brien's firm has contracted to sell a ten-year-old ranch home that is located on five acres of rolling land about eight miles from town. She wants to sell this home to Bill and Jane Peterson, and has a 7:30 P.M. appointment to meet with them in their apartment.

Bill and Jane Peterson are both twenty-eight years old and teach at the local high school in town—Bill in English and Jane in science. They have no children but plan to have one or two within the next few years. Their combined income is about $33,000 a year. They are currently living in Westfield Apartments and like the location's closeness to the high school. After hunting in a very systematic fashion, they have decided to remain in their apartment because of the high cost of homes, rising interest rates, and ever-increasing prices for gasoline. They see the persuader as a pleasant but "typical" real estate sales representative who desires to get a top sales commission, especially since sales of homes have been very slow for months.

A Postsurgery Counseling Program

Janice Lopez, thirty-five years old and head of the surgical nursing staff at St. Anthony Hospital, has become increasingly concerned about the postsurgery experiences of patients. Surgeons tend to spend little time with patients beyond "checking in" on them and checking progress records. Patients ask Janice and the other surgical nurses many questions about what they will and will not be able to do in the future, how long it will take for full recovery, what postoperative complications they might face, and so on. The nurses want to answer many of these questions, but surgeons tend to frown upon nurses who "play doctor." Janice also feels that many patients keep questions to themselves and leave the hospital filled with fears and possible misconceptions.

Janice has made an apointment with George Witherspoon, fifty-five years old and chief surgeon at St. Anthony Hospital, to present a need for a postsurgery counseling program to be developed and conducted by the surgical nursing staff. George Witherspoon respects Janice Lopez for her nursing skills and dedication but sees her as typical of the modern nurse who does not "know her place." Physicians, George believes strongly, must remain in charge of patient care and must develop necessary programs. Physicians will tell nurses what they can and cannot do, and one of the cannots is "playing doctor." George Witherspoon feels that too many patients are "cry babies" and expect surgeons to spend their valuable time sitting around holding their hands.

Student Activities

1. Visit several department stores or car dealers and observe the various persuasive approaches employed. How much information about us and our needs/desires do the sales personnel get before making their sales presentations? How do our personal characteristics such as age, sex, race, dress, physical appearance, and apparent wealth seem to affect the persuasive interviews?

2. Read the sample persuasive interview and make a chart of the values appealed to by the persuader. Which ones appear most often and why? Did the persuader fail to employ certain values of potentially high persuasability?

3. Invite a magazine, encyclopedia, or insurance sales representative to your home for a sales effort. Observe the structure of the interview, the strategies and tactics employed, and the values appealed to. How close is persuasion in practice to persuasion in theory? Warning: you might end up with a magazine subscription, a set of encyclopedias, or an insurance policy as a result of this exercise.

4. Select one of the persuasion role-playing cases. If you were going to be the persuader in a real-life case like the one you select, what supporting materials would you need for your interview? What sources could provide you with these materials?

5. Select a current controversial issue and a potential persuadee who feels differently toward this issue than you do. Make a thorough analysis of the persuadee, including physical and mental characteristics, socioeconomic background, psychological makeup, values, and beliefs. Following the analysis, answer these questions: What difficulties did you encounter in finding relevant materials? How did you determine what information was relevant? How would this analysis affect your persuasive strategy?

6. Write the name of one person you like or admire and one you dislike or distrust. The persons may be casual acquaintances, fellow students or workers, relatives, local, national, or international figures. Make a list of traits or characteristics each person, in your estimation, possesses. These traits will be descriptive adjectives such as honest/dishonest, competent/incompetent. Which of these traits are important facets of credibility? What could the disliked person do to change his or her image in your mind? What could the liked person do to lower his or her image in your mind?

Notes

1. This definition of persuasion is developed from ones in Kenneth E. Andersen, *Persuasion: Theory and Practice* (Boston: Allyn and Bacon, 1978); and Herbert W. Simons, *Persuasion: Understanding, Practice, and Analysis* (Reading, Mass.: Addison-Wesley, 1976).

2. For discussion of ethics, see Richard L. Johannesen, ed., *Ethics and Persuasion: Selected Readings* (New York: Random House, 1967).

3. Karl R. Wallace, "An Ethical Basis of Communication," *Speech Teacher* 4 (January 1955): 6–9.

4. Wayne C. Minnick, *The Art of Persuasion* (Boston: Houghton-Mifflin, 1968), p. 285.

5. Kenneth E. Andersen, *Persuasion: Theory and Practice* (Boston: Allyn and Bacon, 1971), p. 327.

6. These criteria are based on materials developed by W. Charles Redding and the Purdue University staff, some of which are treated in Robert S. Goyer, W. Charles Redding, and John T. Rickey, *Interviewing Principles and Techniques: A Project Text* (Dubuque, Iowa: Wm. C. Brown Co. Publishers, 1968), pp. 49–54. See also Robert B. Zajonc, "The Concepts of Balance, Congruity, and Dissonance," *Public Opinion Quarterly* 24 (Summer 1960): 280–96; and Gerald R. Miller, "Communication and Persuasion Research: Current Problems and Prospects," *Quarterly Journal of Speech* 54 (October 1968): 268–76.

7. This figure is based on one in Robert L. Kahn and Charles F. Cannell, *The Dynamics of Interviewing* (New York: John Wiley & Sons, 1964), p. 103. Reprinted by permission of John Wiley & Sons.

8. Marvin Karlins and Herbert I. Abelson, *Persuasion: How Opinions and Attitudes Are Changed* (New York: Springer, 1970), pp. 89–91; Thomas M. Schiedel, "Sex and Persuasability," *Speech Monographs* 30 (November 1963): 353–58.

9. Karlins and Abelson, *Persuasion,* pp. 97–105.

10. Milton Rokeach, *The Open and Closed Mind* (New York: Basic Books, 1960).

11. Edward D. Steele and W. Charles Redding, "The American Value System: Premises for Persuasion," *Western Speech* 26 (Spring 1962): 83–91; Milton Rokeach, *Beliefs, Attitudes, and Values* (San Francisco: Jossey-Bass, 1968), p. 124.

12. For lists and discussions of values and motives, see Steele and Redding, "The American Value System," pp. 83–91; Milton Rokeach and Seymour Parker, "Values as Social Indicators of Poverty and Race in America," *Annals of the American Academy of Political and Social Sciences* 388 (March 1970): 101–2; Richard M. Baker, Jr., and Gregg Phifer, *Salesmanship: Communication, Persuasion, Perception* (Boston: Allyn and Bacon, 1966), pp. 334–44; and Charles A. Kirkpatrick, *Salesmanship: Helping Prospects Buy* (Cincinnati: South-Western, 1956), pp. 229–64.

13. See for example Andersen, *Persuasion,* pp. 217–46; Lester Thonssen and A. Craig Baird, *Speech Criticism: The Development of Standards for Rhetorical Appraisal* (New York: Ronald Press, 1948), pp. 383–91; and Kenneth Andersen and Theodore Clevenger, Jr., "A Summary of Experimental Research in Ethos," *Speech Monographs* 30 (June 1963): 59–78.

14. Erwin P. Bettinghaus, *Persuasive Communication* (New York: Holt, Rinehart and Winston, 1968), pp. 101–17; John R. Bittner, "Communication Efforts of the Indiana State Police Public Information Division: A Study of Police Image," Unpublished doctoral dissertation, Purdue University, 1972, pp. 2–6; Karlins and Abelson, *Persuasion,* pp. 108–32.

15. Mark L. Knapp, "The Field of Nonverbal Communication: An Overview," On Speech Communication, ed., Charles J. Stewart, (New York: Holt, Rinehart and Winston, 1972), pp. 57–72.

16. Benjamin Pope and Aron W. Siegeman, "Interviewer Warmth in Relation to Interviewee Verbal Behavior," Journal of Consulting and Clinical Psychology 32 (1968): 588–91.

17. The types of supporting materials and tests of supporting materials are based on discussions in Alan H. Monroe, Principles and Types of Speech (Chicago: Scott Foresman, 1962), pp. 197–205; and Donald C. Bryant and Karl R. Wallace, Fundamentals of Public Speaking (New York: Appleton-Century-Crofts, 1960), pp. 351–52.

18. For another example of a critical persuadee, see Philip Zimbardo and Ebbe Ebbeson, Influencing Attitudes and Changing Behavior (Reading, Mass.: Addison-Wesley, 1969), p. 103.

19. Karlins and Abelson, Persuasion, p. 120.

20. For discussion of climax vs. anticlimax and primacy vs. recency see Ralph L. Rosnow and Edward J. Robinson, Experiments in Persuasion (New York: Academic Books, 1967), pp. 99–104.

21. Karlins and Abelson, Persuasion, pp. 22–26.

22. For an excellent discussion of patterns of reasoning, see Monroe C. Beardsley, Thinking Straight (Englewood Cliffs, N.J.: Prentice-Hall, 1966).

23. For discussion of persuasive tactics and devices, see W. H. Werkmeister, An Introduction to Critical Thinking (Lincoln, Neb.: Johnsen, 1957), pp. 80–87; Charles Lomas, The Agitator in American Society (Englewood Cliffs, N.J.: Prentice-Hall, 1968); and Roderick P. Hart, Gustav W. Friedrich, and William D. Brooks, Public Communication (New York: Harper & Row, 1975).

24. For an excellent discussion of questions in persuasive interviews, see V. R. Buzzotta, R. E. Lefton, and Manuel Sherberg, Effective Selling through Psychology (New York: Wiley Interscience, 1972), pp. 225–40.

25. For further elaboration on this approach see Goyer, Redding, and Rickey, Interviewing Principles; Buzzotta, Lefton, and Sherberg, Effective Selling through Psychology; and Baker and Phifer, Salesmanship.

26. Goyer, Redding, and Rickey, Interviewing Principles, pp. 50–51.

27. This outline is based on one prepared by Kay Stucker, a former student at Purdue University.

28. This outline is based on one used by Don Weber, a former student at Purdue University.

29. For ways to meet objections, see Kirkpatrick, Salesmanship, pp. 427–59.

30. We wish to express our appreciation to Chief Dick Coddington of the West Lafayette, Indiana, Fire Department for his valuable assistance with this interview.

Suggested Readings

Andersen, Kenneth E. Persuasion: Theory and Practice. Boston: Allyn and Bacon, 1978.
Baker, Richard M., Jr., and Phifer, Gregg. Salesmanship: Communication, Persuasion, Perception. Boston: Allyn and Bacon, 1966.
Beardsley, Monroe C. Thinking Straight. Englewood Cliffs, N.J.: Prentice-Hall, 1975.
Bem, Daryl J. Beliefs, Attitudes, and Human Affairs. Belmont, Calif.: Brooks/Cole, 1970.
Brown, J. A. C. Techniques of Persuasion. Baltimore: Penguin Books, 1963.
Buzzotta, V. R.; Lefton, R. E. and Sherberg, Manuel. Effective Selling through Psychology: Dimensional Sales and Sales Management Strategies. New York: Wiley Interscience, 1972.
Fotheringham, Wallace C. Perspectives on Persuasion. Boston: Allyn and Bacon, 1966.
Karlins, Marvin, and Abelson, Herbert I. Persuasion: How Opinions and Attitudes Are Changed. New York: Springer, 1970.
Kirkpatrick, Charles A. Salesmanship: Helping Prospects Buy. Cincinnati: South-Western, 1971.
Larson, Charles U. Persuasion: Reception and Responsibility. Belmont, Calif.: Wadsworth, 1979.
Lerbinger, Otto. Designs for Persuasive Communication. Englewood Cliffs, N.J.: Prentice-Hall, 1972.
Minnick, Wayne C. The Art of Persuasion. Boston: Houghton-Mifflin, 1968.
Newman, Robert P., and Newman, Dale R. Evidence. Boston: Houghton-Mifflin, 1969.
Rokeach, Milton. The Open and Closed Mind. New York: Basic Books, 1960.
Rosnow, Ralph L., and Robinson, Edward J. Experiments in Persuasion. New York: Academic Books, 1967.
Simons, Herbert W. Persuasion: Understanding, Practice, and Analysis. Reading, Mass.: Addison-Wesley, 1976.
Zimbardo, Philip; Ebbesen, Ebbe B.; and Maslach, Christna. Influencing Attitudes and Changing Behavior. Reading, Mass.: Addison-Wesley, 1977.

Index

A

Abelson, Herbert I., 313, 314
Adams, J. S., 135
Affirmative Action, 164
Allen, I. L., 102
Alloway, Thomas, 55, 56
Alwin, Duane F., 135
Analogy, 287, 293
Andersen, Kenneth E., 276, 313, 314
Anderson, David, 162
Anderson, Rob, 162
Annual planning interview (*See* Appraisal interviewing)
Answers, 8, 83–85, 92
Appraisal interviewing
  annual interview, 229
  behavior anchoring approach, 212
  closing of, 226–27
  conducting, 219–27
  counseling during, 221, 224
  feedback, 222–23
  history of, 211–12
  human relations factors, 225–26
  management by objectives (*See* MBO)
  MBO, 212–14
  MBO performance appraisal model, 215
  measuring performance, 214–17
  opening of, 223, 224
  perceptions, 225
  performance appraisal quiz, 209–11
  preparing for, 219–21
  principles of measuring human performance, 216–17
  process of, 214–17
  research findings, references for, 240
  research findings on, 228–29
  retrenchment effect, 222
  review form, 219
  setting objectives, 218
  structure, 224–25
  taking part in, the appraisee, 227–28
Arbuckle, Dugald S., 270
Assumptions, 4, 37, 84, 91, 92, 93, 103, 276, 297
Atkinson, Jean, 135
Attitudes, 22, 281–82
Ault, Philip H., 145, 162

B

Babbie, Earl R., 135
Bain, Robert K., 162
Baird, A. Craig, 313
Baird, John E., 208
Baird, John W., 19
Baker, Richard M., 313, 314
Balinsky, Benjamin, 56
Bandwagon technique, 87
Barker, Larry L., 19, 41, 43, 55, 56
Bassett, Glenn A., 208
Battles, Michaele Snyder, 207
Baxter/Travenol Laboratories, 239

H

Haase, Richard F., 56
Hackney, Harold, 270
Harris, Louis, 14, 121
Hart, Roderick P., 73, 74, 314
Hartsough, Donald M., 252, 253, 265, 270
Hawk, Donald L., 240
Hellriegel, Don, 240
Herron, Timothy P., 56
Highly scheduled interviews, 66–67
Highly scheduled standardized interviews, 66–67
Hillmar, Ellis D., 240
Hirsch, Robert O., 55
Hohenberg, John, 162
Hostility, 149
Huegli, Jon L., 240
Humor, 57
Huseman, Richard C., 19
Hutchinson, Marilyn A., 208
Hyman, Herbert H., 135

I

Image of interviewer, 281–82
Information-gathering interviews, 11
Information-giving interviews, 11
Information level and questions, 92–93
Interactions, 9
Interchanges, 4
    behavior, 8, 24–25
    intentional-unintentional, 32, 36–37
    levels of, 28–32
    nonverbal, 33–37
    verbal, 32–33
Interpersonal communication, 5
Interrogation interviews, 6, 8
Interval scales, 115
Interviewees
    confused, 150–51
    embarrassing, 150
    emotional, 149
    evasive, 150
    hostile, 149
    reticent, 149
Interviewer bias, 65, 67, 87, 88, 91, 103, 112, 116, 119, 144

Interviewers, criticisms of, 118–19
Interview guide, 62–63
Interviewing
    approaches to, 14–16, 45–46
    Cash-Stewart model of, 45
    defined, 7, 18
    digressions in, 7
    directive, 13, 14–16, 242–44
    guides, 62–65
    initiation of, 49-50
    interchanging behavior, 8, 24–25
    nondirective interviews, 13, 14–16
    note taking during, 44, 138–39, 146–47, 172
    other forms of communication and, 9–10
    perceptions, role of, 7, 25–27
    programming of parties, 22–24, 32
    ratio of speaking to listening, 10
    reliability of, 17
    role of interviewer and interviewee, 8, 48–49
    role relationships, 47–48
    schedules, 64–68
    seating arrangements, 46–48
    situational variables, 44–50
    tape recording during, 138–39, 146–48, 172
    telephone interviews, 119–21
    two parties, 7, 21–22
    types of, 11–14
    uses of, 16–17
Intimate dyad, 7, 10
Intimate interaction, 6
Introductions (*See* Openings)
Inverted funnel sequence of questions, 96–97
Investigation interviews, 11

J

Jackson, Matthew, 208
Jaffe, Peggy E., 270
Janes, Harold, 182, 184, 208
Janiak, Chris, 239
Johannesen, Richard L., 313
Johari Window, 239
Johnson, David W., 19, 55, 56

Johnson, Wendell, 55
Jourard, Sidney M., 6, 19, 270
Journalistic interviewing, 11, 49, 116
  analysis of results, 151
  atmosphere of, 145
  body of, 142
  closing of, 143
  conducting, 145–51
  difficult situations, 148–51
  guides, 63, 106, 138, 141
  key informants, 139
  leading questions, 150, 152
  news conferences (*See* Press
    conferences)
  note taking during, 138–39, 146–47
  opening of, 141–42
  precision journalism, 103
  preparing the story, 151
  press conferences, 65, 137–38, 140,
    143
  purpose of, 49, 137–38
  questions, criteria for, 143
  question sequences, 142
  research for, 140–41
  respondents, 148–51, 152–53
  responses during, 152–53
  role relationships, 144–45, 152
  schedules of questions, 65, 67, 142
  secondary questions during, 143–44
  selecting interviewees, 139–40
  selecting interviewers, 144–45
  situational variables, 137–39
  stages of, 137–38
  structure of, 141–43
  tape recording during, 139, 146–48
  telephone, 148
  types of, 137–38

K

Kahn, Robert L., 19, 84, 86, 90, 102,
  135, 162, 313
Karlins, Marvin, 313, 314
Katz, Daniel L., 135
Kegeles, S. Stephen, 135
Keltner, John, 19, 27
Kennedy, Eugene, 280
Kibler, Robert J., 56

Killenberg, George M., 162
Kindall, Alva F., 228
Kirkpatrick, Charles A., 313, 314
Kirscht, John P., 135
Kitchens, James T., 56
Klein, David, 74, 102
Knapp, Mark, 55, 56, 73, 74, 314
Krames, Lester, 55, 56
Krivonos, Paul D., 73, 74

L

Lagemann, J. K., 102
Lair, Jess, 22, 55, 56
Language, 4, 8, 32–33, 40, 43–44, 51
  denotative meanings, 32
  listening and, 33
  nonverbal interchanges and, 33–37
  programming, 8, 22–23
  questions and, 84, 89–91
  sources of meaning, 32
  suggestions for handling, 32–33
  symbols, 32
Larson, Charles U., 314
Layer, Robert, 239
Lazer, Robert I., 239
Leading questions, 86–89, 112, 150
Leading question strategy, 114
Leathers, Dale, 19
Leave taking (*See* Closings)
Lefton, R. E., 314
Lerbinger, Otto, 314
Levinson, Harry, 240
Likert scales, 113, 115
Lindzey, Gardner, 135
Linkletter, Art, 150, 162
Listening, 4, 8, 33, 39, 40–44, 46, 84,
    91, 153
  active listening, 40–41
  active listening functions, 40
  critical listening, 40, 44
  empathic listening, 41, 44, 256
  model of, 43
  problems and principles of critical
    listening, 42
  recommendations for improving, 44
Loaded questions, 87–88, 150

Logue, Cal N., 19
Lomas, Charles, 314
Lombard, George F. F., 243, 253, 254, 265, 270
Long, Lynette, 102
Long, Thomas J., 102
Longitudinal surveys, 105

M

McCarthy, Philip J., 135
McCombs, Maxwell, 162
McGowen, John F., 271
Maclean's, 154, 162
Mahler, Walter R., 240
Maier, Norman R. F., 228, 240
Management By Objectives (MBO), 212–14
Margin of error, 107, 108, 124
Martin, Ernest, 19
Maslach, Christina, 314
Mass media compared to interviewing, 9
Mauch, Sandy, 239
Medical interviews, 6
Metzler, Ken, 162
Meyer, John L., 208
Meyer, Philip C., 108, 135, 162
Middlebrook, Patricia N., 55
Miller, Gerald R., 313
Minnick, Wayne C., 275, 313, 314
Minter, Robert L., 55, 240
Mirror questions, 84, 88, 144, 296
Mitchener, Steven C., 197, 208
Moderately scheduled interviews, 65–66
Moeller, Dorothy, 55
Monroe, Alan H., 314
Moody's Manuals, 184
Moore, Bruce V., 19, 74
Morals, 22
Mordan, Mary I., 208
Morrisey, George I., 240
Mortensen, C. David, 56
Motivation, 29, 30–31, 46, 57, 59, 60, 86, 96, 139–40
Motives, 279
Multiple questions, 94
Murray, Elwood, 55

N

Neutral questions, 86, 87–88
Newman, Dale, 314
Newman, Mildred, 19
News conference (*See* Press conference)
News feature story, 137
Nichols, Ralph G., 55
Nixon, Richard M., 150
Nominal scales, 115
Nondirective interviews, 13, 14–16, 45–46
Nonscheduled interview, 64–65
Nonverbal
    association with verbal
        communication, 33–37, 71
    communication, 33–36, 39, 40, 43–44, 46, 52, 57, 82, 86, 87, 119, 255
    interchanges, 8, 33–37
North, David, 154
Note taking during interviews, 44, 138–39, 146–47, 172
Nudging probing questions, 82

O

Odiorne, George, 239
Open-ended questions, 61, 75–77, 96, 97
Openings, 57–62
    establishing rapport, 57–58, 61, 142
    journalistic, 141–42
    opening questions, 61–62
    orientation, 57–58, 61
    primary functions of, 57
    quiz on, 62
    survey interviews, 109–10
    types of, 58–62
Open-mindedness, 279
Oppenheim, A. N., 135
Ordinal scales, 115
Owen, Jean, 19
Owen, Randall, 270

P

Q

telephone surveys, 119–21, 122
training interviewers, 121–22
uses of, 103
versus questionnaires, 121
Symposiums and interviews, 9

T

Tactics, persuasive, 293–95
Tape recording interviews, 138–39,
  146–48, 172
Telephone interviewing, 17, 119–21, 122,
  148
Testimony, 287
Thonssen, Lester, 313
Time sequence, 63
Topical sequence, 63
Tosi, H. L., 239
Transfer interview, 13
Truax, Charles B., 271
Truby, J. David, 55
Trust, 16, 29, 31, 57, 68, 70, 76, 92, 94,
  116, 139, 141, 142, 145, 253
Tubbs, Stewart L., 19
Tunnel question sequence, 97
Turner, Arthur N., 243, 253, 254, 265,
  270
Tyrrell, Robert, 162

V

Values, 22, 24, 279–80
Verbal interchanges (*See* Language)
Vested interests, 48
Video talk back system, 17

W

Wallace, Karl R., 275, 314
Wall Street Journal, 38
Webb, Eugene, 140, 162
Weber, Don, 314
Weil, Raymond, 240
Weinberg, Sanford B., 55
Werkmeister, W. H., 314
Wheately, Bruce, 19
Winstanley, Nathan B., 240
Wirkstrom, Walter S., 239
Wohlford, Bob, 56
Wyatt, D. F., 135

Z

Zarie, H., 270
Zazonc, Robert B., 313
Zimbardo, Philip, 314
Zunin, Leonard, 73, 74
Zunin, Natalie, 73, 74